ROUTLEDGE LIBRARY EDITIONS: FOOD SUPPLY AND POLICY

Volume 3

THE POLITICAL ECONOMY OF AFRICAN FAMINE

THE POLITICAL ECONOMY OF AFRICAN FAMINE

Edited by
R. E. DOWNS, DONNA O. KERNER
AND STEPHEN P. REYNA

R Routledge
Taylor & Francis Group

LONDON AND NEW YORK

First published in 1991 by Gordon and Breach

This edition first published in 2020
by Routledge
2 Park Square, Milton Park, Abingdon, Oxon OX14 4RN

and by Routledge
52 Vanderbilt Avenue, New York, NY 10017

Routledge is an imprint of the Taylor & Francis Group, an informa business

© 1991 OPA (Amsterdam) B.V.

British Library Cataloguing in Publication Data
A catalogue record for this book is available from the British Library

ISBN: 978-0-367-26640-0 (Set)
ISBN: 978-0-429-29433-4 (Set) (ebk)
ISBN: 978-0-367-27572-3 (Volume 3) (hbk)
ISBN: 978-0-367-27590-7 (Volume 3) (pbk)
ISBN: 978-0-429-29672-7 (Volume 3) (ebk)

Publisher's Note
The publisher has gone to great lengths to ensure the quality of this reprint but points out that some imperfections in the original copies may be apparent.

Disclaimer
The publisher has made every effort to trace copyright holders and would welcome correspondence from those they have been unable to trace.

THE POLITICAL ECONOMY OF AFRICAN FAMINE

edited by

R. E. Downs
University of New Hampshire
Durham

Donna O. Kerner
Wheaton College
Norton, Massachusetts

Stephen P. Reyna
University of New Hampshire
Durham

Gordon and Breach Science Publishers
Philadelphia Reading Paris Montreux Tokyo Melbourne

Gordon and Breach Science Publishers

5301 Tacony Street, Drawer 330
Philadelphia, Pennsylvania 19137
United States of America

Post Office Box 90
Reading, Berkshire RG1 8JL
United Kingdom

58, rue Lhomond
75005 Paris
France

Post Office Box 161
1820 Montreux 2
Switzerland

3-14-9, Okubo
Shinjuku-ku, Tokyo 169
Japan

Private Bag 8
Camberwell, Victoria 3124
Australia

Library of Congress Cataloging-in-Publication Data

The Political economy of African famine / edited by R.E. Downs, Donna
   O. Kerner, Stephen P. Reyna.
      p.   cm. – – (Food and nutrition in history and anthropology ;
   v. 9)
      Includes bibliographical references.
      ISBN 2–88124–476–9 (hardcover). – – ISBN 2–88124–477–7 (softcover)
      1. Food supply – – Africa.   2. Produce trade – – Africa.
3. Agriculture – – Africa.   4. Famines – – Africa.   5. Africa – – Economic
conditions – – 1960 –   I. Downs, R. E.   II. Kerner, Donna, O.
III. Reyna, Stephen P.   IV. Series.
HD9017.A2P63   1991
363.8'096 – – dc20   91–36631

CONTENTS

Introduction

R. E. Downs
Donna O. Kerner
Stephen P. Reyna

The tragic picture of African famine in the 1970s and 1980s is now familiar to those who are least affected by it—Western observers. The horror scenes of drought-parched landscapes, refugee camps, and withered, starving bodies presented by the news media have forcibly brought the west to a realization that 200 million people in the some 20 sub-Saharan African countries affected by famine (Strong, 1989) live a life that is, as one commentator put it, "the closest thing to hell...."

If the dimensions of the tragedy are clear, its causes and possible solutions are still hotly debated. As Kathleen Staudt has trenchantly observed, "there is certainly no famine in the food-crisis-in Africa literature" (1987:37). This volume, third in the series, "African Food Systems in Crisis," represents a continuation of anthropological efforts to understand the causes of famine and to frame policy recommendations to manage and prevent food crises. Its contributions may be said to reflect a new political economy of famine, one that is broadly "anthropological" in approach and which appears to provide a promising avenue for addressing food crises. Crucial to this approach are considerations of power and gender. The remainder of the introduction is organized as follows. The first section introduces each of the essays; the second discusses the implications of the essays as they bear upon questions of political economy, gender, and policy.

1.

The essays are grouped into three sections. The first, entitled *Theoretical Perspectives*, consists of a single essay, Michael Watt's "Heat of Darkness: Reflections on Famine and Starvation in Africa." The essay is notable for three reasons. First, it deftly analyzes an enormous literature dealing with both famine theory and efforts to fight hunger. Second, it proposes a rationale for what might be a "next step" in famine theory. Third, it suggests what may be required to terminate African famines.

Attempts to understand famine from the point of view of the environment, poverty, coping-strategies, markets, entitlements, and even phenomenology are reviewed. The analysis of Sen's influential entitlement approach is especially useful, both for showing why it is so useful yet why it needs to be complemented by a more macroscopic perspective. Watts calls for a particular "sources of social power" variant of such an approach. This position has as its central axiom the proposition that "famines are all about politics and the exercise of power..," which implies that a history of "the sources of social power" is essential "to understand not simply the occurrence of famine, but its recurrence."

Watts draws on the example of India when considering ways of combating food-crises. He notes that India has avoided famine since the end of the colonial period as a result of the successful implementation of policies involving the storage of massive grain buffer stocks and early warning, food distribution, and public works systems. However, and this is critical, he believes that such policies can only be successful with democratization of the political arena, which in Africa would allow peasants considerably greater power than they presently enjoy.

The second section in the volume, *Development Practice and Hunger*, explores the positive and negative impacts of different development activities on hunger. The two chapters discuss development programs that were supposed to enhance the production of livestock and grain respectively. Stephen Reyna's "Cultural Construction in a 'Garden of Eden': The Influence of Ontological Acquiescence in an African Development Project and its Implications for Food Security," analyzes a type of livestock development project that was common in Africa throughout the 1960s and 1970s, in which billions of dollars were spent, and *all* of which failed. The particular instance of development sin examined was a project in Chad. Failure resulted in part, it is argued, because Western planners, acquiescing in their own cultural notions, stipulated a reality for the people and the economy of the area of the project that did not exist, and consequently proceeded to devise innovations that threatened ways of maintaining food security in the reality that did exist.

The second essay in this section is William Torry's "Rainfed Agricultural Development Project Performance in the Context of Drought: The Western Savannah Project, South Darfur, Sudan, and the Drought of 1984-1985." Different types of rainfed agriculture feed more people in Africa than any other type of farming system; hence improvements in rainfed agriculture are critical to reducing food insecurity during droughts. Torry analyzes a type of agricultural project in the western part of the Sudan that has been believed by many, especially institutions funding development like the World Bank, to be a model for improving rainfed farming systems. Torry shows how "except possibly for its wateryard rehabilitation program, WSP was not a significant crisis prophylactic or provider of relief within the project area." The failure of this project, which appears to have been overwhelmed by a number of social, organizational, and environmental factors, is unfortunately all too typical of similar ones, which suggests that there may well be some muddles in the rainfed agricultural models for combating hunger.

The third section of the volume, *The African Scene*, analyzes instances of famine and hunger in Niger, Ethiopia, the Sudan, Guinea-Bissau, Tanzania, Ghana, Cameroon, and Chad. A sub-section pays special attention to the role of gender in questions of food security.

Cynthia White's contribution, "Increased Vulnerability to Food Shortage among Fulani Nomads in Niger," begins this section. This essay is the result of remarkable ethnographic field research conducted among Fulani nomads during the late 1970s and 1980s. It considers certain consequences of agricultural and political change upon pastoral production systems. White shows how livestock production is dependent upon the market in ways that in times of drought make it especially vulnerable to reduced food entitlements. This vulnerability is played out in the face of changes both in the farming sector that hinder animal production and in the political arena that further disrupt pastoral life. This has led to the loss of "traditional" activities and the addition of "modern" ones, both of which act to reduce the herders' ability to continue animal production in the face of droughts. As a consequence, they lose their animals, are unable to reconstitute their herds, and become a sort of rural semi-proletariat. Thus her central conclusion is somber. Herders are now more vulnerable to drought and hunger than in the past. If the trends White describes are occurring elsewhere, nomadic pastoral production may well be a thing of the past; and, as she documents, its replacement may be a form of sedentary livestock production that is environmentally malign.

Jason Clay takes readers to Ethiopia, the scene of the most ghastly famines in Africa in the 1980s. "Western Assistance and the Ethiopian Famine: Implications for Humanitarian Assistance" has a critical finding, namely that the origin of the 1984-85 famine in Ethiopia was "political." There are two reasons for this conclusion. First, Clay suggests that Ethiopian government policies, especially those involving villagization and resettlement, were the most significant forces producing famine conditions in 1984–85; and second, that the politics of various donor agencies exacerbated the effects of these disastrous Ethiopian policies. Clay's contribution is significant, even controversial, for three reasons. First, although the "politics" of the authors differ considerably, Clay's finding lends support to Watts' contention that famines are first and foremost about power. Second, the villagization and resettlement policies of which Clay is most critical were those of a Marxist regime. This might be interpreted by some as confirming that communism leads to famine, but before the cockles of rightist hearts are warmed by such a conclusion, it should be realized that villagization and resettlement are by no means restricted to Marxist political systems. Indeed, American military forces in Viet Nam applied a variant of these policies. A third significance of Clay's essay is an unpleasant irony: if the humanitarian relief operations did exacerbate the famine, then—in Clay's words—"the help hurt."

Jay O'Brien and Ellen Gruenbaum's "A Social History of Food, Famine, and Gender in Twentieth Century Sudan" addresses a conundrum. When other sahelian nations experienced drought and famine in the 1960s and 70s, the Sudan suffered the drought but avoided the famine, yet in the mid-1980s, when drought again visited the sahel, the Sudan experienced the severest of famines. The question is, what had changed so radically in the intervening years? O'Brien and Gruenbaum answer it by applying Alain de Janvry's views of Third World capital accumulation. They argue that the Sudan shifted from a pattern of internally articulated growth and capital accumulation to one of disarticulated growth and development in the period just prior to the famine of the 1980s. This occurred when the Sudan radically altered its agricultural development priorities to emphasize crop exports, a policy that tended to sever, or disarticulate, the "dynamic linkage between wages as source of demand for the products of the system and profitability within the system." Of course, and this is the crux of the matter, such disarticulation meant that low wages were not necessarily so bad for business, because profits were made from the sale of products in markets external to the Sudan. O'Brien and Gruenbaum document different factors leading to the stagnation or even decline of farm incomes, thereby reducing the farmers' ability to cope with the drought when it came.

In her paper, "Labor, Economic Power, and Gender: Coping with Food Shortage in Guinea Bissau," Ursula Funk shows how the strategies adopted in coping with food shortages vary according to socio-economic status, urban vs. rural contexts, and gender, though gender inequalities are less in the case of the Brassa, where there is a complementary division of labor, than among the Bejáa. Also contributing to the problems faced are tensions between governmental authorities and the masses with respect to centrally controlled agricultural land development policies.

In "Food Trading and Food Security in Ghana," which deals with market women in Kumasi, Gracia Glark examines the supply side of the entitlement picture during food shortages. Drought and declining crop yields are compounded by economic, political, and transport crises during famine. Market traders are often targeted by governments for supposedly exacerbating food shortages through hoarding and price manipulation. Clark's extensive analysis of female traders' activities indicates that the real constraints on their ability to increase or threaten food security are due to lack of facilities and capital for long-term storage. The same conditions which militate against Ghanaian market women's ability to contribute to long-term food security also restrict their ability to profit from scarcity. Instead, she argues that the flexibility in the Kumasi market system enables it to minimize seasonal food shortages and political shocks by shifting capital and labor to farms in periods of shortage and to the city in times of plenty. She concludes that because traders' activities are so heavily dependent upon the system of rural production, building diverse capacities in the everyday food system, rather than tightening control of the market by the state, should be the paramount policy initiative for famine prevention.

"Gender, Hunger, and Crisis in Tanzania," by Donna Kerner and Kristy Cook, describes how the erosion of entitlements to subsistence farmland and livestock use rights, particularly for poor and middle Chagga peasant women, has increased nutritional risk during food crises. Historically, women have had less access to formal education and wage employment opportunities than men, which has weakened their bargaining power in conjugal households and their exercise of public power in community forums. During the drought and food crisis of the mid-1980s, women collectively organized themselves to protest the threatened loss of exchange entitlements (through beer brewing and access to food relief) upon which they were dependent for subsistence. Gender conflicts thus transcended the private domestic level into the public forum of political consciousness, but Chagga men resisted this attempt by their kinswomen to clear the "fog of ambiguity" enshrouding the illusory complementarity of the productive roles of men and women. The authors suggest that the awakening of political consciousness and collective action, although mobilized as a short-term coping strategy, may have long-term transformative implications for food production capacities.

In "Ideology, Gender, and Change: Social Relations of Production and Reproduction in Nso, Cameroon," Miriam Goheen finds that although women are the backbone of subsistence production, poorer rural women and their dependents are increasingly at risk due to the commoditization of land and its concentration in the hands of "modern big men" as part of a process of rapidly growing rural stratification. As women lose their entitlement to prime farmland they are forced to trek further to their fields and reduce fallow periods, which leads to declining yields. Nso cultural categories, which portray women as caretakers/provisioners and men as warriors/hunters/status-seekers, are reflected in differential patterns of income, expenditure, and investment. Men and women do not necessarily combine their time and resources to maximize the commodity output of the household.

Ellen Brown's periodization of famine stages in "Sex and Starvation: Famine and Three Chadian Societies" (asset preserving, asset stripping, destitution, and reconstruction) provides counter-intuitive evidence concerning class and gender as predictors of destitution. Coping strategies among women and men of different classes during crisis involved the intensification of activities already known to them and the use of entitlements (including knowledge and skills) which were considered gender appropriate. Wealthier women (especially those in seclusion), who were not allowed to learn and practice economically practical skills, suffered more than poor women. Wealthy men, who relied on livestock assets during early stages of famine, were reduced to poverty when severe water and food shortages affected their grazing areas. Women in certain groups were able to survive during the destitution phase of famine, either because they were able to mobilize extra-household support linkages (with brothers), or had acquired food collecting and processing skills. Brown's data indicate that survival during famine involves a complex diversity of economically productive skills and entitlements. This case presents a powerful illustration of how cultural definitions of gender affect an individual's ability to exercise a range of possible life-sustaining options.

The last two articles constitute the fourth section of the volume and contemplate *Prospects for the Future.*

David Cleveland's "New Crop Varieties in a Green Revolution for Africa: Implications for Sustainability and Equity," presents a critical appraisal of proposals for a Green Revolution in Africa, questioning not only their technical feasibility, but two of their basic assumptions: 1) the "unilineal evolution of world culture and agriculture following an idealized Western model," and 2) "the necessity of unlimited economic growth, along with the availability of the resources to support it, on which that evolution is based." He insists that Western social and biological sciences must be grounded in the ecological and sociocultural realities of Africa in a collaborative effort to produce a sustainable agriculture for that continent.

Stephen Reyna's "What is to Be Done?" poses the question Lenin asked for Russia at the beginning of the 20th century for the Third World, and especially Africa, in the late 20th and early 21st centuries. The essay proposes a theory that combines elements of world systems with entitlement theory. It suggests that over the next century the increasing scarcity of resources required by the capitalist economies of the Great Powers will motivate them to control more effectively the sovereignty of Third World nations. This neo-imperialism will tend to maintain or increase warfare in the periphery, producing steep declines in the entitlement sets of people living in, or near violence, thereby provoking famine. The conclusion to this final essay is dismal. Either its analysis is so flawed that its conclusions are dismally wrong, or if they are substantially correct, then what is to be done is to perform the dismal chore of burying the dead.

2.

It is now time to discuss certain questions raised by the different contributors. The first has to do with the need for a new political economy.

Political Economy

African famine has been commonly attributed to acts of nature. None of the contributors, it should be absolutely clear, takes seriously such mono-causal environmental explanations. Rather they have paid special attention to historical trajectories of political and economic processes which have caused and exacerbated famine in Africa. Changes in productive relations (particularly the emergence of wage labor) and the expansion or contraction of factors of production (changes in the ecological base, land tenure practices, and the introduction of western technology) were found to be critical to understanding the predicament of the African communities under study. At the same time, most authors have taken care to emphasize how changes in the international capitalist economy have had an impact on regional, national, and local relations of production, distribution, and consumption.

What is singularly important in many of these contributions and what enlarges our understanding of paradigms that currently inform the food crisis debate is their focus on how local actors cope with and sometimes manage to resist those political and economic changes which threaten their survival (cf. critiques by Vaughn, 1987; Sen, 1981, 1984, and 1988 of the new-Malthusian/food availability decline argument; Berry, 1984 and Staudt, 1987 on rational peasants/imperfect structures; Le Marchand, 1986 and Staudt, 1987 on the economy of affection/irrational peasantry position). They also make clear that endowments and entitlements are differentiated by age and class as well as by cultural values regarding the appropriate sexual division of labor, all of which affect both the overall availability of food and access to it by particularly vulnerable groups.

This focus upon how more macroscopic political and economic processes change microscopic social relations, which in their turn influence local actors' consciousnesses, is a new twist in the political economy of famine, one that is critical for understanding the direction and magnitude of the transformations that affect the ability to produce food and the entitlements necessary to command its consumption. The holistic perspective of anthropology, with its attention to the details of social reproduction through cultural norms and values as well as its insistence upon the full particulars of the integration of the individual into the social and the local into the national spheres, provides a useful framework for analyzing such transformations. It is for this reason that we suggest that this volume reflects an emergence in famine studies of a more "anthropological" political economy.

Gender

In its essence, culture is gendered. Socially appropriate expectations and opportunities ascribed to biological sex by a given society rationalize the moral economy of gender so that socially constituted difference is construed as having a §natural" biological basis (Rubin, 1972). Socialization into a particular culture presupposes the gradual conceptual grasp of these "natural" differences between women and men and thus provides the basis for sometimes complementary, sometimes conflictual, world-views and the acquisition of different skills, knowledge, and power by male and female actors. Yet women within any particular society enter into the division of labor and circuits of distribution and consumption differentially based on age and class. As a result all women and their dependents are not equally vulnerable to food shortages. This complex view of the intersection of gender, age, class, and ethnicity informs many of the essays contributed to this volume. The remarks below are intended to highlight some of the fruitful lines of research on gender and hunger which are currently underway.

The contribution of women to agricultural production is greater in Africa than anywhere else in the world. Current estimates generally cite figures of 45–80% (Dixon, 1982; Gladwin and McMillan, 1989; and Spring, 1986). Not all agricultural production is for subsistence, and there are numerous local variations in the gender division of labor for export and food crops. The extent to which women are the primary food producers in the sub-Saharan African countryside is now well known, despite the erpsistence of statistical under-reporting (see Dixon, 1982 for a critique of ILO, FAO, and national census procedures; Funk, this volume), so that most investigators are constrained to pay lipservice to the conceptualization of the African farmer as "she." Yet, contrary to empirical evidence, census takers, extension workers, state marketing boards, agricultural research institutes, credit agencies, donors, and too may researchers persist in addressing the problem of African food production as if farmers were male.

What accounts for this bias and how does it affect current perceptions of the food crisis? A number of authors point to the persistence of sex-stratified norms, values, and institutions (in the West as well as in sub-Saharan Africa) which cloud the picture of women's participation in agriculture by under-estimating female, unpaid family labor (Dixon, 1982; Mbilinyi, 1990; Safilios-Rothschild, 1985; Staudt, 1987; Whitehead, 1990). While it is generally acknowledged that African women are almost solely responsible for the drawing of water, hewing of wood, cooking of food, and a whole host of other domestic activities, their important role in producing, processing, and trading the harvest and their input into decision-making in the farm household are just beginning to be documented (see Guyer, 1984; Lewis, 1981; Pala, 1976; and Spring, 1986 for comprehensive overviews of variations by regions and the chapters by Brown, Funk, Goheen, Kerner and Cook, O'Brien and Gruenbaum, and White in this volume for comparative case material). Increased attention to women's agricultural contributions in the 1970s and 1980s was sparked by Boserup's (1970) pioneering analysis of African female-farming systems. Recent critiques of Boserup's model of the pristine dualism of the gendered division of labor (with men growing cash crops using modern techniques and women producing subsistence crops with traditional methods) have pointed to the historical specificity of this division (Guyer, 1984; Richards, 1983). Colonial agricultural policies had everything to do with changes in land use/tenure, the provision of credit and inputs, systems of taxation and labor recruitment, and marketing structures that favored male participation in export crop production and reliance on women's activities in subsistence crop production to satisfy home consumption. However, it is important to specify that there have been variations in the implementation of such policies which bear significantly on current divisions of labor.

In this volume Brown contrasts the domestic and food processing activities of Kanembou and Maba women with the high level of food crop production (also used for sale) by Sara women in Chad. Funk contrasts the sexual division of labor among the Bejáa of Guinea Bissau, where men and women grow different varieties of food crops for subsistence and sale, with Brassa wet-rice cultivation, wherein gender serves as a basis for assigning different tasks. Nso women in Cameroon studied by Goheen grow over ninety percent of the food consumed in the household, yet surveys indicate that they contribute over twenty-five percent of the household expenditures from the sale of their food crops. Kerner and Cook describe how Chagga women in Tanzania were systematically excluded from coffee production by colonial authorities, but their access to land for food crop production for subsistence and sale varies by class. Middle peasant women seek to expand income-earning opportunities through the processing of bananas and grain into beer for sale. Asante women are the mainstay of food crop production in Ghana according to Clark, although Asante men are also active farmers. Asante men expect to sell the bulk of the produce, while women, who are heavily dependent upon market trading of their produce, must first provide for the household. Sudanese women are primarily responsible for food crop production, but O'Brien and Gruenbaum demonstrate that in times of crisis, women and children are increasingly drawn into wage labor or commodity production to supplement household income. Pastoralist WoDaaBe women in Niger, studied by White, own few animals, and although their husbands are formally responsible for the household's millet supply, it is the women who acquire the food to feed the household and enable it to survive without the sale of livestock by exchanging milk and milk products, which they control, for grain.

Thus, the stereotypical view of African women as relegated merely to the subsistence sector of production, supported by current interventions under the umbrella of Women in Development programs (see the recent critique by Mbilinyi, 1987), presents a distortion almost as serious as one which neglects the importance of women's agricultural role altogether. As Whitehead argues, the recent interest in the gendered division of labor in African agriculture presupposes that, "food crises have arisen because the economic changes of the twentieth century have relegated rural women to food production within an under-resourced 'subsistence sector' of small-scale agriculture" (1990:54). This vision ignores several critical issues: (1) food crops are often sold as cash crops; (2) food crops and cash crops are grown by a variety of methods; (3) women are heavily involved in rural agricultural wage labor on cash crop plantations; and (4) there are numerous cases of women managing farms for cash and food crop production, either in the absence of, or in conjunction with, their spouses.

A focus on the production side of the African food crisis, however, presents only one half of the picture of how families feed themselves and survive in times of shortage. Researchers who have concentrated on the agricultural production activities of women are inevitably drawn into a consideration of women's involvement in the marketing of crops, their ability to influence the disposal of income generated from sales, the non-agricultural labor demands on their time, and their opportunities for earning non-farm income to care for themselves and their dependents.

There is widespread recognition among anthropologists that men and women in African families are not guided by the unitary interest which supposedly characterizes the household decision-making model described by Western economists. However, so many of the macro-level approaches taken in the famine literature read as if women's and men's activities in distribution and consumption are entirely complementary. Even "internalist" theories of the food crisis which purport to locate the decline in food production in the moral economy of the peasantry, rational or otherwise (see Staudt's 1987 critique of Bates, 1981; Hyden, 1980, 1983; Lofchie and Bates, 1980), fail to examine the different strategies pursued by men and women to sustain basic survival. What accounts for the refusal to see the "hearthhold" (the unit of a woman and her children centered around her hearth, home, granary, livestock, and gardens: see Vaughn, 1987) as located in the contested area of larger (and often competing) household interests? Is this a matter of male bias in the models employed by Western researchers—models which complement an idealized male-dominant vision of the African family held by local actors (Ardner, 1972)? or, as Whitehead (1990) suggests, are Africans and "Africanists" doubtful that domestic conflict represents a legitimate area of political economy investigation (see Collier's 1974 essay, which lays the groundwork for this type of analysis)? Whatever the reason, it is now more critical than ever to harness the wealth of recent empirical research on African families and households (see the exhaustive review by Guyer, 1981) for the analysis of the special vulnerability of women and children to chronic and acute food shortages.

As pointed out by Cohen and Odhiambo (1989) in their poignant description of hunger in Kenya's Siaya district, women in the countryside face an increasing struggle to stretch their income to the limit. The value and quantity of goods purchased in local markets are steadily declining in the rural areas of Africa, and this has profound effects on the production of meals and the sociability surrounding food consumption. The zero-zero-one ration, described by Nigerian women at the 1988 African regional meeting of DAWN (Development Alternatives with Women for a New Era [Thomas-Emeagwali, 1988]), indicates that the mid-day meal has all but disappeared from the rural African diet. Meal preparation at night and food consumption in the privacy of the hearthhold may be the only option available to women in order to stretch the meager grain stores essential to the survival of her dependents. The exclusion of kin and neighbors from nucleated food consumption further weakens claims to wider resources and cooperative labor arrangements.

Changing patterns of wage labor and increased urban migration may be reflected in demographic shifts in rural farm populations. In some areas of East Africa, for example (see Cohen and Odhiambo, 1989; Kerner and Cook, this volume), it is the elderly, women, and young children who are the mainstay of food crop production. In the not-so-distant past, families split between the city and the country maintained a unified consumption unit through the transfer of staple grains, fish, and meat to the urban areas and the shuttle of purchased commodities and cash to the rural areas. Declining grain surpluses in the countryside leave little or nothing to spare, and the declining purchasing power of the urban wage has steadily decreased the volume and value of remittances from spouses and adult children. The fragility of the rural-urban network has obvious negative long-term effects for conjugal and inter-generational cooperation and food security.

One of the premises of a gender-sensitive political economy approach to famine is that special attention must be directed to understanding why certain sectors of a population starve and others do not during a food crisis. Sen's influential work, *Poverty and Famines: An Essay on Entitlement and Deprivation* (1981) addresses this issue. Sen argues that starvation is linked to changes in entitlement. Entitlement consists of the set of alternative commodity "bundles" that are acquired through the legal channels open to a person who holds a particular status. Entitlement is determined in two ways. It consists first of an original bundle of ownership (the endowment) which accrues to the status of the individual, and second, of alternative bundles that are acquired through trade and production (exchange entitlement mapping). Famines occur through entitlement failures related either to endowment decline (e.g., alienation of land or loss of grazing rights) or to exchange entitlement decline (e.g., loss of employment, failure of money wages to keep up with food prices, failure of prices of animal products or craft products or services to keep up with basic food prices, or all of these [Sen, 1985:208-209]}. People starve when their entitlement set does not include any commodity bundle with enough food.

Sen admits that his approach does not explain why widespread failures in entitlement occur (see critiques by Raikes, 1988 and Reyna and Watts, in this volume). His early work is more-or-less gender blind and relies heavily on a market model that does not work adequately for many African cases where entitlement may be based on "less secure claims on food and (other resources) which derive from social obligations other than wages, produce sales, and ownership of property" (Raikes, 1988:83). In a later piece, Sen (1985) applies entitlement analysis to intra-family divisions of labor, and in his reformulation of economic decision-making models he is forced to confront the ideological (extra-economic) dimension of entitlements. Social arrangements of labor within households are based on both cooperation and conflict in this revised model. Moreover, cooperation may be more of an illusion (adapted perception) than a reality. Adapted perception leads to systematic failure to see certain intra-family inequalities and to the viewpoint that extraordinary asymmetries are normal and legitimate. There is a "fog of ambiguity" surrounding certain roles (particularly unpaid female labor) in the labor process which affects entitlement claims to household resources. By entering gender into the equation, Sen is led to expand the concept of entitlement to include claims to use as well as exchange rights. Inclusion of "cultural phenomena" enables him to consider "..the productive contributions that are in effect made by labour expended in activities that are not directly involved in production, narrowly defined" (1985:198). The greater proportion of African women's productive and socially reproductive activities concern the basic survival needs of the household. Therefore, it is critical to consider the conditions under which a woman's legitimate claim to resources is eroded and leads to a weakening in her fall-back options and bargaining leverage in the household, which will ultimately threaten hearthhold survival.

Sen's conceptual framework is useful for anthropological and social historical research on famine trajectories (see for example, Vaughn's 1987 analysis of the Malawi famine of 1949) precisely because it problematizes cultural constructions of gender in relation to losses in entitlement. The behavior of women and their families in times of food shortage, as illustrated in the case studies presented in this volume, is rendered comprehensible once the structure of entitlements and endowments by gender, class, and age is laid out. Two examples may serve to illustrate this process.

In their analysis of the capitalist expansion of agriculture and the impact of economic crisis on rural producers in the Gezira cotton-growing scheme in the Sudan, O'Brien and Gruenbaum note the disruption of traditional divisions of labor and the destruction of autonomous systems of social reproduction. However, the introduction of new technologies, which have commercialized domestic work, and new wage employment opportunities have not proved to liberate secluded women. Instead, the individualization and nucleation of production units have led to dependency on uncertain wage labor opportunities, loss of the safety net of storable surpluses, and (through ecological degradation) loss of the security of surrounding forest resources. Cultural codes that place a high premium on women's honor take on intensified value when families migrate for wage labor on these cotton growing schemes. In the past, a woman's personal autonomy was embedded in cooperative field or pastoral labor with communities of kin. Migration has led to new work/residential patterns among strangers of different ethnic groups.

Ideological pressures to guard female family honor in such cases may lead to an even greater seclusion of women. Women also face greater pressures to increase their fertility in order to sustain acceptable levels of food production in the face of losses due to changes in rotation/fallow and the drain of members of the household through migrant wage labor.

White's WoDaaBe case (Niger) provides a tragic example of how recurrent drought and famine have led to decapitalization and ultimately to total reliance on food relief. In the past, women were the providers of milk and cereal products to the household (purchased through milk product exchange). When drought reduced herd size, milk surpluses became rare. While in times of plenty WoDaaBe women were able to accumulate small numbers of cattle through gifts from male kin and purchase from milk sales, decreased herd size during the drought eroded their endowment and entitlement exchange. By the early 1980s, ninety percent of the household's grain needs were being supplied through livestock sale. The downward spiral was exacerbated by the sale of reproducing female animals, which further reduced milk supplies, necessitating more cereal purchases, higher cash needs, increased animal sales, and fewer calves.

Policy

Unfortunately most measures to remedy famines are little more than bandaids. They have obviously not worked; nor will they, for they are irrelevant to the enormous changes that must occur if hunger is to be eliminated—changes in the realms of gender, politics, and ethics.

The studies of gender and hunger just reviewed suggest certain considerations that are relevant to the prevention and containment of famine. They indicate that policies to ensure food security that rely simply on increasing the overall availability of food are unlikely to prevent hunger. Carrot and stick solutions (offering incentives to grow more food by getting prices right or policies designed to reform the irrational tendencies of peasants and the avariciousness of traders) miss the complex variation in the way farmers are differentially incorporated into wage labor production by gender and class. Such disarticulation intersects with ecologically damaging practices, climatic fluctuation, and political shocks. Combined, these factors have an effect on the expansion of entitlements for some and the contraction of entitlements for others. Entitlement decline for certain groups places them at risk, chronically during seasonal fluctuations, and acutely in time of war or natural disaster.

Clearly, an initial step in the formulation of national food security policies involves the proper documentation of the productive activities of women.

The contribution of women to farming, and particularly their largely invisible contribution to rural wage labor on commercial plantations and farm schemes, should be assessed. This involves a revision of census-taking instruments and the re-training of enumerators. The availability of agricultural extension services, credit, and inputs of women and poor farmers in general should be accurately evaluated. Agricultural research on food crops should receive the same emphasis as export crops. Shifts in land tenure practices, which erode the entitlement to subsistence farmland for women, grazing land for pastoralists, or arable plots for poor farmers in general, bear careful review. Pricing policy for food crops requires an understanding of local consumption preferences as well as the production and processing demands which different crops imply for women. A clear understanding of the extent of women's involvement in farm management and household decision-making will enhance the likelihood of success of price incentives. Ecologically threatening cultivation practices must be considered within the context of the commoditization of land, the potential loss to the household labor pool through migrant wage labor, and declining remittances form urban-based kin.

Income-generating opportunities for rural women should be increased, but the current practice of providing low-level skills training and inputs for petty crafts production favored by many WID initiatives needs to be re-assessed. As many of our case studies indicate, women need more substantial educational opportunities and a steady source of additional cash income to offset entitlement losses in land and livestock. Control over income from non-farm projects may be contested within the family or in public arenas. The introduction of new technologies to alleviate domestic labor and new income opportunities are likely to increase the autonomy of women of certain classes or ethnic groups, but may increase the dependency of others.

A subtle understanding of how cultural codes limit or expand entitlement options, thus affecting the division of labor and consumption patterns for women and men, seems key to predicting when shifts in the overall political economy are likely to intersect with natural disasters or political shocks and lead to famine. The early signs of chronic inability to maintain consumption at the level of the hearthhold are manifest in the rise in domestic conflicts over food and income within the household. These deserve recognition as reflecting resistance to deepening asymmetries that place women and children at increased risk. The fragile structure of women's entitlement bears special consideration in the initial stages of acute shortage when the sale of assets not only increases the vulnerability of women and their dependents, but is likely to have long-range effects for men as well. Once a crisis is in full sway, the entire fabric of entitlements (especially those in the non-commoditized form of claims) is in danger of being ripped asunder. An identification of the special knowledge and skills possessed by men and women to sustain survival is critical to alleviating a short-term food crisis. The necessity of population containment (prevention of migration) and the complexities of providing food relief are well known. However, it is important to reiterate that the delivery of food relief to the most vulnerable groups often depends upon initial entitlement claims.

The predominant media image of African famine features the starvation of women and children. All women and children do not starve during a crisis, but food security policies which take a gendered approach to culture into account will ensure that fewer of them will go hungry in the future.

However, more is required than the protection of the most vulnerable. Radical changes in the relation of the First World to the Third World are essential if famines are to be avoided, and here, as is the case with all social change, politics and the exercise of power are fundamental. Five facts regarding the distribution of food stand out. First, competent authorities agree that there is sufficient food in the world to feed its people. Second, there are enormous numbers of people, largely in the Third World, who lack the ability to produce, or otherwise to acquire, the barest minimum of food. Third, there are also a large number of persons in the world, especially in the West and among Third World elites, who have the ability to produce enormous quantities of food and/or the ability otherwise to acquire and control it. These people, or their agents, also control the political institutions that make and enforce the rules governing access to the resources needed to produce food or to acquire it in other ways. People in this latter group, thus, have the capacity to provide for their own nutrition as well as that of others. Fourth, those with this capacity often act to ensure that those lacking it cannot acquire the food or resources needed to produce food in order to maintain adequate subsistence. Fifth, as a consequence of this distribution of resources and exercise of power some eighteen million people perish annually from hunger related causes. The amelioration of such a situation is hardly easy. It requires fundamental transformations in the distribution of power and the ethics of its use.

Power transformations are vastly complex and far from completely understood. Frequently they involve the vigorous application of violence, as in the case of the French Revolution. On the other hand they may take place peacefully, as in the case of recent changes in much of the socialist block of Eastern Europe.

All such changes involve changes in the cultural codes of the societies concerned. These codes, though they are, of course, influenced by underlying economic conditions, are expressed most clearly in a society's religious and legal institutions. Explicit rules of what is, and what is not, appropriate behavior—i.e., rules of good and evil—basic to these institutions are a society's ethical system. Attitudes in the West appear to be ambivalent with regard to starvation and suffering. On the one hand massive humanitarian efforts are mounted to alleviate gross examples of suffering, as in the Sudan and Ethiopia, but on the other hand it appears that for the most part the prevailing ethics in wealthy, Western nations—those with the potential to end hunger—do not label as evil many acts that maintain, or create, hunger.

This is because for the most part Western legal systems do not tend to judge negatively the acts of individuals in positions of power in major economic or political institutions. What explains the indifference in Western ethical codes to the acts of political officials that indirectly but ultimately kill? The current world distribution of power described dramatically by one author (Haviland, 1991) as "global apartheid," is such that less than one third of the world's citizens (those living in the West) control the vast majority of the world's resources and have a near monopoly over its weapons of destruction. This unequal distribution of power and wealth is increasingly the cause of structural violence. Such violence, committed against a disenfranchised majority of the people of the world, is the cause of unconscionably high levels of poverty, hunger, disease, and death. To individuals in the West, such violence would *appear* to be result of social, political, and economic structures, rather than the direct result of particular political decisions. Such ethical indifference to the consequences of the exercise of power has enormous implications for the causes, and maintenance, of Third World food crises. This is because it allows governments to ignore, or actively promote, the creation of hunger in the pursuit of policies regarded as in their national interests.

The problem with the morality codified in Western legal systems is that those who suggest that powerful officials who kill are bad are often themselves dismissed as bad. So long as such cultural codes predominate, the use of political institutions to create hunger will not be considered evil. Nor will the use of these same political institutions to prevent hunger be considered a great good. The Industrial Revolution had its Protestant Ethic. The revolution against famine needs a Hunger Ethic: a belief that it is unthinkable that people should go hungry.

If such a revolution does not occur, then the world will be left with enormous numbers of people living in hunger. There have been approximately 120 wars since 1945 (Kende, 1978, 1983). All but five of these were in developing nations. The West has little hunger. The Third World is hungry. Such statistics suggest, as Steinbach puts it, that "struggles" occur when the "basic needs" of a population are not met (1983:22). This, in turn, suggests that prospects for violence will increase if the changes in cultural codes and the distribution of political and economic power necessary to reduce hunger are not achieved.

REFERENCES

Ardner, E.
  1972 Belief and the Problem of Women, in J. S. LaFontaine, ed., The Interpretation of Ritual: Essays in Honour of A. I. Richards. London.
Bates, R. N.
  1981 Markets and States in Tropical Africa: The Political Basis of Agricultural Policies. Berkeley: University of California Press.
Berry, S.
  1984 The Food Crisis and Agrarian Change in Africa: A Review Essay, African Studies Review, 27:2:59-112.
Boserup, E.
  1970 Women's Role in Economic Development. NY: St. Martin's Press.
Cohen, D. W. and E. S. A. Odhiambo
  1989 Siaya, the Historical Anthropology of an African Landscape. Athens: Ohio University Press.
Collier, J.
  1974 Women in Politics, in S. Rosaldo and L. Lamphere, eds., Female, Male, and Society. Stanford: Stanford University Press.
Dey, J.
  1981 Gambian Women: Unequal Partners in Rice Development Projects? Journal of Development Studies, 17:3:109-122.
Dixon, R. B.
  1982 Women in agriculture: Counting the Labor Force in Developing Countries, Population and Development Review, 8:3:539-566.
Guyer, J.
  1981 Household and Community in African Studies, African Studies Review, 24:2/3;87-138.
  1984 Women in African Rural Economies: Contemporary Variations, in J. Hay and S. Stichter, eds., African Women South of the Sahara. London: Longman.
Haviland, WIlliam A.
  1991 Anthropology (6th edition). Chicago: Holt, Rinehart, & Winston, Inc.
Hyden, G.
  1980 Beyond Ujamaa in Tanzania. Berkeley: University of California Press.
  1983 No Shortcuts to Progress: African Development Management in Perspective. Berkeley: University of California Press.
Kende, I.
  1978 Wars of Ten Years 1967-1976. Journal of Peace Research, 3(XV)L:227-241.
Lappe, F. M.
  1986 World Hunger: Twelve Myths. New York: Grove Press.

Lemarchand, R.
   1986   The Political Economy of Food Issues, in A. Hansen and D. E. McMillan,
          eds., Food in Sub-Saharan Africa. Boulder: Lynne Reinner Publishers,
          Inc., 25-42.
Lewis, B.
   1981   Invisible Farmers: Women and the Crisis in Agriculture, Washington,
          D.C.: AID Office of Women in Development.
Lofchie, M. and R. Bates, eds.
   1980   Agricultural Development in Africa. New York: Preager.
Mbilinyi, M.
   1987   Women in Development: Ideology and the Marketplace, in V. Miner and
          H. E. Longino, eds., Competition: A Feminist Taboo. New York: Feminist
          Press, 106-120.
   1990   Structural Adjustment, Agribusiness and Rural Women in Tanziania, in H.
          Bernstein, B. Crow, M. Macintosh, and C. Martin, eds., The Food Ques-
          tion: Profits Versus People? London: Earthscan Publications, Ltd.,
          111-124.
Pala, A.
   1976   African Women in Rural Development: Research Trends and Priorities,
          Washington, D.C.: Overseas Liaison Committee, number 12.
Raikes, P.
   1988   Modernizing Hunger. Portsmouth, NH: Heinemann Press.
Richards, P.
   1983   Ecological change and the Politics of African Land Use, African Studies
          Review, 26:2.
Rubin, G.
   1972   The Traffic in Women: Notes Towards a Political Economy of Sex-Gen-
          der, in R. Reiter, ed., Towards an Anthropology of Women. New York:
          Monthly Review Press.
Safilios-Rothschild, C.
   1985   The Persistence of Women's Invisibility in Agriculture: Theoretical and
          Policy Lessons in Lesotho and Sierra Leone, Economic Development and
          Cultura Change, 33:299-317.
Sen, A.
   1981   Poverty and Famines: An Essay on Entitlement and Deprivation. Oxford:
          Clarendon Press.
   1984   Resources, Values, and Development. Cambridge, MA: Harvard Univer-
          sity Press.
   1985   Women, Technology, and Sexual Divisions, Trade and Development,
          6:195-223.
   1988   Hunger and Entitlements, World Institute for Development Economics re-
          search, United Nations University.
Spring, A.
   1986   Women Farmers and Food in Africa: Some Considerations and Suggested
          Solutions, in A. Hansen and D. E. McMillan, eds., Food in Sub-Saharan
          Africa. Boulder: Lynne Reinner Publications, Ltd., 332-348.
Staudt, K.
   1987   Uncaptured or Unmotivated? Women and the Food Crisis in Africa, Rural
          Sociology, 52:1:37-55.

Strong, M.
  1989 Africa Beyond the Famine: The Case for Hope, Boston University: Working Papers in African Studies, number 135.
Thomas-Emeagwali, E.
  1988 Development Alternatives with Women: Food and the Debt Crisis, ROAPE, 43:94.
Vaughn, M.
  1987 The Story of an African Famine: Gender and Famine in Twentieth Century Malawi. Cambridge: Cambridge University Press.
Whitehead, A.
  1990 Food Crisis and Gender Conflict in the African Countryside, in H. Bernstein, B. Crow, M. Macintosh, and C. Martin, eds., The Food Question: Profits Versus People? London: Earthscan Publications, Ltd., 54-68.

PART A

Theoretical Perspectives

CHAPTER 1

Heart of Darkness: Reflections on Famine and Starvation in Africa

Michael Watts

The history of Man from the beginning has been the history of the struggle for daily bread.
Josue de Castro (1977:49)

The disaster ruins everything, all the while leaving everything intact.
Maurice Blanchot (1986:1)

In a modernist slogan with imperial overtones, USA for Africa proclaimed in 1985 that "We are the World" and kicked off the largest food relief effort in history. Underwritten in large part by an influential community—the rock music industry—not exactly distinguished by its political or ethical maturity, this unprecedented humanitarian assistance was triggered by the 1984-1985 Ethiopian famine. The terrifying images of the Korem relief camp in Wollo Province transmitted in October 1984 by a BBC broadcast are generally credited with having broken through the Chinese wall of silence surrounding mass starvation in The Horn. Michael Buerk, in a chilling and memorable narrative captured the awful power of the images: "Dawn, as the sun breaks through the piercing chill of night, on a plain outside Korem . . . a biblical famine in the twentieth century;" an earthy landscape but in reality "the closest thing to hell"—tropes of the African condition.

But landscapes can also be deceptive; they can be, as John Berger (Berger and Mohr, 1967:1) says, less a setting than a curtain behind which struggles, achievements, and accidents take place.

The African food crises of the 1980s have been distinguished by something of a seachange in international perceptions of famine. A major publish-

23

ing house took on the Report for the Independent Commission on International Humanitarian Issues, *Famine: A Man-Made Disaster* (ICIHI, 1985), which posited, as have other popular books by The World Commission on Environment and Development (1987) and Food First (Twose and Goldwater, 1986), that famine was "man-made." In sharp constradistinction to the Club of Rome (Meadows, Meadows, Randers, and Behrens, 1972) and the Brandt Commission (1980), *Famine: A Man-Made Disaster* rejects the meterological and demographic explanations of African hunger. A foreword by Dr. David Owen, former head of Britain's Liberal Party, makes for startling reading, perhaps because it resembles a measured Marxist reading of Robert Chambers and Amartya Sen: famine emerges, he says, from the particular conjunction of a colonial legacy, the ineptitude of "development experts," and human mismanagement of the market, not from a malevolent Nature. Paul Richards' intriguing observation (1987a:113) that this new political perception of famine, and in particular the discussion of humanitarian versus economic pressures in famine eradication, is in some respects similar to debates over the ending of the slave trade reaffirms how central famine is to human experience. In our historical lexicon, famine is indelible, emotive, and pervasive. As a type of disaster, famine is "that which does not have the ultimate as a limit but bears the ultimate away in the disaster" (Blanchot, 1986:vii).

Famine is, and always has been, the very stuff of history. In talking of food crises we are not, to employ David Arnold's colorful language (1988:4), tracking the rare trajectory of a Halley's comet across the historical firmament. Subsistence struggles are woven into the very fabric of history. China had close to 2000 famines between 300 B.C. and 1911, and Britain has been afflicted by mass starvation at least 180 times since A.D. 10. Famines and mass hunger have been motors of social transformations, important historical markers in the almanac of the long durée, and in some cases political icons in the historical imagination: the Paris Commune in 1871, the Ukraine's harvest of sorrow in 1932–1933, the "Great Leap Forward" famine in China in 1958. It is the exceptional yet recursive quality of famine which leaves its imprint on the collective memory. French peasants in the seventeenth century could expect to experience at least one famine in their lifetime; Hausa peasants talk of the great hungers of the past, the *babban yunwa* encapsulated in oral tradition, song, and anecdote, as living entities with distinctive personalities (Watts, 1983). Famines are, after all, named. Like much in peasant "histories," their meanings transmit an immediacy; in popular speech and reference, they might have transpired yesterday (cf., Berger and Mohr, 1982). Mass starvation, especially in peasant societies in which famine is endemic, is a powerful instance of what Michel Foucault calls "the history of the present;" famine is rooted in the normal, in the prosaic, and in the everyday (Scheper-Hughes, 1988).

In this sense subsistence crises, whatever their particular causality or cultural articulations, are extensions of lived experience, what David Arnold (1988:91) refers to as "intensifiers." Famine contains the terror of the possible; in the words of Maurice Blanchot (1986:1) "the disaster is its imminence." However horrific and traumatic, societies will not, indeed cannot, act entirely out of character during famines. Food crises are exceptional events, but are rooted in the subterranean structures of the present. As R. H. Tawney (1966:77) observed half a century ago, famine is the final stage of a disease which, though not always conspicuous, is ever present. And in this sense, to make use of March Bloch's metaphor, calamities afford us the opportunity to grasp in a more profound sense the structure of society itself in the same way that disease permits the physician better to understand the secret life of the body.

Yet the secret life of famine remains in shadow if not entirely hidden. If there is a growing sentiment that African hunger is "man-made,"[2] Rangasami is surely close to the mark when she observes that our biggest failing remains "the inability to recognize the political, economic and social determinants that mark the onset of the process" (1985:1747). It is ironic that such a failing marks an era that has "the odious distinction of being the period when more people will die of famine than in any previous century" (Cahill, 1982:1).[3] It is an era, moreover, in which famine is more preventable than ever, in which abundance and surplus in the advanced capitalist states have reached unprecedented levels, and in which North-South inequities are ever more vivid and untenable. In 1988 an estimated 480 million people lived in countries where local crop production and import capacity failed to meet their usual levels of consumption and five countries with a combined population of 204 millions failed to prevent famine within their national borders (Brown University World Hunger Program, 1989:5). 455 million people live in households too poor to obtain the energy sufficient for minimal activity among adults and for the healthy growth of children. These food poor, improvished households are primarily in Africa and South Asia and their number has almost certainly grown.

However laudable the humanitarian efforts, it is salutary to recall that the Ethopian famine relief of BANDAID and We are the World raised $120 million, roughly the value of an F30 frigate. Official food assistance from the US Government to Ethiopia totaled 300,000 tons ($200 million), much less than half a stealth bomber. The total Ethiopian relief effort in 1984–1985—the largest in history—was equivalent to one quarter of global *daily* expenditures for military purposes over the same period (Sivard, 1987). In 1988–89 the appalling starvation in southern Sudan and northern Somalia was all but ignored internationally.[4]

In this essay I shall meander across the broad terrain of famine studies. In part this reflects the burgeoning of scholarship stimulated by Sen's book (1981) and the proliferation of food shortages in Africa over the last two decades. But this journey also provides me with an opportunity to rethink my own work on food crises in northern Nigeria, not least to clarify what I have come to believe are critical aspects of famine dynamics, namely *how the market develops* and the *social logic of agrarian relations* (Watts, forthcoming). I am motivated in this respect by the belief that Sen's brilliant work cannot throw much light on either the longer term processes of social reproduction in contradistinction to the proximate causes of crisis, or on the struggles between dominant and subaltern classes which ultimately determine exchange entitlements. Beginning with some observations on how famines are represented in Africa, I go on to discuss the basis of famine proneness, the internal architecture of famine, the relations between drought and food shortage, and the significance of entitlements and the market in the famine genesis. I conclude with some remarks on famine and popular consciousness and on the centrality of democracy and civil society in famine prevention.

REPRESENTING AND DECODING STARVATION

It is paradoxical, but hardly surprising, that the right to food has been endorsed more often and with greater unanimity and urgency than most other human rights, while at the same time being violated more comprehensively and systematically than ... any other right. Peter Alston (1984:9)

We are bombarded with images of hunger and starvation. This is particularly the case for Africa. Famine in its popular representation has emerged as the icon of African collapse, a sort of effigy of the deep and enduring "crisis" of post-Independence development (Watts, 1989). Images provide powerful representations of crisis, but of a special sort. Photographs, for example, say things beyond the reach of words. This is a source of great power, yet also of ambiguity. Images of starving Tigrean mothers and children appear in the pages of the *New York Times* usually jumbled together with glamorous advertisements for sable jackets and the latest symbols of middle class consumer sovereignty. The contrast contained in such a juxtaposition is itself a sign of a certain sort of madness, but, as John Berger (1980) astutely remarks, these overwhelming images of deprivation also have a dispelling quality. The photograph is weak in intention and meaning; it is ambiguous because it represents a single choice and a discontinuity; that is to say a photograph ruptures the continuity of [public] history or individual [private] life stories.

Photographs supply information—'bursts' of information as Walter Benjamin (1969) says—without a language of their own; they "quote from appearance" (Berger and Mohr, 1982:96; Barthes, 1977:45). The photograph produces a truth which is only partly defensible (an event without context), but often through the use of words this ambiguity is often replaced by dogmatic assertion.

As famine photographs appear in the press, the event of starvation is ambiguous "except to those whose personal relations to the event are such that their own lives supply the missing continuity" (Berger and Mohr, 1982;128). And most of us cannot, of course, provide the missing link; most of us do not even know hunger directly. But powerful images of famine frequently have a continuity provided for us however: they have a dispelling effect, blaming everyone and no-one, they have no history. The discontinuity of the photograph is, in other words, healed by a sort of diffuse causality. The event depicted retains its enormous power because it documents a truth: the violation of a universal right, namely the right to food. And yet for reasons perhaps hinted at in the meanings attributed to images of the personal agony of famine victims in refugee camps, this right is systematically abrogated.

The power and ambiguity of famine images combined with the moral weight of the right to food open food crises to explicitly political, indeed propagandistic, interpretations and meanings. In the context of the recent Cold War and the resurgence of the nationalities question in the USSR, the Ukrainian famine in the early 1930s has become a compelling illustration of such extreme politicization. The film *Harvest of Despair* (1985) employed photographic material which proved to be fraudulent to make a case that the Ukrainian famine was a case of genocide, a "holocaust"—the "greatest holocaust of the century" according to William F. Buckley on *Firing Line*—engineered by Stalin to crush nationalist sentiment (Jeff Coplon, 1988:28). Robert Conquest's book, *Harvest of Sorrow*, funded by the Ukrainian Research Institute and published in 1986, added a patina of scholarly legitimacy to the genocide argument, resting in large measure on notoriously biased emigré accounts. The purveyors of famine genocide have pressed their case on human rights into curricula available to every tenth grade social studies teacher in New York State (U.S. Commission on the Ukraine Famine, 1988). *Glasnost* has in fact contributed to a reopening of the debate over numbers, including some astonishing claims by Roy Medvedev (Mace, 1989).[5] Without denying the veracity of the event and its political-economic origins, there is no evidence to claim that the Ukrainian famine (or the Ethiopian activities in Eritrea and Tigre in 1984-1985) was genocidal.[6] To paraphrase Lévi-Strauss, famines can be good to think with.[7] In this ideological climate, Ukraine in 1932, Ethiopia in the 1980s, and China in 1958 starkly reveal socialism as an evil empire, providing a counterweight to what is seen as the growing hegemony of a deterministic dependency theory ("capitalism causes famine").

It needs to be asserted, nevertheless, that if famine "exposes us to a certain idea of passivity" (Blanchot, 1986:3) and if its ideological uses bear odious political meanings, images of starvation in a free press have regularly mobilized state and international support for famine relief. Indeed, it is not easy to find an example of a famine in a country in which a free press, harnessing the power of famine images and the moral weight of the right to be free from hunger, has not been capable of mobilizing popular support and political opposition (Dreze, 1988; Sen, 1987; Dreze and Sen, 1989).

TELLING FAMINE STORIES:
THEORIES, TROPES, AND METAPHORS

We tell ourselves stories in order to live. Joan Didion (1979:1)

Famine is what Raymond William (1977) calls a "keyword;" its meanings are tightly bound up with the problems it is used to discuss. They are binding words, "indicative of certain forms of thought" (ibid., p. 13), ways of seeing culture and society. Famines are used to challenge cozy consensuses on purportedly golden ages of "primitive abundance" in the past and to shape the ways in which we envisage the future. Famine is, as David Arnold says (1988:5), a "formative influence in our understanding of the modern world." Famine as an instance of widespread scarcity is naturally central to the discipline of economics. In Walrasian competitive theory the notion of a structural failure of individuals to obtain what they want (employment, food) is anathema. Desai (1987:397) has observed that in a pure Walrasian general equilibrium theory, entitlements are secure in a trade-interdependent way such that the possibility of death due to insufficient entitlement claims is ruled out. An optimizing peasant in the face of an indeterminate harvest would make insurance arrangements. In the absence of trade barriers imposed by the state, private markets perform adequately, and hence W. O. Jones of the Stanford Food Research Institute can confidently claim that Nigeria only experienced famine once this century (!)—during the Civil War—"which demonstrates that private marketing systems can be relied upon to feed the population" (1980:340). But what for many economists is an anomaly or aberration—or for the likes of Jones simply does not exist—is the central problematic in famine studies (minimum subsistence is not met for large sections of society). The particular significance of Sen's (1981) storytelling is precisely to question the economists' conventional story by positing economic relations and the market as socially and politically constituted. This may not appear terribly earth shattering either to Marxists or to famine victims.

There are other stories to be told, of course. Climate, "overpopulation," and war, while potentially significant as proximate or trigger factors (Torry, 1989b:8), have been substantially discredited as primary factors.[8] Essentialist explanations of famine in which nature (broadly understood) or natural laws are invoked, have, in other words, been socialized. This shift represents for some a significant theoretical shift and the growing hegemony of a new story, that of dependence (Torry, 1986b), imperialism (Gartrell 1985), and radicalism (Bryceson, 1980).[9] Bill Torry jumbles together an unusually heterogeneous literature—Sen (1981), Scott (1976), Watts (1983)—that apparently argues that poverty causes famine, that capitalism causes poverty and that "entire classes and nations lose control over their productive resources" (1986b:5). Dependency stories are deterministic, privileging ultimate causes (and ignoring proximate or triggering events) and treating the Third world poor as hapless victims of a vampiric capitalism (*see also* Rahmato, 1988). Torry believes dependency to be a sort of Beast of the Apocalypse, a body of theory constituted by rigid, theoretical laws which are weak when it comes to explaining the complexity of particular events. Apparently my own work (Watts, 1983) is a compelling example of this beastly story.[10] Gartrell (1985) accuses Mamdani (1985) of similar sins, romanticizing a pre-colonial past, refusing to accept the occurrence of pre-capitalist famines, and building a rickety causal structure on, God forbid, unilinear modes of evolution and reified imperialism.

These stories tend to produce universalistic theories of famine causation or to relativize explanations by adding "causes." There are quite reasonable grounds for Rahmato's claim (1988:338) that "the problem of famine causation is more complicated," but his own treatment of these debates is quite insubstantial. Like others writing on famine he posits simple dualisms: internal versus external, state versus market, capitalism versus socialism, moral versus political economy. Rahmato employs the empirical record that famine has occurred in a variety of contexts—socialist and capitalist, colonial and non-colonial, dependent and peripheral—to invoke complexity, but it is unclear what sort of theory is implied. Rahmato and Gartrell err toward a listing of "factors," a seamless web of influences producing a generic famine, in the same way that Currey (1984) refers to a "complex concatenation of factors." But *the circumstances under which factors become causes*—Mamdani (1986b:89) refers to the inability to distinguish primary from secondary social processes and determinant from contributory historical causes—are rather murky.

What sort of famine theory should one aspire to? Clearly there is a need for a "comparative phenomenology of famine" (Arnold, 1988:2)—that is to say comparative studies of the construction, understanding, and experience of famine—but there is a danger, seen in the best of comparative studies, of assuming all cases of extreme food shortage to be members of the same class of events (i.e., a sort of misplaced categorization). In other words, a generic view of famine identifies these social crises as species of the same phenomenon having the same antecedent conditions. This freezes history in such a way that famines are removed from the evolving world history of which they are organically part. The danger, then, is that necessary and sufficient conditions for famine are collapsed, and hence, it is not clear what *social processes* make factors into causes. My own belief is that one has to harness (i) long-term structural processes—what I would call tendencies producing certain patterns of vulnerability—(ii) the contingent or proximate events producing reductions in food supply and changes in entitlement (i.e., production and exchange failures, Swift, 1989), and (iii) the locally specific social or molecular processes that give them a particular rhythm, motion, and timbre.[11] The structural context for much of the modern period is provided by the development of capitalism linked to long-term entitlement change through market expansion, increasing divisions of labor, and proletarianization, and the growth of centralized states, which have both initiated and mediated entitlement changes (Tilly, 1983). The uneven development of capitalism is such that is transplants itself onto foreign soil and combines with differing social and power structures to produce different configurations of class and entitlement so that famines assume distinctive national i.e. 'local' characters.

Famines are all about politics and the exercise of power, specifically the power to command food through a variety of market and non-market institutional means (Cliffe et al., 1989). Sen (1981), for example, has shown how a theory of entitlement necessarily raises questions of politics and differential power. But in addition, to the extent that it is the poor who are typically at risk and are famine victims, the study of food crises provides an opportunity to grasp the ways in which subaltern groups are both subordinate to, and capable of resisting, dominant relations of power. Famines constitute one moment in the struggle for food, and any theory of mass starvation must come to terms with the political, social, and judicial contexts of the economy, what Sen (1987:64) calls "the entire system of property rights." Fathoming famines demands, but rarely makes use of, a sophisticated theory of power.

THINGS FALL APART:
AFRICAN CRISIS AND FAMINE PRONENESS

"This [peasant] life is a long drawn out question between a crop and a crop. "
Rudyard Kipling (in Lewin, 1984:175)

In popular representations of Africa, the leitmotif for the continent is crisis and decay.[12] Consumed by unrelenting poverty, war, massive debt, and political chaos, Africa has discovered a new heart of darkness. Witness the vertiginous descent:

> The African world has fallen apart. The countryside is ravaged by drought, locusts and pestilence; there is an AIDS epidemic. People flock from the rural areas to cities unable to cope. . . . National economies are near bankruptcy. Foreign exchange is exhausted. Food is in short supply. Fuelwood is becoming depleted. . . . Governments are constantly changing through coups. . . . There is an aura of . . . decay nepotism, corruption, coercion. . . .The cruel reality is exacerbated by rapid growth of population . . .soil erosion and land degradation. Above all millions are facing poverty and starvation. . . . The present is grim and the future even bleaker (Riddell, 1987:387-8).

The doom-laden qualities of Africa are certainly rooted in what is generally seen as a crisis in agriculture (low productivity, limited per capita growth in output), but also in a sort of African exceptionalism. The presumption is that across much of the Third World, famine as a recursive phenomenon has gradually disappeared, though hunger and malnutrition may of course remain and indeed worsen. Historically speaking this is not simply a pattern of the recent past. Gallant (1989) has argued that in the *poleis* of Greece during the Hellenistic period (323-144 B.C.) structural changes wrought by the creation of large-scale empires sounded the death-knell to famines but eroded "risk buffering mechanisms" of the peasantry and hence increased subsistence insecurity (*see also* Garnsey, 1987). A similar argument has been made for South Asia: India's "success story" (the eradication of famine but the persistence of appalling poverty) stands in sharp contrast to the "persistent drama of famine in Africa" (Dreze, 1988:102). African famine is seen as iconic of the failure of agriculture—indeed post-colonialism generally—and confirms her exceptionalism.[13]

John Iliffe in his new book, *The African Poor*, draws from the same intellectual lineage. Drawing upon a distinction between structural poverty—"long term poverty of individuals due to their social or personal circumstances"—and conjunctural poverty—"the temporary poverty into which ordinarily self-sufficient people may be thrown by crisis" (1988:4)—Ilffe suggests that Africa has experienced two major shifts in relation to poverty. The first, in keeping with the recent histories of Europe and Asia, is the transition from labor scarcity as a source of poverty in pre-colo-

nial Africa to land scarcity (fed by the demographic boom from the 1930s) of
the contemporary era. The second is the disappearance of famine (for Iliffe
meaning 'mass' mortality) from the 1920s,[14] but—and here is the exceptionalism—the terrifying "return of conjunctural poverty in the form of mass
famine mortality" after Independence induced by drought and political conflict (Ibid., p. 250). It is a position with some support from Marxists like Bill
Warren (1980:130) who salutes the progressive impact of colonial capitalism. But aside from the problems of defining the "mass" mortality, the existence of major crises in some parts of Africa in the 1940s and 1950s and the
fact that Iliffe's own view of famine causality is associated with drought,
which was relatively insignificant in the small pluvial of the 1950-1965 period, there is a great danger of theoretically divorcing the structural from the
conjunctural. Iliffe can, in this regard, suggest that as a cause of conjunctural
poverty "the international depression was trivial when compared with famine" (1988:156).

As a particular form of crisis, famines can be usefully situated with respect
to current debates over crisis theory (Offe, 1984). The classical definition of
crisis refers to the turning point of an illness in which the organism's self-
healing powers are called into question. But Offe has suggested that this can
generate at least two different crisis concepts: the first, which he calls a sporadic concept, represents a system endangered by acute catastrophic events
similar to Iliffe's conception of famine. The second refers to a social system
whose "grammar" may be endangered but in which crisis is seen dynami-
cally and processually as "developmental tendencies that can be confronted
with counter-acting tendencies which means that the outcome of the crisis is
quite unpredictable" (Offe, 1984:37). For Offe the latter focuses on what he
refers to as "crisis proneness." Structural tendencies and crisis proneness
strike to the heart of a conjunctural theory of famine, but move us beyond
Iliffe's neo-Malthusian notion of structure as a population-resource equation
(1988:4-7, 161-163).

In what respects can one talk of famine proneness in Africa? This is naturally deserving of a comprehensive analysis in itself, but in brief I wish to
suggest four axes of vulnerability in Africa. The first is *poverty* (Mellor and
Gavian, 1987) or, perhaps more properly, *power and need*. This is not to suggest that famine cannot occur in the midst of plenty (Sen, 1981; Spitz, 1980),
but rather that large numbers of individuals who are materially poor face ex-
cessive food insecurities even during normal periods (Bryceson, 1984; Wisner, 1988). Poverty is a diffuse structural explanation of famine, however,
and analytically one must grasp how the power to command food—*that is to
say the specific social structure of access to and control over resources*—is
abrogated in concrete historical circumstances.[15] This subsumes power in

the market but also the power of subaltern classes in relation to the state and other institutions. Nevertheless, the major relief agencies [the World Food Programme, the United Nations Food and Agriculture Organization] show dramatically that in terms of national food consumption, food production, sources of food, and income levels twenty-seven African countries can be defined as at risk, that is to say vulnerable to famine (see IDS, 1989; Curtis, Hubbard, and Shepherd, 1988:13–27).[16] Notwithstanding the fact that many of the statistics are probably fictional and so inaccurate as to be of dubious value (!), most of these states are particularly vulnerable to drought, war, or both.

The second axis is *the fiscal crisis of the state and import capacity*. Curtis, Hubbard, and Shepherd (1988:13) show that states suffering reduction in national income and import capacity are famine prone both in terms of long-term famine prevention and in terms of relief. Reductions in employment and purchasing power, state expenditures on infrastructure, health, and ecological restoration, and particularly declining import capacity increase famine risk (Demery and Addison, 1987).[17] The 1980s have been, in this regard, a nightmare for sub-Saharan Africa. GDP per capita declined by 20%, the terms of trade by 34%, and real minimum wages by 20% between 1980 and 1986 (Ghai and de Alacantara, 1989). Imports per capita declined by 65% over the same period. These trends are on average between two and three times worse than in Latin America. In 1988 Africa's debt-service burden accounted for 60% of export earnings and African countries paid to the IMF about a billion dollars more then they received. Some 23 states were relying on short-term capital (import credits in large part) either to sustain imports or prevent them falling in the 1980s. Austerity in the form of state reduction in health services, limited capacity to import food in crisis situations, growing income inequality and unemployment, and a compelling pressure to generate export revenues from the rural sector, in tandem constitute the very anithesis of a famine-resistant economy. In Africa "life is poor, nasty . . . and short and likely to remain so" (*The Economist*, March 4th, 1989, p. 15).[18]

The third axis is *war and geo-political conflict*, something largely ignored by Sen (1981). Without wishing to condone simplistic generalizations that civil wars across the continent can be explained by African political immaturity or "tribalism," the reality is that the extent of war, war related deaths, and destruction over the last two decades have been substantial (*see Figure 1*). In the last four years we have witnessed the hideous calamity of Sudanese and Eritrean/Tigrean refugees shuttling back and forth across the Sudan-Somali-Ethiopian borders fleeing military conflict. In the last year, large swaths of northwest Somalia have been depopulated by armed attacks from the Somali state, while in Ethiopia it is estimated that nine million have been dis-

	Civil Only	Civil/ International	International Only	Religious/ Ethnic	U.N Involved	Superpower Involved	Total Deaths
AFRICA							
Angola		•		•	•	•	213,000 since 1975
Burundi	•			•			5,000+ in 1988
Chad		•			•	•	7,000 since 1980
Ethiopia-Eritrea		•		•		•	546,000 since 1974
Ethiopia-Other	•			•			ca. 500,000 since 1974
Morocco-Western Sahara		•		•	•	•	10,000 since 1975
Mozambique		•		•	•		400,000+ since 1981
Namibia		•		•	•		25,000 since 1970
South Africa	•			•	•		3,000 since 1985
Somalia	•						ca. 25,000 in 1988
Sudan	•			•			100,000+ since 1984
Uganda	•			•			102,000 since 1981

Source: *The Nation*, January 9, 1989, p. 47; Sivard, 1987, p. 31.

Figure 1. War and War Related Deaths 1970–1988

placed (internally and externally) by war and famine over the last decade (Giorgis, 1989:370). War no more produces mass starvation as a necessity than does drought or entitlement change, but the physical displacement of large numbers of peasants, the destruction of communications and health infrastructure, and the dependency of a deracinated population on structures of relief made vulnerable by the fiscal crises of the state, vastly intensify famine proneness among improvished war victims. The scale and cost of displacement, and the important relations between domestic conflicts and external aggression, is most vivid in the Dante-esque world of southern Africa. The monetary cost of destabilization between 1980 and 1986 is over $30 billion; six of the nine states are among the poorest 25 states in the world with average debt-service ratios of 120%. The brutal activities of Renamo in Mozambique have created conditions of the most appalling poverty: 400–600,000 have died in the war, two million have fled, and six million currently face food shortage (Finnegan, 1989:43).[19] According to the UN one million in the region require food and health aid (Brittain, 1988:118). In war situations there is always a transfer of food from civilian to fighting forces, from social to military budgets (the 1988 Ethiopian defense budget was 54% of gross income), and from subaltern to dominant groups. In the case of the latter, war may, through its inflationary effects, erode the purchasing power of the poor, but in civil wars hunger can also be employed to weaken recalcitrant civilian or ethnic populations (Kula, 1988). In southern Sudan, where some two million have been made homeless and 250,000 have died since 1984, the movement of food relief has been interrupted by the SPLA and the Sadiq government (Bonner, 1989).[20]

And finally there is the *partial commoditization of peasant societies.* A distinctive aspect of sub-Saharan Africa is the continued dominance of peasant production and the persistence of what Spitz (1980) calls self-provisioning. This is not to suggest a Rousseauian world of self-sufficiency as the notion of an uncaptured peasantry implies. By the early 1960s, for example, 56% of total calories in the cocoa belt in Nigeria were purchased, and a more recent study by Pinstrup-Anderson (1985) shows how a 10% increase in food prices in rural northern Nigeria decreases the income of the rural poor by 9%, confirming earlier studies that 45% of monetary expenditures by peasants was spent on food (for a review of food purchases among African peasants, *see* Bryceson, 1984). It is not simply that "famine is embedded in the low levels of productivity . . . of pre capitalist modes of production" (Bryceson, 1980:90) or that famine has a structural relationship with peasant societies (Arnold, 1988:4). Rather I want to suggest that in Africa a central analytic axis is the struggle between forces of retention [self-provisioning] and forces of extraction [commoditization] (Spitz, 1980:1), which has two sorts of im-

36   M. WATTS

plications for famine: first that the manner in which the market develops (the how rather than the if) produces particular vulnerabilities. And second, that the partial commoditization of peasant life suggests that non-market functions performed by complex social and institutional arrangements, contracts, and inter-linked transactions shape famine proneness.

THE INTERNAL ARCHITECTURE OF FAMINE

> *Coping with crisis is an important aspect of peasant life . . . [and] crisis antici-pation forms a central part of peasant agronomy and . . . rural communities.*
> Dessalegn Rahmato (1988:155)

Peter Cutler (1985:12) suggests that "famine is an *abnormal event*, charac-terized by a *breakdown* in social relationships giving rise to *epidemic starva-tion and excess mortality*" (emphasis mine). This particular famine lexicon must, of course, be employed with great care. Famine is a complex process not an event; it is about abnormality and collapse, but it also implies an exten-sion and intensification of the status quo. It is defined by disease and mass death, which is terminal and biological, but famine is also made up of eco-nomic, political, and social pressures of growing intensity and hence cannot be defined by death or starvation alone (Rangasami, 1985:1749). These po-larities and the language of famine are not narrowly semantic because, as I hope to show, they contain assumptions about human agency, the role of the collectivity, and the recursive qualities of subsistence crises.

Sen's theory of entitlement change rests on a quite sharp distinction be-tween poverty and famine; the latter appears as episodic (rather than recur-sive) and is a biological episode or aberration rather than a process (Ati, 1988; Vincent, 1987). Further, Sen's model of famine mortality—destitution leads to starvation leads to death—posits a linear and relatively un-problematic sequence from food scarcity to biological death from starvation. But it is clear that even in biological terms the adaptive capability of the body generates stages (and a complexing "plateauing") of physiological deteriora-tion. The starvation in the Netherlands prompted by the German Occupation occurred over a four year period during the Second World War, and Cutler (1986) has detailed a five or six year degeneration in the Horn. In addition, de Waal (1989) has argued that a food crisis may lead to destitution, but it is a crisis of health—increasing exposure and/or susceptibility to fatal dis-eases—which tends to produce famine mortalities. Famines can, and often are, long and drawn out interactive social and biological process accompa-nied by transformations in the mental and emotional states of victims and of social networks in which they are embedded (Swift, 1989).

In what sense, then, is famine a process? Rangasami (1985:1749) has offered a tripartite model in which "forces of deepening intensity" deprive individuals of assets and endowments: the onset she refers to as "dearth" (in essence high prices), the second phase as "famishment" (the process of being starved), and finally "morbidity." A great strength of this vision is that it privileges action and agency. Famines at some point may fell the subaltern classes, but not before the rural (and sometimes urban) world is "turned into a scene of frenzied activity" (Rahmato, 1988:32). The recognition that individuals struggle for food is not exactly original, having been noted over a hundred years ago in the Indian Famine Codes, which documented the premonitory signs of famine. In the last decade our understanding of what is variously referred to as coping mechanisms, household or survival strategies, and adaptive responses (*see* Mortimore, 1989; IDS, 1986; Longhurst, 1986; Chastanet, 1982; de Garine and Harrison, 1988, for overviews) has expanded considerably, particularly in relation to African famines. One can now constructively compare, for example, the village study by Richards (1986) in Sierra Leone with that of Watts (1983) in northern Nigeria. In spite of striking differences in ecology, climate, and population density, each case asserts the centrality of both anticipatory and counter-acting crisis tendencies. In each community the on-farm flexibility of local agronomy, the innovative deployment of household labor, and a graduated sequence of asset liquidation and money raising associated with seasonal price rises in local grain markets are plainly in evidence. In the Mende community, however, limited land pressures and partial commoditization in conjunction with a robust moral economy rooted in intense political competition among local patrons work to the advantage of the rural poor. In Hausaland a vibrant mercantile system driving complex inter-linked commodity markets (grain, labor, and money) and marked endowment differences work to reproduce structural vulnerability, but not necessarily dispossession in a Leninist sense, among some peasants.

Across the divide of local and regional variability[21], however, one can construct a sort of behavioral bridge; the famine survival strategies conform, in other words, to a rough and ready pattern (*see* Watts, 1983; Cutler, 1985; Leatherman, 1987; Ati, 1988; IDS, 1989; Halderman, 1987; Downing, 1988; Herlehy, 1984), recognizing, of course, that the rhythms and speed of the onset of shortage may vary dramatically.[22] Famines, like peasant rebellions or revolutions, are particular couplings of structures of power and human agency and are rarely exactly alike.[23] On the basis of four detailed accounts, Corbett (1988) posits a three stage model of "household coping strategies." The first stage (*insurance mechanisms*) embraces cropping strategies, wild food collection, sale of possessions such as jewelry, local employment opportunities, and interhousehold loans. In relation to past famines people often find *new ways* to survive—characteristically via the market, which provides new opportunities (Rahmato, 1988; Mortimore, 1989; Downing, 1988)—"but they are in new, even more precarious positions" (Pankhurst, 1988:26).[24] The second stage (*disposal of productive assets*) entails the liquidation of livestock, tools and land, consumption reductions, and credit from moneylenders. Stage three is *destitution, distress migration, and death*.[25] At the terminus of the famine—in the heart of darkness itself—there is, to employ Blanchot's (1986:6) powerful imagery, "the calm of the disaster."

A recognition that households may pass along a sort of response gradient has stimulated considerable discussion on the use of socio-economic indicators for famine early warning systems, and most especially to sustain individuals sliding down the slippery slope to destitution and refugee status.[26] It is axiomatic, of course, that the extent to which the market forces shape specific responses and the flexibility and freedom of choice exercised by families varies geographically[27] and by class. It is the latter which is often least understood, however (cf., Mortimore, 1989). Akong'a and Downing (1988), in a spatially sensitive study of responses to the 1984 Kenya food crisis, crudely lump together all "smallholders" (peasants with less than 40 acres!) who are presumed to be "satisfyzers" (p. 221) balancing labor and capital for a "reasonable level of productivity." Coping strategies are also historical phenomena constantly shaped and eroded by local struggles and state policies and grounded in a food system often in the throes of transformation. In the rough and tumble of actual famines, the identification of a broad social and temporal logic lays the foundation, at least, for strategic intervention.

The ways in which societies reproduce themselves in the course of the famine process seem reasonably clear, but there are several important caveats to be raised. First, the sequencing is ordered in such a way that human responses to shortage can be graduated with respect to time, reversibility, and commitment of domestic resources (Watts, 1983; Mabbs-Zeno, 1987). The *structure* of responses implies that famine can function to dispossess peasants of assets, particularly land, in a way that is more or less irreversible (a sort of ratchet effect). Second, the responding unit is ordinarily presumed to be the household (*see* Corbett, 1988; Longhurst, 1986) defined in a solidary Chayanovian sense. But households have their own architecture and are sites of competing interests and struggles; gender and generational struggles may be exacerbated in times of crisis (Vaughn, 1987; McCann, 1987). The household may gradually fracture, and this suggests a decomposition of that are putatively taken to be domestic entitlements (i.e., the household welfare function; *see* Folbre, 1986). In the Fula communities in which I worked in eastern Gambia, farmers refer specifically to the moment during extreme hungry seasons when "individuals have to look after themselves." Third, famine response is victim-centric. But it needs to be reiterated that households respond differently (*see* McCann, 1987, for example) and that famines involve accumulation as well as liquidation. The discourse of famines solely in terms of the victim (and of starvation rather than disease), however morally necessary, nonetheless constitutes only one part of the story. Finally, coping—popularly conveying passivity or the imagery of individuated scavenging—is irreducibly collective and political, and not in the prosaic sense of occasional food theft or riots (Arnold, 1984; Tilly, 1983). In my opinion the sequence of responses represents struggles over the command of food; entitlements may be defended, fought over (however unsuccessfully), won and lost.[28] Famine victims are, after all, victimized, a process encompassing the moral and political weight of peasant solidarity, moral indignation, collectivity, and subaltern power.[29] The image of destitution and powerless supplicants represents a terminal point and, as Arnold (1984:74) notes, "depoliticizes and dehumanizes [famine sufferers] by reducing their behavior to the unthinking reflexes of Pavlov's salivating dogs."

If there is a growing consensus on the architecture of famine responses, there is something of an intellectual fracture over the purported *abnormality* of famine conditions. The "breakdown" view emphasizes social collapse (at some point) to the point of pathology (Currey, 1984). Cutler (1985), for example, paints a gory canvas of the 1984 Ethiopian famine: slavery, child abandonment, prostitution, murder, and even cannibalism all mark the dissolution of civility. Rahmato (1988:292) rejects such pathologies as "nonsense," positing that famines and the recursive quality of subsistence crises in everyday life reaffirm that he calls the "traditional values of survival . . . diligence, frugality, co-operation" (p. 153). This is what I call the 'elastic theory' of famine, a point similar to Torry's (1986a) important claim that famine adjustments "extend ordinary conventions" (p. 126). A processual view of famine such as I have outlined naturally implies that famines intensify and deepen what may be "normal exploitation" (cf., Scott, 1985), but Torry pushes this insight to extraordinarily dubious extremes. In his view (1989a:150) "researchers have misunderstood peasant adjustments to famine" because (i) high risk constituencies acquiesce to harms imposed upon them as part of the moral order, (ii) the recovery process is not as socially traumatic as Westerners suppose, and (iii) individuals excuse or tolerate life endangering actions performed against them as "leading to a healing of . . . psychic wounds" (p. 152). Torry is referring to what he sees as a fatalistic Hindu society, but his claims are often empirically unsubstantiated (psychic healing, for example) and, to be generous, strike one as unrepresentative even in India. There is an important truth in both positions, nevertheless, which can be resolved by returning to the notion of process. Famine as a social and biological process is rooted in the "normal"—crises heighten social realities and rarely negate them, as Arnold (1984:64) observes—yet at its zenith it is of exceptional potency and destructive power, as is vividly portrayed in Satyajit Ray's film *Distant Thunder*. To use the metaphor of Tigreans, famine is the time when brothers betray brothers.

CLIMATES OF UNCERTAINTY: A NOTE ON DROUGHT AND AGRARIAN PERFORMANCE

> *Agriculture as performance is part of the wider performance of social life. . . .*
> *[It] is an expert performance by lay actors and as social action it is not corrigible by outside actors.* Paul Richards (1987:3)

Perhaps more than in other parts of the Third World, the contribution of the African climate as an exogenous agent in the production of famine has drawn a great deal of scholarly attention. This scholarship has prompted a shift from prosaic sorts of environmental determinism and nature blaming—droughts cause famine—to a recognition that "droughts do not generate disequilibrium, they merely reveal a pre-existing one" (Gracia, 1981:12). Climatic perturbations function as triggers or proximate causes whose effects (which may or may not generate reductions in supply and harvested output) are transmitted through the market via entitlements. The significance of context in assessing climatic impact has been a central problematic in geographical studies of environmental hazards and society-nature interactions more generally (*see* Kates, 1985). This body of research began with simple and naïve models of perception-human response, but it has been pushed to address, though often inadequately, conceptions of society and adaptation-adjustment. Kates (1985), for example, refers to, but does not really demonstrate, the importance of understanding social vulnerability and the capacity of social systems to resist harm; Whyte (1986) employs the cybernetic language of adaptation (long-term responses to hazards) and adjustments (short-term responses) to assess the capacities of systems to buffer climatic variations. In the cases of drought-prone peasant societies, "climatic impact assessments" have generated a more sophisticated understanding of adjustments in self-provisioning societies (Swinton, 1988; Jodha and Mascarenhas, 1985). Often using models of risk aversion and household modeling derived from agricultural economics, geographers and anthropologists have identified diversified production strategies, including soil and moisture conservation, polycultural and varietal planting strategies, and flexible consumption patterns, which mediate the potentially disruptive (production) consequences of drought.

Peasant agrarian systems may have a substantial capacity to absorb drought effects, resisting displacement from extant levels of social reproduction through properties referred to as "endurance" of "absorptive capacity." Whatever the implications of such findings for famine prevention policies, the body of theory on which it rests (see the SCOPE volume *Climatic Impact Assessment* edited by Kates et al., 1985) remains quite inadequate. Drought cannot be meaningfully isolated from social systems, but the conceptions of society employed by Kates and his colleagues are, to be generous, quite underdeveloped, and their resistance to jettison the cybernetic and biological concepts of adaptation reproduces the static dualism of Nature and Society.[30] Another body of work has provided an alternative vision of drought as a moment in the labor process (see Mamdani, 1986a; Watts, 1983). The brilliant work of Paul Richards (1986) in Mendeland offers one avenue by viewing agriculture as a sort of performance. First, Mende farmers respond to drought as a series of rolling adjustments (including varietal and multispecies intercropping, moisture conservation, exploitation of microenvironments, and so on). I have tried to make a similar argument about Hausa peasants; rather than instituting a farm plan every year—what Richards (1987b) calls a combinatorial logic of intercropping—the responses reflect a specific space-time performance in relation to local (i.e. field specific) conditions. And second, the manner in which these rolling adjustments are made is not technical but social and political; in a profound sense nature is made through the labor process. The central issue for Mende farmers, according to Richards, was the ability to mobilize labor, a process grounded in the ability to raise work parties and to exercise claims over kin and non-kin and patrons. Not only is agriculture and response to drought necessarily rooted in the social field, but for resource-poor farmers simple reproduction is "often a brilliantly innovative achievement" (Richards, 1987b:5).

In situating responses to drought in this social field one moves beyond the realm of knowledge—"peasant science"—and the language of biology, to the ways in which farming households are constituted. Much of the new agrarian studies (Guyer, 1988; Guyer and Peters, 1987) shows that households are constructed through negotiations and contracts and that claims on labor are tied to domestic units as sites of competing interests. What Richards refers to as performance strikes to the heart of constrained agency in human systems. This frames not only how families can farm (and respond to climatic perturbation) but more generally how the process of famine is not simply a question of vulnerability, but sees peasants as embedded in social relations of production which are simultaneously realms of possibility and constraint. Harrell-Bond's (1986) work on refugees shows dramatically how refugee survival is a skilled social achievement.

ENTITLEMENTS: ENDOWMENT MAPPING IN HISTORY

*[The] phase of economic development after the emergence of a large class of
wage laborers but before the development of social security arrangements is
potentially a deeply vulnerable one.* Amartya Sen (1981:146)

Amartya Sen's *Poverty and Famines* (1981) has done more than any other
single publication to prompt debate and discussion on theories of famine causation. Reflecting perhaps his formative intellectual influences (Maurice
Dobb and Kenneth Arrow), Sen's economics begins unconventionally with
entitlements—the rules governing the acquisition, use, and transfer of property rights—and with what in orthodox neo-classical theory is taken to be
trivial or logically incomplete (i.e. explanations of mass starvation) (*see*
Srinavasan, 1983). An entitlement system is related to an individual's command over food in two senses. First, it heavily shapes the initial endowment
through inheritance; second, it frames the transformation of endowments
into goods through production, trade, employment, and so on—what Sen
calls exchange entitlement mapping. E-mapping and initial endowment (his/
her ownership bundle) determine an individual's exchange entitlement.
Famines develop when these entitlements collapse for large segments of society, which implies that starvation can occur without there being a shortage
of food. The Great Bengal Famine of 1943 is, according to Sen, a case of
entitlement change without FAD (food availability decline), having dire consequences for some three million victims due to (i) a requisition-induced inflationary spiral and (ii) limited markets for what some rural non-food
producers had to sell (*see also* Brennan, 1988).[31] Sen's theory does not imply
that food imports are irrelevant for famine relief (as Bowbrick, 1986, 1987
believes); rather that they are necessary but not sufficient, whereas food
availability decline is neither necessary nor sufficient to precipitate a famine
(Desai, 1987).

It has been suggested, with good reason, that Sen's entitlement theory is
the formalization of a very old idea. The famine debates in India discussed
"famines of work" in the 1860s and the Famine Commission Report of 1880
is a superb example of entitlements and class analysis (Dreze, 1988; Rangasami, 1985). With some deserved hostility, Ashok Mitra noted that "our
great-grandmothers who . . . were altogether innocent of the notion of 'non-
negative orthant of n—dimensional real space' knew about these common
factors underlying famines" (1982;78). Nonetheless, entitlement approaches
have the formidable merit of focusing on the *specific relations between people and food* and why some groups are affected and others hardly touched.
Megan Vaughn (1987) has employed this approach with extraordinary
power in her discussion of the 1949 Nyasaland famine. She vividly docu-

ments the differing fortunes of tenants on the estates, brick makers, millers, and freeholding peasants, but most particularly she documents the entitlement changes among women (something largely neglected by Sen), who are invisible in the historical record. Some women were more vulnerable than others, a function of their relative dependence on food (and beer) production, on wages, and on the status of their husbands (salaried officials versus migrant laborers). Gender subordination, embedded in the social relations of society prior to the famine, explains why women were neglected, abandoned, divorced, and sold into prostitution in the interests of male survival. Turshen (1984) actually suggests that during famines some men in Tanzania actually acquired wives as parents were prepared to part with their daughters for small dowries.

The gender basis of entitlement (*see* Schroeder, 1987; Smale-Heisey, 1987; IDS, 1986; Moore and Vaughn, 1987; and Funk, this volume) raises the more general issue of intra-household food access and distribution. Sen (1987:63) sees this as a non-ownership problem, since "food owned by the family is shared," but a good deal of the work on African households would suggest otherwise. In any event age and gender bias has been shown to be central to discussions of nutrition and health (Watson and Harriss, 1985), and it is of equal significance for an understanding of domestic entitlements, the vulnerabilities of the young and old, and for questions of maternal detachment (Scheper-Hughes, 1986).[32] All this said, the Indian studies and the Sudanese data for 1984–1985 (de Waal, 1989) suggest that male mortality due to starvation and disease was higher than that of women during the nineteenth century famines, which suggests that women's "coping" "contested their victim status" (Arnold, 1988:90).

Sen is on somewhat shakier ground when he turns to history. In his book— but less in his subsequent work (1987)—entitlements provide a *theory of conjunctures*. It focuses on the immediate relationship between food and certain sorts of people. Sen's history is derivative of proximate trigger effects, such as state requisition, which perturb entitlements and less on the processes producing a crisis of social reproduction, i.e., the historical political economy by which certain sorts of entitlements come to be socially distributed (Basu, 1986). In this sense it is questionable what sort of causality Sen has identified insofar as, for example, his account of Bangladesh is singularly lacking in sensitivity to the decline and social transformation of the Bangladeshi food sector, a critical part of what Marxists call the agrarian question. Of course, Sen himself notes that entitlements are mediated by legal and property relations, which demand a detailed examination of the socio-economic structure of society and of what he tantalizingly refers to in passing as "modes of production."[33] History of a different sort—namely the sources of social power—is required to understand not simply the occurrence of famine but its recurrence (Crow, 1986).

To invoke history in this way is not to summon up the demon of the market or capitalism and to assert unequivocally that they "cause famine." To assert, as Gartell does (1985), that Mamdani ignores pre-colonial famines and hence his explanation ("imperialism") is wrong-headed really doesn't get us very far. The point is that the famines in Uganda in 1850 and 1950 were qualitatively different phenomena. These differences must be accounted for precisely in terms of transformations of entitlements, property rights, and so on. The question surely must be how the specific forms of peripheral capitalism which provide the central dynamic in Uganda over the last century produced periodic crises of reproduction of a certain sort. Mamdani's theoretical edifice—or my own built to explain the run of quite different famines in Nigeria between 1850 and the present—is not pulled asunder by the discovery that "socialism or pre-capitalist states cause famines too." To make my own Marxist position quite clear, I take Sen's reference to modes of production quite literally to imply that material production is a social and political process. If famine is about command over food, it is about power and politics broadly understood, which are embedded in a multiplicity of arenas from the domestic (patriarchal politics) to the nation/state (how ruling classes and subaltern groups acquire and defend certain rights). In social systems dominated by capitalism, ownership through private property determines exchange entitlements, which is to say that class and class struggle shape the genesis and the outcomes of the property-hunger equation. At the same time capitalism has developed unevenly on a world scale, with the result that there are *national capitalisms* (colored by differing configurations of class and international geopolitics) which provide the building blocks for distinguishing different species, and consequences, of subsistence crises. Actually existing socialisms have class and other interests, too, and perhaps other property rights consequent on political action and "socialistic" regimes of accumulation. The same can be said for pre-capitalisms for which the moral economy of the poor may be constitutive of some important entitlement claims. In all such cases, however, one needs to know how enforceable and legitimate are the legal and property relations which mediate entitlements and to recognize that all such rights are negotiated and fought over. Such struggles are not peripheral to famine but strike to its core. And it is perhaps quite proper that Sen himself in this recent work (1987) has turned to the question of the politics of the "right not to be hungry."

THE MARKET AND ANTI-MARKET MENTALITY

A price is a reflection of what is to Marx a contradiction of capitalism. It is both the organizing and rationalizing guide for production decisions and at the same time a reflection of the antagonistic social relations among buyers and sellers. Diane Elson (1988:27)

The influence of Sen's analysis has irrevocably shifted the terms of the debate from shortage of food supply to the intervening variables between food production and consumption. The market has, as a consequence, become the icon of contemporary famine analysis. While Kautsky's (1906:167) observation that the peasant is driven to increasing dependence on the market "which he finds even more moody and incalculable than the weather," is an apt commentary on market risk, there has been a broad and subtle shift to exchange determinism. Seaman and Holt (1980:296) argue, for example, that "a shift from a 'communal' to a 'market' economy does in general . . . mark a shift toward greater vulnerability to and severity of famine." They themselves note that this is a crude division, but the market-centric view is now deeply etched in famine discourse.[34] It is certainly seen in some strains of the moral economy story in which commercialization unproblematically erodes *tout court* a putative subsistence ethic.[35] As a counterweight, the anti-market mentality is matched, of course, by a glorification of the market, the so-called structure-conduct-performance approach by which African markets are seen as "efficient, responsive and self-financing" (Hopcraft, 1987; Jones, 1980).

The issue here is not to dismiss or extol the market but to reassess the very notion of the market itself, and specifically to see markets as social and material institutions (Elson, 1988). Markets are conventionally rendered as a system of freely negotiated chosen contracts (bargaining), an auction in which buyers and sellers bid against one another, or a broker-organized market. All of these usages are of limited substance. As Elson (1988:10) says, a market is a nexus between buyers and sellers but "*this nexus has to be made . . .* a market implies one or more agents who act as market makers, setting prices, providing information . . . bringing buyers and sellers together" (emphasis mine). This is neither the invisible hand of Adam Smith's market nor the bureaucratic "market" of Alfred Chandler's visible hand. How markets develop and how they are "socialized"—the nature of the market antagonisms as Marx put it—become extremely relevant (Mackintosh 1989). In the case of the Third World, in which commoditization is incomplete and the intersection of markets with other institutions is integral to agrarian structure, the making of markets presages exchange-mapping and hence famine dynamics. The question of the social development and construction of the market has been brilliantly explored by Barbara Harriss (1988, 1989) in her discussions of merchant capital in India and its "impurities", i.e. its relation to production, usurer's capital, and interlinkages with industrial enterprises. Crow's (1987) study of what he calls the history of the development of the market in Bangladesh (especially the source of traders' working capital) and the interlinkage of commodity markets is also a path-breaking account of how price formation and trading practices create market specific structures and not markets in the abstract (see also Bush, 1988).[36]

This "alternative" market focus on famines has generated some excellent studies of food systems and the social relations of exchange in Africa. These market ethnographies reflect less an anti-market mentality than a sensitivity to the social development of the market and in particular the politics of exchange and the interlinkages of commodity markets. Clough (1985) and Saul (1987) both document complex crop advance systems organized by local merchants, the tying of markets in money, grain, and labor, and a segmented grains trade in which speculative activity and market collusion by large wholesalers reproduce local patterns of vulnerability for rural poor. Saul's Burkina research documents restricted competition at local and national levels and an extreme concentration of inter-seasonal grain storage. Clough identifies distinctive rhythms of seasonal grain acquisition and disposal by class: poor peasants are compelled to sell early and take interest bearing loans later in the season, a pattern of distress sales and purchase intensified during famines.

The question of the social relations of trade and production strikes to the heart of contemporary famine vulnerability within the pastoral sector in drought-prone ecosystems (Samatar, 1989; Sutter, 1987; Starr, 1987; White, 1986; Bonfiglioli, 1988). Seasonal stresses are frequently exacerbated by volatile terms of trade and growing inter-household inequality. In Sahelian systems it is well documented that animal-grain terms of trade are central to any understanding of the pastoral sector and that serious droughts, which affect both cereal harvests and milk production via range quality, greatly enhance off-take rates (Hesse, 1987). Increased animal sales (usually small ruminants in phase I, see McCabe, 1987) combined with higher animal mortality rates can be associated with market slumps and price collapses. Herders are forced into distress sales of younger males and eventually reproductive stock. As markets are flooded, herders' purchasing power collapses and herds are rapidly depleted (phase II). In famine conditions these processes may be synergistic, with devastating consequences. Herd reconstitution, due to high animal prices in the aftermath of large-scale herd liquidation and mortalities (phase III), may be problematic if not altogether impossible (Hogg, 1985).

Processes of herd viability and vulnerability are shaped by new patterns of stock alienation and social stratification in the 1980s (Blenche, 1985), themselves a product, in part, of previous famine conditions. Households owning smaller herds and strapped by inadequate milk production depend on non-livestock income sources, increasingly evanescent secondary sources (such as gathering and laboring), and commercialization strategies characterized by heavy culling of males and forced sales of cows and heifers.[37] During a severe drought and/or high grain prices, poor herders massively decapitalize and experience gradual "proletarianization." Decapitalization among the poor may be matched by heavy buying and accumulation on the part of wealthy herders and entrepreneurs. Large diversified herds appear at the same time that absentee ownership and new forms of animal contracting and debt-traps signal new relations of production in the pastoral economy (Glantz, 1987; White, this volume). Wealthy herders make use of the services of effectively propertyless herders, profit from the fruits of a lucrative cattle trade, and may be able to consolidate their power through privatizations of rangeland and wells (Mazonde, 1987; Behnke, 1988). Changing patterns of ownership and production relations account for the particular exposure of some herding families and the differential capacities for herd reconstitution (Toulmin, 1987; Sutter, 1987). Hogg (1985) notes the emergence of an especially risk-prone class of Boran herders with few animals and heavy dependence on food relief, even in non-famine conditions. Sperling (1987) shows how in the 1984 drought in Kenya such improvished herders found themselves with few secondary sources (i.e., few coping mechanisms) and unable to decapitalize their small herds because of constrained market opportunities. Food relief was activated only when well-to-do Samburu voiced their needs, by which time the poor had suffered animal losses of 75% and had felt the pinch of food shortages for at least four months.

POLITICS AND FAMINE:
RELIEF AND REFUGEES IN THE HORN

[T]here was perhaps some truth in Trotsky's remark that the world revolution failed because of the faith created by Hoover's food aid.
David Arnold (1988:139)

This is not the place to rehearse the substantial body of literature on famine relief and state interventions to protect entitlements (*see* Harriss, 1988; Ravallion, 1987; and Clay, 1988 for a review). Whatever the particular constellation of supply and/or entitlement changes, state intervention to administer food relief is, at some point, absolutely pivotal. The politics of state-subsistence relations is, of course, of great antiquity, and famine "relief" as such is not simply a product of capitalist democracy. The most compelling tradition of efforts to guarantee some form of food entitlement is found in China. Manchu emperors granted peasants few political rights, but the imperial state depended on peasant surpluses for political stability and it was held accountable in respect to subsistence by the realities of massive subaltern dissent. State paternalism was, as Scott (1976) noted long ago, shackled by technical and intrastructural constraints and by the limited capacities of soft states, but the achievements of food security policies (environmental management, public granaries, and so on) were substantial. Iliffe (1988) has argued that such institutional means of relief were lacking in precolonial Africa, particularly for the poor, who relied largely on personal charity, though there are some significant exceptions (*see* Watts 1983).

In the contemporary epoch, famine relief represents one element in a panoply of public interventions to provide food entitlements to vulnerable groups (most visible perhaps in South Asia). A central axis in debates over famine relief has been the relative merits of rationing and other food entitlement schemes subsuming food security with income transfers, Food for Work Programs, and "vulnerable group" feeding (*see* Clay, 1988). In the course of the last twenty years a great deal has been learned about the rough and tumble of relief administration and the practical considerations of any sort of disaster relief operations. I wish to address, however, another facet of state food interventions, namely their politics. Politics in two senses: first, questions of state performance and capacity are fundamentally about the exercise of power and interest and they will naturally shape targeting, exclusion, and selection of food entitlements in times of crisis. And second, since the mid-nineteenth century, when international relief emerged as a means by which states could obtain grain supplies (*see* Arnold, 1988), the capability to acquire food from multilateral or bilateral sources is frequently a political question. Hoover, and Presidents Ford and Reagan after him, systematically employed food relief in an unashamedly political way.

The politics of subsistence is thrown into dramatic relief in The Horn. The role of superpower conflicts and geopolitics, the longstanding nationalities question, the politicization of relief, state predations in the name of agrarian socialism in Ethiopia since 1974, and the mad civil conflicts in northwestern Somalia and southern Sudan must be part of any discussion of famine etiology. In his admirably balanced assessment, Griffin (1987) notes that long prior to the 1974 revolution, Ethiopia was characterized by sluggish growth, production instabilities, and a fragmented market. Indeed, McCann (1987) shows conclusively how the conditions of material life in the northeastern provinces "deteriorated precipitously" (p. 173) between 1900 and 1935.

Demographic growth, proletarianization, and inheritance practice further compounded an intolerable situation throughout the 1960s, producing a massive "shortage of productive resources" (p. 206). This historical context has often been woefully absent from the rabid state-bashing that has characterized discussions of famine in The Horn in the 1980s.

In the last decade, most discussions about famine in The Horn have centered directly on politics (MERIP, 1987; ROAPE, 1985). Preston (1986) and Gill (1986) both focus on super-power rivalry, shifting alliances sustained by the Cold War, and the international environment in which Western donors might greet Ethiopian requests for assistance with extreme (anti-socialist?) skepticism or indifference. In the US, the Hickenlooper Amendment prohibited economic development assistance to Ethiopia (part of a wider marginalization of Ethiopia in the international community after 1974), and a White House memorandum of May 1984 revealed the Reagan administration to be aware of the need for massive food relief although it remained inactive for six months (Smith, 1987). The recent hue and cry over US neglect of internecine strife in The Sudan and Somalia are cut from the same cloth. Preston is able to show how the geopolitical theatre in The Horn has intensified militarism, which necessarily compounds the difficulties of relief efforts. The generous provision of aid to Somalia by the US conversely has buffered some of the consequences of drought, but not of food insecurities induced by war. *An African Winter* (Preston, 1986) is a powerful reminder of how directly or indirectly "politics" creates particular risks, but the book cannot in itself answer the question of why international relations are more or less crucial among different states, a problem which naturally rests upon a political economy of a different sort.

Another tack—perhaps more visible politically—has focused not unexpectedly on internal politics and the machinations of the state (Giorgis, 1989; Lemma, 1985; Dejene, 1987; Cohen and Isaksson, 1988). On the basis of interviews conducted among Tigrean and Eritrean refugees in Sudanese camps, Clay and Holcombe (1985, *see also* Clay, Steingraber, and Niggli, 1988) argue that the government was "the major cause of [famine] deaths in the country" (p. 195). Forced labor (*see* Rahmato, 1988:144), grain appropriation, expanded taxation, and useless expenditures on state farms cumulatively manufactured famine in northeastern provinces hostile to Amharic rule. The famine relief effort simply legitimated major resettlement efforts and assisted a poorly disguised paramilitary strategy to crush longstanding internal dissent. Food relief was refracted through the prism of the nationalities question such that Tigre, with 18% of famine victims, received 5.6% of wheat shipments in 1985 (Cutler, 1985). According to Smith (1987) one million starved in the guerrilla held areas.

Gill (1986) shows, however, that there was a "guerrilla war" of another sort between famine relief agencies. A careful reading of Jansson et al. (1987) and Giorgis (1989) reveals not only the extraordinary turf battles in the 'disaster community' (with dire consequences in an already intolerable situation) but the extreme politicization of relief agencies. *War on Want* and *Mèdecins Sans Frontiéres* are two well publicized cases in relation to the Tigrean movement and resettlement respectively, but these conflicts contributed more broadly to what is now widely documented as sadly biased media reportage (*see*, for example, Kaplan, 1988). My point is that there is not only a politics of famine but a politics of information and interpretation.[38] Without papering over the effects of the waste and profligacy of the Ethiopian state and its collectivization program, state-bashing does not constitute a sufficient explanation of famine either (Clarke, 1986; *see also* Pankhurst ,1988 on The Sudan). Clay and Holcombe (1985), while correctly attacking the Ethiopian state and its project, ultimately rely, like Conquest (1986) in his discussion of the Ukrainian famine in Russia, heavily on the testimony of refugees and draw direct connections (and in my opinion unsubstantiated causal claims) between state appropriation and famine. History and geopolitics are certainly kept in very low profile. The ghastly face of socialism on the other hand is projected onto a much larger screen. The product is an extremely ideological debate (*see Anthropology Today* 1986–1987) reaching a quite ridiculous scale in Kaplan's (1988) irresponsible book, which is filled with "killing fields," "holocausts," and the observation that Ethiopia is more deplorable than apartheid in South Africa.

The obvious point is that The Horn is at war and has been for some time. This cannot be understood as a local struggle, and it creates conditions (dislocation, food shortages, distributional nightmares) which may create and/or intensify famine. What must be grasped, then, are both the origins of this political conflict and its precise analytic connections to food entitlement changes. Yet what is so often at stake in the debate is capitalism versus socialism. Some commentators find both wanting and plump for a populism of "fourth world people's struggles" or some undisclosed "alternative development." Indeed, what is distinctive about Kaplan's anti-Marxist narrative is the neglect of the political content of movements, not least of the Tigrean movement itself, whose virtues he claims to extol.

Of course, in the short term the prospects in The Horn are grim if not dreadful. All sides of the Ethiopian struggle are using food relief and their own relief agencies to further their own relief agencies to further their political fortunes. The Eritrean guerrillas have begun destroying international food relief to their own people because the Ethiopian state has sanctioned the convoys, and the Red Cross terminated its operations in June 1988, unable to reach an agreement with the Dergue (*Manchester Guardian*, June 7th, 1988, p. 15). The prospects in The Sudan, even with the two month ceasefire declared in May 1989, look equally grim for the hundreds of thousands of refugees in Juba and the countless millions facing food shortages across the south of the country (*New York Times*, April 9th, 1989, p. 6).

FAMINE, RESISTANCE, AND CONSCIOUSNESS

> *In these dark times*
> *Will there also be singing?*
> *Yes there will also be singing*
> *About these hard times.*
> Bertolt Brecht (1972:167)

"We are on the edge of disaster without being able to situate it in the future; it is rather always already past, and yet we are on the edge or under the threat. . .". So says Maurice Blanchot (1986:1). Embedded in his disaster narrative is the configuration of famine in what one might call popular consciousness. One of the advantages conferred by a processual and active view of food crisis is that its political content and collective character are rendered especially visible. Rain-making rites as a collective expression of subaltern sentiment during periods of drought are well documented in Africa, and as the food shortage intensifies, acts of petty theft, gang robbery, and popular appropriation constitute the forms by which the popular classes vent their political frustrations and articulate entitlement claims. As famine deepens, crime and violence—whether collective insurgence or individual acts of desperation—are gradually overwhelmed by the despair and desolation of starvation.

The ideology of subsistence and its relation to class power is of course at the heart of reflections on justice and the so-called moral economy of the poor (Moore, 1970; Scott, 1976). David Arnold (1984:78) is mistaken, I believe, when he says that their moral economy "denies the relevance of class identities and class conflict;" rather it addresses how notions of justice rooted in subsistence claims for fair prices emerged from the delicate polarities of class forces, from the fragile hegemonies manufactured in all class societies. The structural similarities between, for example, the "people's armies" in the *ancien régime* in France and subsistence dacoity in nineteenth century India are well documented. Although the historical record for Africa is much thinner (*see* Watts 1983, Iliffe 1988), the lineaments of a moral economy are certainly in evidence in the food riots of the 1980s in Khartoum, Tunis, and Lagos triggered by IMF austerity measures, but the subject demands much more systematic study.

52   M. WATTS

Famine has also entered political discourse in another arena, however. The instances of nineteenth century Ireland and India reveal dramatically how famine sustained and nourished nationalist and anti-imperialist sentiment. In 1848 a young Irish leader declared that the famine was after all a "fearful murder" committed on the Irish, and Jawaharal Nehru, imprisoned in 1944, saw the Great Bengal Famine as the high-water mark of imperial indifference and complacency (Arnold, 1988, pp. 115–117). Experience of famine may have grown from the fertile soil of local exploitation, but it frequently flowered into a critique of state power, promising a world—indeed a development strategy to use the modern lexicon—of a quite different order.

Situating famine in peasant consciousness and action is to resurrect the old debate over hunger and peasant insurgency. David Arnold (1984:112) poses this relation as "a single underlying consciousness [which] employed a single vocabulary of expression and drew upon a basic, limited store of belief . . ." In his view the genesis of famine throws into relief attitudes and identities that "lay dormant . . .in more normal times," it "enhanced [popular] awareness of exploitation" and entitled people to act. Arnold's analysis is problematic, but his own vision actually affirms the need to search out both the meaning of famine in the collective memory and the exercise of power in "normal periods." The question of meaning and famine is enormously complex (and relatively unexplored in Africa), but an important avenue has been opened up by Scheper-Hughes (1988) in her discussion of how a common complaint in northeastern Brazil —nervoso—is the metaphorization of hunger and famine. In the traditional idiom of delerio de foem, hunger exploded into rage and peasant rebellion and banditry in the backlands of Pernambuco, but in the 1980s nervoso has been medicalized and domesticated to pacify a recalcitrant population. Hunger anxiety is expressed through the cultural idiom of nervoso, and it is now medically treated by phalanxes of practitioners armed with psychotropic medication rather than expressed politically.

It is in the realm of normal exploitation that Scott's (1985) book on peasant resistance provided an opportunity to weld subaltern consciousness to famine. Scott refers to the "euphemization of power" (1985:309), a socially recognized form of domination, in which rich and poor engage in a complex practical and symbolic struggle. It is within this crucible that local entitlements—generosity, stinginess, assistance, and justice, to use Scott's language—are forged, fought over, won and lost. Where Scott errs, I think, is in his discussion of the local and quotidian forms of state power and their implications for how everyday resistance can or cannot construct food entitlements.

In this regard famine consciousness is not dormant in normal times; indeed, as Scott (1985:317) puts it, subaltern classes resist and demystify hegemonic relations "on the basis of their daily material experience." Famine provides a means by which an idealized hegemonic ideology can be criticized on its own terms. As Mick Taussig observes (1984:468) in his commentary on terror, famine is "a wide space whose breadth offers positions of advance as well as those of extinction" and as such it is crucial to the creation of meaning and consciousness.

PEACE, DEMOCRATIZATION AND THE RIGHTS OF THE POOR

Claims of right or entitlement . . .carry only as much weight as the legitimacy of the institution will bear. Thomas Nagel (1977:57)

Unless obligations to feed the hungry are a matter of allocated justice rather than indeterminate beneficence, a so-called "right to food" . . .will only be a "manifesto right." ONora O'Neill (1986:101)

In comparing the current African crisis to conditions in an increasingly heterogeneous Third World, several authors (e.g., Dreze, 1988; Sen, 1987) have drawn a sharp distinction between India and sub-Saharan Africa. In spite of the almost pharaonic sequence of famines throughout Indian history, the period from the termination of the Second World War has been, despite the existence of conditions which might trigger major food crises, famine free. Since 1947 the government of India, working with the legacy of the Famine Codes of the late nineteenth century, have enacted laws and instituted a famine relief system intended to bolster and protect food entitlements among the popular classes. The Famine Codes (systematized in the 1970s as Scarcity Manuals) contained early warning and food distribution systems, but their cornerstone was a panoply of public works (i.e. income transfers to enhance purchasing power) and a massive long-term buffer stock of grain, standing in 1990 at some 20 million tons. The imperial famine prevention system has been reinforced by state interventions in agrarian structure (asset protection, labor and wage legislation), infrastructure, and a decentralized relief administration system (Harriss, 1988). Of course, it needs to be added that if India has averted food crises, it has done little to remedy chronic malnutrition: nearly half the world's malnutrition is said to be in that one country. Further, one should not exaggerate the extent to which women's subordination, the protection of assets, urban bias, or corruption in the food relief have been systematically eradicated. Yet famine aversion—particularly in relative to its resurgence in Africa since 1970—is no mean achievement.

Jean Dreze (1988), in his assessment of famine relief in India, has highlighted the contribution of a long bureaucratic tradition, an effective local administration, and the importance of contingency planning, experimentation, and learning. But what is central to the genesis of famine prevention—and entitlement protection—is, of course, politics. This is not simply a case of appreciating that relief is a form of "investment," as Dreze puts it; neither is it entirely a reflection of moral rights and obligations (O'Neil, 1986). Sen (1987) is, however, closer to the mark when he observes that a free press has both helped produce, legitimate, and maintain the relief system. Food entitlements—themselves expressions of power—emerge precisely from political claims, obligations reflecting a commitment or compulsion to sustain vulnerable classes (Dreze and Sen, 1989). Obligations to protect entitlements and to keep the hungry alive, if they are to be more than rhetorical or manifesto rights, must be matters of what Alston and Tomasevski (1984:124) call allocative justice; that is to say they are political achievements. Political representation and struggle are not, in other words, marginal to discussions of famine prevention.

It is in this regard that the problem of democracy and peace strike to the heart of Africa's "famine problem." There are, of course, macroeconomic, bureaucratic, and infrastructural contrasts between Africa and South Asia, but the heart of the contrast between Africa and South Asia is the political exclusion of peasants and the fact that "control of political power . . .is a [subject] of armed conflict in which food is a weapon of war" (Harriss, 1988:169). Access to the state is a precondition for membership in the African bourgeoisie—and the state exploits peasants through extra-economic coercion—which, as Mamdani (1986a:47) notes, "gives a life and death character to the political struggles within it." In this context democratization must remove the straitjacket which stifles the peasantry, because any popular movement to transform political life must sever the hold that ruling classes exercise over rural producers.

The need for what Curtis, Hubbard, and Shepherd (1988:196) call social entitlements, i.e., the control of assets as a basis for famine prevention, is deeply embedded in civil society and democratization, a project which in my opinion can best emerge by organization from below. All of this should not paper over the important success stories in African famine relief; indeed, local administration and public works programs have seemed to work best under crisis conditions (Clarke, 1986; Reddy, 1988; Downing et al., 1989; Hay, 1988). In fact the oft-cited Botswana famine prevention program (replacement of lost income and asset protection) can in part be grounded in competitive politics and local democratic representation that was responsive to local needs (Holm and Morgan, 1985).[39] But the likelihood of entitlement protection for the millions of rural poor in Africa—equitable access to arable and pasture land, the provision of legal status to women as major food producers, institutional mechanisms for the regulation of public goods, and the serious commitment to public works and market regulation—cannot be divorced from "the creativity of popular activity" (Mamdani, 1986:49). Famine prevention in Africa, by what Ben Wisner (1988) calls the "strong Basic Needs Approach," is rooted in power and need in the doubtless long and contradictory struggle for democracy, and in the creation of a robust civil society.

ACKNOWLEDGMENTS

I am grateful to Steve Reyna for his equanimity in accepting my shoddy excuses for a tardy delivery of this chapter. Reyna and R. E. Downs also provided extensive editorial comments. I have been particularly challenged by the recent work of Amartya Sen as a basis for reassessing my own thinking on famine. Even though they almost certainly are unaware of it, I have been deeply influenced in this regard by David Arnold, Michael Burawoy, John Berger, Paul Richards, Jane Guyer, Peter Taylor, and Donna Harraway.

NOTES

1. This chapter is certainly not intended to be a comprehensive review of "famine studies." I have quite arbitrarily identified some issues which have emerged in the period since Amartya Sen's seminal book, *Poverty and Famines*, was published in 1981.
2. A recent contribution by Seavoy (1986) argues for the human origins of famine but of a rather different order, namely that peasants are lazy and suffer from an intrinsic propensity to reproduce up to the Malthusian limit.
3. According to the Brown University World Hunger Program *Hunger Report 1988*, the trend in famines since 1945 is "clearly downward" (p. 8). This trend refers, however, to "average population residing in countries reported with famine as reported in the *New York Times*" and is in my opinion open to serious dispute. See *The Hunger Report: Update 1989* (Brown University World Hunger Program, 1989).
4. An excellent exception is Raymond Bonner, 1989.
5. Medvedev claims (*New York Times*, February 4th, 1989, cited in Cockburn, 1989, p. 294) that 20 millions perished under Stalin due to collectivization and famine, a figure roundly condemned by demographers. The Soviet historian Victor Danilov, no favorite of the Soviet authorities, claimed in *Pravda* that 3-4 millions perished in the Ukrainian famine, a figure roughly half of that proposed by a partisan US Commission on the Ukraine Famine (1988). As Alex Cockburn observed, these estimates have "a regulatory ideological function" such that "any computation that does not soar past 10 million is . . .taken as being soft on Stalin" (Cockburn, 1989:295).
6. In spite of the claims of Vice-President Bush in 1985 that famine relief was used explicitly by the Ethiopian state as an instrument of war and genocide in Eritrea and Tigre, this has been denied by Dawit Wolde Giorgis, the émigré and former head of Ethiopian Relief and Rehabilitation Commission, who is certainly no friend of the Dergue (Kaplan, 1989:311).
7. Miriam Kahn (1984) provides a wonderful case study of thinking with famine drawn from Melanesia, in which famine does not refer to food deprivation but "as a statement about their willingness to invest in social relationships" (p. 151). Famine is a comment on the relationship between individual desires and collective needs.
8. But the recent disclosures and debates over ozone depletion and greenhouse effects have given climatic explanations of starvation a new lease on life.

9. Bryceson (1981:79) identifies the radical cliché that international capital and transnational corporate investment have undermined food production.
10. I have provided elsewhere a systematic critique of Torry's analysis of dependency theory; see Watts, 1988.
11. I am including here the *active* processes—men and women making history, but not under circumstances of their own choosing—by which individuals and classes "adjust," and "adapt," and "respond to" shortage and struggle over access to food.
12. The *New York Times* Kenya correspondent, Sheila Rule, wrote a piece for the *New York Times Magazine* (Rule, 1989:36) marking the end of her sojourn in Africa, which was dominated by an all-powerful image of a Sudanese refugee camp. The FAO "Images of Africa" Conference in Rome in 1988 found that the same stereotypes of Africa as "the famine ravaged continent" dominated Western Media (*West Africa*, December 19th–25th, 1988, pp. 2381–2382).
13. I believe that many discussions of the current "crisis" in Africa reveal with some clarity the received wisdom, the static images of *Africanism* (cf., Edward Said on Orientalism), a discourse which "has less to do with [Africa] than with 'our' world" (Said, 1978:12). The crisis of the 1980s is often presented as though there were no crises prior to 1960 and that the present conjuncture is the tragic playing out of deeply sedimented African traditions (the economy of affection, the absence of a landlord class, the "soft state," and so on). See Watts, 1989 for an elaboration.
14. But which, as he makes clear, saw the genesis of chronic subsistence insecurity and endemic malnutrition.
15. Raikes (1988:70) rightly identifies three components to the poverty-famine equation: access to land and other productive resources, availability and security of employment, and effectiveness and stability of social networks. This is a quite different notion of famine-risk than, for example, the notion of "vulnerability" proposed by Bates (1988), which is measured by (i) skill in managing food stores and shortages, (ii) population increase, and (iii) the shift from pastoralism to arable production.
16. According to Lipton (1983:54) 10–20% of Africans are *ultra-poor* (i.e., too poor to avoid risk of undernutrition) in contradistinction to being poor (i.e., risk hunger). They are particularly at risk during the hungry season and move further into risk during bad years (p. 56). Lipton believes that ultra-poverty is more prevalent in rural areas, where "greater seasonality of work and income aggravates the relative nutritional disadvantage created for rural people by lower income, remoteness, medical care, regulated markets, etc." (p. 66).
17. In Madagascar child mortality appears to have doubled between 1982 and 1985; the real income of the average African is said to be 10% lower now than in 1970 (*The Economist*, March 9th, 1989, p. 15; *African News*, 31/6, April 3rd, 1989, p. 4).
18. The World Bank study on Africa (1989) suggests, however, that things are not so bad at all, especially among those states which have adopted IMF austerity reforms. The figures and trends are extremely dubious (see the *Left Business Observer*, #28, May 15th, 1989 on the IMF and World Bank's capacities to cook up the numbers). The World Bank report believes that the African crisis is not a result of an "adverse international climate" (p. 2); indeed, the catastrophic collapse of commodity prices since 1980 is not such a bad thing (!) and the downturn represents a return to "the long term trend." The report also excludes the impacts of price shocks and war as "exceptional" events.
19. Wuyts (1989) rightly points out that since 1975 Mozambique has been a war economy facing the daunting task of economic recovery, emergency relief, and now structural adjustment.
20. Domestic politicization of food relief is rarely detached from global geo-politics. Until August 1988, the Reagan administration exerted no pressure on the Sudanese government, which was diverting food relief from the South. In July 1988 The House Select Committee on Hunger denounced that Ethiopian efforts at famine relief (which were actu-

ally praise from the UN) and only referred to the logistical problems of relief in the Sudan (Bonner, 1989:92).

21. Reardon, Matlon, and Delgado (1988), for example, show how household strategies are diversified regionally and sectorally in Burkina Faso. In the Sahelian zone, 75% of average household income came from non-cropping sources (substantially more than the Sudanian zone). Greater food aid is targeted to the Sahel in spite of the fact that purchasing power (and food security) appear higher and more stable than in the southerly regions.

22. Mortimore (1989), in his rather curious study of northern Nigeria, goes against much of this literature and, on the basis of quite limited evidence, suggests that there is no diachronic or synchronic pattern to famine response.

23. Cutler (1985:12) notes that lead times to famine in Bangladesh (3–4 months) and Ethiopia (up to five years) contrast markedly, and "when this happens little can be said with certainty about the length of time it takes for a person to starve to death."

24. Downing (1988), like Watts (1983) for northern Nigeria, argues that the range of coping strategies in Kenya has lessened, while the most effective strategies involve access to cash and reliance on local food markets.

25. There is good reason to include a fourth stage, namely a post-emergency 'rehabilitation' phase (see Harrell-Bond, 1986 and Brown, this volume).

26. See Cutler (1985, 1986), McCorkle (1987), and the activities of the Relief and Development Institute (Formerly the International Disasters Institute) in London, much of which has been published in their journal Disasters.

27. In his excellent study, de Waal (1989:17) shows how the mortality impact of migratory responses to famine in Darfur were primarily a function "not of what people did but where they did it."

28. Paul Richards' (1986:128) discussion of patronage, political competition, and entitlements is especially relevant here.

29. This is important because it provides a counterweight to what I take to be the deeply problematic biological derivation of "adaptation" or "coping" theory (see Watts, 1983).

30. Kates (1985:25) does recognize what he calls cultural adaptations by peasants to drought, but sees them as "largely unconscious." Mortimore (1989) provides a good critique of this position.

31. Basu (1986) has shown, however, that Sen's presumption that increases public works increased income for an underfed class whose new demand exhausted the possible supply is untenable. It rests on certain assumptions of the income elasticity of the beneficiaries and the existence of a free market without rationing, both of which Basu shows to be dubious.

32. The empirical (and ethical) question of documenting such intra-household dynamics during famines is extremely problematic. Wheeler and Abdullah (1988) argue, however, that while malnourishment is shaped by age and gender in Malawian and Indian households, men eat less during periods of scarcity and protect children. Lipton (1983:54) argues that it is rare to find gender discrimination against women in intra-household food allocation, slightly less rare against children, and least rare against girls 0–4 years.

33. In his book Sen really discusses the value of entitlements and less their structure, form, origins, and relative importance. See Joshi, 1981.

34. In the same way there is no simple causal relationship between commercialization or commoditization and nutritional status: see Cowen, 1983; Bryceson, 1984; von Braun, 1988; Kennedy and Cogill, 1987.

35. This does not endorse the rather silly commentary of Cohen (1988), who believes that any hint of moral economy is to invoke a Third World wonderland of "primitive affluence," benevolent patrons, and indigenous welfare.

36. These views are not unrelated to those of the institutional economists who refer to informal relationships in the market nexus and to the important body of work on contracts and interlinkages, forced commerce, and the like in peasant agriculture.

37. White's (1986 and this volume) brilliant study of the WoDaaBe revealed that only 10% of households owned herds sufficient for subsistence. Poor herders with limited animal and

58   M. WATTS

landed property lost labor as men migrated, further deepening their own labor shortages
(and contributing to poor herd management). Migration and animal contracting from outsiders (*jokereeji*) reinforce poverty, unviable herds, dependence on food aid, and extreme
vulnerability.
38. Jansson et al. (1987) document some of these fictions (see pp. 68-73) and their political
context.
39. According to Downing et al. (1989) the successful 1984 response to the Kenyan drought-
food crisis was due to political leadership rather than a systematic food monitoring system. Bates (1989) documents a more uneven performance, however, and a severe famine
in Meru in 1984, where food relief was tardy for reasons he cannot explain.

REFERENCES

Much of the relevant literature on famine is compiled in the excellent bibliographies
by Seeley (1986) and Leftwich and Harvie (1986).

Africa News
     1989 Making Its Own Miracles. 31(6):4-7.
Akong'a, J., and T. Downing
     1988 Smallholder Vulnerability and Response to Drought. In M. Parry, T. Car-
           ter, and N. Tonijn, eds., The Impact of Climatic Variations on Agriculture,
           pp. 221-248. Boston: Kluwer.
Alston, P.
     1984 International Law and the Human Right to Food. In P. Alston and K.
           Tomasevski, eds., The Right to Food, pp. 9-68. Dordrecht: Nijhoff.
Alston, P., and K. Tomasevski, eds.
     1984 The Right to Food. Dordecht: Nijhoff.
Anthropology Today
     1986-1987 An Exchange on the Ethiopian Famine, 2:11-14.
Arnold, D.
     1984 Famine in Peasant Consciousness and Peasant Action. In R. Guha, ed.,
           Subaltern Studies III, pp. 62-115. New York: Oxford University Press.
     1988 Famine. Oxford: Blackwell.
Ati, H. A.
     1988 The Process of Famine: Causes and Consequences in Sudan. Development
           and Change 19:267-300.
Barthes, R.
     1977 Image-Music-Text. London: Fontana.
Basu, D.
     1986 Sen's Analysis of Famine. Journal of Development Studies 22:598-602.
Bates, R.
     1988 From Drought to Famine in Kenya. In R. Cohen, ed., Satisfying Africa's
           Food Needs, pp. 103-120. Boulder: Rienner.
     1989 Famine: Meru, 1984. Working Paper #12, Duke University, Program in In-
           ternational Political Economy.
Behnke, R.
     1988 Range Enclosure in Central Somalia, ODI, Pastoral Network, Paper #25b.
Benjamin, W.
     1969 Illuminations. New York: Harper.

Berger, J.
  1980 About Looking. New York: Pantheon.
Berger, J., and J. Mohr
  1967 An Unfortunate Man. New York: Pantheon.
  1982 Another Way of Telling. New York: Pantheon.
Blanchot, M.
  1986 The Writing of Disaster. Lincoln: University of Nebraska Press.
Blenche, R.
  1985 Pastoral Labor and Stock Alienation in the Subhumid and Arid Zones of
        West Africa. ODI, Pastoral Network, Paper #19.
Bonfiglioli, A.
  1988 Dudal: Histoire de famille et histoire de troupeau chez un groupe de
        Wodaabe du Niger. Cambridge: Cambridge University Press.
Bonner, R.
  1989 A Reporter at Large: Famine. New Yorker, March 13, pp. 85-101.
Bowbrick, P.
  1986 The Causes of Famine: A Refutation of Professor Sen's Theory. Food Pol-
        icy 11:105-124.
  1987 Rejoinder: An Untenable Hypothesis on the Causes of Famine. Food Pol-
        icy 12:5-9.
Brandt Commission
  1980 A Programme for Survival: The Brandt Commission on North-South Is-
        sues. London: Oxford University Press.
Brecht, B.
  1972 Collected Works, vol. 7. New York: Vintage.
Brennan, L.
  1988 Government Famine Relief in Bengal, 1943. Journal of Asian Studies
        47:542-567.
Brittain, V.
  1988 Cuba and Southern Africa. New Left Review 172:117-124.
Brown University World Hunger Program
  1988 The Hunger Report. Providence, RI: Brown University.
  1989 The Hunger Report: Update. Providence, RI: Brown University.
Bryceson, D.
  1981 Colonial Famine Response. Food Policy 6:78-90.
  1984 Nutrition and the Commoditization of Food systems in Sub-Saharan Af-
        rica. Unpublished manuscript, Oxford University.
Bush, R.
  1988 Hunger in Sudan: The Case of Darfur. African Affairs 87:5-24.
Cahill, G., ed.
  1982 Famine. New York: Orsis.
Chastanet, M.
  1982 Les crises de subsistance dans les villages Soninké du Cercle de Bakel de
        1858-1945. Dakar-Hann: ORSTOM.
Clarke, J.
  1986 Resettlement and Rehabilitation: Ethiopia's Campaign against Famine.
        London: Harney and Jones.

Clay, E.
   1988   Assessment of Food Entitlement Interventions in South Asia. In D. Curtis
          et al., eds., Preventing Famine, pp. 141-155. New York: Routledge.
Clay, J., and B. Holcolmb
   1985   Politics and the Ethiopian Famine 1984-1985. Cambridge, MA: Cultural
          Survival.
Clay, J., S. Steingraber, and P. Niggli
   1988   The Spoils of Famine: Ethiopian Famine Policy and Peasant Agriculture.
          Cambridge, MA: Cultural Survival.
Cliffe, L., R. Bush, D. Pankhurst, and D. Littlejohn
   1989   The Survival Crisis in Southern Africa. London: ROAPE.
Clough, P.
   1985   Grain Marketing in Northern Nigeria. Review of African Political Econ-
          omy 34:16-34.
Cockburn, A.
   1989   A Million Here: A Million There. The Nation, March 6th:294-295.
Cohen, J., and N. Isaksson
   1988   Food Production Strategy Debates in Revolutionary Ethiopia. World De-
          velopment 16:322-348.
Cohen, R., ed.
   1988   Satisfying Africa's Food Needs. Boulder: Westview.
Conquest, R.
   1986   The Harvest of Sorrow: Soviet Collectivisation and the Famine. London:
          Oxford University Press.
Coplon, J.
   1988   Soviet Holocaust. The Village Voice, January 12th:28-34.
Corbett, J.
   1988   Famine and Household Coping Strategies. World Development
          16:1099-1112.
Cowen, M.
   1983   The Commercialization of Food Production in East Africa after 1945. In R.
          Rotberg, ed., Imperialism, Colonialism and Hunger. Lexington: Heath, pp.
          187-205.
Crow, B.
   1986   U.S. Policies in Bangladesh: The Making and Breaking of Famine. DPP
          Working Paper #4, Milton Keynes, The Open University.
   1987   Plain Tales from the Rice Trade. DPP Working Paper #6, Milton Keynes,
          The Open University.
Currey, B.
   1984   Coping with Complexity in Food Crisis Management. In B. Currey and G.
          Hugo, eds., Famine as a Geographical Phenomenon. Dordrecht: Reidel,
          pp. 1231-133.
Curtis, D., M. Hubbard, and A. Shepherd, eds.
   1988   Preventing Famine. London: Routledge.
Cutler, P.
   1985   The Use of Economic and Social Information in Famine Prediction and Re-
          sponse. Food Emergencies Unit, London School of Hygiene and Tropical
          Medicine.

1986 The Response to Drought of Beja Famine Refugees in Sudan. Disaster 10:181-188.

DeCastro, J.
1977 The Geopolitics of Hunger. New York: Monthly Press.

De Garine, I., and G. Harrison, eds.
1988 Coping with Uncertainty in Food Supply. Oxford: Oxford University Press.

Dejene, A.
1987 Peasants, Socialism and Rural Development. Boulder: Westview.

Demery, L., and Addison, T.
1987 Food Security and Adjustment Policies in Sub-Saharan Africa. Development Policy Review 15:177-196.

Desai, M.
1987 Storytelling and Formalism in Economics: The Instance of Famine. International Social Science Journal 113:387-400.

de Waal, A.
1989 Famine Mortality: A Case Study of Darfur, Sudan 1984-1985. Population Studies 43:5-24.

Didion, J.
1979 The White Album. New York: Vintage.

Downing, T.
1988 Climatic Variability, Food Security and Smallholder Agricultures in Six Districts in Central and Eastern Kenya. Ph.D. Dissertation, Clark University.

Downing, T., K. Gitu, and C. Kamau, eds.
1989 Coping with Drought in Kenya: National and Local Stratigies. Boulder: Reinner.

Dreze, J.
1988 Famine Prevention in India. Paper #3, Development Economics Research Programme, London School of Economics.

Dreze, J., and A. Sen
1989 Hunger and Public Action. Oxford: Oxford University Press.

Elson, D.
1988 Market Socialism or Socialization of the Market? New Left Review 172:3-42.

Finnegan, W.
1989 A Reporter at Large: Mozambique. New Yorker, May 22:43-76 and May 29:69-96.

Folbre, N.
1986 Hearts and Spades. World Development 14:245-256.

Gallant, T.
1989 Crisis and Response: Risk-Buffering Behavior in Hellenistic Greece. Journal of Interdisciplinary History XIX:393-413.

Garcia, R.
1981 Nature Pleads Not Guilty. New York: Pergamon.

Garnsey, P.
1987 Famine and Food Supply in the Graeco-Roman World. Cambridge: Cambridge University Press.

Gartrell, B.
    1985 The Roots of Famine in Karamoja. Review of African Political Economy
          33:102-110.
Ghai, D., and de Alacantara
    1989 The Crisis of the 1980s in Africa and Latin America. Paper delivered to
          ISER/UNRISD Conference, Economic Crisis and Third World Countries,
          Kingston, Jamaica.
Gill, P.
    1986 A Year in the Death of Africa. London: Paladin.
Giorgis, D.
    1989 Read Tears. Trenton: Red Sea Press.
Glantz, M., ed.
    1987 Drought and Hunger in Africa. Cambridge: Cambridge University Press.
Griffin, K.
    1987 World Hunger and the World Economy. New York: Holmes and Meier.
Guyer, J.
    1988 Multiplication of Labor. Current Anthropology **29**:247-260.
Guyer, J., and P. Peters, eds.
    1987 Conceptualizing the Household. Development and Change, **18**.
Halderman, M.
    1987 Development and Famine Risk in Kenya. Ph.D. Dissertation, University of
          California, Berkeley.
Harper, M.
    1988 Images of Africa. West Africa, December 19th-25th:2381-2382.
Harrell-Bond, B.
    1986 Imposing Aid: Emergency Assistance for African Refugees. Oxford: Ox-
          ford University Press.
Harriss, B.
    1988 Limitations of the Lessons from India. In D. Curtis et al., eds., Famine Pre-
          vention. London: Routledge, pp. 157-170.
    1989 Merchants, Capital, and Class Formation in South Asia. Paper delivered to
          the Association of American Geographers, Baltimore.
Hay, R.
    1988 Famine Incomes and Employment. World Development **16**:1113-1125.
Herlehy, T.
    1984 Historical Dimensions of the Food Crisis in Africa: Surviving Famines
          along the Kenya Coast. Working Paper #87, African Studies Center, Bos-
          ton University.
Hesse, C.
    1987 Livestock Data as an Early Warning Indicator of Stress in a Pastoral Econ-
          omy. ODI, Pastoral Network, Paper #24.
Hogg, R.
    1985 The Politics of Drought. Disasters **9**:39-43.
Holm, J., and R. Morgan
    1985 Coping with Drought in Botswana: An African Success. Journal of Mod-
          ern African Studies **23**:463-482.
Hopcraft, P.
    1987 Grain Marketing, Policies, and Institutions in Africa. Finance and Devel-
          opment **24**:31-38.

IDS
  1986   Seasonality and Poverty: Special Issue. IDS Bulletin 17
  1989   Vulnerability: How the Poor Cope. Special Issue. IDS Bulletin 20
Iliffe, J.
  1988   The African Poor: A History. Cambridge: Cambridge University Press.
Independent Commission on International Humanitarian Issues
  1985   Famine: A Man-Made Disaster. London: Pan Books.
Jansson, K., M. Harris, and A. Penros
  1987   The Ethiopian Famine. London: Zed Press.
Jodha, N., and Mascarenhas, A.
  1985   Adjustment in Self-Provisioning Societies. In R. Kates et al., eds., Climate
         Impact Assessment. New York: Wiley, pp. 437-468.
Jones, W.
  1980   Agricultural Trade within Tropical Africa. In R. Bates and M. Lofchie,
         eds., Agricultural Development in Africa. New York: Praeger, pp.
         311-348.
Joshi, V.
  1981   Enough to Eat. London Review of Books, 19th December:13-14.
Kaplan, R.
  1988   Surrender or Starve: The Wars behind the Famine. Boulder: Westview.
Kates, R.
  1985   The Interaction of Climate and Society. In R. Kates et al., eds., Climate
         Impact Assessment. New York: Wiley, pp. 3-36.
Kates, R., J. Ausubel, and M. Berberian, eds.
  1985   Climate Impact Assessment. New York: Wiley.
Kahn, M.
  1984   Always Hungry, Never Greedy. Cambridge: Cambridge University Press.
Kautsky, K.
  1906   La question agraire. Paris: Maspero.
Kennedy, E., and Cogill, B.
  1987   Income and Nutritional Effects of the Commercialization of Agriculture in
         South Western Kenya. Research Report #63. Washington, D.C.: IFPRI.
Kula, E.
  1988   The Inadequacy of the Entitlement Approach to Explain and Remedy Fam-
         ine. Journal of Development Studies 25:112-116.
Leatherman, T.
  1987   Illness, Work and Social Relations in the Southern Peruvian Highlands.
         Ph.D. Dissertation, University of Massachusetts, Amherst.
Left Business Observer
  1989   IMF Staffer Defects 28:4-5.
Leftwich, A., and Harvie, D.
  1986   The Political Economy of Famine. Discussion Paper #116, Institute for Re-
         search in the Social Sciences, University of York.
Lemma, H.
  1985   The Politics of Famine in Ethiopia. Review of African Political Economy
         33:44-58.
Lewin, M.
  1984   Rural Society in Twentieth Century Russia. Social History 9(2):171-180.

Lipton, M.
    1983 Poverty, Undernutrition and Hunger. Staff Working Paper #597. Washington, D.C.: The World Bank.
Longhurst, R.
    1986 Household Food Strategies in Response to Seasonality and Famine. IDS Bulletin 17:27-35.
Mabbs-Zeno, C.
    1987 Long Term Impacts of Famine. Economic Research Service. Wshington, D.C.: Department of Agriculture.
Mace, J.
    1989 Soviet Attempts to Confront the Famine of 1932-33 during 1988-89. Manuscript, Ukrainian Commission, Washington, D.C.
Mackintosh, M.
    1989 Gender, Class and Rural Transition. London: Zed.
Mamdani, M.
    1985 Disaster Prevention. Review of African Political Economy 33:92-96.
    1986a Peasants and Democracy in Africa. New Left Review 156:37-50.
    1986b A Rejoinder. Review of African Political Economy 36:85-93.
Mazonde, I.
    1987 The Development of Ranching and Economic Enterprise in Eastern Botswana. Ph.D. Dissertation, Manchester University.
McCabe, T.
    1987 Drought and Recovery. Human Ecology 15:371-389.
McCann, J.
    1987 From Poverty to Famine in Northeast Ethiopia. Philadelphia: University of Pennsylvania Press.
McCorkle, C.
    1987 Foodgrain Disposals as Early Warning Famine Signals. Disaster 11:273-281.
Meadows, D. H., Meadows, D. L., Randers, R., and Behrens, W.
    1972 The Limits to Growth. New York: Universe Books.
Mellor, J., and S. Gavian
    1987 Famine: Causes, Prevention and Relief. Science 235:539-545.
MERIP
    1987 The Struggle for Food. Middle East Report, #145.
Mitra, A.
    1982 The Meaning of Meaning. Economic and Political Weekly XVII, 13:78-79.
Moore, B.
    1970 Reflections on the Causes on Human Misery. Boston: Beacon.
Moore, H., and M. Vaughn
    1987 Cutting Down Trees: Women, Nutrition and Agricultural Change in the Northern Province of Zambia 1920-1986. African Affairs 86:523-540.
Mortimore, M.
    1989 Adapting to Drought: Farmers, Famines and Desertification in West Africa. Cambridge: Cambridge University Press.
Nagel, T.
    1977 Poverty and Food. In P. Brown and H. Shue, eds., Food Policy. New York: Free Press, pp. 43-61.

Offe, C.
1984 The Contradictions of the Welfare State. Cambridge, MA: MIT Press.
O'Neill, O.
1986 Faces of Hunger. London: Allen and Unwin.
Pankhurst, D.
1988 Hunger in Western Sudan. Capital and Class 35:19-28.
Pinstrup-Anderson, P.
1985 Food Prices and the Poor in Developing Countries. Review of Agricultural Economics 12:156-189.
Preston, P.
1986 An African Winter. Harmondsworth: Penguin.
Rahmato, D.
1988 Famine and Survival Strategies: A Case Study from Northeast Ethiopia. Institute for Development Studies, University of Addis Ababa.
Raikes, P.
1988 Modernizing Hunger. Toronto: Currey.
Rangasami, A.
1985 Failure of Exchange Entitlements Theory of Famine: I. Economic and Political Weekly 41:1747-1752; 42:1797-1800.
Ravallion, M.
1987 Markets and Famines. Oxford: Clarendon Press.
Reardon, T., P. Matlon, and C. Delgado
1988 Coping with Household Level Food Insecurity in Drought Affected Areas of Burkina Faso. World Development 16:1065-1074.
Reddy, S.
1988 An Independent Press Working against Famine: The Nigerian Experience. Journal of Modern African Studies 26:337-346.
Richards, P.
1986 Coping with Hunger. London: Allen and Unwin.
1987a The Politics of Famine. African Affairs 86:111-116.
1987b Agriculture as Performance. IDS Workshop, Sussex University.
Riddell, B. N.
1987 The African Malaise. Canadian Journal of Development Studies 8:387-392.
ROAPE
1985 War and Famine (Special Issue). Review of African Political Economy 33.
Rule, S.
1989 Africa Up Close. New York Times Magazine, April 30th:36-39.
Said, E.
1978 Orientalism. New York: Harper and Row.
Samatar, A.
1989 The State and Rural Transformation in Northern Somalia. Madison: University of Wisconsin Press.
Saul, M.
1987 The Organization of a West African Grain Market. American Anthropologist 89:74-95.
Scheper-Hughes, N.
1986 Culture, Scarcity and Maternal Thinking. Ethos 23:291-317.

1988   The Madness of Hunger. Paper delivered to the Wenner Gren Conference
       on Analysis in Medical Anthropology, Lisbon, Portugal.
Schroeder, R.
1987   Gender Vulnerability to Drought: A Case Study of the Hausa Social Envi-
       ronment. Working Paper #58, Institute of Behavioral Science, Boulder.
Scott, J.
1976   The Moral Economy of the Peasantry. New Haven: Yale University Press.
1985   Weapons of the Weak. New Haven: Yale University Press.
Seaman, J., and Holt, J.
1980   Markets and Famines in the Third world. Disasters 4:283-297.
Seavoy, R.
1986   Famine in Peasant Societies. New York: Greenwood.
Seeley, J.
1986   Famine in Africa: A Bibliographic Guide, 2 vols. African Studies Centre,
       Cambridge University Press.
Sen, A.
1981   Poverty and Famines: An Essay on Entitlements. Oxford, Oxford Univer-
       sity Press.
1987   Property and Hunger. Economics and Philosophy 4:57-68.
Sivard, R.
1987   World Military and Social Expenditures 1987-1988. Washington, D.C.:
       World Priorities.
Smale-Heisey, M.
1987   Intrahousehold Allocation of Resources during Drought. Paper #w/S4417.
       Rome: FAO.
Smith, G.
1987   Ethiopia and the Politics of Famine Relief. MERIP Reports 145:31-37.
Sperling, L.
1987   Food Acquisition during the Kenyan Drought of 1983-1984. Disasters
       11:241-272.
Spitz, P.
1980   Drought and Self Provisioning. Working Paper, Food Systems and Soci-
       ety. Geneva: UNRISD.
Srinavasan, T.
1983   Review of A. Sen (1981). American Journal of Agricultural Economics
       43:143-146.
Starr, M.
1987   Risk, Environmental Variability and Drought Induced Improvishment. Af-
       rica 57:29-57.
Sutter, J.
1987   Cattle and Inequality. Africa 57:196-218.
Swift, J.
1989   Why Are Rural People Vulnerable to Famine? IDS Bulletin 20(2):8-15.
Swinton, S.
1988   Drought Survival Tactics and Subsistence Farmers in Niger. Human Ecol-
       ogy 16(2):123-144.
Taussig, M.
1984   Culture of Terror, Space of Death. Comparative Studies in Society and
       History 26:467-497.

Tawney, R. H.
    1966 Land and Labor in China. Boston: Beacon.
Tilly, L.
    1983 Food Entitlement, Famine and Conflict. In R. Rotberg and T. Rabb, eds.,
          Hunger and History. Cambridge: Cambridge University Press, pp.
          135-152.
Torry, W.
    1986a Morality and Harm: Hindu Peasant Adjustments to Famines. Social Sci-
          ence Information 25:125-160.
    1986b Economic Development, Drought and Famines: Some Limits of Depend-
          ency Explanations. GeoJournal 12:5-18.
Toulmin, C.
    1987 Drought and the Farming Sector. Development Policy Review 5:125-148.
Turshen, M.
    1984 The Political Ecology of Disease in Tanzania. New Brunswick: Rutgers
          University Press.
Twose, N., and M. Goldwater
    1986 Fighting the Famine. San Francisco: Food First.
United States Commission on the Ukraine Famine
    1988 Report to Congress, Investigation of the Ukrainian Famine 1932-1933.
          Washington, D.C.: Government Printing Office.
Vaughn, M.
    1987 The Story of an African Famine: Famine and Gender in Malawi.
          Cambridge: Cambridge University Press.
Vincent, C.
    1987 The Politics of Hunger: The Allied Blockade of Germany 1915-1919.
          Athens: Ohio University Press.
von Braun, J.
    1988 Effects of Technological Change in Agriculture on Food Consumption and
          Nutrition: Rice in a West African Setting. World Development
          16:1083-1098.
Warren, B.
    1980 Imperialism: Pioneer of Capitalism. London: Verso.
Watson, E., and Harriss, B.
    1985 Health, Nutrition and Work. Discussion Paper #179, School of Develop-
          ment Studies, University of East Anglia.
Watts, M.
    1983 Silent Violence: Food, Famine and Peasantry in Northern Nigeria.
          Berkeley: University of California Press.
    1988 The Faces of Famine. GeoJournal 17:145-149.
    1989 The Agrarian Question in Africa. Progress in Human Geography 13:1-41.
    Forthcoming. Manufacturing Discontent: Production Politics in a Peasant Soci-
          ety. London: Heinemann.
Wheeler, E., and M. Abdullah
    1988 Food Allocation within the Family. In I. de Garine and G. Harrisson, eds.,
          Coping with Uncertainty in Food Supply. Oxford: Oxford University
          Press, pp. 437-451.

White, C.
  1986 Food Shortage and Seasonality in WoDaabe Communities in Niger. IDS
       Bulletin 17:19-26.
Whyte, A.
  1986 From Hazard Perception to Human Ecology. In R. Kates and I. Burton,
       eds., Geography, Resources, and Environment II. Chicago: University of
       Chicago Press, pp. 242-271.
Williams, R.
  1977 Keywords. Oxford: Oxford University Press.
  Wisner, B.
  1988 Power and Need in Africa. London: Earthscan.
World Bank
  1989 Africa's Adjustment and Growth in the 1980s. Washington, D.C.: IBRD.
World Commission on the Environment and Development
  1987 Our Common Future. London: Oxford University Press.
Wuyts, M.
  1989 Economic Management and adjustment Policies in Mozambique. Paper
       delivered to the ISER/UNRISD Conference on Economic Crisis in Third
       World Countries, Kingston, Jamaica.

PART B

Development Practice and Hunger

CHAPTER 2

Cultural Construction in a 'Garden of Eden': The Influence of Ontological Acquiescence in an African Development Project and its Implications for Food Security

Stephen P. Reyna

During the afternoon of New Year's Eve, 1977, a group of development experts on a mission to formulate a development strategy for the Chad Basin conferred in the bar of the only luxury hotel in N'Djamena, Chad. They planned a speedy, three-hour trip to the bush to evaluate native conditions, possibly to see some game, and by these good works, to justify their anticipated nocturnal revels. The younger ones asked a senior member of the group, one whose judgment had proved invaluable concerning whiskies, varieties of bottled water, and what to say to taxi drivers if you required a *poule de luxe*, what he thought of the plan.

In response to their query, the gentleman—ready to party in impeccable black trousers, a dazzling Christian Dior shirt, and a tastefully understated leather belt with gold buckle—raised a bottle of Johnny Walker (red) aloft, in a manner faintly reminiscent of the Pope about to give an audience, and intoned: "I am a scientific expert, I do not need to go. I have seen it." Being an anthropologist who had done time in the bush, and in possession of the knowledge that the gentlemen had never left the hotel, I felt affronted by his claim that he had "seen" it.

But I now know what he had seen. How I came to such knowledge and what some of its implications are form the basis of the present inquiry, which analyzes an unremarkable development project in the Chad Basin that came to an unnoticed demise—and whose significance lies in the fact that it was so ordinary. The argument is at two levels. First, I suggest that a form of cultural construction of the project's planners, which I call ontological acquiescence, helped create a project that if "successful" might have decreased rather than increased its beneficiaries' food security. Then, on the basis of this instance I explore the possibility that this mode of constructing reality might contribute more generally to African food security problems.

The analysis is organized as follows. The first section introduces the notion of ontological acquiescene. It also describes the project. The second section suggests that such acquiescence played a role in this project's design. The third section explains first why this design failed and second how if implemented it might have increased food production risks. The final section explores more generally certain implications of such thought for African hunger.

Two asides: one concerns acronyms, the other, my qualifications to undertake the present analysis. Ethnographers pride themselves on "experience near" descriptions (Geertz, 1977:481), by which they usually mean the reporting of events as closely as possible to the way they are experienced. One often hears kin terms in the speech of rural, Third World folk, because such peoples' lives are lived among relatives. So anthropologists carefully report the meaning of these terms. Similarly one is struck by the many acronyms dominating development bureaucrats' chatter, because here lives are played out among the agencies denoted by this babel of letters. Readers should accordingly brace themselves for a dose of "experience near" acronyms.

To introduce a first acronym, it might be noted that I was the project anthropologist for the CLP—the Chadian Livestock Project—from 1973 through 1974. During this time I conducted participant observation and survey research in eighteen villages. I returned to the region, though not the project, in 1975, 1977, 1978, 1980—and thus was able to observe something of its progress.[1]

1.

When you ask development experts what makes them so "expert" they often respond, as did the gentleman in the previous section, by saying that they are scientists, implying that scientists know better than others. Such an implication raises the question: can scientific thought be distinguished from other forms of thought?

Thinking about thinking has been central to social analysis since the beginning of the 19th century, during which time a tradition has emerged suggesting, among other things, that reality is constructed. This tradition, which might be termed phenomenological, includes Husserl (1900-01, 1913), Shutz (1967), and Berger and Luckman (1966) in philosophy and sociology as well as Sapir (1928), Whorf (1956), Goodenough (1957), Geertz (1973), and those of a more interpretive turn (Rabinow and Sullivan, 1987) in American cultural anthropology. Its members are united in their adherence to a particular view of ontology. Ontology, broadly speaking, is "the study of being..." (OED, 1989, vol. X:824). It is the analysis of the way things are, of reality. Construction is a trope for creation, in the sense of building something. An axiom shared by phenomenologists is that reality is a construction of peoples' modes of thought. Further, cultural anthropologists might insist that when people build up their views of reality they do so on the basis of "folk," "native," or "indigenous" models derived from their culture (Lutz, 1988:10), so that when this occurs it is appropriate to speak of a cultural construction of reality.

If there is no "objective" reality because people construct reality—the world "out there"—by thinking about it, and if, when they construct such worlds, they do so on the basis of commonly agreed upon cultural conceptions about what it is that is out there, then people are, in effect, simply accepting the nature of the phenomenal world as so determined. Propositions about the nature of things arrived at as a result of tacitly or passively accepting what one's culture directly, or by implication, states about reality are an aspect of cultural construction that I call "*ontological acquiescence*." Trobriand Island culture stipulates that the ancestors of their matriclans crawled from holes in the earth. Trobriand Islanders accept this view of their origins as natural and correct. Mundurucu culture classifies humanity into people, restricted to the Mundurucu themselves, and *pariwats*, all others (Murphy and Murphy, 1985:80). Mundurucu take for granted this, to them, utterly obvious reality. Both are examples of ontological acquiescence.[2] Much ontological thought would appear to derive from such agreements between members of a society as to the nature of being. When this occurs the old proverb "seeing is believing" might be reversed to read "believing is seeing."

It should be noted that there is a difference between ontological acquiescence and science. This is in part because the practitioners of each evaluate the validity of their propositions in radically different manners. Propositions are valid under ontological acquiescence so long as people continue to accept them. Propositions are valid in science only if what goes on in the world is consistent with what the propositions specify goes on in the world. This means, as Malinowski noted, that the utility of scientific propositions is "founded on observation" (1948:87).

Observation is "not so simple a matter…" (Cohen and Nagel, 1934:215). However, the root of the term means "to see," suggesting that is is most fundamentally about sensing reality. Specifically, observation compares sensory data concerning events in the world with the specifications of general and abstract propositions as to what those sensory data should be like. Propositions have some utility if sensory impressions of reality correspond *exactly* to what the propositions say they should be.

It might be said that observation also plays a role in ontological acquiescence, and to some extent this is true. However, here it involves a sensing of the world that is different from that in the sciences. In science before a proposition is accepted there must be a sensing of events bearing upon all concepts and relations between the concepts comprising the proposition. In ontological acquiescence such complete sensing is irrelevant to the acceptance of the proposition.

Some have likened observation to voyeurism (Kaplan, 1964:127). It is, however, a very specialized kind of voyeurism: one that either deduces propositions from theory and, then, through interpretation, instrumentation, scaling, and sampling decides what sort of sense impressions are required to evaluate these propositions; or one that through measurement, sample summarization, and parameter estimation of sense impressions formulates new propositions (Wallace, 1971). Propositions evaluated in the first manner are called hypotheses; those formed in the second manner are called empirical generalizations. Activities leading to the testing or forming of such propositions are termed empirical analyses, and are necessary for establishing their scientific validity.

In ontological acquiescence, on the other hand, what largely determines the utility of propositions is the effectiveness of the institutions that enculturate belief. For example, members of certain Christian sects refuse to visit doctors even, as occurred in one recent case, if it means that a sick child dies in agony. This is because officials of that church skillfully teach the proposition: "Christ heals!" In this case, the officials' pastoral activities are so powerful that they enculturate acceptance of a "reality" even the most casual observation suggests is to contrary to fact.

Thus there appear to be two different ways of constructing reality. Most people spend most of their lives passively complying with the different notions of being found in their culture. This is ontological acquiescence.[3] Sometimes, however, some people think scientifically, and here propositions are constructed through systematic observation. When the gentleman in the bar, and for that matter other development practitioners, justify their actions by saying they are scientists, what they are implying is that they have "seen" according to the standards of contemporary empirical analysis, and based their judgments upon such seeing. However, have they really been seeing as scientists or as practitioners of ontological acquiescence? This is precisely the question posed by the CLP.

CLP was funded by three major sources of development investments—the United Nations Development Program (UNDP), the United States Agency for International Development (AID), and the French *Fonds d'Assistance et Coopération* (FAC). These donors' financial contributions were on the order of $3,300,000, which was sufficient for a middle sized project in the early 1970s. The Lake Chad Basin Commission (LCBC), an African development agency formed by the governments of the countries bordering Lake Chad, was chosen to implement the project. CLP began operations in 1973 and ran for five years in the Assale region of Chad and the adjacent Serbewel district of Cameroon. The project was spread over 5,300 square kilometers immediately south of Lake Chad, mostly in the Serbewel. The region was sahelian: rigorously flat, acacia dominated tree and shrub savanna, baked in blazing heat. Temperatures ranged from a mean of 22 degrees centigrade in the cold season (December/January) to on of 31 degrees during the hottest time (April/May), when highs of 43 degrees were common. The area received an average of 475 millimeters of rainfall distributed in two to three months of precipitation from July to September.

Prior to the project, Assale-Serbewel was inhabited by approximately 81,000 people thought to be largely Kotoko or Arab in ethnic affiliation. Arabs were known to be the most numerous ethnic group. They were understood to be pastoralists who owned large amounts of livestock, estimated to include 130,000 cattle, 75,000 sheep and goats, and 8,500 donkeys and horses. As the Assale-Serbewel was not only a pastoral zone but was close to the Chadian capital, N'Djamena, which promised to simplify logistic problems, it was thought to be an appropriate place to locate a livestock development project.

The project was part of a second round of livestock development activities in francophone Africa. The first round, which had lasted through the colonial and immediate post-colonial period, stressed the provision of veterinary services. It was realized, as an AID planning document expressed it, that these "efforts to improve livestock production have not been typically marked by success" (AID, 1971:4). It was further believed that one reason why these projects had failed, as the same AID document put it, was because "Past efforts to improve livestock production...[had] largely ignored...[a] critical human factor...Instead past programs...[had] concentrated largely on the animal itself... (AID, 1971:4). The CLP would succeed, its planners hoped, by bringing people back in and concentrating upon the "human factor."

CLP's "overall aim," according to the main document that the Lake Chad Basin Commission used to guide project operations, was to be "the development of animal production, particularly of cattle..." in the project zone (LCBC, 1971:22). However, it was feared that the pasture in the Assale-Serbewel was beginning to be over-utilized. This meant that development could not proceed on the basis of increased numbers of animals. Rather, it would have to result from enhanced herd productivity and offtake that would follow from "improvement of [herd] sanitary conditions..., [and] improvement of marketing..." (LCBC, 1971:22). Herd composition would be altered to provide the maximum number of market animals, with herders concentrating only on cattle. These would be herded on a new pasture rotation scheme. They would be fed fodder. They would be given extensive veterinary care. They would be sent to feedlots for fattening.

Just as "modern" farming tends toward mono-cropping, so the CLP herder would narrowly specialize. He—and it was only men that the project planners were thinking about—would be expected to raise a single race of a single species: cattle. In sum, the way Assale-Serbewel pastoralists went about the livestock business was to be revolutionized. They were to become cowboys in the mold of the Euro-American livestock industry. However, consistent with the emphasis on the human factor, "the fundamental characteristic of the proposed actions" was that they would be undertaken "in conjunction with the livestock owners themselves" (LCBC, 1971:22). Let us explore the degree to which this was the case during actual planning of the CLP.

2.

CLP appears to have been planned largely by a single person who was an officer of a UN agency. This person went about his chores late in 1970 at the request of the LCBC. His mission seems to have lasted for a few months. Throughout my stay in the project area I continually asked people if they had ever heard of or actually seen this gentleman. Nobody ever had. No local official or herder that I met in the Assale-Serbewel had ever been asked by anybody what he thought about a livestock development project in his area. For that matter, most people in the LCBC could not remember who had planned the CLP. Nor had they ever been asked what they thought about such a project. There were, and are, a few social scientists familiar with the societies of the Assale-Serbewel, but only two with any expertise with respect to the pastoralists at that time (Hagenboucher, 1973, 1974; Zeltner, 1970). They played no part in the planning of the CLP. In short, the design of the project could not have involved extensive participation of the people in the project area. Nor, for that matter, could it have been based upon thorough observation. There was nobody there to do the observing.

Nevertheless, the person responsible for the main design of the project and the other officials with whom he worked in the donor agencies that would fund the CLP expressed a number of ontological statements about the way things were in the Assale-Serbewel, especially with regard to social realities, in the various documents used to plan or implement the project. The most extraordinary of these statements was a Comtean insistence that the herders were not *rationnels*, so they would have to be, as the French version of LCBC's planning document put it, led to a *plus rationnelle* form of livestock management. English speakers dealing with the project tended to use the concept of traditionality in place of that irrationality, when discussing the Assale-Serbewel. In doing so they were complying with two deeply held American cultural notions: that people in less developed areas are more traditional; and that more traditional folk are less rational. Thus English versions of both the AID and the LCBC planning documents continually referred to the area's pastoralists as "traditional" (AID, 1971:1). A second proposition was that "individual property is non-existent" in the Assale-Serbewel (LCBC, 1970:9). A third proposition, getting down to the specifics of pastoralism, stated that the livestock raising "more of less completely" assured "the lives of the pastoralists" (LCBC, 1970:1), who were recognized to be "Arab Shawas" (LCBC, 1970:7).[4] The ontology, then, which emerges from these documents for Assale-Serbewel pastoralists was that they were a bunch of not two swift guys, in the iron grip of tradition, subsisting entirely from pastoral activities.

By my time with the project, nobody—not AID, UN, FAC, or LCBC personnel who had anything to do with the project—knew where this ontology had originated. Nor did they themselves spend any time in the Assale-Serbewel actually observing the people and the land. But they believed the ontology! French speakers would say, "*c'est comme ca...*" Americans would say, "that's the way things are with them, you see..." In a sense, what these Americans were asking me to do was to "see" just as they did. This meant not to see in the sense of making visual observations, but to agree, in the sense of assenting to their conceptions of the Assale-Serbewel reality. So when I was asked to "see" something, really what I was being urged to do was to be a good sport and to acquiesce in their ontological stipulations.

When I asked an American official what it meant to be traditional he responded, "You know, they do what their customs tell them. Not like us, we're modern—except for my mother, of course." He then referred me to Eugene Rostow's *The Conditions of Economic Growth* for a confirmation that Assale-Serbewel pastoralists were traditionalists. And that was precisely the point. Dr. Rostow would be the first to admit that he has never observed the Assale-Serbewel. Members of the LCBC and the donor agencies had never observed the Assale-Serbewel. The original planner of the CLP, who was supposed to include the human factor, had never observed the Assale-Serbewel. But they had ideas about the way things were, and in the end they simply pictured the Assale-Serbewel in ways that were consistent with their culture's ontology of the Third World. Rostow, expressing the earlier noted American cultural notions about less developed areas, says Third World people are traditional; the people of the Assale-Serbewel are in the Third World; therefore the Assale-Serbewel pastoralists are traditional.

Such thinking is a clear example of what I call ontological acquiescence. A consequence of such acquiescence is ontological stipulation; because the project planners and personnel, by accepting their own cultural notions, in effect demanded or stipulated that the people in the Assale-Serbewel had a particular reality. In the following section we will see some of the Assale-Serbewel reality, and one reason the project failed because of it.

I argue that development projects can enjoy at least two types of success and failure. "Tactical" success or failure refers to the fate of the project itself/ If the innovations a project proposes are successfully introduced, then it is a tactical success; while if the innovations are rejected, then it is a tactical failure. However, project activities typically have consequences beyond the innovations they seek to introduce. If these are beneficial, the project may be considered a "strategic" success; while if they are harmful, it must be judged a strategic failure. Consider, for example, a project that successfully introduces a new crop, whose sale prices unfortunately are so low as to reduce total income. This project, thus, would have implemented a planned innovation, the crop, that produced unfortunate results, the income decline. Such a project would be a tactical success but a strategic failure. It will be argued that the CLP was a tactical failure and that ironically this made it a strategic success, in the unusual sense that its tactical debacle maintained existing beneficial practices.

Not all of the CLP's interventions were rejected. Over the project's life some of the veterinary interventions and the new wells were accepted and may have initially improved animal health. These, however, were not really innovations so much as improvements upon existing techniques or practices. Herders had been searching for, and constructing, wells throughout their existence. CLP simply offered them new, cemented models. Similarly, herders had been using veterinary measures based upon their own medical notions for centuries. CLP merely offered them different procedures based upon Western medical conceptions.[5]

When I spoke with herders in 1980 it was clear that little had changed. They were still herding a number of species. They had not appreciably altered herd compositions. They were pasturing animals and transhuming them in the same ways. They were giving them the same feeds. They were not growing fodders. There were no feedlots. They were selling animals at more or less the same ages, through the marketing arrangements that had existed before the project. They were, thus, raising animals, utilizing range, and marketing in the same pre-project ways. CLP was a tactical failure in the sense that herders continued in the livestock business after the project had ended pretty much as they had done before the project had ever begun. How this was, at least in part, due to the ontology stipulated for the herders by project personnel is now explored.

Remember that the project stipulated that the herders were "traditional" and therefore not "rational." This seemed to me questionable, because I continually witnessed efforts by livestock people to calculate their utilities. Frequently their perceived utilities involved economic advantages, and often their calculations of these advantages seemed sensible to me, as—and this is the crux of the matter—their calculations were based upon a productive strategy which offered greater survival and income prospects than those proposed by the project.

Arabs have been occupying the Assale-Serbewel since the 15th or 16th century. By the 1970s most groups that were in the project zone had been there for at least two centuries. They had drifted in largely as nomads. Perhaps this migratory drift had been stimulated by a drier spell beginning after 1200 AD that transformed much of the region to the north of Lake Chad from dry savanna to desert (Maley, 1977). The groups which arrived in the Assale-Serbewel found an environment which offered far richer opportunities than the arid lands they had left, and so they appear to have altered their production strategies to enjoy the new opportunities offered by the new land.

The plains in the Assale-Serbewel have far more surface water than is normally found in sahelian regions. There is permanent water in the Shari River and Lake Chad, and there are a number of seasonally flowing streams such as the Serbewel. There are flood plains along these rivers that have heavy, dark clayish soils—called either *berbéré* or *firki*. Vegetation tends to be thick here—the remains of gallery forest. The land ever so imperceptibly rises between the streams. Soils are sandy here. Grasses and acacia thorn bushes tend to predominate. Interspersed between the sandy plains and the flood plains are depressions. These result from the action of ancient streams which in moister times were part of the filigree of water-courses that formed the delta of Lake Chad. At present they do not flow, though they do accumulate water during the rains. Depression soils are also called *berbéré* or *firki*, but owing to their origin as old river beds, they are often heavier and occasionally more fertile than the younger similar soils in the flood plains (Dabin, 1969).

The ecological anthropologist, R. Carneiro, calls such a situation one of resource concentration (1987), i.e., the juxtaposition of different micro-environments—river and lake, flood-plain, sandy plain, low swamps—in walking distance from each other. It was this concentration that created the different opportunities in the Assale-Serbewel, because each micro environment offered different food-producing possibilities which would be absent, or vastly more difficult, in arid zones.

Two related food-production strategies evolved to exploit these opportunities. The first is currently favored by the Kotoko. This involves the use of the rivers and lakes for fishing and the use of different land surfaces for cereal production. The second is that of the Arabs. It exploits the rivers and lakes as water sources for their animals and, as do the Kotoko, the different land surfaces for cereal production. We will explore the farming system resulting from this second food production strategy in greater detail, because it was the reality upon which the CLP had tried to impose its own ontology. However, before this farming system can be appreciated we need to know more about the Assale-Serbewel environment.

The lands immediately south of Lake Chad are in the southern Sahelian bioclimatic zone. This is a region of high uncertainty, i.e., of considerable, and unpredictable, variation in the ecological components of the various micro-habitats which comprise the area. Inter- and intra-annual variation is exhibited in the fungi, plants, animals, and climate in the area; and fluctuations in each of these can, singly or in combination, influence agricultural production. A high incidence of certain fungi can produce certain smuts, such as covered smut or loose smut, which are major diseases affecting millets and sorghums. A large infestation of the semi-parasitic weed *striga* can lead to the destruction of most of the millets or sorghums in the fields (Kowal and Kassam, 1978:245–49). Similarly, birds or monkeys will attack different cereals as they mature.

However, by far the most important and unreliable component of the environment is precipitation. The average rainfall in the southern Sahel is sufficient for millets and some sorghums, but yearly rainfall variations are so considerable that it is only a rare year that receives the average. For example, Matlock and Cockrum (1974:75) estimated annual deviations from the mean precipitation in the Sahel to be on the order of plus or minus 30–45 percent. A total annual rainfall that is 45 percent less than the southern Sahelian mean of 475 millimeters would be about 260 millimeters, not really enough moisture for even millets, the most drought resistant of cereal plants. Figure 1 shows

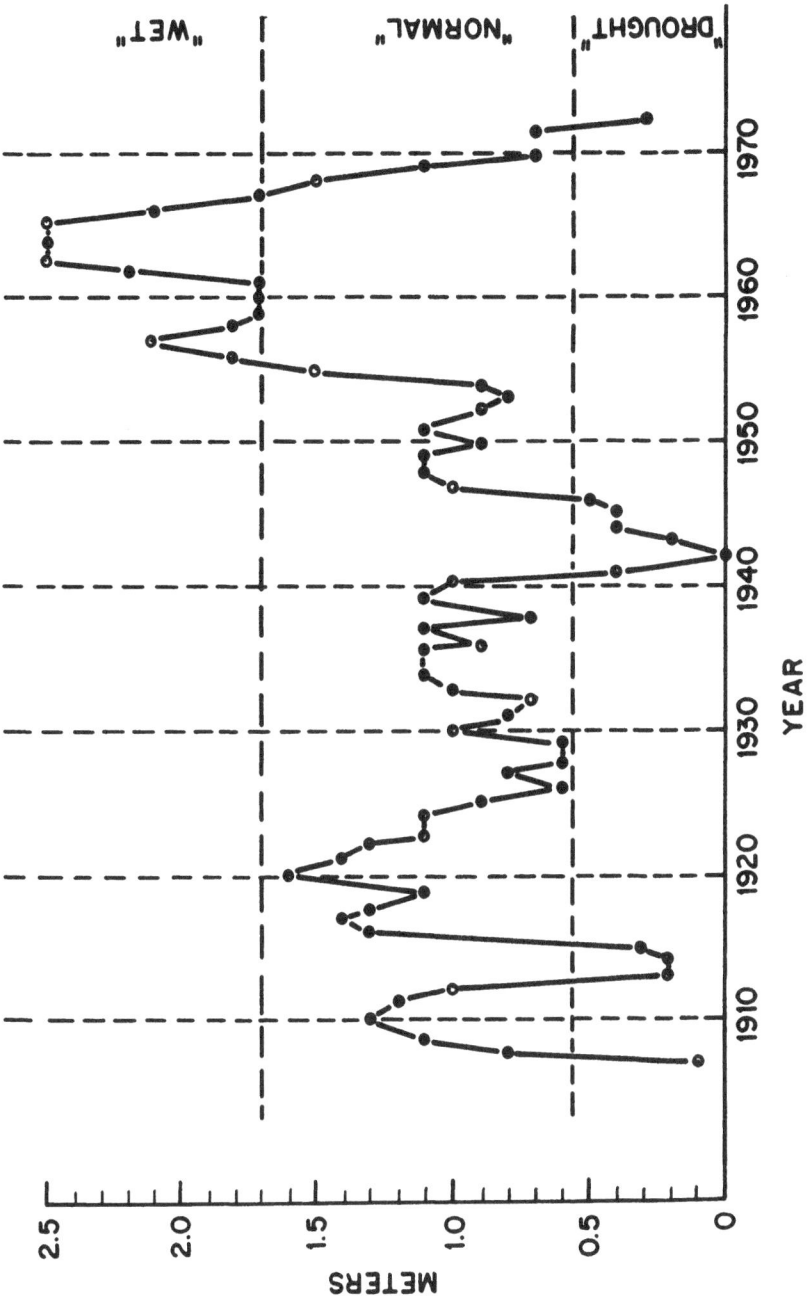

Figure 1   Variations in Maximum Levels of Lake Chad

the variations in the levels of Lake Chad in the period between 1907 and 1972.

High lake levels indicate greater than average and low levels less than average precipitation. The figure zigs and zags from peaks to valleys recording variations in rainfall. It is a picture of climatic uncertainty; and, because moisture is the *sine qua non* of agriculture, such uncertainty poses "high risks" to food production (Kowal and Kassam, 1978:204). This means that nutritional security requires risk-aversive food production strategies.

The Arabs address the environmental uncertainty by producing a relatively large number of food-stuffs in the different micro-habitats in the Assale-Serbewel. Each year each household (*zeribet*, sing.), the farm unit, regularly performs seven major production activities—four in farming, three in livestock. These are cultivating vegetable gardens, millets, sorghums, and corns as well as raising sheep, goats, and cattle. Vegetable gardens are cultivated in plots that surround households. Millets are cultivated in the sandy lands which often surround villages. Sorghums and corns are grown in the heavier soils of the flood plains and depressions. Cattle are raised during the rainy season in pastures adjacent to villages (*hille*, sing.). Then, in the dry season, villages transhume to locations near permanent water sources. There they reside in dry-season camps (*ferik*, sing.). Dry season pastures are in the flood plains near the water sources. Sheep and goats scavenge grasses and leaves where ever people happen to reside.

These different food-production activities have different labor requirements, occur at slightly different times in the agricultural calendar, and—most critically—produce harvests under different rainfall conditions. Millet (*dukhn*) requires relatively little labor because it is grown on light soils which reduce the time needed to clear land. Millet is a drought resistant crop and will continue to produce if there is as little as 300 mm of rainfall. Millet is, however, sensitive to rusts and various parasitic weeds, such as the earlier mentioned *striga*, which increase with rainfall.

Corns (*masar*) and certain sorghums (often called *berbéré, masakwa*, or *dura*) that are grown in the flood plains and depressions require considerable labor. This is because the vegetation on the flood plains tends to be thick and because the flood plains tend to be located far away from villages and camps. This means that the transportation to and clearing of flood plain fields are time consuming. Similarly, because flood plain soils are more fertile than sandy ones, weeds grow more vigorously there and more time is therefore required for weeding. Corn and sorghum take more water than millet, but if there is too much precipitation neither crop will produce, because the flood-plains would be over-flooded, and the maturing plants would be drowned.

Cultivation in the depressions and flood plains is carried out by two forms of so-called flood recession-techniques that appear to have been practiced in the region for at least a thousand years (Connah, 1981:195). The term flood-recession is used because crops are planted in soils that have been flooded, but only after the waters have begun to recede. The plants' long roots follow the lowering water table. In the flood plains no agricultural works are required. However, in the depressions, while other fields are maturing, those destined for flood-recession farming are surrounded with a low dike of earth (*jirif*). Bunds, parallel to each other and extending the entire length of the field, are then often constructed within the diked area. Such fields capture the rains in admirable fashion. When the rains have stopped, and the soil has drained to a suitable degree, the fields are planted with sorghum seedlings which have been raised to perhaps a foot in height in nurseries.[7] This form of agriculture struggles under drought conditions because the fields do not receive enough water to retain sufficient moisture to supply the plants after the rains have ceased. It will produce, however, under *both* medium and maximum rainfall conditions. This is important because both millet and flood plain crops tend to be threatened by too much precipitation. Farmers simply wait longer for the flood to recede in their fields when there is a lot of rain. Flood-recession farming can be especially laborious in the early phases, when the dikes which retain the waters are constructed.

It should thus be appreciated that these three types of cereals will yield under three different rainfall conditions prevailing in the Assale-Serbewel: millet will flourish under conditions of low rainfall, flood plain sorghum and corn under medium conditions, and swamp flood-recession sorghum under medium and heavy conditions.

It should equally be understood that the different species of animals which the Arabs raise tend to survive under different rainfall conditions. Cattle are primarily grazing animals. Sheep and goats are browsers as well as grazers. Cattle being larger animals require more water to drink then sheep and goats. This means that cattle are less drought resistant animals than sheep and goats. Further, small ruminants have shorter gestation periods than cows. They often also twin, which occurs more rarely among cows. This means that sheep and goat herds can be replaced more quickly after droughts.

Thus, the Arabs appear to have a diversified, risk-aversive farming system which produces dairy products, meat, and cereals in different micro-habitats of the Assale-Serbewel under varying conditions of precipitation. Such a farming system should be called "mixed" because it combines the production of a number of plant and animal species, and it allows them to address their single greatest production problem—rainfall uncertainty.

It should also be noted, however, that this farming system allows its practitioners to earn cash in either of two ways. The first is through the sale of male cattle. That such sales were heavy is indicated by an age-pyramid of cattle, derived from my study of certain Assale-Serbewel herds, that showed only two percent of the male animals to be five years old or older (Reyna, 1974). Where had all the males gone? Sold.[8]

The second way to earn cash was through the sale of cereals—especially flood-recession corn and sorghum. The closeness of the Assale-Serbewel to N'Djamena meant that there was demand for cereals. The growth of the city from under 100,000 in 1954 to approximately 500,000 by the mid 1970s meant that this demand was rapidly increasing. The market in millets and sorghums was not controlled by government decree, so prices rose continually. Arabs were aware of these rising cereal prices, which rose roughly two hundred and twenty-eight percent between 1968 and 1974.[9] This meant that the terms of trade between cattle and cereals in the Assale-Serbewel, as was the case throughout the West African Sahel during the drought of 1973–1974, decisively turned against cattle in favor of cereals. There was much profit to be had in cereals. Perhaps this was why my informants seemed far more enthusiastic about raising and selling cereals than cattle. Their attitude, as one fellow put it, was "cattle, old hat—boring! cereals—big money!"

We are now in a position to understand why the CLP's innovations were rejected. To put it bluntly, they were based upon a postulated economic reality for the Arabs in the Assale-Serbewel that did not exist. Remember that the project's planners and other personnel had assumed that Arab livelihood was "completely" assured by livestock production. However, high rainfall variation meant that people in the southern Sahel had to be interested in risk reduction; and this was accomplished, as just shown, through a mixed farming system, cultivating plant and animal species that flourished under different rainfall conditions in different micro-habitats. Furthermore, Arabs were eagerly interested in on-farm income opportunities. These could most profitably be realized through sorghum and corn production. In short, the project insisted that the Arabs were pure pastoralists when in fact they were mixed farmers. This is like insisting that New Jersey truck farmers are Texas ranchers.

It is important to understand that many pure pastoralists suffered more from the 1973–1974 drought in the Chad Basin than did mixed farmers like the Assale-Serbewel Arabs. Kreda, for example, who herd in the lands to the north and east of the Assale-Serbewel, and who tend to be exclusively animal breeders, were especially hard hit by the drought. Assale-Serbewel Arabs, in recognition of this, gave the year 1973 the name "the year Kreda cows came to die" (Chapelle, 1980:100). This was in wry acknowledgment of the fact that once stripped of their animals by the drought, the Kreda had no other way to produce food, and as a result, they themselves came to starve.

In that same year the Assale-Serbewel Arabs with who I lived lost many cattle. Their millet fields withered. The depression flood-recession fields did not produce. Things were desperate. Houses were pulled down, and the thatch from them fed to starving animals. People began to migrate, anywhere. Some went to N'Djamena, some to Lagos, some decided upon the *hadj*. But the fields—at least some of them—in the flood plains by the river did manage a small harvest. So they barely eked through, praying for rain and eating a single meal a day, and knowing that it was far worse for the Kreda.

Mixed farming would have had to cease for the CLP to be a tactical success, something of which the project was utterly oblivious, because it assumed that the Assale-Serbewel Arabs were exclusively pastoralists. Loss of the mixed farming system would have removed its risk reduction features and reduced incomes. The project was unaware of these possibilities, so it lacked either a strategy or the resources to mitigate the effects of lost risk reduction techniques or incomes. Because the Arabs would have experienced decreased food security, the project, by any standard, would have been a strategic failure.

I once asked an Assale-Serbewel Arab if he would ever contemplate giving up all his economic activities save for cattle breeding. He looked me straight in the eye, and pronounced me *luti*, Arabic for "nuts." Perhaps, in part, due to attitudes like this, the CLP was a tactical failure; but its very failure made it *malgré lui* a strategic success—at least in the sense that the Arabs continued to maintain a successful mixed farming system, one that reduced risk, while generating income.

4.

Resource concentration in the Assale-Serbewel makes the region, especially when contrasted with the desert and sub-desert to the north and east, something of a Garden of Eden. The CLP failed, in part because its planners, due to their acquiescence in certain of their cultural notions, stipulated an ontology for this Garden that did not exist, and then, on the basis of this stipulation, devised innovations which threatened what did. This to the Arabs was *luti*, "nuts," which they declined to be.

One must be cautious in extrapolating the lessons of a particular instance to a general situation, but there was absolutely nothing atypical about the CLP. Even if this were the case, it—at the very least—suggests that three related propositions warrant consideration. The first is that many African agricultural development projects are designed on the basis of ontological acquiescence, i.e., as a result of the passive acceptance by their designers of their own culture's notions of being. The second is that such projects tend to reflect ignorance of the ways that food security is maintained, because acquiescence to one culture's presuppositions about another's realities is an inappropriate way of understanding these realities. The third suggests that such ignorance increases the risks of disturbing existing ways of maintaining food security.

The following gives some idea of the dimensions and consequences of such ignorance. M. Horowitz recently concluded, subsequent to a review of World Bank and other major donor funded pastoral projects, first, that about $600,000,000 was spent over the period of 1965-80 on livestock projects; and, second, that "none of the interventions" in these projects "increased production, enhanced producer income, retarded environmental degradation, or provided a satisfactory economic rate of return on investment" (1989:12). He further discovered that these donors' project portfolios emphasized "top-down development in which supposed beneficiaries are passive recipients of externally conceived and directed interventions" (ibid.:27). "Externally conceived" projects are likely to be those driven by ontological acquiescence. All of which suggests that gentlemen such as the one described at the outset—ready to party with Johnny Walker—are designing and directing huge enterprises that squander vast sums, while much of Africa goes hungry.

NOTES

1. A version of this essay was presented at the 85th Annual Meeting of the American Anthropological Association, Philadelphia, 1986. I gratefully acknowledge the comments on different versions of it by R. E. Downs, E. Evans, S. Fuchs, and M. Horowitz. All errors, of course, are my own. A summary of my findings concerning the peoples in the project areas and the project itself can be found in Reyna (1974, 1979, 1984).

2. There are antecedents to the notion of ontological acquiescence. Husserl's "dogmatism of the natural attitude" (1912), Gadamer's "prejudices" underlying *verstehen* (1976), and Garfinekl's "certainties" of "mundane reasoning" (1967) correspond to it. I suggest that ontological acquiescence is an appropriate term because it focuses attention on what produces what: if people acquiesce to a line of thought, then they tend to follow it, and—as a consequence of this—they become dogmatic or prejudiced.

3. The position argued in the text may seem to be that of a naive positivist. I am aware of a number of critiques of science (for example Gadamer, 1975; Feyerabend, 1975; Rorty, 1982). These raise serious questions about the methodlogical foundations of scientific activity. However, they have not in any way produced a body of procedure that clearly surpasses those of science. Thus,

while I recognize that the rationale for science is no longer as compelling as once thought, I prefer to rely on scientific methods. This makes me not so much a naive positivist as a pragmatic one.

4. Project documents contained a number of propositions other than those mentioned here. These included a somewhat racist assertion that the Kotoko were "aristocratic," "mixed-blooded," with a caste form of organization (LCBC, 1971:6). This is muddled. It should be further noted that they could not get their main beneficiaries' name straight. One document called them "Shawas." There are no "Shawas" roaming the savanna around Lake Chad. There are people who call themselves Arabs, who are pejoratively called Shuwa by their neighbors. The project, then, referred to its main beneficiaries by a deformed version of an insulting label applied to them by outsiders.

5. Wells provided by the CLP, and, for that matter, by other projects, were appreciated when they worked. However, they quickly broke down, could not be maintained by the herders themselves or the local authorities, and thus were of questionable value. CLP veterinary measures were greatly appreciated, but the project was leery of providing them at the levels demanded, because it was afraid that improved animal health would lead to increased pasture degradation.

6. *Berbéré* can refer either to a soil type or certain sorghums grown on these soils.

7. The flood-recession farming described in the text is occasionally referred to in the literature as "falling flood" farming (Connah, 1981).

8. It should be observed that male calf mortality was not higher than that of females.

9. Retail millet prices in the N'Djamena market went from an annual average of about 1600 F CFA per sack (90 to 100 pounds) to about 5250 F CFA per sack in 1974 (CRED, 1977:71). Over this same period the retail price for cattle in the N'Djamena market collapsed. This was because the market was flooded with the animals of herders desperate to sell them before they died from the drought. The point being made here is not that cattle ceased to be an important income source, but that Arabs were well aware that cereals were becoming an increasingly attractive alternative source of income, one that in times of drought did not lose its value.

REFERENCES

AID
1971 Noncapital Project Paper: Central African Livestock and Meat Production Pilot Project. Washington, D.C., Africa Bureau: Agency for International Development.
Berger, P. and T. Luckman
1966 The Social Construction of Reality. Garden City, NY: Doubleday.
Carneiro, R.
1987 "Further Reflections on Resources Concentration and its Role in the Rise of the State" In L. Manzanilla (ed.) Studies in the Neolithic and Urban Revolutions. Oxford: British Archaeological Reports. International Series.
Chapelle, J.
1980 Le peuple Tchadien: ses racines et sa vie quotidienne. Paris: Harmattan.

88   S. P. REYNA

Cohen, M. and E. Nagel
  1934 An Introduction to Logic and the Scientific Method. NY: Harcourt.
Connah, G.
  1981 Three Thousand Years in Africa: Man and his Environment in the Lake
        Chad Region of Nigeria. Cambridge: Cambridge University Press.
CRED
  1977 Marketing, Price Policy, and Food Grains in the Sahel. Vol. 2. Ann Arbor,
        Michigan: Center for Research in Economic Development. University of
        Michigan.
Dabin, M.
  1969 Etude générale des conditions d'utilization des sols de la cuvette
        tchadienne. Travaux et Documents de l'ORSTOM. #2. Paris: ORSTOM.
Feyerabend, P.
  1975 Against Method: Outline of an Anarchistic Theory of Knowledge. London:
        New Left Books.
Gadamer, H. G.
  1975 Truth and Method. NY: Seabury Press.
  1976 Philosophical hermeneutics. Berkely: University of California Press.
Garfinkel, H.
  1967 Studies in Ethnomethodology. Englewood Cliffs, NJ: Prentice Hall.
Geertz, C.
  1973 The Interpretation of Cultures: Selected Essays. NY: Basic Books.
  1977 "'From the natives Point of View:' On Anthropological Understanding."
        In J. Doplgin, D. Kemnitzer, and D. Scheider (eds.), Symbolic Anthropl-
        ogy. NY: Columbia University Press.
Goodenough, W. H.
  1957 "Cultural Anthropology and Linguistics." In P. Garvin (ed.) Report of the
        7th Annual Roundtable Meeting in Linguistics and Language Study.
        Washington, D.C.: Georgetown University.
Hagenboucher, F.
  1973 Les Arabes dits "Shuwa" du Nord Cameroun. ORSTOM (N'Djamena)
        1-24.
  1974 Magi and sorcellerie chex les Arabes Suwa (Rive sud du Lac Tchad.)
        ORSTOM: 1-32.
Horowitz, M. M.
  1989 Donors and Deserts: The Political Ecology of Destructive Development in
        the Sahel.
Husserl, E.
  1900-01 Logische untersuchungen. Tubingen: M. Niemeyer.
  1912 Ideen zu reinen Phänomenologie und phanomenologischen philosophie.
        Halle: M. Neimeyer.
Kaplan, A.
  1964 The Conduct of Inquiry. San Francisco: Chandler.
Kowal, J. M. and A. H. Kassen
  1973 Agricultural Ecology of the Savanna: A Study of West Africa. London:
        Oxford University Press.
LCBC
  1971 Animal Production Development in the Assale District (Chad) and Ser-
        bewel (Cameroon). N'Djamena: Lake Chad Basin Commission.

Lutz, C. A.
1988 Unnatural Emotions: Everyday Sentiments on a Micronesian Atoll and Their Challenge to Western Theory. Chicago: University of Chicago Press.

Maley, J.
1977 Analyses polleniques et paléoclimatologues des derniers millenaires du Bassin du Tchad (Afrique Centrale). Birmingham, England. Comité Français pour le Dixième Congrès de l'INQUA.

Malinowski, B.
1948 Magic, Science and Religion and Other Essays. NY: Free Press.

Murphy, Y. and R. F. Murphy
1985 Women of the Forest. 2nd. ed. New York: Columbia University Press.

O.E.D.
1989 The Oxford English Dictionary. Oxford: Clarendon Press.

Rabinow, P. and W. M. Sullivan
1987 Interpretive Social Science: A Second Look. Los Angeles: University of California Press.

Reyna, S. P.
1974 Etude de l'economie et des populations de l'Assale-Serbewel. N'Djamena, Chad. Lake Chad Basin Commission.
1979 Social Evolution: A Learning Theory Approach. Journal of Anthropological Research. 35(3): 336-349.
1984 Chadian Arabs. In R. V. Weekes ed. Muslim Peoples: A World Ethnographic Survey. Westport, Connecticut: Greenwood Press.

Rorty, R.
1982 Consequences of Pragmatism. Minneapolis: University of Minnesota Press.

Schutz, A.
1967 The Phenomenology of the Social World. Evanston, IL: Northwestern University Press.

Wallace, W.
1971 The Logic of Science in Sociology. Chicago: Aldine.

Whorf, B. L.
1956 Language, Thought, and Reality. Cambridge, MA: MIT Press.

Zeltner, J. C.
1970 Histoire des Arabes sur les rives du lac Tchad. Annales de l'Université d'A'bidjan. Série F. 2(2):109-237.

CHAPTER 3

Rainfed Agricultural Development Project Performance in the Context of Drought: The Western Savannah Project, South Darfur, Sudan, and the Drought of 1984–1985

William I. Torry

INTRODUCTION

Drought in 1984 severely affected 8.8 million persons, or 41% of Sudan's 21.6 million population. Seven of the country's eight administrative regions suffered more than nominally (UNOEOA, 1986:58). In the aftermath the Western Savannah Development Corporation (WSDC) declared: "It is only through projects such as WSP [Western Savannah Project] that future disasters will be avoided" (WSDC, 1985:2). Examining this claim comprises the analysis which follows.

WSDC's pronouncement does hold good in principle. Neither governments nor villagers, with the resources normally at their command, can appreciably diminish famine vulnerability in Sahelian countries beset chronically by the incidence of drought. For now, it seems, development projects such as WSP, backed with external funds and expertise, form a front line defense of peasant food security. Increased farmer productivity and purchasing power, project managers hope, will stop famine somewhere down the road. But what will assure this end-state if droughts recur, causing damage in the rainfed sector that investments in heavily capitalized segments of the economy cannot offset? At issue is what rainfed development projects can do to preempt drought disasters and how fast and far disaster experiences defer project goals. Specifically, this paper evaluates: (a) advantages, if any, WSP bestowed on project households in 1984/85; (b) drought impacts on the project's own sustainability. Considering the magnitude of agricultural losses that drought can inflict, one wonders why researchers in the fields of economic development and social theory rarely raise such issues.

A pilot study, planned in October/November 1985, was undertaken in December 1985/January 1986 in South Darfur, Sudan, where the World Bank assisted WSP operates. Much in WSP's setup recommends it for a study of drought-development project interactions. It is among Sahelian Africa's largest rainfed projects. The Government of Sudan and international lenders, futhermore, conceived WSP expressly for cushioning farmers and herders from stresses created by drought and desertification (World Bank, 1985a,b). Hence, if WSP could protect its farmers better than they could protect themselves from droughts, the 1984 drought would provide a telling litmus test of this capability. Finally, WSP incorporates multiple resource management components and South Darfur attracts varied land-use modes with long traditions. These factors promised compariability between WSP/South Darfur's experiences with drought and development and experiences acquired elsewhere in Africa's Sahel, lending the findings high generalizability.

Drought affects rainfed projects both directly and indirectly. Anything droughts do in the way of making peasant economic problems more tenacious and more expensive for project programs to eradicate entails indirect effects. Direct effects come down immediately on project rather than on peasant resources, where the two are evidently distinct. Both direct and indirect effects are, among other things, functions of drought severity, sufficiency of relief measures, and peasant economic resilience. The paper selectively examines each of these factors.

THE WESTERN SAVANNAH PROJECT

The WSP, administered by the Western Savannah Development Corporation (WSDC), a public corporation associated closely with the Sudan Ministry of Agriculture, became operative in July 1982. It began as a pilot operation to introduce improvements in farming methods and animal husbandry, develop water resources, and control environmental degradation. Within this framework of goals, the project subsumes several implementing components, among which are four controlled settlements for 1,500 settler families and plans for starting up at least three additional units. Tenants acquire 20-year leases, receive agricultural inputs at concessionary rates, and obtain help putting in place social services in exchange for a nominal rent and compliance with the restrictive covenants of their lease agreements. Experiments are underway for enlisting nomads and sedentary farmers in programs of rotational grazing and for reseeding overgrazed rangelands.

With cooperating agencies of government, WSDC had rehabilitated 150 of the 233 wateryards (containing 328 boreholes)[1] in the project area and has supplied rinderpest vaccine to livestock owners. The three agricultural development centers run by the corporation conduct experiments with animal traction, test new varieties of seeds, and perform trials on phosphate fertilizer applications. Tests involving mechanized cultivation of hard alluvial soils are also in progress. Work with the Forestry Department will rehabilitate small nurseries and emplace shelterbelts for revegetating denuded areas. Road and track improvements can be counted as other project achievements.

The project extends over an area of 135,000 km², from 23°15' to 27°45' longitude and from 9°30' to 13°0' latitude, covering almost all of South Darfur province. WSP and the small (35,000 km²) Jebel Marra Development Project are the only major agricultural schemes being run in Darfur Region. Rainfall increases from 300 mm in the north to 800 mm in the south, but these isohyets reflect long-run averages and obscure the drier climate regime having taken hold for two decades now. Sandy soils dominate, with silts and clays overlaying the alluvial belts and skeletal strata mantling the Basement land system. The 1.7 million people inhabiting South Darfur are predominantly shifting millet cultivators, planting some sorghum and cultivating groundnuts and sesame as primary cash crops. Pure nomadism is almost extinct, although transhumant cattle and small stock herding endures. Many farmers own livestock. Donkeys are the transportation mainstay, with merchants and better-off farmers also owning camels.

DROUGHT AND FAMINE IN 1984–85

Major famine indicators, namely migration, asset losses, human and livestock mortalities, family food consumption, and, with one Oxfam et al. (1985) study excepted, individual nutrition, were not quantified systematically in 1984 by anyone working in South Darfur. Absences and dismissals depleted the WSDC staff, and petrol and vehicle scarcities precluded wide-ranging survey exercises (WSDC, 1985). Regional ministries were no better equipped for monitoring the famine's advance, and emergency food and medical deliveries bogged down Save the Children Fund, Médecins Sans Frontiéres, Oxfam, and Across operators stationed in South Darfur. In lieu of direct socio-economic evidence from surveys made in the field, famine occurrence is described here in terms of crude agro-climatic parameters and farmers' and administrators' estimates of impacts from drought. Indirect though it may be, this evidence clearly illustrates what South Darfur residents were up against when drought took hold of their land.

Rainfall

Generally, millet requires no less than 250 mm of timely downpours for full growth attainment on sandy soils and 300 mm on clays; sorghum needs even more moisture. Over much of North Darfur, the 1984 rains fell short of this agronomic minimum, with some areas not receiving any rainfall (Ibrahim, 1984; JMRDP, 1985a). South Darfur fared better, but not by much. In four South Darfur locations for which information is available, the rainfall figures for 1984 were 198 mm, 352 mm, 245 mm, and 243 mm.

Crop Production

In evidence for North and South Darfur are exceptionally low cereal yields for the drought year of 1984. In kg/ha, millet yields in South Darfur declined by more than half (52%) over the preceding two year average. Average per capita production of millet in the WSP project area amounted to 307.4 kg in 1981 and 208.9 kg in 1982. Sorghum yields averaged 100.4 kg. and 65 kg. for those years. Total per capita production of cereals (millet and sorghum combined) was 407.8 kg in 1981 and 273 kg in 1982. Assuming a 150 kg. annual per capita subsistence requirement (Oxfam et al., 1985:12), it is clear that, if these figures are to be given credence, farmers in the project area were acquiring a 190.4 kg. (42%)/capita food surplus in the early 1980s (1981 plus 1982). Drought dissipated this margin in 1984 as food production plummeted to 124.7 kg/capita, or a fall of 17% below the 150 kg subsistence limit.[2] The regional sorghum crop was said by the WSDC staff who were interviewed to have failed almost completely in much of South Darfur, thus accentuating the severity of the millet shortfall.

Projecting back from the 1983 province-wide estimate of millet production (324 kg), and again using average household and millet acreage statistics for the years 1981 and 1982, in 1983 average per capita millet yields were about 225 kg, or just 74 kg above the subsistence threshold. So going into the 1984 agricultural season, the average household would have retained little carryover stock of millet after grain sales, labor hire, and seed layaways were deducted from its cereal budget. The situation would have been no better, and was probably worse, for the minority of predominantly sorghum producing households in South Darfur.

With household grain consumption requirements taken into account, 1984 production declines in millet proved devastating for North Darfurans. 1982 and 1983 millet yields averaged a meager 143 kg/ha. Sorghum production turned out to be a mere 52 kg/ha in 1982 and 207 kg/ha in 1983, but few households, in fact, harvested any sorghum. Finally, livestock losses were very high in 1983 and 1984. Evidently North Darfurans carried few or no reserves of food grain into the 1984 drought crisis (see also Ibrahim, 1984).[3] Extrapolation from Ibrahim's data (1984) collected late in the 1970s and in the early 1980s would indicate that northerners experienced a millet deficit of 63%, while southerners fell 23% below the 150 kg/capita norm in 1984. Judging by these *averages*, numerous households growing millet predominantly had to come to grips all over Darfur with a total failure of their primary crop.

There is no way one can distill deep and reliable sociological insights from the crude agro-economic statistics at hand. Yet these data may well be the most suitable foundation available for quantifiably portraying climatic impacts on cereal production in 1984. Most of all, the data put official numbers to largely anecdotal characterizations of subsistence crisis reported in the literature and conveyed to the author by diverse sources throughout the term of his fieldwork. The data lend themselves to the following generalizations.

(1) The 1984 drought made South Darfur into a food deficit zone. A poor crop year in 1983 failed to equip the average household with stock sufficient to stave off famine in 1984. By January 1985, when the harvest season would normally close, many farms had already spent their grain stores.

(2) The foodgrain availability situation in North Darfur looked far graver. However heavily the drought fell upon South Darfur, the province enjoyed greater sufficiency in food than North Darfur. Starving families from the north saw South Darfur as a sanctuary. Anticipated supplies of food were not the only pull factor luring North Darfurans south. North Darfur's arable land base was slipping away, while South Darfur's resources could still accommodate new settlers, and North Darfur's long run of drought years had been especially oppressive for rainfed farmers, many of whom were ready now for a permanent move (Ibrahim, 1984).

Migration From North Darfur and Chad

Collating projections from assorted agencies, Fuller (1985:40) produces a qualified estimate of 200,000 to 300,000 migrants to South Darfur from North Darfur and Chad.

EMERGENCY FOOD AID TO SOUTH DARFUR AND WSDC

Emergency food aid moved into South Darfur in 1985 via three main conduits. During the first half of the year the regional government supplied limited stocks of grain. Through its regional contractor, Save the Children Fund (SCF), USAID, the largest provider of food relief to Darfur, dispatched 152,927 mt of sorghum in addition to supplementary foods.[4] SCF made deliveries to rural centers and village communities. WSDC arranged with the World Food Program (WFP) for taking the delivery of several thousand metric tons of wheat and other food commodities to its settlements and experiment stations (WSDC Food Aid Files, Khartoum Office). In addition, 3000 mt of millet and sorghum seed purchased in the eastern Sudan were distributed to farmers in North Darfur in May–July 1985. Farmers in North and South Darfur received another 500 mt of millet seed purchased locally with EEC funding. WSDC procured seed from Darfur and the eastern regions for tenants in its new settlements.

At the time of the field study neither USAID nor SCF could furnish figures on grain disbursements broken down by rural and village council units. The sufficiency of these deliveries for meeting the nutritional requirements of targeted beneficiaries can be estimated roughly with the very partial data at hand for the Buram area of South Darfur. A total of 6,202 mt of USAID sorghum went to this area, where two of the four WSDC settlements were located, and where the field tour was carried out. Census estimates for 1983 put the Buram populace at around 202,000. If population size held steady or increased during the drought, the grain apportioned from USAID (31 kg/capita) would not have of itself been anywhere near a sufficient retardant of hunger for families lacking food stores and plentiful assets. That would be all the more the case if the claims from many quarters could be authenticated of large-scale leakages of grain out of the distribution system.

Grain deliveries ranging from 15 to 100 (45 kilo) sacks were taking place almost monthly from rural and village council depositories to the WSDC settlements. They were earmarked for a population of about 292 families (ca. 2044 persons) in the Nakara settlement and 249 families (ca. 1743 persons) in the El Amud al Akhdar settlement. Settlers and villagers alike said supplies did not go far toward alleviating hunger. WSDC deliveries did not reach the settlements until October 1985. Up to that point the settlement leaders and WSDC staff had applied to the area and rural councils of Buram for emergency supplies of food. The first written request for assistance from WSP appears in a letter from the acting Director General of WSDC, dated April 27, 1985. It is worth noting that WSDC realized the gravity of the situation it was facing as early as December 1984: the harvest was well below normal and its settlers and its own stores lacked reserves of grain. Why so many months were to elapse before the WSDC moved forward with an official appeal for WFP cooperation could not be ascertained in the field.

Two of the settlements were three-quarters full and two were approximately half full when the April 27 letter was being drafted. WSDC had expected all four to be filled by June 25. A series of meetings began toward late April, and in the weeks that followed WSDC management, WFP staff, and officials from the Ministry of Agriculture and the Ministry of Economic Planning worked out an agreement involving consignments of WFP food targeted within a framework of food-for-work enjoinders. WSDC put its requests across with urgency, sensing the rapid approach of the rainy season, then only one month away. If food relief waited until the rains, several more weeks would go by before deliveries could resume, since the roads would become impassable. Meanwhile, settlers, weakened by hunger, would have trouble putting in a crop, and families which postponed moving into the settlements would probably hold off even longer.

WSDC thought it needed a two-year supply of food aid but was content to request a six-month supply of food from WFP for feeding 11,000 persons. The beneficiaries included all settlers, as well as project field staff and their families. The food would be stored in containers at WSDC headquarters and allocated under the supervision of the settlement committees and WSDC management. The final terms of the contract stipulated that:

(a) For each allotment, settlers would pay LSd 10 and staff LSd 25. An allotment would consist of one 50 kilo sack of grain, 10 lbs of powdered milk, and 2 gallons of cooking oil. These payments would fund development and training programs for the settlements.

(b) WSDC establish a food-for-work program for putting settlement infrastructure in place and for prompting farmers to work quickly at setting up house, preparing land for cultivation, clearing paths through the villages, maintaining wateryard grounds, and building schools and other community facilities.

(c) WSDC devise a system of checks for monitoring compliance with work norms applicable to food-for-work beneficiaries, and report progress of the program to the food-for-work officer in Khartoum.

The first shipments arrived in October and plans were underway for periodic deliveries to each settlement from February through the end of the planting season, 1986. WSDC had also arranged for waiving fees at the settlement wateryards until October, well into the 1985 harvest season.

EFFECTS AND EFFECTIVENESS OF FAMINE RELIEF

Regional ministries and public corporations in the western Sudan are not endowed with infrastructure, supplies, and personnel for interdicting the advance of a famine. Nothing exists even resembling a distribution system in foodgrains equipped with procurement devices, price controls, granaries, and ration shops. Darfur at the time also lacked a famine surveillance capability. Staff could not be spared for health, nutritional, migration, crop-livestock, and other surveys during the drought of 1984, and civil servants with requisite statistical training were scarce. For all the same reasons it would be fanciful to imagine a massive food-for-work program going into effect.

Getting in supplies where needed and expeditiously getting out reliable information necessitate administrative grounding at sub-regional levels of civil service. Here, too, Darfur was wanting. Rural and area councils[5] were end points in the line of conveyance of emergency food supplied by foreign donors during the drought emergency. WSDC staff, RICSU (1985) reports, Save the Children field operators, and Buram area villagers expressed convergent views, holding councils to blame for slighting drought refugees seeking help within their territories. Another opinion with considerable currency heaped censure on councils which denied food to politically weak ethnic minorities and villages and nomad camps stationed far from designated supply depots. Occasionally councils seemed unaware of the location of points of greatest need. Charges were brought to bear on council authorities for pilfering, but with less conviction than other accusations recorded.

Whatever credence these criticisms merit, they should in fairness be tempered with some understanding of the constraints that council bodies came up against. Council territories may bracket several hundred square kilometer areas and claim registered populations running into the thousands. Most roads are simply bush trails, and composition in council divisions is exceptionally fluid. In 1984 part of the established population migrated out for wage employment, while, as indicated earlier, thousands of families fled into the region from harsher semi-desert zones further north and west, settling within walking distance of boreholes, often in or near villages inhabited by kinsmen or ethnic compatriots.

Council members in dire straits themselves took off for work on irrigation schemes and in cities further east. Finally, the councils were not enjoined by government to distribute food to families other than those registered in their administrative domains. With all of these factors at work, councils could not possibly have kept themselves adequately informed during the drought as to the numbers and sizes of families within their territorial jurisdictions; even less could they apprise themselves accurately of each family's needs. Nor did law compel or political expediency necessarily dictate a policy of equal distribution for all. Still, the brunt of the work of organizing food aid deliveries to drought-affected villages in Darfur fell to the councils.

Food and seed aid supplied by the government and WSDC may have had a very slight moderating effect on famine distress. If these agencies rightfully had anything to boast about in regard to the food emergency, it would be for their efforts in water resource development. WSDC's self acclaim may indeed be well founded (WSDC, 1984):

> There is little doubt that if it had not been for the rapid progress made under the WSDC's wateryard rehabilitation program the [drought] situation would have been many times worse.

Mention should be made briefly of WSDC's seed distribution program earmarked for new settlements. In the judgment of WSDC management, "many farmers with no seed of their own would have been unable to sow at all without help provided through the project" (WSDC, 1985:21). Nevertheless, WSDC prepared itself poorly for the seed crisis. It took action and purchased millet seed in the markets of Nyala, El Daien, and in areas north of the rail lines only at the last moment. Quite a bit of this imported stock comprised a short maturing variety of millet known locally as *dimbi*, whereas the variety in greatest demand near the settlements was the longer maturing *Wad el Labow*. Evidently *dimbi* could not effectively capitalize on showers falling very late, and some of it came infested with downy mildew. By one WSDC officer's estimate, *dimbi* users produced 1/2 to 1 sack of millet/mukhamas[6] in 1985, against a 3 sack/mukhamas output associated with the longer maturing variety harvested ordinarily on sandy soil after a fair growing season.

Famine relief on top of the drought interfered with WSDC operations and plans. Drought impacts are taken up in detail shortly. As far as famine relief is concerned, direct impacts entailed for the most part certain minor inconveniences. WSDC is a respository of information about the region and its people and has a relatively large number of English-speakers on its staff. Hence visitors from Western relief and development agencies sought WSDC assistance on their missions to South Darfur. The WSDC Land Use Planning Units' 1985 visitor roster alone recorded over 40 individuals and groups in need of maps, census tract data for sampling frame design, and other resources.[7] At times this barrage of guests placed considerable strain on the capacity of WSDC's small staff.

And there were other problems. Equipped with the lure of good salaries, NGO relief agencies that branched out to Nyala attracted drivers and mechanics from WSDC's labor force. Chronically short of competent workers from these ranks anyway, WSDC could not find suitable replacements quickly, and it was making do with several vacancies at the time of the field study.

Indirect impacts may have been more substantial. The unprecedented international attention the drought had focused on South Darfur and the WSDC gave project management cause for concern about the fate of its long-range plans. UNDP, Quaker Peace and Service, Across, Oxfam, and the Ford Foundation, among others, saw in South Darfur significant development potential. But WSDC officials were plainly worried that an influx of new and uncoordinated projects, formulated in haste, might derail its own development initiatives. A conviction was evident at WSDC headquarters that as years of spade work were just not showing results, it would be inappropriate for other agencies with limited background in South Darfur to rush ahead with programs before WSDC's experiences were well in hand and properly evaluated.

Prompt and complete deliveries of WFP supplies would have been salutary for WSP's important controlled settlement program. Instead, food aid shipments, stalled for months, threw the critical food-for-work program off track, costing WSP a package of self-help incentives which might have gotten settlers quickly into a mode of community structured work projects. Settlement plans were set back several months, in part for this reason. Timely and generous dispatches of food and other aid to villages outside the project area, furthermore, might have averted the enormous incursion of refugees into South Darfur. These refugees, as will be noted, added pressure on a resource base that is under WSDC's partial stewardship.

DROUGHT EFFECTS ON HOUSEHOLDS AND ON REGIONAL INSTITUTIONS

Project adaptations to drought cannot be assessed independently of changes in the conditions of existence surrounding the people and institutions to which the project is devoted. Drought effects on projects entail costs which project investors and managers incur while abating these conditions in the aftermath of a drought. Should conditions of living deteriorate appreciably without a concomitant renewal and enhancement of project resources, then there is no way around the conclusion that drought has affected project capabilities more than trivially. In effect the project will have failed to catch up with new economic realities.

Parameters of change in the economic and social conditions prevailing in South Darfur before and after the 1984 drought are seldom quantified or are quantified without rigor. Assorted data will be adduced for several important diagnostics of change. Crude figures appear in some instances to illustrate orders of magnitude. Documented evidence of a pejorative tendency observed during the 1968-1973 drought fortifies in other instances purely anecdotal accounts recorded in 1984 of that same tendency. And trends for South Darfur are projected from similar trends more concretely described elsewhere in the Sahel. At the very least this piecing together of fragmentary evidence should mark out the parameters for which WSDC would need data in order to apprise itself of whether and how badly droughts can unhinge the achievements and prospects of its development programs.

Seeds

Droughts impede the growth and dissemination of agricultural seeds in areas of rainfed farming. As a result three primary sources of local supply become affected. Seed production declines in farmers' fields and seed stocks stored in private granaries dwindle. Disruptions to growth cycles limit seed availability on the farm, constrict flows of information among farmers about seed supply and performance, and make seed purchases very expensive for poorer households and women.

Under extreme circumstances, drought might drive entire varieties of cultivators out of existence in specific areas if hungry farmers sell their seed stocks over a run of unproductive years, and should plant growth stop repeatedly before the seed bearing stage is reached. Seed extinction may not be likely anytime soon in rainfed belts of Darfur and Kordofan. Nevertheless, portents of plant extermination in drought pockets of central Ethiopia, for example, emerge in the western Sudan. One sign is that farmers are experiencing difficulty generating seed stocks from their fields. In northern Kordofan, 45% of farmers surveyed in one study purchased millet seed, having consumed their stock the preceding season as a result of hunger. Millet seed purchases are becoming standard practice in this area (Reeves and Frankenberger, 1982:35). Recently, farmers in great numbers in South Darfur exhausted their seed stocks before the 1985 growing season (author's notes). The precise amount of seed exhausted in an area suffering protracted drought and the replacement rate of this seed in subsequent years are not known. The fact that many farmers now make a habit of buying seed suggests that indigenous seed stocks are, overall, not increasing. Unusual sub-species adapted to highly localized conditions are becoming scarcer, possibly because environmental conditions are worsening.

When farmers use up their stocks of seed a number of problems arise. The most serious entails a lack of seeds for the next rainy season. A situation this desperate would be improbable on a large scale in the western Sudan, at least in regard to first plantings. Seeds can usually be obtained from other farmers, or from the market, the government, or international agencies. Often, however, seed gifts or loans will not be enough to allow for second plantings, should the first planting fail, unless the acreage desired is reduced. Darfur farms witnessed these problems during the 1985 crop season. Increasingly, commercial and institutional outlets will become more important suppliers of seeds than networks of friends and kinsmen over closely spaced years of low rainfall. Yet, by acquiring seeds through these channels, the household assumes certain risks.

Farmers generally buy seeds from merchants, barring other options that enlarge their range of choice. They obviously prefer collecting seeds from their fields rather than paying for them in the marketplace, especially under pain of debt. Quality standards may pose as great a concern as costs. Because merchants deal in grain rather than in seeds, farmers do not receive pure varieties of the type suited best to the microenvironments of their fields (e.g., Coughenour and Nazhat, 1985:ix). In the case of new seeds, merchants may be fairly ignorant about growth and productivity characteristics under local conditions, or may deliberately misinform a prospective buyer who happens to be a stranger from a distant village and/or other tribal group (*ibid.*).

Likewise, emergency seeds that drought victims get from government or multinational agencies often come from market outlets. Seeds that WSDC passed along to its settlers in 1985 were acquired in this manner, with rather disturbing results. Many farmers complained, and project staff acknowledged, that these seed varieties were not well adapted to the soil/climate regimes of their South Darfur destination points. As noted earlier, farmers who utilized these seeds suffered a pronounced shortfall in crop yields later that year.

Drought, Production Methods, and Desertification

Darfur farmers aspire to put more land into production in years of low rainfall in the hope of securing some return on their crop(s) (Ibrahim, 1984:110,118); Scott-Villiers, 1984:3; Mangouri, 1985:15). Of the 240 farmers interviewed by Mangouri, for example, 65% increased the area they cultivated in 1984. (Unfortunately, the studies reviewed could not quantify these increments.) Field area expansion serves to increase surface area exposed to sun bake and wind erosion when low rainfall begrudges cleared land a full crop cover. Hence: "This expansion of cultivation to counteract the decrease of rainfall acts as a catalyst for the process of desertification" (Ibrahim, 1984:118).

There is yet another reason why cultivated land will expand during drought. It follows from a postulate which holds that "the labor available to the family is the number one factor controlling the acreage of cultivation" (Mohamed et al., 1982:60). Others promulgate this thesis more cautiously, advising that "This relationship between size of landholding and labor bears further investigation" (Reeves and Frankenberger, 1982:39). If field size and labor availability correlate positively and significantly, *ceteris paribus*, labor flow from drought-impacted to neighboring drought-free areas will avail farmers in the latter an enlarged pool of cheap labor for augmenting the size and/or number of cultivated fields (and in the process depleting regional stocks of unfarmed land) or for intensifying cultivation on land already in use (and possibly curtailing fallow cycles). That that form of exploitation was taking place during the 1984 drought is in evidence in and near Sough Darfur (cf. Fuller, 1985).

Characteristically, western Sahelian farmers deal with meteorological risk and uncertainty by cutting back the production of cash crops in favor of food crops (Normal et al., 1982:176). Time series data recorded over a continuum of drought and non-drought years were unavailable in the studies consulted. If the subsistence security thesis posited by Norman and his colleagues holds up equally in Darfur, it would mean the virtual monocropping of millet or sorghum by many farmers several times during, say, a 10- or 15-year cycle. Monocropping cereals on a parcel of land may make good sense judged against *immediate* household survival requirements, but deferring the rotation and intercropping of cereals and legumes abrogates sound long-term management procedure (Kowal and Kassam, 1978: Hall et al., 1979).

Other undemonstrated yet plausible relationships involving drought and agriculture associate labor requirements and desertification. Drought is a recognized impetus to labor migration in the western Sudan (Holy, 1980; Reeves and Frankenberger, 1982). It may be supposed that post-drought years see: (a) increased seasonal labor migration; (b) an earlier-than-normal departure for off-farm employment in anticipation of large seasonal job demand in towns and mechanized agricultural schemes. Either situation *alone* can prompt farmers to clear virgin or fallowed land two or three months in advance of sowing it, as early as February or March (Reeves and Frankenberger, 1982). The longer the interval between clearing and crop growth, the greater the danger of wind eroding those exposed parcels of land (Ibrahim, 1984).

Certain changes in the livestock sector subsequent to the 1984 drought can be projected in light of the low rainfall years of the early 1970s and 1980s. Shifts from cattle or cattle/sheep production to goat husbandry were in evidence at points up and down Kordofan and Darfur (Ibrahim, 1984:156;

Awadalla, 1985; Coughenour and Nazhat, 1985:16; Abdul-Jalil, 1979:185). Holy (1980:69) alone supplies estimates. Berti cattle herds shrank by 30% from 1965 to 1977—an interval transected by five years of drought—and sheep holdings dropped 13%, while goat numbers almost quadrupled. Goat destruction of forage is well known, giving planners reason for concern that drought in 1984 has accelerated this tendency.

Water

Most western Sudanese households and livestock will acquire water from boreholes housed in wateryards through part of the dry season and during periods of drought. Regional herds are, accordingly, redeployed from farflung reservoirs, pools, and shallow wells. When this pattern repeats itself often at boreholes visited by sizeable migrating herds, it may happen that villagers take notice of declining supplies of water at their wells. Water table depression poses a serious problem at sites in North Darfur and North Kordofan (Mangouri, 1985; Mohamed et al., 1982). South Darfur may be similarly at risk, since western Sudan livestock in vast numbers spend several months of the drought cycle massed within this province.

Drought or not, boreholes break down frequently, largely because the national Water Authority lacks a well-planned, properly financed, and proficiently administered wateryard maintenance program. Needing repairs and renovations of engines, pumps, pumpjacks, distribution piping, trough, building, and fences, half the wateryards in a province may be out of order at any given time (Mohamed et al., 1982; AACMC, 1984:67; author's notes). Droughts lie behind an even greater number of borehole failures lasting days on end. Droughts subsequently elevate regional government appropriation requests for wateryard rehabilitation, and livestock mortalities increase.

Finally, droughts drive up wateryard fees. Wateryard consumption expenditures erode household opportunities for investing in farm improvements and for hiring-in agricultural labor. Perhaps more so in Kordofan than in Darfur, moreover, water rates are "In many cases the key variable in determining whether farmers migrate for seasonal labor..." (Reeves and Frankenberger, 1982:24). To earn enough money to defray water bills back home, more than 75% of adult males migrate from some villages in search of work (ibid.:19,27). Such tendencies signal stresses for South Darfur residents that may not be a long way off.

Acacia Senegal Mortalities

Acacia senegal is no bit player in Darfur's agricultural economy. The gum arabic extruded by these trees earns peasants cash. Granted, labor investment in *A. senegal* has taken a back seat to groundnuts and other farm-grown cash crops since the early 1970s, and the tree grows less prolifically in the more southerly savannahs than in semi-desert bands extending over North Kordofan and North Darfur (Haaland, 1982). *A. senegal* can nevertheless furnish a respectable supplementary income to farmers, who may travel far afield to draw and sell their harvested gum (WSDC, 1982, 1983). Ecological benefits deserve attention also. This leguminous tree fixes nitrogen in soils, draws surface water into soil pores, and binds soil particles (UNSO, 1984). For these reasons and the trees' commercial value, WSDC, and especially the Western Sudan Agricultural Research Program (WSARP), are promoting on-farm plantings of *A. senegal*. Finally, *de jure* rights to living *A. senegal* still guarantee tree owners in some areas *de facto* rights over land surrounding the trees through the term of fallow (El Mukhtar and Runger-Gabelmann, 1985). By protecting farmed land from cultivation while it recovers, *A. senegal* supports a sound system of land management.

A. senegal thrives in a dry climate, growing on sandy (*goz*) soils between the 180–450 mm isohyets, approximately, but it is not immune from drought (Olsson, 1984:30). Precipitation below 280 mm stops gum arabic production and can kill mature trees. Large *A. senegal* mortalities were reported in the northern regions of western Sudan through the drought years of 1968–73 (Hammer-Digernes, 1977; Holy, 1980:69). Droughts can also release white ant invasions, which damage *A. senegal* root systems *Hammer-Digernes, 1977. Finally, nomads escaping climatic conditions inimical to livestock survival in their northern homelands pollard branches of *A. senegal* to feed emaciated livestock and dismantle trees prepared for commercial sale when they move onto *A. senegal*-rich tracts (HTS, 1977:3; Awadalla, 1985:34). Certainly the economic consequences of *A. senegal's* susceptibility to drought devastation requires serious scrutiny.

Migration

Drought ushered several thousand households into South Darfur during 1984 and 1985. With unabated political unrest in Chad, relief from low rainfall and desertification not in sight for North Darfur anytime soon, and an accommodating attitude toward famine refugees on the part of regional authorities, it is almost certain that migrants in large numbers will stay in South Darfur indefinitely (Provincial Government of South Darfur n.d.; Ibrahim, 1984). Migration and resident population increases combined boost annual population growth rates as high as 5% in South Darfur (AACMC, 1985:2). This trend should trouble development planners managing a shrinking resource base of acutely limited productivity. An immediate dilemma will be the feasibility of uprooting migrant families in the event that settlement authorities at WSDC elect to appropriate their land. By the time these areas are designated for registration, moreover, they may be too badly degraded to be suitable for settlement purposes.

Sedentarization

There is no telling how many families bereft of livestock because of drought resigned from transhumant and nomadic herding for a sedentary mode of livelihood. Drastic forage depletion, long trekking distances to water points, and staggering wateryard fees took, by all accounts, a heavy toll of migratory livestock. Distress sales also pared down livestock holdings. Zaghawa experiences with drought over the past two decades illustrate the damage that these factors have created for pastoral economies.

According to one authority (Ibrahim, 1984), almost 90,000 Zaghawa have migrated from their desiccated homelands in northwestern Darfur since 1983, when the population stood at 148,000. Ibrahim, who has followed this diaspora closely, estimates that "Ninety percent of the migrants abandoned their semi-nomadic mode of living and livestock raising and became settled millet farmers in the Goz areas of Darfur…[while] 10% live in towns now…" (*Ibid.*, 156). Over a span of 28 years, between 1955 and 1983, the nomad population, comprising mainly Kababish, Kawahla, and Hawawir of Kababish Rural Council, North Kordofan, has dropped by about 70%, from a high of 137,523 to 29,461 individuals. Over the same period, the settled population has increased almost threefold (El Sammani, 1984:22). Droughts have been a major catalyst for these transformations.

Sedentarized nomads create problems for integrated agricultural projects. Settled herders accelerate agricultural encroachment on fragile rangelands. More families fill the ranks of an expanding agricultural sector, and family size on average increases. There is some evidence that, compared to a nomadic household, farming families marry at an earlier age and allow more adult males a chance to marry, thus endowing them with higher rates of fertility (Henin, 1969). Such tendencies can do nothing but aggravate WSP's problems in trying to manage South Darfur's finite agricultural resources. A shrinking herding sector will also give the WSDC livestock division pause for reflection if it means, eventually, decreased regional revenues from livestock sales, changes in setional herd composition, relaxed pasture rotation discipline, and weakened range trespass controls (Behnke, 1985).

Local Government Infrastructure

South Darfur was the most underfunded of all the provinces in the country in the mid-1970s (HTS, 1974). In 1978/79 South Darfur ranked second to last among the country's northern provinces in the amount of revenues allocated by the central government, holding the same position in the category of total revenues (Alassam, 1981). Rainfed small farmer agriculture and subsistence herding still dominate its economy. Crop and livestock export earnings add but marginally to the region's net revenue base.

Darfur local governments, in short, operate with sparse budget outlays for planning and executing development programs and enforcing laws. Opportunities for leaders to acquire administrative and fiscal expertise come with taking part actively in the process of setting up schools, dispensaries, roads, and other vital services. Chronically starved of funding, councils usually find themselves deprived of such opportunities. These performance barriers restrain counselors from acquiring leadership credibility with ordinary citizens, who frequently judge the promises of participatory government, embodied in the local council organization, with resounding skepticism. All too often the councils turn into symbols of unfulfilled promises. Peasants cannot readily appreciate the apparent impotence of their elected representatives as evidence of harsh fiscal constraints on staffing, salaries, and funding, rather than purely as manifestations of incompetence (which sometimes is the case) or corruption.

Droughts weaken local council organization further by whittling down revenues that fund estimable projects. This would not necessarily be the case if droughts in the western Sudan were to attract large public works projects for which councils could take some responsibility. The stringencies forced on South Darfur council government by the 1984 drought can be inferred from a quick look at the role of agricultural taxes in the provincial economy. These taxes have been called the "backbone" of South Darfur's internal revenues (Glentworth and Idris, 1976:75). HTS surveys for 1970-72 gave an estimate of crop and livestock taxes that added up to 75% of South Darfur's total revenue base (HTS, 1974:85). In 1975-76 agricultural taxes amounted to 28% of the revenues generated by the province and 8% of the total provincial budget, including central aid. 1976-77 figures were 27% and 10%, respectively (Glentworth and Idris, 1976:71). More current statistics are not available. Locally generated revenues, however, averaged almost 32% of total revenues in 1978-80 (Alassam, 1981). If precedent offers reliable guidance, agricultural taxes, it would suggest, still represent a sizable fraction of revenues in South Darfur and in other western rainfed regions of the country.

Any likelihood of local government revenues escaping the ravages of the 1984 drought would be remote. Livestock and crop losses, and particularly cash crop losses, reduce taxable revenues sharply, and drought exacerbates problems of animal tax collection. Food aid distribution constricts the time sheikhs can devote to locating delinquent individuals who push south with their herds toward the Bahr el Arab river or beyond, into the Central African Republic. Tax enforcement will be more lax, considering peasants' defiant regard for tax exactions of any kind during a food crisis. Incidents of tax evasion, it stands to reason, will only escalate. If drought runs concurrently with schedule rate revisions, the new tax must take into account any excess stock mortalities, which depress revenues available from this tax.

Donkey Deaths

Donkeys are the number-one beast of burden in South Darfur. They haul water, firewood, fodder, crops, trade goods, and people. Peasants who lose their donkeys may face serious hardships getting to distant fields and boreholes and maintaining their rhythm of buying and selling in the network of local markets. And farmers may go into debt to borrow a donkey temporarily. Almost every household head interviewed bewailed the loss of his donkeys during the 1984 drought. Farmers and WSDC staff alike reported high mortalities of donkey stock in South Darfur, and expected the effects to persist for some time.

The Western Savannah Project was planned astride a raft of baseline surveys compiled in the early and middle 1970s by Hunting Technical Services. There has been little subsequent documentation of changes in the province's economic resources, especially at the household level. Some small-scale but useful surveys undertaken by the WSDC Project Monitoring and Evaluation Unit (PMEU) have spurred rough projections of social and ecological transformations. The findings predict for South Darfur a decline in standards of living in the event that development projects fail to hold their ground. The facts and arguments reviewed above suggest how serial years of low rainfall, culminating in the drought of 1984, may be forcing a stepped-up tempo of poverty and natural resource degradation along the following lines.

(1) Mass migration into South Darfur of new long-term residents, compounded by expansion of cultivated fields during and in the aftermath of the drought, will lower stocks of unsettled land needed for sustaining future development projects and programs.

(2) Land scarcity in some areas will aggravate the problem of fallow curtailment and may further encourage range enclosure movements spearheaded by farmers.

(3) The drought has lowered watertables of aquifers tapped by boreholes.

(4) The drought itself, the limited availability of emergency relief, and poverty accompanying farmers and herders into the crisis will further retard the peasants' accumulation of capital and savings for agricultural investment.

(5) Local government, fiscally, has no doubt emerged from the drought in a weakened position. Local and regional livestock and crop losses and the national scale of the disaster in an economically depressed country have dealt a blow to prospects of local leaders and political institutions playing a major role any time soon in agricultural and natural resource management reforms. Woefully small budgets for development will continue to foster program-poor environments that stifle strong, innovative, and self-confident leadership at or near the community level.

(6) Overgrazing at boreholes and dry-season pastures as well as natural and human-induced destruction of tree stocks—for which the drought was a chief instigating factor—may be impossible to roll back at current levels of development project funding in South Darfur.

IMPACTS OF THE DROUGHT ON DEVELOPMENT PROJECTS

Development projects cannot control climate, only its effects. Research all too often takes little explicit account of drought impacts on projects, as if project-environment relations were strictly one-way. Western Sudan research is no exception in terms of failing to register development project performance quantitatively over different climatic situations. This much can be said. Arguably, drought at best retards the progress projects make in years of good or moderate rainfall. While resilience to drought, for now, cannot be evaluated with any degree of rigor, it is still useful to indicate generally how key project operations function during trials imposed by droughts.

This section draws from information about the 1984-85 drought experiences of WSDC, along with those of the Western Sudan Agricultural Research Project (WSARP), headquartered in North Kordofan and serving Kordofan region and portions of Darfur, and the Jebel Marra Rural Development Project (JMRDP), occupying 35,000 km of land in the northwestern extremity of South Darfur. All three projects are administered by public corporations affiliated chiefly with the Government of Sudan Ministry of Agriculture and co-financed with loans from international agencies. The reason for juxtaposing WSP with WSARP and JMRDP in this discussion is that drought impact data in all three areas are tenuous. Since the land and people served by each project are significantly comparable, there is logic to regarding the documented and alleged problems which had beset a given component of one project at the time of the drought as predictive of unanalyzed problems encountered by a like component of another project during that same drought. Hopefully, detailed studies of each project will span some future drought so that deeper and more comprehensive comparisons, establishing similarities and differences in project adjustment capabilities, can be achieved. Some significant drought impacts on projects can now be discussed.

Multiplying Appropriate Seed Varieties

A regime of lowered rainfall and shortened growing seasons has held sway since the late 1960s. Crop production has not caught up with this transformation. The more popular millet varieties in South Darfur are long-growing lines taking as many as 140 days to mature. It has been suggested that the seeds were selected "in an area with a longer growing season than the present area of production" (HTS, 1976:21). However, these varieties are just as likely to be indigenous, having evolved during a moister phase of climate history with longer seasons. Shorter-term, higher-yielding lines are already in cultivation in the project area, but quantities are very limited (WSDC, n.d.). Droughts have shown many western Sudan farmers the advantages to growing short-maturing varieties of millet and sorghum in addition to their traditional strains. Supplying farmers' needs has been the problem. JMRDP, WSP's northern neighbor, faces the same situation (JMRDP, 1985c:2):

> Most farmers in the Project area have in the past not been convinced of the merits of growing either Dabar or Gadam el Haman [both early maturing varieties], but after their experiences of the 1985–85 season it is possible that demand for these varieties will increase substantially...If there is a substantial increase in demand the Project is in a poor position to satisfy it. The Project obtains its Dabar and Gadam el Haman seed from Sennar, and as Sennar have difficulty meeting the Project's present seed requirements, it will almost certainly not be able to meet any extra demand from the Project for planting in the 1985–86 season. The only other Sudanese sources of this seed in large quantities are from the mechanized farming schemes to the east of the country, and this is not a guaranteed source.

The demand for shorter maturing and hardier varieties is also evident in North Kordofan, where "the dire consequences of low yields of long maturing crops in recent years have impelled farmers to search frantically for better adapted, i.e., early maturing, varieties" (Coughenour and Nazhat, 1985:23). While the length of the dependable growing period is about 70 days in North Kordofan and 100 days in South Kordofan, farmers plant 90-120 days varieties of millet and sorghum in the north and 120-150 day varieties in the south (Berhe and Waldetatios, 1986). Furnishing Kordofan farmers enough of these seeds is a problem (Reeves and Frankenberger, 1982). In sum, droughts put enormous pressure on WSDC and other western Sudan agencies to bring household crop production capabilities into harmony with ecological reality.

Droughts Can Abort Agriculture and Range Experiments

Reports prepared by WSDC and WSARP agriculture divisions covering 1984-85 are littered with references to miscarried trials for seeds, fertilizers, and animal traction. Cereal experiments on 118 farms situated on clay (*naga'a*) soils in the WSP project area were disrupted seriously because of low rainfall (WSDC, 1985:20). Rotational grazing plans, enclosure construction projects, and ground cover estimates, which were part of WSP's two range management schemes, suffered setbacks from poor forage growth and livestock movements away from the schemes. A consulting agronomist for WSDC remarked that "the on-farm testing of the donkey drawn seeder weeder planned for the 1985 season did not occur on the planned scale because so many of the farmers lost their donkeys during the dry season" (Ogborn, 1986:8). Further, inadequate rainfall rendered experimental data obtained from assorted phosphate fertilizer trials inconclusive (op. cit., 1986). Similarly, at WSARP's El Obeid site in North Kordofan, "no meaningful data were collected..." in 1984 owing to drought (Berhe, 1986:5; see also Berhe and Jain, 1986). For the same reason fertilizer trials were inconsistent.

All of this is to say that droughts hamper seed research and reduce seed production from experimental programs, as well as retarding other experimental activities. Low rainfall also discourages communication of information to farmers about seeds (and presumably other inputs). More scientific experience with new seeds generally accumulates with more trials, especially in early stages of experimentation. In addition, the greater the number of trial runs, the more exposure farmers have to information about seed performance off the farm, thus increasing their propensity to adopt successful varieties. INSORMIL researchers discovered that in North Kordofan cooperating farmers withhold information about new seed products until their success has been demonstrated, and remark that "recent droughts have handicapped the evacuations and slowed the spread of information" (Coughenour and Nazhat, 1985:vi).

Drought, Female Farmers, and Extension Agents

Harris noticed several years ago the difficulty women farmers experienced in certain Islamic West African countries assimilating innovations in tillage "because of agricultural extension oriented to males exclusively" (1979:272). Western Sudan Muslim culture throws up communication barriers similarly, such that it is "virtually impossible for women producers to meet with male extension agents or to discuss credit with male officials" (Holcombe, 1986:8—for Darfur; see also Coughenour and Nazhat, 1985:vii for Kordofan). WSARP extension reports for Darfur and Kordofan, curiously, do not bring up this issue (Trial, 1985a; 1985b).

Nevertheless, the documents cited and conversations between the author and female farmers make a plausible case that: (1) gender role segregation in Sudan Muslim culture restricts communication between male extension agents and female clients; (2) that droughts compounds these restrictions. Male household head migration during drought years leaves females as acting home managers for a greater length of time than usual. Consequently, extension agents' tasks involving the dissemination of agricultural information to villagers will be hindered for months on end by prolonged male absenteeism from the household. For the present, this has to stand as a working hypothesis, but one that is not without support.

Droughts and Uncertainty in Planning

Droughts, it was pointed out, deny projects information. They can also obscure information which planners use to establish norms and trends for allocating resources. Land-use planning is particularly susceptible to complications stemming from indeterminate records. While project management and extension agents can adjust fertilizer and seed allotments somewhat in accordance with changing environmental and socio-economic constraints, land tenure covenants cannot be revamped so readily. WSDC staff and consultants have for years been grappling with optimum plot size criteria for WSP's controlled settlements. How much land, they ask, should tenants on settlements be allowed to rent and what proportion of land in these blocks ought tenants be permitted to cultivate each year? Factored into calculations typically are average household size, per capita consumption requirements, soil characteristics, and average crop yield. Climate decisively modifies the values of some of these variables, which can swing wildly from one year to the next. What then should be the standard land holding unit and area of cultivation? A lengthy quote from Fuller (1985:59) will put the issue into context.

There are two key considerations in deciding how much land each family should be allocated: (1) how much land does each family need to cultivate each year? and (2) how long should the fallow period be compared to the period of cultivation?

It is proposed that the answer to the first question is "10 feddans" and the answer to the second should be the fallow period should be three times as long as the period of cultivation.

Ten feddans is viewed a a generous portion of land for annual cultivation for two reasons. First, most farmers in Southern Darfur cultivated less than 10 feddans. Second, 10 feddans is normally enough for a family to produce a surplus of grain. It is roughly estimated that a 6-person family needs 12 sacks of grain per year for subsistence. If the yield is only 2 sacks per feddan, say because of poor rainfall, 10 feddans is still adequate. Even if the farmers devote 3 or 4 feddans to a cash crop and get 2 sacks of grain from each remaining feddan, 6 or 7 feddans would produce enough grain for one family's needs.

It should be noted that in a drought year such as 1984, 10 feddans would probably not produce enough grain for household consumption; however, planning on the basis of years as dry as 1984 would be infeasible, both in terms of cost and the amount of land required. Survival in drought years similar to 1984 will need to be dependent upon savings rather than the years of productivity.

Fuller pegs optimum plot size to crop yields. Yield estimates for planning purposes, he argues, should except data gathered during drought years. Land-use planners should instead match holding/field size with survival requirements by making use of data for low harvest years. In years as bad as 1984, when no amount of land would secure a crop, households have to lean on their savings, which would presumably include grain laid away in reserve. Fuller's argument that drought years must not be counted is not entirely correct. Grain reserve levels may be artifacts of drought damage from a previous year, in two respects. First, grain lost to drought in year X limits grain quantities carried through to current year Z. Second, the amount of land cropped in year Y, coming after year X, and the yield carried from Y to Z may reflect decisions affected by losses in year X. To the extent that land-use planning ought to incorporate survival needs through crop yield estimates, no-yield and poor yield years together should be reckoned.

Fuller's calculations do not sort out these factors. The 2 sacks (45 kg/sack) per feddan (.42 ha) yield in low rainfall years should amount to a 900 kg harvest on 10 feddans (4.2 ha) of land. This 214-kg/ha yield for a family of 6.8 (which is nearer to average household size in South Darfur than Fuller's figure of 6) translates into a 132-kg/capita/annum during a poor growing season (to say nothing of a drought year). Hence Fuller's 10 feddans[8] would be insufficient for meeting the average family's consumption requirements in the province during a not-unusual year of production (i.e., of fair to poor yields), and even less sufficient if carryover stocks from a previous drought year are zero. Without further qualification, the 10-feddan standard might allow too small a subsistence safety margin for self-reliant households even in non-drought years.

What acreage standards are the most suitable, taking into consideration all the relevant variables, cannot be settled here. That issue is still a matter of debate at WSDC. This section has taken up a simpler problem. South Darfur planners have tended to construct their land-use models on results from one or two fair-to-average harvest seasons. Inasmuch as crop yield data supply inputs to land-use planners, then multi-annual yields in runs of poor- and zero-yield years must not be lost sight of. These data make norms and standards harder to set. But the end result will be land allotment more in keeping with tenants' actual survival requirement.

Depletion of Project Area Resources

Large influxes of drought migrants, it was explained, are reducing reserves of unoccupied land that could be earmarked for future development projects. Migrants, furthermore, add greatly to the pressures being exerted on the project area's limited social services infrastructure. Making matters worse is that by bleeding government agencies of revenues, the drought itself has halted or diminished construction on flour mills, roads, and wateryards, and at medical clinics, hospitals, and schools. Although no evidence shows conclusively that water tables are being lowered to critical levels, this possibility must not be ruled out.

CONCLUSIONS AND RECOMMENDATIONS

A look at 1984, the year of widespread crop failure, will indicate that WSP's activities slowed down appreciably and that South Darfurans found themselves worse off a year later than they had been in 1982 when WSP-I was officially activated, or in 1983, for that matter, on the eve of the drought. Until a more complete assessment can be made, the following conclusions from the preceding analysis may have to stand.

(1)   Except possibly for its wateryard rehabilitation program, WSP was not a significant crisis prophylactic or provider of relief within the project area.

(2)   WSP lost resources because of the drought. In some areas, land it might eventually want for range and agricultural experimentation and for community development has been preempted by drought refugees. A year's worth of some important information from research stations is

irretrievably lost. And the depletion of water supplies here and there may be worrisome.

(3)   The general lowering of living standards over the area will make development work more difficult and expensive during WSP-II and possibly thereafter. In view of these circumstances there is no telling if the $2.1 million for settlements or $5.2 million for forestry, or other estimates of costs projected by project underwriters, are realistic, and how far afield they may stand when measured by social soundness standards.

ACKNOWLEDGMENTS

Research for this paper would not have been possible without support from the AGRES and EAPNA divisions of the World Bank. Colleagues at the Bank supplied valuable reports that would otherwise have been difficult or impossible to obtain and made arrangements for financial assistance enabling a two-month tour of South Darfur, Sudan during December 1985 and January 1986.

NOTES

1.   Wateryards are fenced stations containing two or three boreholes, taps, and troughs. They are staffed by a government clerk who collects water fees from yard users.
2.   These calculations are derived from Elhanan (1985), citing GOS Ministry of Agriculture statistics, and from figures presented in Fuller (1985), who also bases his information on Ministry of Agriculture data.
3.   Whereas prior to the 1968–1973 droughts North Darfur farmers might have laid away enough grain to stay them through an abnormally dry year, they have subsequently not found it possible to build up multi-annual buffer stocks (Holy, 1980; Abdul-Jalil, 1979; Tully, 1984). JMRDP staff notes that "even in normal years, farmers in North Darfur cannot usually meet their subsistence requirements from grain production alone" (1985b:5).
4.   USAID data were supplied by staff at the USAID mission in Khartoum.
5.   A procession of laws affecting regional government reorganization coincides with the drought years of the 1970s and 1980s. The most recent modifications preceding Sudan's 1986 elections include the People's Local Government Act of 1981 and the Regional Government Act of 1980. These laws mandate parcelling the country into regions, then into provinces whose executive officer,t he Provincial Commissioner, shares power with the most inclusive echelon of administration, the district (area) councils. South Darfur established seven district councils and North Darfur six. These corporate bodies prepare their own budgets and collect revenues from investments, commercial services, taxes, fees, and fines. District councils have oversight of rural councils outside of towns and cit-

ies. Rural councils in turn subsume nomadic and village councils, forming the lowest tier of regional administration. The latter enjoy no budgetary discretion and implement tasks delegated from the district. Recruitment at all three levels of administration is by election.
6. One mukhamas is approximately .5 ha.
7. It was observed that "with the advent of numerous missions from development organizations and relief agencies it has become almost impossible to keep a full record of visitors..." (WSDC, 1985:4).
8. One feddan is .42 ha. The 10 feddans represents the total allowable cultivated area per year on a standard 40-feddan block.

REFERENCES

Abdul-Jalil, M. A.
   1979   The Dynamics of Ethnic Identification and Ethnic and Group Relations among the People of 'Dur', Northern Darfur, Sudan, Ph.D. Dissertation, Anthropology, University of Edinburgh.
Allassam, M.
   1981   Decentralization and Development: The Sudanese Experience. U.N. Seminar for Development, September. Khartoum (mimeo).
Austrialian Agricultural Consulting and Management Company (AACMC)
   1984   Western Savannah Project Evaluation. Sudan.
   1985   Western Savannah Project Phase 2, Preparation: Main Report. Sudan.
Awadalla, S. A.
   1985   Tegali District, Southern Kordofan (Sudan). Monitoring Report No. 2 ETMA Program, Institute of Environmental Studies, University of Khartoum, Sudan.
Behnke, R. H.
   1985   Rangeland Development and the Improvement of Livestock Production: Policy Issues and Recommendations for the Western Savannah Project, South Darfur, Sudan. Sudan.
Berhe, T.
   1986   Notes on Rainfall Patterns and Their Influence on Sorghum/Millet Research and Production in Kordofan, Western Sudan. Department of Agronomy, Kansas State University, Manhattan, Kansas (mimeo).
Berhe, T. and R. P. Jain
   1986   A Pearl Millet Variety for Western Sudan. Agronomy Department Report, Kansas State University, Manhattan, Kansas. March (mimeo).
Berhe, T. and T. Woldetatios
   1986   Recommendations for Agronomic Crops Research Priorities in Kordofan Region, Western Sudan. February (mimeo).
Coughenour, C. M. and S. M. Nazhat
   1985   Recent Changes in Villages and Rainfed Agriculture in Northern Central Kordofan: Communication Process and Constraints. INSORMIL Report 4. Institute of Agriculture and Natural Resources, University of Nebraska, Lincoln, Nebraska.

E. Mukhtar, M. H. A. and M. Runder-Gabelmann
1985 Agricultural Development and Land Tenue Issues in Darfur. Report Prepared for the Task Force No. 2 on Land Tenure as Part of the Rainfed Sector Initiated by the World Bank (mimeo).
Elhanan, M. M.
1985 Production Cost and Profitability of the Major Crops in the rainfed Mechanized Sector, Sudan. Rainfed Agriculture Development Strategy Task Force 4, Marketing, Pricing and Incentives. Ministry of Finance and Economic Planning and Ministry of Agriculture and Natural Resources, GOS, Khartoum (mimeo).
El Sammani, M. O.
1984 The Impact of Water Supply Centers on Ecosystems with A Suggested Strategy for Action. Department of Geography, University of Khartoum (mimeo).
Fuller, T. D.
1985 Resettlement as a Desertification Control Measure: Feasibility Study and Proposal of Appropriate Strategies for Darfur Region, Sudan. Paper Prepared for United Nations Sudano-Sahelian Office (UNSO) (mimeo).
Glentworth, H. and M. S. Idris
1976 Report of the Administrative Survey of the Province, 1976. Vol. 2, Local Government and Development in the Sudan: The Experience of Southern Darfur Province. Academy of Administrative and Professional Sciences, University of Khartoum.
Haaland, G.
1982 Social Organization and Ecological Pressure in South Darfur. In Problems of Savannah Development. G. Haaland, ed., p. 55-106. Occasional Paper No. 19, Department of Social Anthropology, University of Bergen, Norway.
Hall, A. E., G. H. Cannell, and H. W. Lawton
1979 Agriculture in Semi-Arid Environments. Berlin, Springer-Verlag.
Hammer-Digernes, T.
1977 Wood for Fuel—Energy Crisis Implying Desertification: The Case of Bara, the Sudan. Geografisk Institute, University of Bergen.
Harris, B.
1979 Going Against the Grain. In Proceedings of the International Workshop on Socioeconomic Constraints to Development of Semi-Arid Tropical Agriculture. G. J. Ryan and H. L. Thompson, eds., pp. 265-288. International Crops Research Institute for the Semi-Arid Tropics, India.
Henin, R. A.
1969 Marriage Patterns and Trends in the Nomadic and Settled Population in the Sudan. Africa 39: 238-259.
Holcombe, S. H.
1986 Strengthening Rural Women Producers in Darfur Region: Constraints and Opportunities (mimeo).
Holy, L.
1980 Drought and Change in a Tribal Economy: The Berti of Northern Darfur. Disasters 4(1): 65-71.

Hunting Technical Services, Ltd. (HTS)
    1974 Southern Darfur Land-Use Planning Survey. Annex 6: Economics and
          Project Evaluation. For GOS, England.
    1976 Savanna Development Project, Phase II. For GOS and FAO, England.
    1977 Agricultural Development in the Jebel Marra Area. Annex V: Social Or-
          ganization and Structure. For GOS and FAO, England.
Ibrahim, F. N.
    1984 Ecological Imbalance in the Republic of the Sudan with Reference to
          Desertification in Darfur. Bayreuther Geowissenschaftliche Arbeiten Vol.
          6. Bayreuth, Germany.
Jebel Marra Rural Development Project (JMRDP)
    1985a Migrants in the Project Area. Monitoring and Evaluation Department, An-
          nual Review, 1985. Sudan (mimeo).
    1985b Preliminary Grain Production Estimates (1985) for the Project Area.
          Monitoring and Evaluation Department (mimeo).
    1985c Suggested Schemes for the Alleviation of the Problems Caused by Drought
          (mimeo).
Kowal, J. M. and A. H. Kassam
    1978 Agricultural Ecology of Savanna: a Study of West Africa. Oxford, Claren-
          don Press.
Mangouri, H. A.
    1985 Umm Kaddada District (Northern Darfur Province). Institute of Environ-
          mental Studies, University of Khartoum, Sudan.
Mohamed, Y. A., M. O. El Sammani, and M. Z. Shadad
    1982 The Northern Kordofan Rural Water Supply Baseline Survey. Institute of
          Environmental Studies, University of Khartoum, Sudan.
Norman, D. W., E. B. Simmons, and H. M. Hays
    1982 Farming Systems in the Nigerian Savanna. Boulder, Westview Press.
Ogborn, J.
    1985 An Agronomic Outline for a New Settlement in Qoz areas. Agricultural
          Division, WSDC, Nyala, Sudan (mimeo).
    1986 WSDC Nyala Agronomy Section Annual Report for 1985 Season, Janu-
          ary, 1986. Nyala, Sudan (mimeo).
Olsson, K.
    1984 Long-Term Changes in Woody Vegetation in North Kordofan, the Sudan.
          Laboratory of Remote Sensing, Department of Physical Geography, Uni-
          versity of Lund, Sweden.
Oxfam, UNICEF, and Darfur Regional Government
    1985 Nutritional Surveillance and Drought Monitoring Project. Report on Pro-
          ject Activities, May, 1985. June (mimeo).
Provincial Government of South Darfur
    n.d. Final Report of the Technical Committee for Migration Organization
          (translated from Arabic) (mimeo).
Reeves, E. B. and T. Frankenberger
    1982 Farming Systems Research in North Kordofan, Sudan. INSORMIL Report
          2. University of Kentucky, Lexington.
Relief Information and Coordination Support Unit (RICSU)
    1985 Sudan Drought Emergency Country Brief. Darfur, UN Headquarters,
          Khartoum (mimeo).

Scott-Villiers, H.
1984 Land-Use Change in Qoz Ma'aliya 1972-1984. Nyala, WSCD (mimeo).
Trial, T. F.
1985a Strengthening Research—Extension and Linkages in Kordofan region, Sudan. WSARP Pub. No. 50. Pullman, Washington State University.
1985b Extension in Darfur Region, Sudan. WSARP, Government of Sudan, Khartoum.
Tully, D.
1984 Culture and Context: The Process of Market Incorporation in Dar Masalit, Sudan. Ph.D. Dissertation, Anthropology, University of Washington. University of Michigan Microfilms, Ann Arbor.
United Nations Office for Emergency Operations in Africa (UNOEOA)
1986 Special Report on the Emergency Situation in Africa: Review of 1985 and 1986 Emergency Needs. January 20, New York.
United Nations Sudano-Sahelian Office (UNSO)
1984 Restocking the Gum Belt for Desertification Control, Phase II (mimeo).
The Work Bank
1985a Sudan: Western Savanna Project—Phase II. Staff Appraisal Report, November 12.
1985b Project Completion Report. Sudan Western Savannah Project. Eastern and Southern African Region, Northern Agricultural Division (mimeo).
Western Sudan Development Corporation (WSDC)
1982 1982 Farmer Survey. PMEU Report 1. Nyala, Sudan (mimeo).
1983 1983 Farmer Survey. PMEU Report 2. Nyala, Sudan (mimeo).
1984 Annual Report July 1983-June 1984. Nyala, Sudan (mimeo).
1985 Agricultural Services Division Annual Report 1985-85 (mimeo).
n.d. Annex IX. The Climatic Potential for the WSDC Project Area. Land-Use Planning Unit (mimeo).

PART C

The African Scene

CHAPTER 4

Increased Vulnerability to Food Shortages among Fulani Nomads in Niger

Cynthia White

INTRODUCTION[1]

Nomadic pastoralists are particularly vulnerable to famine. Over the past century nomads throughout sub-Saharan Africa have been pushed gradually into increasingly marginal ecological areas as more fertile land is taken over by expanding agriculture, irrigation schemes, commercial ranching, or game reserves. The aridity of regions used by nomads is compounded by unpredictable rainfall fluctuations. In the Sahel, as one moves north toward the Sahara, mean rainfall levels fall, and the coefficient of variation rises substantially (Sen, 1981:115). These are often cereal-deficit areas whose low agricultural potential explains their availability to nomads.

Even when there are adequate food stocks in the market, pastoralists are vulnerable to fluctuating terms of trade. Sahelian pastoralists rarely eat meat and only part of their diet is made up of milk.[2] They therefore depend on the sale or barter of animals and animal products for cereals, which provide cheaper calories than meat or milk and are the bulk of their diet.[3] Terms of exchange between animals and cereals vary seasonally. The price of cereals is high at the end of the dry season, when pastoralists' cereal needs are highest and their animals are in poor condition and fetch low prices.[4] There are also less regular shifts in relative prices due to factors other than the seasons, as well as inter-annual variations. These are caused by factors such as agricultural yield levels, currency exchange rates, disposable incomes, and government policy (for example on prices, imports, and exports). In a drought, cereal prices rise and livestock prices collapse. Pastoralists then have to sell

REPUBLIC OF NIGER

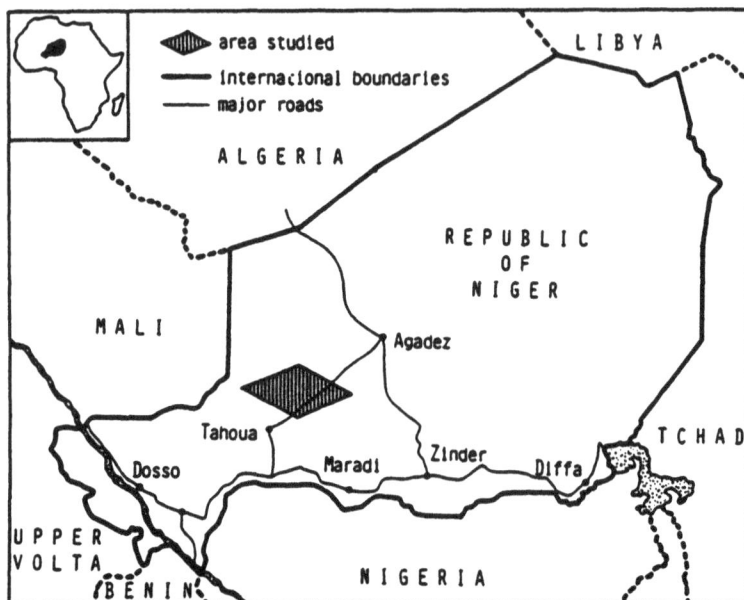

more animals to obtain the cash to buy a given quantity of grain. The poor condition of these animals due to poor pasture further lowers herders' purchasing power. The intersection of curves for livestock and cereal prices is a good indication that famine conditions are a serious threat.

Herders then are vulnerable because they do not produce what they eat. Furthermore their means of production, their herd, can be entirely wiped out at any time either by drought or by disease. Although a Sahelian farmer is equally subject to crop loss, this does not represent a loss of his productive assets (unless, of course, he is obliged to consume his seeds).

Interventions that could prevent a drought from turning into a famine are even less likely to be timely and well targeted for pastoralists than for other rural peoples. The regions pastoralists use are often isolated and the central authorities are poorly informed about their conditions. Droughts in the Sahel are usually highly localized. The situation in the pastoral zone can be different from that in the agricultural zone. 1913, for example, was a year of disastrous crop failure throughout the Sahel. However, pasture conditions in Niger that year were not particularly bad. Other years can be worse for pasture than for crops. Accurate assessment of local conditions in isolated areas is further hindered by poor lines of communication between herders and government services. There is frequently mistrust on both sides. In most African states pastoralists are both ethnic and occupational minorities, with little political bargaining power. Only in Somalia and Mauritania are people from nomadic backgrounds well represented in government structures. Even when there is not deliberate neglect, a general lack of knowledge about conditions in pastoral areas and problems confronting herders prevails.

Nomadic pastoralists often are considered backward and ignorant, and are sometimes seen as fearsome marauders. Not only local governments but often international donors and experts deplore their lack of participation in the market economy, their accumulation of animals for ritual or prestige, and their destructive use of the environment. Their herds are thought to be responsible for overgrazing and desertification.[5] These misconceptions lead to inappropriate policies and justify lack of support for nomadic pastoralism.

There is often an historic and political dimension to the division between nomadic and sedentary populations. In Niger the ethnic group with largely dominant political power (the Djerma) and the one with the most economic influence (the Hausa) were the former slaves of the Twareg, the principal nomadic group in the country. This has left a strong residue of bitterness and fear that affects current policy and is periodically exacerbated by Libya, Niger's neighbor to the northeast. Mali and Chad used the 1968-1974 drought to break the strength of nomadic groups opposed to their governments (Somerville, 1986:31). Sen (1981:122) refers to evidence of discriminating treatment against pastoral nomadic people in the 1973-1974 relief camps, and "a firm suggestion that the Sahelian governments were closely tied to (and more responsive to the needs of) the majority sedentary communities."[6]

Nomads' geographical, political, and cultural marginalization, their dependence on the market, the collapse of their purchasing power during a drought, and their lack of immunity to many common diseases due to dispersed living conditions all contribute to their vulnerability to famine. Nomads suffered considerably more in terms of mortality and nutritional deficiency in 1968-1974 than sedentary populations.[7]

At the same time much less is known about pastoral production systems than about farming systems. The first step toward famine prevention is a thorough understanding of how local economies operate in normal times to identify constraints to production and measures that can be taken to strengthen existing risk avoidance and insurance strategies. Many "drought-proofing" mechanisms are abandoned due to poverty (White, 1987). Chronic malnourishment because of poverty is increasingly widespread among African pastoralists. Examination of the processes of improvishment and identification of possible interventions and policy changes provide a key to equipping societies to face, withstand, and recover from drought.[8]

We must look at what Vaughan has called "long-term changes as well as short-term strain" (Vaughan, 1987:134). "If we are to understand why some people starve and not others, then we need to know the individual's economic entitlements both in normal and crisis times, but also to see how these are meshed with social relations" (Vaughan, 1987:3). This includes looking at gender relations to avoid the "tendency to give an exaggerated priority to the individual unit of production" (Harris and Young, 1984:124). As Dahl (1987:5) points out, "the domestic unit is not undifferentiated with respect to access to resources, productive efforts and appropriation of produce." At the same time some understanding of the changing political and economic conditions through which a particular community is linked to wider structures is necessary.

I will consider aspects of these issues by taking a specific case: that of WoDaaBe cattle herders in central Niger.[9] The WoDaaBe are a sub-group of the Fulani, who are found throughout West Africa and as far east as the Sudan. The WoDaaBe do not cultivate. They raise cattle and some sheep and goats, and use camels and donkeys for transport. They do not live in villages or build houses or huts or use tents. They are highly mobile, adapting to rainfall variability by camping with their herds where pasture is best.

Throughout this chapter I refer to quantitative data.[10] All data were collected from each individual member (including women and children) within sample households, and exchanges between households were recorded. Labor data were aggregated into age/sex categories for analysis and budget data were analyzed by household. In spite of the many drawbacks to using the household as a unit of analysis, it is nonetheless important to examine what is going on at this level, particularly for a discussion of famine. It is well recognized that aggregate food production and food availability figures are not indicators of famine as much as individuals' access to food. Attaining national food self-sufficiency or increasing food production do not guarantee access or equitable distribution or necessarily benefit the hungry.[11] If the pitfalls of using the household as an economic unit are taken into consideration (for example by observing intra- and inter-household exchanges), this level of analysis can reveal realities that are masked by aggregate figures but that are nevertheless extremely important for policy. For example, ten years after the 1968-1974 drought the national cattle herd in Niger was estimated to be 60 percent reconstituted. Herders were thought by government and donors to be wealthy once again, to have large herds, and to be overstocking. Data I collected at the household level, however, showed that because of significant shifts in livestock property ownership due to the drought, a large proportion of the animals in the pastoral zone belonged to outsiders and many herders were destitute (White, 1984a:462-529).

SUBSISTENCE AND ENTITLEMENT

As we have seen, grain procurement is an important aspect of a pastoral economy. For the WoDaaBe it has become increasingly critical as their herds have diminished: a larger portion of their diet must be purchased grain to compensate for dwindling milk supplies.

Marguerite Dupire, who did fieldwork amongst the WoDaaBe in 1951-1952 and 1961, describes their economy as based on the exchange of milk and milk products for cereals (1971:80). WoDaaBe women own few animals, which are inherited by a man's sons and brothers. However, women milk allotted household animals, deciding about the proportions of milk to be left for the calves (with an important effect on their health, growth rate, and the future productivity of the herd), and that for human consumption. It is the women who distribute milk and prepared cereals within the household and to guests. They also set aside milk in excess of consumption needs for gifts, barter, or sale. Proceeds from milk products belong to women. Dupire (1962:127) explains that although supplying the household with millet is the husband's formal responsibility, cereal stocks were actually provided by wives through the exchange of milk and butter for cereals to avoid having to sell animals. Dupire (1971:80) states that in the rainy season (in the 1950s) no cereals were consumed. Rainy season milk supplies were sufficient for subsistence needs. Only in the dry season, when milk production is lower due to poor pasture conditions, was it necessary to supplement milk with cereals.

Now, however, smaller household herds rarely produce milk surpluses. Data I collected twenty years later show that even in the rainy season 25 percent of the WoDaaBe's diet is composed of cereals (see Table 1). Cereals account for 53 percent of sample families' annual consumption (White, 1984a:520-521). These cereals are now bought (87%) by men rather than obtained through barter (9%) by women (see Table 2). Animals are the WoDaaBe's main source of cash for cereal purchases. Ninety percent of average household cash income is from animal sales (see Table 3). Obtaining cereals from animal sales rather than by exchange for milk leads to a process of decapitalization.

Less available milk due to smaller herds clearly reduces WoDaaBe women's resources. In the past women were able to accumulate small flocks of sheep and goats with their milk and butter earnings. However, WoDaaBe women's rights to milk cattle have always been almost entirely dependent on men. Although women have never had direct control (alienation rights, not

Table 1.   Sources of Food Intake in WoDaaBe Model Production Unit

	Percent of calories intake by origin				
	rains	cold	hot	transition	year
Milk	68	39	21	22	40
Cereals	25	54	71	71	53
Sugar	7	7	8	7	7
Total	100	100	100	100	100

Table 2.   WoDaaBe Sample: Proportion of Net Cereal Inflows from Different Sources (%)

	Season				Year Total
	rains	cold	hot	transition	
Purchase	83	77	98	93	87
Barter	17	20	—	—	9
Gift	—	3	2	7	4
Total	100	100	100	100	100

Table 3.   WoDaaBe Sample: Main Cash Incomes

	Mean cash income (CFA/household) in season:				Year	
	rains	cold	hot	transition	CFA	(%)
Animals	124,662	178,447	195,036	65,251	563,396	(91)
Salaries	286	179	25,928	—	26,393	(4)
Misc.	3,356	8,988	14,536	7,178	34,058	(5)
Total	128,304	187,614	235,500	72,429	623,847	(100)
	(20)	(30)	(38)	(12)	(100)	

simply usufruct rights) over many animals, they are able to market those that they do own. Independent access to the market by women is as important a consideration as ownership rights.[12] Now, however, with smaller WoDaaBe herds, women have no opportunity to accumulate savings from milk sales to invest in livestock. The few institutionalized transfers of animals they received in the past (gift from father at marriage, gift from brothers' inheritance) have dropped due to poverty.

Data I collected from 1980 to 1983 showed that household herds had become inadequate for subsistence. To meet their cash needs to buy cereals and other necessities,[13] WoDaaBe households were selling animals essential to the on-going production of the herd (White, 1984b). Sales of reproducing female animals had begun, which is a clear sign of distress in a pastoral economy. They represent a loss of the most important productive assets. Sales of females result in fewer calves and lower milk supplies, necessitating more cereal purchases, which raise cash needs and therefore increase animal sales. The small herd that necessitated sales of females in the first place has become even smaller. This quickly creates a downward spiral.

The contrast between Dupire's findings, which described herds adequate for household consumption, and my own can be traced to the 1968-1974 drought, which decimated WoDaaBe herds. This drought constituted a turning point for the WoDaaBe, since which they have had to contend with insufficient herds. However, the impact of the drought and, perhaps more important, its aftermath were determined by processes set in motion well before the drought. This was not the first drought to ravage the Sahel, nor was it the most severe. The WoDaaBe have complex risk avoidance and security mechanisms that had helped them reduce losses as well as successfully reconstitute their herds when previous droughts struck (White, 1984a and 1987). Ten years after the 1968-1974 drought (even before the disastrous year of 1984), however, they not only had not begun the process of reconstituting, but were decapitalizing.

THE IMPACT AND AFTERMATH OF DROUGHT

To understand both why this drought had more of an impact on the WoDaaBe than previous droughts, as well as their continuing poverty and increased vulnerability to following droughts, we must examine not only what happens during a drought (i.e., how a drought becomes a famine), but also the processes underway before the drought and the mechanisms available for recovery.

Since the beginning of this century, cultivated surfaces in Niger have been expanding due to a combination of demographic pressure, increased cash needs, and reduced soil fertility. Gradually pasture used by nomads for grazing their animals became fields as farmers were obliged to move further north into more arid, less agriculturally productive areas.[14] Rainfall in the decade preceding the 1968–1974 drought was high. The unusually high rainfall and a program of well-digging encouraged the WoDaaBe to move into even more northerly and more habitually arid regions to use uncultivated pasture.

The shift north had a series of consequences. The areas the WoDaaBe were pushed into are well beyond the normal limit (350 mm. of annual rainfall) of rainfed agriculture, so they no longer had regular and mutually beneficially exchanges with farmers, such as manure for crop residues. The government-dug wells allow public access and upset traditional land use patterns, which are based on pasture control through private well ownership. Localized overgrazing appeared around boreholes. Most important, the WoDaaBe's mobility, which is the most critical security mechanism for nomads in a risky environment, was restricted. When the rains failed they were unable to move to their southern fall back pastures, which had become cultivated fields.

A series of years of low rainfall, beginning in 1968, caused grain prices to rise and animals in poor condition to flood the market as herders' purchasing power collapsed. Nomads lost animals not only through deaths but also through increased sales to buy expensive cereals. Their economic entitlements[15] were limited, for the WoDaaBe production system is highly specialized. They neither produce nor store wealth in any form other than livestock. They therefore had no other assets to sell to obtain cash. There were no employment opportunities for wage labor. The WoDaaBe do not have marketable skills, and Niger has no industrial sector to absorb surplus labor. Urban centers during the drought were already filled with sedentary wage-seekers with better skills and connections than those of the nomads. The relatively egalitarian distribution of wealth within WoDaaBe society and the isolation of the WoDaaBe from farmers meant that social networks and redistribution systems provided them with little access to food at a time of large-scale loss. Some died; others ended up in refugee camps and feeding centers.

Recovery after a drought is particularly difficult for herders. Their loss of animals is equivalent to a farmer's loss of his land. Even if the rainy season following a drought is good and pasture is abundant, it does not benefit a pastoralist who does not have any animals. When the rains come he cannot replant and obtain a harvest in five months' time. Herd reconstitution even in normal times requires high capital investment. After a drought, animal prices rise sharply because there are few animals on the market.

After previous droughts, when the WoDaaBe had lost as many if not more animals as in 1968-1974, they cultivated fields, gathered bush products[16] for consumption and sale, and women did menial tasks for sedentary neighbors, such as mending calabashes, braiding hair, and pounding millet. The WoDaaBe then gradually reinvested in livestock, beginning with sheep and goats, and in ten to fifteen years were able to rebuild their cattle herds to adequate subsistence levels. After 1974 however, they did not have access to fertile land for agriculture or to the wild foods they had previously used. Farmers were already cultivating even marginal land. The more northerly areas the WoDaaBe were using at the time of the 1968-1974 drought were too dry for reliance on wild foods. The WoDaaBe had no sources of income to reinvest in livestock.

In the ten years following 1974 they were able to survive in the pastoral zone by using three mechanisms: redistributing their remaining animals between households through their traditional system of animal loans (*haBBanae*), herding animals (*jokereeji*) belonging to wealthy non-pastoralists to increase slightly their milk supplies, and dry season labor migration.

It is important to distinguish between the post-drought recuperative mechanisms available to the WoDaaBe after previous droughts and those they were obliged to use after the 1968-1974 drought. Those described above for past droughts (agriculture, gathering, local jobs) were temporary activities which gradually contributed to a return to pastoral production based on herds adequate for subsistence. In contrast, those the WoDaaBe had to resort to after 1974 (*jokereeji*, migrant labor) were stopgap survival mechanisms that do nothing to halt the downward spiral of poverty.

HaBBanae is a traditional redistributive system that has powerful meaning for the WoDaaBe. It expresses much of their collective identity, which is distinctive and particularly important to them. The system is simple: an individual loans a female animal which is cared for by the borrower until she has reproduced three times. She is then returned to the lender. The borrower keeps the three offspring and has the use of the original animal's milk during the period he cares for her.

These "loans," which amount to a transfer of animals, are often given by richer to poorer WoDaaBe. But poor WoDaaBe also initiate *haBBanae* loans, which confer prestige on the lender, bringing admiration for his generosity, and establish an important tie between loaner and borrower. They also provide insurance by spreading an individual's animals over different herds, reducing the chance of loss from animal disease or localized drought. The community, as well as former borrowers, contribute *haBBanae* animals to an individual suffering hardship. There is a strong feeling that it is shameful for the group to allow one of its members to become destitute. At times of large-scale loss, however, this system is not adequate for the reconstitution of all family herds. A minimal nucleus of group animals must survive to be loaned out. While *haBBanae* played an important role in past droughts as well as in 1974, and continues to be used in the vicissitudes of normal pastoral life, at times of major loss it is accompanied by other recuperative mechanisms.

Both *jokereeji* and migrant labor were new to the WoDaaBe in 1974. While *haBBanae* animals are given between WoDaaBe, have an important social content, and contribute to the reconstitution of the borrower's herd, *jokereeji* are quite different. When they herd *jokereeji*, the WoDaaBe provide labor at virtually no cost to the owners, who are non-WoDaaBe and usually non-pastoralists. The WoDaaBe benefit only from the milk.

The owners are usually wealthy farmers, civil servants, or merchants. They use their animals for investment rather than subsistence. They are therefore more likely to have male animals for meat rather than female animals for milk. Destitute herders create good investment possibilities for those with capital. Young animals are readily available cheaply in the market, whereas when herders have viable herds they rarely sell young animals. Poor herders then supply labor until the animal has gained enough weight to make a handsome profit for its owner. Forage is free.

The WoDaaBe take on *jokereeji* when they have no other economic alternatives that allow them to remain in the pastoral zone. There are so many nomads looking for animals to herd that they are unable to demand compensation for their labor other than the little milk that may be produced. The Fulani have always herded for farmers, particularly during the rainy season, taking the animals to fresh pasture and keeping them from damaging the fields their sedentary owners cultivate. This arrangement still exists in other parts of West Africa. But the terms are very different from what is being described here. The traditional system is part of a larger network of exchanges between equals: farming and pastoralist neighbors. Clearly defined payment is given for herding labor in the form of food, clothing, and animals, allowing a poor person to build up a herd.

Jokereeji have definite disadvantages for the nomads. Mobility is reduced, as the sedentary owners often want to supervise their animals. Mobility is essential to find pasture where rainfall is unpredictable and to avoid overgrazing. The village-based *jokereeji* often introduce disease into WoDaaBe herds. Other WoDaaBe are less likely to give *haBBanae* animals to a herder of *jokereeji* to avoid the diseases and the unruliness, leading to wounded animals, of herds with large numbers of males. Potential lenders are also aware that herders with *jokereeji* cannot use as wide a range of pastures. The herder of *jokereeji* is thus cut off from mutual support networks. Even if there are females in the herd of *jokereeji*, they are not necessarily lactating, so the milk obtained does not contribute significantly to household consumption. Cash needs for cereals and other necessities must continue to be met by the sale of the WoDaaBe's own animals. Reduced mobility and less participation in the circulation of animals contribute to long-term vulnerability.

The WoDaaBe resort to migrant labor, like *jokereeji*, reluctantly, recognizing its drawbacks. Wives accompany their husbands on dry season labor migration to the coastal countries. Because the WoDaaBe do not have marketable skills, the wages they are able to obtain barely cover their living expenses.[17] They often have to borrow money for transportation costs or to buy cereals for family members remaining behind. So there is no money left to invest in livestock. The absence of migrants, however, reduces household cereal needs during the critical dry season, thereby limiting the number of animals that must be sold from the diminishing herd. But migration has a serious impact on labor availability, a crucial requirement in the WoDaaBe's strategies for optimal livestock management. Makeshift arrangements are made because of labor shortages, but these contribute to long-term vulnerability.

Jokereeji and migrant labor do not assist herd reconstitution.[18] In fact, they seriously undermine the viability of WoDaaBe economy and society: herd productivity drops, risk avoidance strategies and security mechanisms are abandoned, and ecological degradation is increased (White, 1987). All of these factors increase vulnerability to future droughts, and, indeed, in the drought of 1984, most WoDaaBe lost all their remaining animals and are now dependent on government food aid.

ORGANIZATION OF PRODUCTION

Much has been made in the famine literature of the importance of diversification as a coping strategy. Under risky conditions economic diversification has been a critical safety net for other pastoralists, such as the Twareg, during droughts.[19] The WoDaaBe have, in a sense, used the opposite approach. Rather than diversifying, they have increased labor inputs. It is their extreme specialization in livestock production, their considerable skills, and detailed knowledge that have permitted them to survive in an extremely difficult environment. However, political and economic changes depending on factors beyond their control have altered the context within which they function.

The WoDaaBe's lack of economic diversification can be linked to their particular organization of production. Labor demands are high. Annual work hour totals, about 2,800 hours a year for adult men, 2,900 for adult women (*see Table 4*), are high in comparison to what we know about other Sahelian

Table 4. Annual Labor Hours Performed by WoDaaBe Men and Women at
Different Tasks

| | Mean person hours/year | | | | | |
| | Men | | | Women | | |
	6-14 years	15-40 years	41-60 years	6-14 years	15-40 years	41-60 years
Livestock work	1,314	1,874	876	133	574	378
Food and domestic	224	298	489	792	2,040	1,582
Household maintenance and artisan	—	13	31	1	41	70
Marketing and camp movement	26	258	445	2	102	326
Misc. work and travel	7	300	481	31	124	397
Remainder	8	76	218	14	43	546
Total	1,579	2,819	2,550	973	2,924	3,299

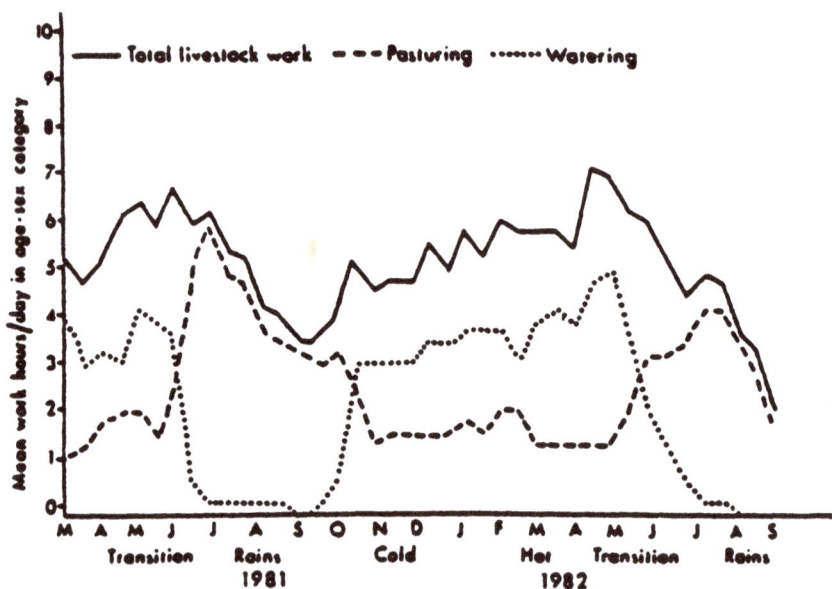

Figure 1. Seasonal distribution of work devoted to all livestock tasks by
WoDaaBe men aged 15 to 40 years.

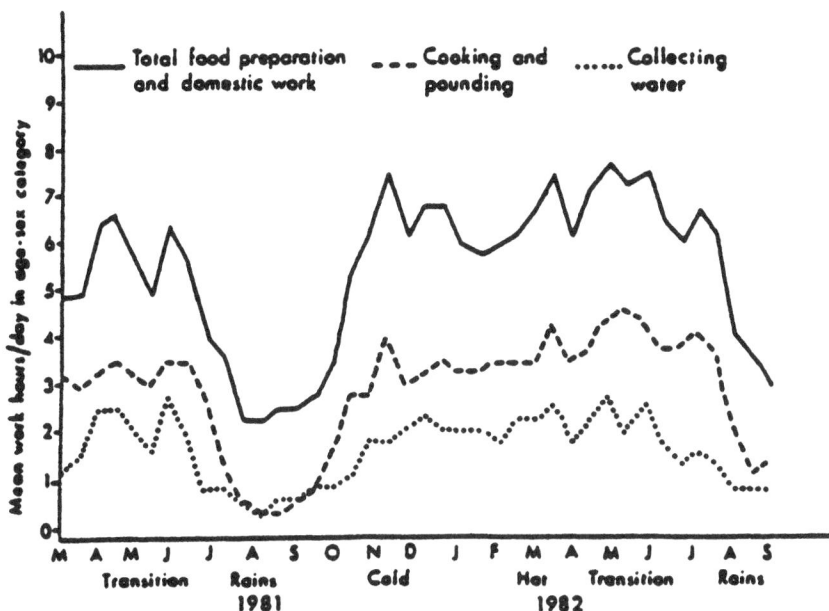

Figure 2.   Seasonal distribution of domestic labor by WoDaaBe women aged 15–40 years.

pastoral and farming economics. These high labor demands can be explained in several ways. There is a clear sexual division of labor (*see Figures 1 and 2*). Although it is not rigid and men and women can help with each other's tasks, the different spheres are well separated. Different tasks must be carried out by different people independently (White, 1984a:408-430 and 484-488). The herd needs continuous supervision, usually by men, while women are doing other tasks: milking, fetching water, preparing meals, caring for children. While the cows are being pastured by one herder, the calves must be tended closer to camp by someone else. Goats are also a separate flock that requires a herder. Production units, consisting of a nuclear or extended family, are small, spatially scattered, and highly mobile, facilitating flexibility in an unpredictable environment. This makes labor cooperation between units difficult, however. Milking, in particular, cannot be done by a woman from another household with whom the cows are not familiar. Even within the household, there is little labor cooperation between co-wives, who milk their own allotted animals and prepare separate daily meals. A co-wife

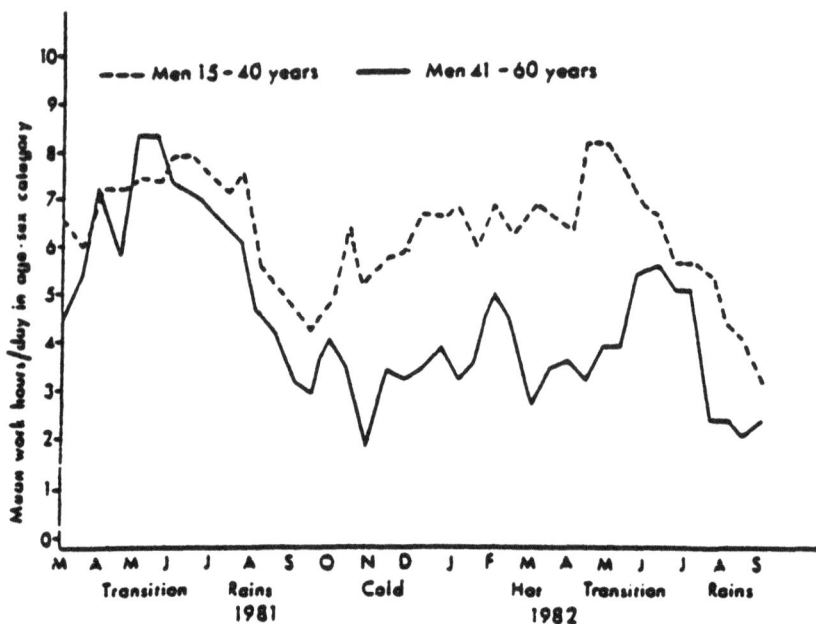

Figure 3.   Seasonal distribution of time spent by adult WoDaaBe men on all productive activities.

is, instead, an economic competitor. She reduces the milk supplies over which each wife has control.

Labor requirements are high throughout the year. In all seasons the herd must be milked and supervised at pasture every day and watered regularly. Although labor hours are lower for both men and women in the rainy season (*see Figures 3 and 4*), there is no slack period, as there is in agriculture, when the herd can be left for "off-farm" wage labor to supplement household incomes. In fact, it is the dry season rather than the rainy season, as is the case for farmers, that is the period of food shortage, high labor demands, and high consumption requirements (White, 1986). Weight loss is high at this time (5.3 percent of body weight for men and 4.6 percent for women). Although women lose less weight in the dry season than men, they recuperate less rapidly during the rainy season (*see Figure 5*) (Loutan and Lamotte, 1984:946). Children make an important labor contribution from an early age (*see Figure 6*) because so many hands are needed, making schooling or training outside the pastoral economy problematic.

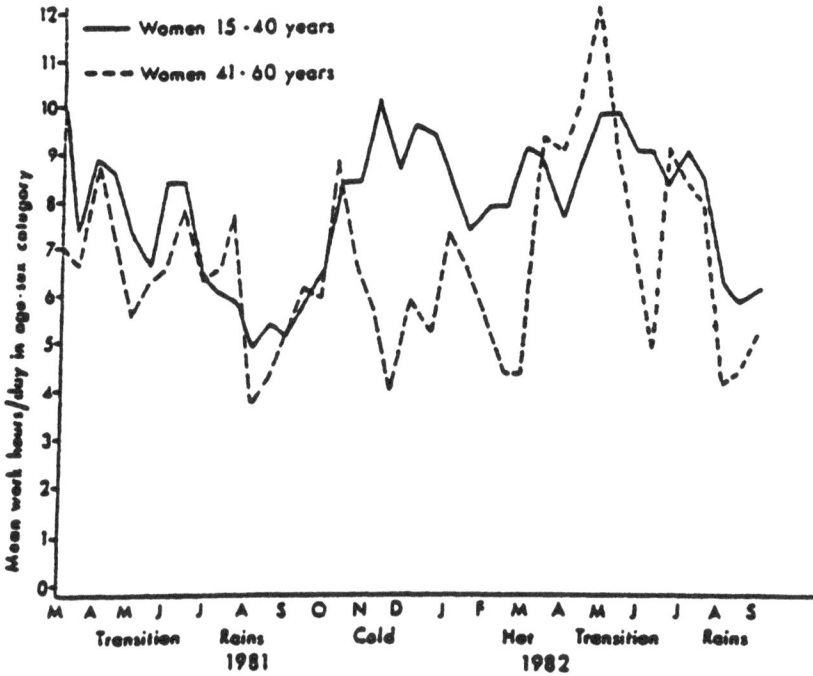

Figure 4.   Seasonal distribution of time spent by adult WoDaaBe women on all productive activities.

The organization of labor is such that even if wage labor were available to men, it is difficult for them to leave the household herd, in contrast to the situation Vaughan found for farmers in Southern Malawi. There, because of male absences for wage labor, women were forced to intensify work on food production to prevent shortages. During the 1949 famine it was men who had links with the formal wage economy that gave them economic entitlements to food, often not shared with their wives (Vaughan, 1987:127-132).

The labor demands of pastoralism tie both men and women to the herd. This is particularly the case for the WoDaaBe, where mobility is high and social relations relatively unstratified. At times of difficulty Twareg herders can often rely upon help from a relative who is a merchant or a civil servant. The WoDaaBe's lack of economic diversity, which therefore entails low entitlements at times of drought, has made the WoDaaBe economy vulnerable to changing conditions.

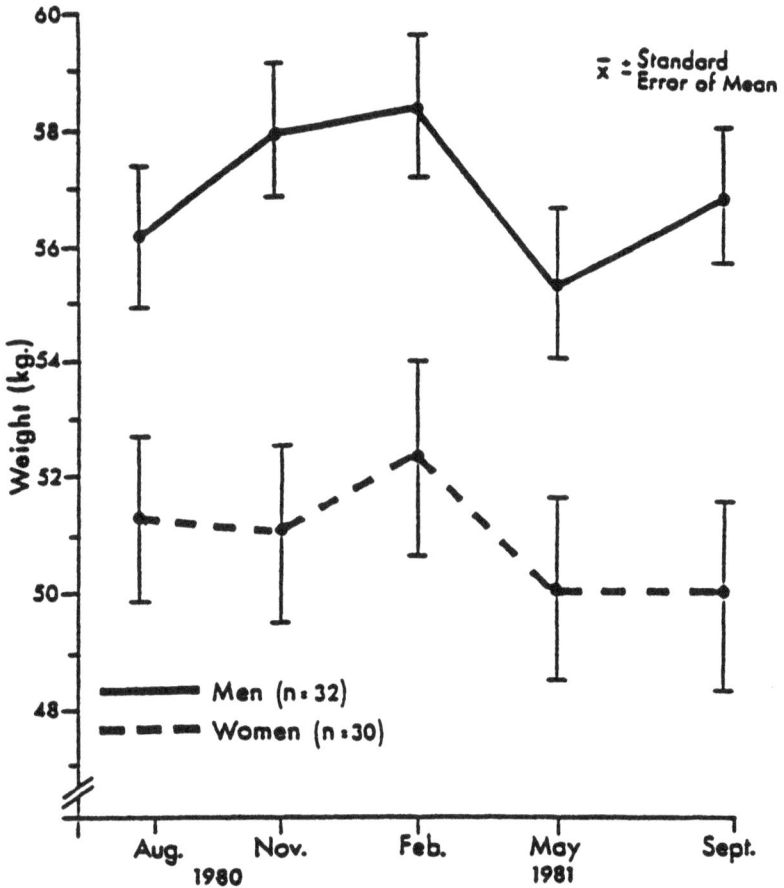

Figure 5.   Seasonal changes in the mean weight of adult WoDaaBe men and women.

But lack of diversification has also given the WoDaaBe a strength. Partly because they have specialized and intensified production in the face of difficult conditions, their social organization has not been affected in the ways identified for many other African societies. Cash crop production, regular wage labor, and more sustained contact with other communities and urban areas have engendered processes of individualization, changed consumption patterns, and increased differentiation, processes that are not as marked for the WoDaaBe. Most recent descriptions of pastoral societies mention the breakdown of mutual support networks and communal responsibility.[20]

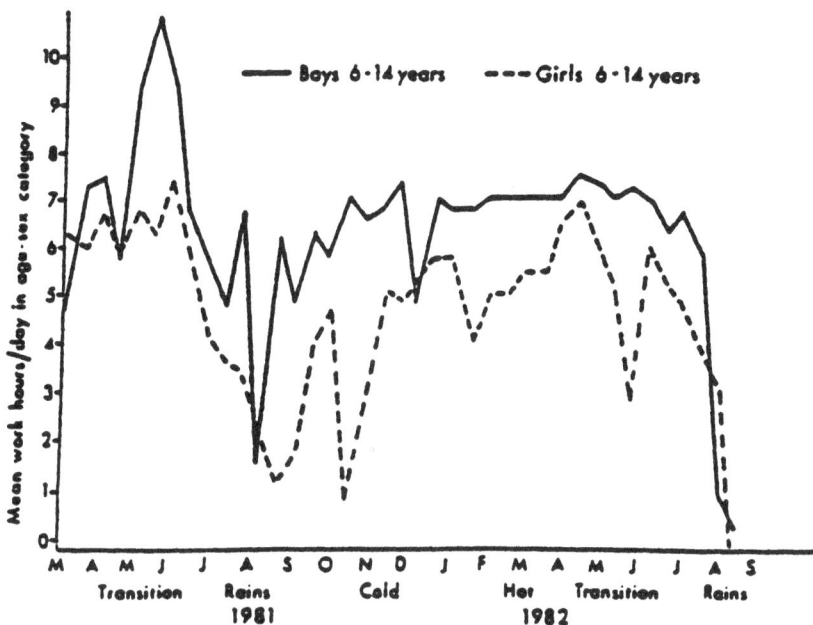

Figure 6.   Seasonal distribution of time spent by WoDaaBe children on all productive tasks.

When the WoDaaBe have the necessary material basis (i.e., adequate herds and access to land) they put into practice a large range of strategies that reduce risk, increase adaptability, and tend to keep all members of the community within pastoralism.[21]

POLICY IMPLICATIONS

The key role of policy in creating or deflecting famine is now well recognized. It is emphasized by striking situations like the export of cash crops from Sahelian countries during the 1968-1974 famine (Glantz, 1987:309) and the fact that food production was actually adequate to prevent starvation in all Sahelian countries at this time (Sen, 1981:118). Pastoralists are in a particularly bad position to make demands on their governments, however, especially groups like the WoDaaBe, none of whom is educated or in the civil service.

Niger, however, can no longer afford the luxury of ignoring the economic role of pastoralism in the national economy. Uranium provided a significant rise in foreign export earnings in the 1970s, but world prices subsequently dropped and uranium from land-locked Niger is no longer competitive. There are no other resources. Only Lesotho and Mauritania had a lower index of food production per capita than Niger for the period 1983-85 (Barbier, 1989:143). USAID and World Bank policy makers have "given up" on the Sahel and are shifting attention to higher rainfall areas (Derman, 1984:92-94).[22] This mirrors the French colonial policy of investing in the more productive coastal countries, creating a structurally dependent hinterland with a stagnant economy (Higgot, 1980).

It is important to move beyond the stereotypes of nomads as wandering romantics accumulating animals for ritual and prestige while destroying the environment. They are food producers both for themselves and others. They sell animals regularly to obtain what they do not produce, and livestock makes an important contribution to badly needed foreign export earnings. There are no other economically and ecologically viable uses for the pastoral zone, which is a natural resource that is wasted if not used by mobile livestock raising. The national economy cannot make use of the labor of destitute herders. There are no other economic alternatives for nomads within or outside the pastoral zone. If they cannot support themselves by raising livestock, they become dependent on the government, which can ill-afford to provide food aid to 17 percent of its population.

The first step is to look very carefully at what pastoralists actually do, and eliminate inappropriate, but nonetheless costly, policies and projects. Incentives and training to convince nomads to destock and increase their market integration for example are useless. Pastoralists sell animals and buy cereals without the advice of experts. They are actually selling so many animals that the reproductive core of their herds is jeopardized. Furthermore, a large proportion of animals using the resources of the pastoral zone do not even belong to nomads who therefore can not sell them. Desperate efforts to promote agriculture and gardening in areas that are utterly unsuited are not only a waste of money but are also ecologically destructive. The commonly advocated range management interventions, designed to teach nomads how to use their resources, can also be damaging (Homewood and Rogers, 1987:119).

What is needed are better policies rather than new technologies. "Appropriate policies can mobilise self-reliant strategies and minimise the cost of, and necessity for interventions" (Mortimore, 1989:15). It is important not to idealize the pre-capitalist past and the "capacity of subsistence economies to withstand natural disaster" (Vaughan, 1987:10). But rather than putting scare resources into convincing herders to do things that they are already doing, or training them to do things they should not be doing given ecological and economic constraints, it makes sense to identify the adaptive strategies they use that should be supported rather than undermined. For example, anything that

restricts the mobility of pastoralists in arid areas should be carefully scruti-
nized. The WoDaaBe's system of traditional loans provides a good basis for
herd reconstitution schemes. Their own herd management strategies, which
are implemented when they have an adequate number of household animals,
are extremely well adapted to ecological conditions.[23] Existing cooperative
structures should be made use of as a basis for any interventions.[24]

Many policies mentioned with respect to famine in agricultural societies
are important for pastoral communities. They should be adjusted to the specifics of pastoral production. For example, asset protection and reconstitution are of critical importance to herders. Price supports for livestock can
help prevent the collapse of purchasing power and limit the need to sell animals. Secure access to reasonably priced cereals, particularly in the dry season, can also reduce decapitalization. At times of large-scale loss, herd
reconstitution is essential. Female animals have the unusual advantage of being simultaneously a means of production for the long-term (by giving birth
to more animals) and immediate suppliers of food (milk) for hungry families.
Security of access to land is also fundamental to reduce vulnerability in general and particularly at times of drought. This last point raises thorny and
politically difficult issues with respect to the conflicting demands and needs
of herders and farmers, yet it is important to recognize the futility of farmers
expanding into marginal arid zones.

Many of these policies overlap with those necessary to strengthen the livestock sector in normal times, which should be a priority to reduce vulnerability. A viable pastoral economy has great resilience to withstand difficult
conditions. But this depends more on political will than on rainfall levels.

NOTES

1. Greatful thanks to Michael Horowitz, Michael Mortimore, Tom Painter, and François
   Piguet for very useful comments, not all of which I have been able to incorporate, on an
   earlier draft. All errors remain mine.
2. Some East African pastoralists use blood as well. Some are less dependent on cereals than
   in West Africa.
3. Agro-pastoralists combine cultivation with herding. They are less dependent on sale or
   exchange for obtaining cereals, but their yields are usually lower than those of agricul-
   turalists.
4. See White (1986).
5. I will discuss market integration in later sections. See Homewood and Rodgers (1987) on
   overgrazing, Mortimore (1989) on desertification, and Peters (1985) on overstocking and
   the "tragedy of the commons" debate. See also Sandford (1983) and Horowitz (1979) on
   these issues.
6. See also Snow and Morris (1984:53) for an example of famine being used for political
   purposes (to sedentarize nomads).

7.   See Sen (1981:120-122 and 126-127); Somerville (1986:27-32); Sheets and Morris (1974:46-50, 53-54, and 133-134).
8.   In this chapter I will be speaking of drought-induced famine, although there are many other causes and although droughts do not necessarily create famines. See Snow and Morris (1984:52) for an example of policy-induced famine.
9.   I did fieldwork from 1979 to 1983 and for another year in 1986. During the first period I worked on the Niger Range and Livestock Project, financed by USAID, and, among other things, collected basic production data (household budgets and labor use). In 1986 I collected data on the impact of the 1984 drought on the families previously studied.
10. See White (1984a:329-430) for sample description, methodology, and full research findings.
11. See Raikes (1986) and Vaughan (1987:18).
12. See Bourgeot (1987:110-111 and 115) and Ensminger (1987:29, 42, and 47).
13. Unlike many communities, the WoDaaBe's consumption patterns are little changed. Although items are more often purchased rather than made or obtained through barter, material goods in WoDaaBe camps in the 1980s were not very different from Dupire's descriptions (apart from some plastic sheets, a few flashlights, and occasional radios).
14. The farmers are condemned to a marginal existence, with yields to be expected only every few years. See Glantz (1987:306-308) on the ecological damage caused by cultivation in arid zones.
15. Sen (1981:1-8) describes entitlements as overall access to food, either through the market (using cash from wages or sales of produce or assets) or through non-market circuits (gifts, exchange, redistribution).
16. Mainly dum palm root (*Hyphaena thebaica*).
17. They get intermittent work as watchmen or sell magical charms. Women braid hair.
18. These mechanisms (*haBBanae, jokereeji*, and migrant labor) and their repercussions are described in more detail in White (1984a:462-529).
19. See Baier (1980) for an historical analysis of the Twareg economy and a description of their alternative system of production during droughts. See also Gartrell (1988:214) for an east African (Karamoja) example of diversified subsistence strategies and dispersal of social ties and trade links between ethnic groups and ecological zones.
20. See papers presented to the workshop on Changing Rights in Property and Pastoral Development, University of Manchester, 23-25 April 1987, *Ethnos* (1987), and Baxter and Hogg, eds. (1990).
21. See Bradburd (1989) for a good discussion of "sloughing off" versus redistribution within pastoral societies.
22. The World Bank now has this under review (Mortimore, personal communication). However these constant shifts in policy underline the importance of Niger's making the most of its own resources.
23. More fully developed in White (1990).
24. See Gartrell (1988:216) for the dangers to indigenous coping systems of relying on state-mediated famine hedges.

REFERENCES

Baier, Stephen
     1980 An Economic History of Central Niger. Oxford: Clarendon Press.
Barbier, Edward B.
     1989 Economics, Natural-Resource Scarcity and Development: Conventional and Alternative Views. London: Earthscan Publications Ltd.

Baxter, P. T. W. with Richard Hogg, eds.
    1990   Manchester: Department of Social Anthropology and International Development Centre, University of Manchester.
Bourgeot, André
    1987   The Twareg Women of Ahaggar and the Creation of Value. In Ethnos 52(1-2):103-118. Stockholm: The Ethnographical Museum of Sweden.
Bradburd, Daniel
    1989   Producing their Fates: why poor Basseri settled but poor Komachi and Yomut did not. American Ethnologist 16(3):502-517.
Dahl, Gudrun
    1987   The Realm of Pastoral Women: an Introduction. In Ethnos 52(1-2):5-7. Stockholm: The Ethnographical Museum of Sweden.
Derman, William
    1984   USAID in the Sahel: Development and Poverty. In Jonathan Baker (ed.), The Politics of Agriculture in Tropical Africa, pp. 77-97. London: Sage Publications Ltd.
Dupire, Marguerite
    1962   Peuls Nomades: Etude Descriptive des WoDaaBe du Sahel Nigérien. Paris: Institut d'Ethnologie.
    1971   The Position of Women in a Pastoral Society. In Denise Paulme (ed.), Women of Tropical Africa, pp. 47-92. Berkeley: University of California Press.
Ensminger, Jean
    1987   Economic and Political Differentiation among Galole Orma Women. In Ethnos 52(1-2):28-49. Stockholm: The Ethnographical Museum of Sweden.
Ethnos
    1987   52(1-2) Special Issue: Women in Pastoral Production. Stockholm: The Ethnographical Museum of Sweden.
Gartrell, Beverly
    1988   Prelude to disaster: the case of Karamoja. In Douglas Johnson and David Anderson (eds.), The Ecology of Survival: Case Studies from Northeast African History, pp. 193-217. London: Lester Crook Academic Publishing.
Glantz, Michael H.
    1987   Drought and Economic Development in sub-Saharan Africa. In Donald A. Wilhite and William E. Easterling (eds.), Planning for Drought: Toward a Reduction of Societal Vulnerability, pp. 297-316. Boulder: Westview Press.
Harris, Olivia and Kate Young
    1984   Engendered Structures: Some Problems in the Analysis of Reproduction. In Joel S. Kahn and Josep R. Llobera (eds.), The Anthropology of Pre-Capitalist Societies, pp. 109-147. London: Macmillan.
Higgot, Richard
    1980   Structural Dependence and Deocolonisation in a West African Land-Locked State: Niger. Review of African Political Economy 17:43-58.

Homewood, Katherine and W. A. Rodgers
  1987 Pastoralism, conservation and the overgrazing controversy. In David Anderson and Richard Grove (eds.), Conservation in Africa: People, Policies and Practice, pp. 111-128. Cambridge: Cambridge University Press.
Horowitz, Michael M.
  1979 The Sociology of Pastoralism and African Livestock Projects. Washington, D.C.: USAID.
Loutan, Louis and Jean-Marie Lamotte
  1984 Seasonal variations in nutrition among a group of nomadic pastoralists in Niger. Lancet i:945-947.
Mortimore, Michael
  1989 Five Faces of Famine: the autonomous sector in the famine process. Paper presented to the study group on Famine Research and Food Production Systems, Freiburg University (FRG), 10-14 November.
Peters, Pauline E.
  1985 Embedded Systems and Rooted Models: The Grazing Lands of Botswana and the "Commons" Debate. Cambridge: Harvard Institute for International Development.
Raikes, Philip
  1986 Flowing with milk and money: food production in Africa and the policies of the EEC. In Peter Lawrence (ed.), World Recession and the Food Crisis in Africa, pp. 160-176. London: James Currey.
Sandford, Stephen
  1983 Management of Pastoral Development in the Third World. Chichester: John Wiley and Sons.
Sen, Amartya
  1981 Poverty and Famines: An Essay on Entitlement and Deprivation. Oxford: Clarendon Press.
Sheets, Hal and Roger Morris
  1974 Disaster in the Desert. Washington, D.C.: Carnegie Endowment for International Peace.
Snow, Robert and Joseph Morris
  1984 Do Relief Efforts Beget Famine? Cultural Survival Quarterly 8(1):51-53.
Somerville, Carolyn M.
  1986 Drought and Aid in the Sahel: A Decade of Development Cooperation. Boulder: Westview Press.
Vaughan, Megan
  1987 The Story of an African Famine: Gender and Famine in Twentieth-Century Malawi. Cambridge: Cambridge University Press.
White, Cynthia
  1984a The WoDaaBe. In Jeremy Swift (ed.), Pastoral Production in Central Niger, pp. 292-430 and 462-529. Niamey: MDR/USAID.
  1984b Herd Reconstitution: the role of credit among WoDaaBe herders in central Niger. Pastoral Development Network paper 18d. London: Overseas Development Institute.
  1986 Food Shortages and Seasonality in WoDaaBe Communities in Niger. IDS Bulletin 17(3):19-26. Sussex: Institute of Development Studies.

1987 Changing Animal Ownership and Access to Land among the WoDaaBe (Fulani) of Central Niger. Paper presented to the workshop on Changing Rights in Property and Pastoral Development, University of Manchester, 23-25 April.
1990 Changing Animal Ownership and Access to Land among the WoDaaBe (Fulani) of Central Niger. In Property, Poverty and People: Changing Rights in Property and Problems of Pastoral Development, P. T. W. Baxter with Richard Hogg, eds., pp. 240-254. Manchester: Department of Social Anthropology and International Development Centre, University of Manchester.

CHAPTER 5

Western Assistance and the Ethiopian Famine; Implications for Humanitarian Assistance

Jason Clay

Since October 1984, when the full impact of the Ethiopian famine became evident to the West, more money has been raised for Ethiopia than for any other emergency humanitarian effort in history. The best evidence suggests that the Ethiopian famine, like many other famines, was mostly man made. The context in which Western assistance was given, the role that assistance played in maintaining and extending the famine, and, consequently, the problems that arose in attempts to deliver the assistance in an impartial manner all raise questions about the nature of truly "humanitarian" assistance. This is not a new issue, nor is it one that can be easily dismissed. Increasingly, states are using famine and humanitarian assistance as weapons. The existence of famine usually indicates that governments or elite groups are extracting too much food from the countryside and offering too little compensation to those producing it. Famine assistance, ironically, often gives power and credibility to those who perpetrated the famine.

The 1984-1985 Ethiopian famine was no exception. The research undertaken with the victims indicates that the most significant causes of famine in Ethiopia were government policies (Clay and Holcomb, 1986; Niggli, 1986; Clay, Steingraber, and Niggli 1988; Keleman 1985; REST 1986; Doble 1986). Farmers report that both agricultural and military policies implemented since the late 1970s made it impossible for them to produce and retain food for their families, let alone surpluses to sell. Inputs (improved seed, credit, fertilizer) were rarely available for private farmers, prices paid to farmers were low, and marketing was increasingly controlled by the state-run Agricultural Marketing Committee (AMC).

In Ethiopia, as elsewhere, famine and famine assistance are political. The failure of humanitarian agencies and donor governments to address this issue directly in Ethiopia resulted in a number of avoidable mistakes. In short, the help hurt. Most of the problems of delivering humanitarian assistance to Ethiopia result from the unwillingness of Western agencies and governments to insist on understanding the context in which the famine occurred and into which the assistance was delivered. Four general problem areas should be underscored. The donors were unwilling to insist that they be allowed independently to :

• determine the causes of the famine,
• assess the extent of the famine,
• monitor the implementation and impact of their programs, and
• evaluate the effectiveness of their programs in treating the root causes of the famine.

Two Ethiopian programs that the government claimed would eliminate famine and provide better services to the rural population now appear to be the leading causes of starvation in Ethiopia (Clay and Holcomb, 1986; *Africa Report* March-April 1986; Clay, 1987; Clay, Steingraber, and Niggli, 1988). Both programs—resettlement and villagization—move people from their homes into planned villages from which the government can monitor their movements and activities. Both programs give the government control over the residents' labor through the immediate or eventual establishment of communal production systems. What farmers plant, as well as what they produce, comes under the increasing control of the state. The overriding intent of these programs is to provide sufficient government-controlled food supplies to guarantee the needs of the military and urban residents—the groups most likely to revolt against the present government in the event of food shortages. Virtually every Western NGO working in Ethiopia was either actively or passively involved in one or both of these programs.

This essay first examines the famine created by the Ethiopian government and then how that government manipulated Western food assistance during the 1984-1985 famine. These brief discussions provide the context for describing and critiquing the role Western humanitarian agencies played in maintaining and spreading the famine. Although the humanitarian task confronting such agencies was enormous, they responded inadequately and, in many instances, indefensibly. Some agencies have acknowledged their mistakes and are currently restructuring their relief and development programs. The events described below have helped to shape the internal debate in such agencies. They may also encourage less reflective agencies, through the threat of public sanction, to begin similar discussions.

BACKGROUND TO THE FAMINE CRISIS

Perhaps the poorest country in the world, Ethiopia has nonetheless been a strategic ally of the West in general and of the US in particular. Located at a crucial geographical and political crossroads between Africa and the Middle East, and between North Africa and sub-Saharan Africa, Ethiopia is a key prize in the superpower struggle for the region. When the US refused to sell weapons to the Ethiopian government in the mid-1970s, Ethiopia turned to the USSR, ending its long-standing alliance with the West. Since that time US officials have sought to reestablish this important alliance.

In late 1984, independent political observers and journalists speculated that the famine would enable the West, and particularly the US, to win Ethiopia back; humanitarian assistance, they suggested, might succeed where diplomacy had failed.[1] This was not to be. Instead, Ethiopia accepted food from the West *and* weapons from the USSR and its allies. In fact, Mengistu Haile Mariam, Ethiopia's head of state, blamed the severity of the famine on the West's failure to respond to the crisis earlier.

Unbeknownst to many Western observers, the US National Security Council (NSC) had known of the impending famine since the early 1980s. At a 1982 meeting on the famine, in fact, the NSC reportedly decided to withhold food from Ethiopia even though it was well known that the country was already suffering serious food shortages. According to one council member who attended the meeting, the consensus of those present was to let the famine occur in the hopes of either destabilizing the Mengistu regime or, at the very least, forcing it to make economic reforms more amenable to the US government (Clay 1989:232).

Although the US eventually allowed some food to be distributed in Ethiopia through US-based agencies in the early 1980s, it did not respond promptly and rarely gave the full quantities of grain requested. The deterioration of food availability in Ethiopia continued through 1984. Fred Cuny, one of the architects of Ethiopia's famine early warning system, suggests that most relief assistance arrived after the death rate from the 1984–1985 famine had started to decline. Yet the Dergue, Ethiopia's ruling military junta, ignored the famine throughout the summer of 1984, banning it from their own media and barring foreign television and film crews from famine-affected areas until after the tenth-anniversary celebrations of the Ethiopian revolution, held in early September 1984.

Regardless of one's views on the US government's decision to ignore the gravity of food shortages in Ethiopia, the US did not create the food shortages. However, it is precisely this question—What caused the shortages?—that is at the heart of the debate concerning the delivery of appropriate humanitarian assistance. At this late date, it is quite difficult to assess accurately the reasons for starvation. Yet this was the fundamental question of the day, a question not asked by Western assistance agencies. Ethiopian officials *claimed* that drought was the main cause of the famine and that insects and warfare also played a role.[2] Westerners—diplomats, relief officials, and journalists—accepted these explanations, *assuming* that they were correct. Unfortunately, they did not see the need for an in-depth examination into the causes of the famine. In this respect, they could not legitimately claim that their help did not serve to reinforce the causes.

As the famine persisted, Ethiopian officials were either embarrassed or unconcerned by it. They certainly were not prepared to make policy changes that would alleviate it. Their priorities lay elsewhere. Famine provided the opportunity—a smokescreen of chaos—to intensify resettlement and villagization, programs intended eventually to relocate most farmers in Ethiopia so that the government could control better the movements *and* production of the country's food producers. Mengistu, for example, did not visit relief camps in Wollo or Tigray, the areas hardest hit by famine, until December 1984. However, in October, just after publicly acknowledging the famine, he toured western and southwestern administrative regions in order to identify resettlement sites.

Another incident places Ethiopia's response to the famine in the proper context. During the fall of 1984, at a meeting with Western diplomats, Ethiopia's foreign minister, Goshu Wolde, insisted that Ethiopia would not allow the West to deliver food to famine victims not living in government-held areas. During the heated discussion, Wolde declared that "food is an element in our strategy" against the insurgents (KORN 1986:5). Resettlement and villagization, too, were part of the government's strategy against the insurgents.

After it became apparent that food would not realign the Ethiopian regime, the US looked for alternative groups that, through humanitarian assistance, could be supported in their struggle against the government. Although the Ethiopian People's Democratic Alliance (EPDA) had received $500,000 worth of "general" assistance per year from the US Central Intelligence Agency since 1981,[3] it was not seen as terribly effective. The Reagan Administration then looked to the Tigrayan People's Liberation Front (TPLF) as a more acceptable alternative. Vice-President Bush and M. Peter Macpherson, head of the US Agency for International Development (AID), visited Sudan to meet with the TPLF and REST (Relief Society of Tigray) in early 1985. In April 1985, however, the TPLF unveiled its Marxist programs, at which point the US withdrew much of its pledged support.

From mid-1985 to the present, the US appears to have taken a "wait and see" attitude regarding its influence on internal policy in Ethiopia. After all, US citizens had demanded that their government send immediate and massive assistance to Ethiopian famine victims, which was accomplished through US-based agencies, primarily Catholic Relief Services (CRS) and World Vision. As a result of the famine, US-based agencies and Americans in general, although still restricted, had more and freer access to rural areas in Ethiopia than at any time since the 1974 revolution.

Ethiopian officials, however, suspected Western relief agencies—particularly those from the US—of spying for their governments. Consequently Ethiopia placed strict conditions on the relief agencies' movements, their presence in rural areas and, once on site, their movement into the surrounding countryside. In their haste to help, humanitarian agencies accepted restrictions that adversely affected their ability to move freely, to assess local conditions and to monitor their programs—in short, to deliver impartial assistance (Clay, 1984, 1987, 1989; Korn, 1986). In some cases, in their efforts to appease local officials, agency personnel further curtailed their activities and movements and, gradually, even their discussions with the media and other outsiders.

While the relationship between US-based agencies working in Ethiopia and US political interests in the area is little known, the relationship does not appear to be essential to an understanding of the politicization of humanitarian assistance during the famine. Although the US certainly withheld assistance for some time in the early 1980s, only three conditions appear to have been attached to assistance once the food was given to US-based agencies to distribute, in an attempt to reduce any manipulation of aid by the Ethiopian government. These conditions are notable because similar stipulations were not placed on the distribution of the food given by the European Economic Commission (EEC). First, the US attempted (and failed) to strike an agreement with Ethiopia that would allow US food to be distributed to famine victims regardless of whether they lived in government-controlled areas (Korn, 1986:5). Second, the US stipulated that none of its assistance could be used to support resettlement. And third—a related point—the US is required by law to ensure that relief assistance to Ethiopia is not used for development.

Ethiopia's contribution to famine relief in the north consisted only of the salaries of Ethiopia's Relief and Rehabilitation Commission (RRC) officials detailed to the area and some equipment, much of which the West or international organizations had donated (Korn 1986:6). What developed, then, was a division of labor: the West provided famine relief in the north, thereby un-wittingly freeing all Ethiopia's resources for the resettlement program.

There were, of course, problems with this arrangement. Trucks, always in short supply in Ethiopia, were allocated to resettlement. Thus, although the West had donated many trucks to transport grain, after January 1985 the ports were never clear of food supplies. In one incident alone, 13,000 tons of grain left standing were destroyed in a rainstorm (Korn, 1986:6). Médecins sans Frontières, a French relief agency (MSF), estimates that if in the first year of the famine the trucks used to move people had been used as in-tended—to move donated food—some 200,000 to 300,000 tons of food, about half the total required, could have been transported north for famine victims (Malhurst, 1985:45; Roni Brauman, personal communication; *New York Times*, 21 January 1985; *Washington Post*, 2 May 1985). The artificial scarcity of trucks also forced Western governments to use air transport, not only to supply remote regions but also Makelle, the capital of Tigray, from October 1984 until mid-summer 1985 (Korn, 1986:6).

The Ethiopian government's politization of humanitarian assistance stems primarily from the relationship of its policies to the Western agencies' pro-grams. Some 90 to 95 percent of all Western assistance—including virtually all US government assistance—intended for Ethiopian famine victims went through government-held areas, even though most victims lived outside the government's control. It was this assistance that the Ethiopian government politicized.

The massive assistance effort in response to the Ethiopian famine came virtually entirely from the West (Korn, 1986:5).[4] Without doubt it saved many lives, although perhaps only a fraction of the number claimed by West-ern agencies and governments. For example, in early 1985, 7 million people were estimated to be at risk. Some relief, but not full rations, was reaching 2.5 to 3 million people. Later, revised World Food Program (WFP) estimates generously pushed the estimate of food recipients to 3.5 and subsequently to 4 million people.[5]

Less well known or perhaps even understood by the agencies, but equally as important, is the fact that the Ethiopian government has used humanitarian assistance to reinforce the conditions that led to the famine (Clay and Hol-comb, 1986; Clay, Steingraber, and Niggli, 1988; Niggli, 1986; Clay, 1985, 1986a, 1986b, 1988). The government even used the assistance to extend the famine into formerly self-sufficient regions. Conservative calculations indi-cate that Western assistance contributed directly to conditions that led to the deaths of 250,000 to 300,000 people between 1984 and 1987.[6] In addition, there is every indication that the conditions now being created throughout the countryside as a result of the forced movement of people will add to the death toll for decades to come.

THE WEST'S RESPONSE TO THE FAMINE

The West's response to the Ethiopian famine was truly massive. The tremendous effort on the part of agencies, journalists, civil servants, and entertainers should not be belittled. The effort was also remarkable both for its technical logistics and for the well-orchestrated cooperation between nongovern-mental organizations (NGOs), governments, and multilateral organizations. That the world's public wanted agencies and governments to rush assistance to Ethiopia as quickly as possible was commendable, and that the agencies and governments could mount an effort of such massive scope so quickly with relatively few problems was remarkable. To a large extent such action was possible because agencies and governments put politics aside—at one level, at least. US AID director MacPherson said at the time, "A starving child knows no politics." Such attitudes carried the day, sweeping all doubts aside.

By late 1984, however, doubts about the causes of the famine as well as the Ethiopian government's so-called eradication programs (e.g., resettlement and villagization) had already begun to surface. Considerable documentation and specific inquiries into the causes of famine were made public.[7] The information called into question the Ethiopian government's "natural causes" explanation for the famine. For the most part, however, agencies working in government-held areas either echoed the government's assertions (e.g., famine is caused by drought and prolonged soil degradation) or were silent, allowing them to go unchallenged. Most agency personnel believed that an open debate on the causes of the famine would lead to donor apathy and reduced contributions.

Many agency personnel were anything but passive in their attempts to limit the debate concerning the famine's causes. In public forums they tried to discredit information that did not support the official explanation of the famine. At one such meeting in the spring of 1986, sponsored by the Refugee Studies Program at Oxford University, the World Vision-UK representative insisted that research on the causes of the famine, although perhaps academically interesting, should not be undertaken. What might be an "ego booster" for the researchers would hurt Ethiopians, the representative claimed, adding that it was "immoral" to publish the findings.

At the same meeting, a representative of Oxfam-UK publicly contradicted a finding that mosques were banned in those new villages being created in eastern Ethiopia in 1985 and 1986 in which Western agencies (such as Oxfam) worked. After the audience left, the same person admitted that of course the new villages he had visited were "show" villages, saying that he did not doubt that religious persecution occurred during villagization, particularly in villages off the main roads. (Most villages are off the main roads.) In fact, Western agencies are present in only a few hundred of more than 10,000 new villages. They were present in even fewer of the more than 30,000 traditional villages that have been destroyed since early 1985.

At a meeting of Canadian NGOs in September 1986, the head of the Irish agency Concern's operations in Ethiopia stated categorically that those who undertook research and whose findings discredited resettlement were "dangerous." The point, then, is that from 1984 through 1986 Western agencies preferred to denounce researchers and their findings rather than confront the difficult issues that the research raised.

Unfortunately, such intimidation by agencies silenced some critics directly, and others indirectly, by discrediting them or their findings. Sadly, the net effect of these efforts by representatives of many NGOs was to limit the debate on the Ethiopian famine precisely when it should have been expanded. An open debate could have improved the agencies' understanding and response to the famine.

Even by 1987 little had changed in this regard. On 11 and 12 December 1986, the Liaison Committee of Development NGOs to the European Communities (EC) met to discuss "The Situation and Possibilities for Aid in Ethiopia." The points of discussion for the agenda on which the organizer, Dr. Hartmut Bauer, thought all NGOs could agree included the following:

(1)   The Ethiopian Government is as before interested in cooperating with Western Governments and donor agencies. It urgently needs their help.

(2)   The NGOs are granted surprisingly wide fields of activities and room for movement.

(3)   The resettlement and villagization programs have been carried out with great determination using brutal methods. After a "phase of consolidation" it is expected that both programs are going to be continued. Corresponding amounts of funds are included in next year's budget.

(4)   During the first drought period the farmers moved southwards. The government used this "advantage of the hour" to start resettlement programs which exceeded by far the sociological necessities.

(5)   It is true that the Ethiopians and their allies primarily took care of the transport of the people but these actions would not have been possible without the food aid from the Western countries.

In the same memo, anticipated future developments were outlined as follows:

(1)   The Ethiopian Government will continue carrying out both the resettlement and villagization programs.

(2)   The Ethiopian Government is relying upon the Western donor agencies to take over part of the activities, e.g., supplying food for resettled people.

(3). Those donor agencies who want to continue engaging themselves for the people in Ethiopia might find that they will also support the activities of the Government—directly or indirectly—that in the long run will cause devastating consequences. The donor agencies will face the situation that—in spite of their good will—they will not succeed in realizing the human aims they stand for.

Considering the difficult situation I am asking myself whether or not the NGOs can come to a mutual understanding [as to] how to realize their aims and to convince the Ethiopian Government of developmental and humanitarian issues. Help can only be given by the NGOs if it is guaranteed that basic principles of aid are observed such as participation of the concerned, voluntariness, sufficient preparation of the activities, adequate scientific investigations, etc. It is obvious that each NGO on its own cannot observe all these points.

In my view, it is the Liaison Committee which is just the right place for such consultations because . . . [of its] connection to the commission of the EC it can be decided according to which principles support may be given to Ethiopia in accordance with the Lome III Agreement.

I believe that we need the support of the European Governments for the sake of achieving our humanitarian aims (Letter from Dr. Hartmut Bauer dated 1 December 1986).

Thus, according to the memo, political clout is needed to deliver the type of assistance in Ethiopia that European agencies could find acceptable.

Not much headway was made at the December meeting. Instead, the group decided to set up an ad hoc committee to discuss possible strategies for delivering humanitarian assistance in Ethiopia. The ad hoc group held its first meeting on 28 January 1987. The points identified in the cited letter were intended to provide the agenda for the meeting.

In the subsequent meeting, however, the mood, as one of the participants reported, quickly shifted from an open discussion of Ethiopia's policies and how the agencies could avoid reinforcing them through their assistance to expressions of grave concern about the disaster that would confront each NGO if the media were to report the link between Western assistance and agricultural collectivization policies in Ethiopia. The representatives declared that they would have to take a different tack immediately if the media expressed interest in the topic. All were concerned as to the best way to conceal their real role in Ethiopia in order to continue their engagement in the country. They did not even discuss the strategies or the leverage that the NGOs and their governments might use to influence Ethiopia's policies.

Although some European agencies are now prepared to acknowledge— privately, at least—the disastrous consequences, both realized and pending, of Ethiopia's policies as well as their own roles in implementing them, by and large they still do not recognize the need for examining the causes of the famine. Yet clues as to the government's hand in the famine had been evident from the beginning.

By 1985, the research presented by Cultural Survival (Clay and Holcomb, 1985; Clay, 1985a, 1985b), as well as oblique reports in the media, should have given the agencies pause; it did not. In fact, without undertaking their own research, agencies vehemently denied reports implicating government policies as the underlying cause of the famine, even though the reports came from the victims themselves.

Instead, during the fall of 1985 and continuing through the summer of 1986, Western humanitarian agencies attempted to fan the flames of compassion by touting the Ethiopian famine as a continuing natural disaster in both the press and their public appeals. By this point, the public was understandably skeptical.[8] Even in the fall of 1984, during the height of the publicity surrounding the famine, telephone interviews with supervisors of the "1-800" telephone fundraising operators indicated that one-fifth to one-third of all callers to six of the largest US-based relief agencies inquired as to how the agencies proposed to avoid the politics of the famine. By the time the second round of fundraising took place, extensive media coverage and the limited research undertaken on the causes of the famine led many potential donors in the West to realize that, at best, the agencies were not telling the whole story. At worst, the agencies were ignorant of what was happening in Ethiopia and therefore were not qualified to receive contributions.

The public skepticism resulted, at least in part, from the literature published and distributed by most agencies. Their so-called public information and education packets were little more than self-serving fundraising mailings. This issue is important. Most agencies claimed to have "public education" programs, but a careful reading of their material on Ethiopia does not reveal an independent, careful assessment of the famine. Rather, it consists of fundraising appeals that repeat the standard, assumed causes of the famine and use descriptions of the agencies' existing programs to raise money for future work. In short, the content of the materials was shaped by existing public awareness and little else.

The lack of confidence in the agencies' portrayal of the famine, and not mere donor apathy, is presently at the heart of the difficulty in raising funds for famine victims, not only in Ethiopia but in other parts of Africa as well. As a result of the problems arising from the West's response to Ethiopia— and following on the heels of similar problems encountered in Kampuchea— humanitarian agencies' abilities to claim apolitical postures, much less deliver apolitical assistance, have been seriously impaired.

What led to this lack of confidence in humanitarian agencies? Apparently, their unwillingness to find out what caused the famine, or, if they were quietly to investigate the causes, their unwillingness to release that information publicly in their own publications or through the media.

FROM RELIEF TO DEVELOPMENT

A separate but related problem arises when humanitarian agencies shift their focus from relief to development or when they see relief as a development tool. Increasingly, NGOs throughout the world, using both public and private funds, are "doing" development. The use of NGOs for development and community-based, grassroots work in the US began in the 1960s and intensified in the 1970s due to hiring ceilings in government. Few relief agencies and not all nonprofit development agencies have sufficient expertise or training to undertake successful development work. Fewer still have even the admittedly lax internal guidelines and regulations (for project review, social and environmental impact assessments, cost-benefit analyses, monitoring, or follow-up evaluations) that exist in such agencies as US AID or the World Bank.

Lutheran World Relief (LWR), considered by some to be one of the more sensitive relief/development organizations, by its own admission does not fund research.[8] But how can such an agency possibly believe that it can solve problems if it doesn't first assess their causes? The LWR is not alone in this regard; most relief agencies apparently believe that research is expensive and time consuming. It need not be either.

Cultural Survival's research on the causes of the Ethiopian famine is the largest and most systematic, duplicative piece of research undertaken on the topic.[10] The research cost less than $15,000, a small amount compared to the more than $1.5 billion the West spent on famine assistance in Ethiopia from 1984-1986. Although it took four months to raise the money (only one agency contributed—the rest was in public donations), the research took only two months to complete. Since most agencies stressed the need to attack the "root causes" of the famine, their reluctance to undertake or fund any kind of research on the causes of the famine is puzzling.

For Western agencies, both private and public, research on the impact of their assistance during the famine was limited to monitoring the flow of grain form its point of origin to the point at which it left their hands—i.e., tracing the path of Kansas wheat through its long journey into the hands of an Ethiopian famine victim.[11] This system does not constitute adequate monitoring because the *context* of the grain's journey must be understood. The Ethiopian government used food as bait to trap people into taking part in "voluntary" programs. When governments or agencies willingly or unwittingly collaborate in such programs, they must assume responsibility for the resulting deaths.

Put another way, good intentions are not an appropriate foundation for good programs. Agencies' attempts to ignore the context of the famine by burying their heads in the sand and claiming political neutrality cannot be accepted. An agency's only hope for remaining neutral is to research its programs thoroughly; to ignore politics is in itself a political act. To use a sports analogy, agencies involved in famine aid must serve as referees, neutral agents who are thoroughly educated in the rules of the game and are watching the actions of all participants at all times.

Naturally, however, each NGO is political, and therefore not impartial. Each has its own agenda, albeit hidden, its own ideological leanings, and its own ideas on appropriate relief and development activities. Unfortunately, few agencies are above board about these positions, apparently for two reasons: first, it is rare that the agencies' own positions have been clearly outlined, and second, each agency fears a drop in its fundraising constituency due to such a public disclosure and debate. Some of the smaller agencies experience additional problems: their programs can be traced to the agendas of specific individuals who do not even discuss their rationale for programs, much less their overall agenda, with other members of the staff.

This is not to suggest that assistance should have been withheld from famine victims until even superficial or cursory assessments of the problems were undertaken. Rather, agencies should have negotiated with the government so that as they began to provide relief assistance, they could also have begun to understand the nature and the scope of the problem as well as its overall context. Even if such conditions could have been negotiated with the Ethiopian government, each agency, as its understanding of the causes of the famine increased, could have modified its programs accordingly.

Such research need not be expensive. Doctors, nurses and administrators are good observers;[12] considerable information can be brought to light in feeding centers, food distribution centers, villages, refugee camps or even from local officials, drivers, and residents. However, someone must collect and analyze the information systematically in order to make it as representative as possible. Even though this task would have taken one person per agency at most—to travel to program areas, witness the abuses associated with resettlement or identify patterns regarding the causes of famine or the abuse of Western assistance, villagization, or the problems associated with the delivery of assistance and talk with other agency staff. Nevertheless, this did not happen in Ethiopia.

THE EXTENT OF THE FAMINE

If Western agencies had examined the Ethiopian famine closely, they would have discovered how Ethiopia calculated the "at risk" population. According to former RRC officials who controlled not only Ethiopia's famine relief agency but also the distribution of all relief assistance in the country, the "at risk" calculations were based, by and large, on rainfall measurements and spot field checks taken at a few dozen points only in government-held areas. The calculation was simple: a 15-percent average decline in rainfall was assumed to indicate that 15 percent of the country's population would not have enough food. Such an equation not only incorrectly assumed that the check points represented accurate rainfall patterns for the entire country, but that a one-to-one relationship exists between rainfall and crop yields. It also assumed that there were never surpluses in Ethiopia.

Furthermore, the calculation was based on a total population figure that is open to debate. The larger the population, the greater the absolute number of people at risk and the greater the need for foreign assistance. The government claimed to have undertaken a census in early 1984—even though its own army could barely penetrate large, densely populated regions, including some of those most affected by famine. The government's census "showed" that 42 to 45 million people lived in the country; the World Bank's estimate for 1981-1982, by comparison, showed the population to be 32.55 million (World Bank, 1984:8). Subsequently, the population figure of 40 to 42 million and the rainfall shortage figure of 15 to 18 percent were apparently negotiated and finally accepted for planning purposes. From these numbers, then, the government calculated that around 7 million people were at risk.[13]

Similar calculations were used to evaluate the effectiveness of famine assistance. One calculation was simple: by early 1986, the government indicated that one million people had died from the famine; it followed logically that 6 million people had been saved during the crisis. Western agencies quickly claimed credit for all 6 million saved.[14] During the crisis, the method of determining the number of famine victims was never made public. Apparently, none of the agencies or their governments was unduly concerned about the calculation because its employees were seeing so many sick and dying people.

Many people were at risk during the famine. The point is not merely to show that the calculation might have been off by x or y percent, but rather to indicate that no one knew how large the at-risk population was, where it lived, and whether it was increasing or decreasing or varied from region to region. The urgency of the moment conditioned the agencies to believe each new government report—100,000 people dying of starvation in this inaccessible region, 10,000 famine orphans in need of immediate assistance, and so on. The agencies were overwhelmed with where and how many, not why.[15]

THE CAUSES OF THE FAMINE

Government taxes and contributions from 1978 to the present (even from famine victims in the period 1984–1986) stripped peasant producers of the cushion (both grain and animals) that they needed to survive anticipated years of bad harvests (Clay and Holcomb, 1986:67, 141–142). Production declined further, both in famine areas and in surplus-producing areas, because the government required farmers to perform unpaid labor on local militia and government officials' lands and on plots that provided produce for the government (Clay and Holcomb, 1986). During the height of the famine in 1984, the artificially low government prices for food crops led many farmers to leave their crops unharvested in the fields (Joseph Collins, personal communication). Even Ethiopia's much-heralded early warning system for predicting food deficits became part of the problem in the 1980s because it allowed the government to define, identify, and expropriate "surpluses" from peasant farmers who had been accused of hoarding grain.

Even the "natural causes" of the famine advanced by the government had greater impact as a result of government policies. Famine victims reported that government programs caused delays in planting, both in liberated areas through attacks during the planting season and in government-held areas through forced labor programs during peak agricultural periods (Clay and Holcomb, 1986:192). Delays in planting allowed both insect (armyworm) and weed pests (striga) to thrive during the time when food crops were in their early, most vulnerable stages (Clay and Holcomb, 1986:192). Likewise, government actions and policies that delayed planting in years when rains stopped early (e.g., 1983 and 1984) intensified the effects of drought. Thus, drought did not *cause* the conditions that resulted in the famine; rather, it exacerbated them—it was the final straw.

THE IMPACT OF WESTERN ASSISTANCE

Ethiopian officials viewed Western assistance as an element essential to the continuance of their famine-producing policies. Furthermore, many officials saw Western assistance as the best way to extend programs (e.g., resettlement and villagization) that, while an official priority for years, had lacked sufficient funding. How, then, was the Western assistance manipulated to achieve these ends? In some cases food from the West proved to be no more than transfer payments to the government. For example, all residents of Ethiopia were required to pay a famine tax—even famine victims. Those who were not famine victims reported receiving food from CARE and using it to pay their required famine taxes, either in kind or by selling it and giving the cash to the government. Some former recipients of food rations indicated that in their areas the famine tax appeared to be pegged to the level of Western assistance that individuals received (Clay, 1987).

Self-sufficient peasant producers in many parts of Ethiopia were required to donate grain to the government even though they did not themselves produce a surplus. Some of those peasants reported that they sold cash crops in order to buy food from CARE in Hararghe, in eastern Ethiopia (Clay, 1989). Other peasants reported that they purchased food from the Catholic Relief Service (CRS) in northern Ethiopia (Clay, 1989), fulfilling their government grain contributions from these stocks. To the extent that this happened, it would have been far simpler if the US government had merely handed over the food to the Ethiopian government at the port, instead of transferring it to the US-based agencies that than gave or sold it to farmers who in turn gave it or its cash value to the Ethiopian government.

Delivering humanitarian assistance to famine victims in Ethiopia also involved a number of direct payments to the governments—e.g., taxes, handling fees, airline tickets, accommodations and office rentals. Although the total amount is not known, these direct payments were apparently not insignificant. The government, for example, purchased four new airplanes for the state-run airlines—with cash (Clay, 1989).

In 1985, during the height of the famine, Ethiopia tripled its foreign currency reserves (Clay, 1989). Famine assistance generated more income than any other source. In a normal year, agricultural exports (mostly coffee) account for about 90 percent of Ethiopia's known foreign exchange earnings. Ethiopia spends most of its hard currency to purchase weapons and equipment needed to carry on wars throughout the country. There is little reason to believe that the hard currency acquired as a result of the famine was used any differently, since the Ethiopian government also uses food as a weapon.

The delivery of relief assistance involved additional transfers of money, which added to the government's coffers. Ethiopians hired as translators, camp assistants, drivers (and in some cases, their vehicles), and assistants all earned foreign exchange for the government. "Famine tours" for the media, diplomats, agency personnel, and interested individuals not only generated income inside the country, but also increased Ethiopian Air occupancy rates by 30 percent (*African Business* May 1986:33).

Many agencies—Save the Children, Oxfam-America/UK, CARE and Live Aid—provided indirect support to the government through programs that the government had designed to reorganize agricultural and rural life. In 1985 Western agencies purchased oxen that were distributed for cooperative production while the government exported 200,000 head of livestock—an export figure four times higher than that of the previous year (Clay, 1989). The agencies also bought and distributed seeds and tools to and through local government organizations (peasant associate, producers' and service cooperatives). Through these organizations the government forced people—without pay—to grow crops destined for government warehouses, and even nationalized produce in areas where agencies had distributed agricultural inputs.

Western agencies gave millions of dollars in cash, personnel, and materials for work with children "separated" from their parents during the famine. Yet some agencies acknowledge that during the resettlement program food was deliberately withheld from children until their parents "volunteered" to be separated and resettled hundreds of miles away. The government recently admitted that some 200,000 children were reunited with their parents more than a year after being "inadvertently" separated during resettlement (*New York Times*, 5 March 1987). Cultural Survival's research indicates that as many as 300,000 to 400,000 children were separated from their parents as a result of resettlement. If only 200,000 children were reunited with their parents, where are the rest? We will never know how many children died *because* they were separated from their parents. Eyewitnesses reported seeing children beaten to death for attempting to climb on departing trucks to stay with one or both parents. The separation, more often than not, was deliberate. This comes as no surprise: from 1978 to 1984 resettlement was undertaken only after separating household heads from their families (Clay, Steingraber, and Niggli 1988:154-156).

Although few Western NGOs or governments overtly supported resettlement, they did indirectly support it by allowing the food they donated to be used to force people to participate in the program. For example, in 1984 the government set up "orphanages" in each of Ethiopia's administrative regions. Many Western agencies provided assistance to these children, in some cases taking over the institutions. Many speculate that the government will now use such institutions to train a new cadre of government supporters.[16] International agencies such as UNICEF, which gave millions of dollars directly to the government for programs with orphans and children separated from their parents, are particularly susceptible to this type of manipulation. However, even smaller groups—such as Save the Children-US, which began to receive massive numbers of donations for Ethiopian famine relief in late 1984 (due to their pictures of starving children) even though it was not operating in the country at the time—went to the government and asked officials to identify the areas in which they could work. This rather naive approach allowed the government to manipulate such agencies.

Finally, Western NGOs allowed themselves to be manipulated in other ways. Refugees in Sudan reported that while staying in Western-run feeding centers in government-held northern areas, they had been given blankets by foreigners who came in white vehicles with red crosses on the sides. As soon as the foreigners left the camp, the blankets were confiscated. Likewise, MSF reported that local authorities confiscated the blankets that it had brought to Ethiopia to distribute to people in its centers. Local officials told MSF workers that they did not want to make life too comfortable in the camp because then famine victims would refuse to be resettled (Malhuret, 1984:45; Roni Brauman, personal communication).

FORCED RELOCATION, STATE BUILDING, AND FAMINE IN ETHIOPIA

Since 1978, Ethiopian government policies aimed at centralizing state power have simultaneously undermined each of the major ethnic groups in the country by nationalizing lands and productive assets and by using a divide-and -conquer strategy in which members of dissident groups are moved from their own areas onto the land or the villages of others. This systematic mixing and consequent destruction of the economic and social fabric of families and even distinct groups within the country is intended to make each community dependent upon a strong central state.

Western assistance aids and abets the government in its program. The government has created, from the top down, local organizations, through which Western NGOs, doing humanitarian and/or development assistance, are required to work. Many peasant farmers view these "local" organizations as state-imposed institutions that reduce their communities' autonomy as well as their ability to feed themselves (Clay and Holcomb, 1986; Clay, 1987).

The government's policies aimed at increasing the power of that state over individual peasants laid the groundwork for the famine of 1984-1985. Yet the famine itself clearly demonstrates that although the state succeeded in rendering such communities dependent and unable to feed themselves, it could not provide sufficient food for all those peasants no longer allowed to feed themselves. Ethiopia's first proposed solution to the starvation it had been instrumental in creating was to resettle 1.85 million alleged famine victims from northern, rebel areas (or pivotal areas that officials feared would become aligned with the rebels) to the southwestern administrative regions of Wollega, Illubabor, and Keffa. The government succeeded in resettling more than one-third of this goal population. Western humanitarian assistance and the gasoline and transport vehicles provided by the USSR and its allies were the two key elements that enabled the government to undertake even the scaled-down version of the resettlement program.

A number of points should be kept in mind when evaluating the resettlement program. First, participation in the program was, for the most part, not voluntary; if given a choice, most residents of resettlement sites would have returned home. Second, the government could produce no studies showing that resettlement was more effective over other, less costly or socially disruptive programs nor any studies suggesting alternatives to the immediate or long-term problems that resettlement posed for those moved, for those "resettled upon," or for the local environment (*Boston Globe*, 13 December 1984; *New York Times*, 21 January 1985, 26 March 1985; Clay and Holcomb, 1986; Clay, Steingraber, and Niggli, 1988). Third, the government did not budget funds from the program until four months after it began, after it had moved more than 100,000 people (Clay, 1989). Even then the appropriations were far less than necessary. For example, some 60 percent of all land cleared for planting (Mengistu claimed that this was 8 percent of Ethiopia's remaining forests) was left barren because the clearing took place too late or because seed was not available for planting.[17]

In February and March 1985, Cultural Survival began its initial research on the famine. The objectives of the research were to investigate the famine's causes and to examine the impact of resettlement on those resettled as well as on the original inhabitants of areas selected for the program. Members of the research team were barred from entering Ethiopia; thus the study was undertaken, by necessity, with refugees in Sudan who had recently fled from the Ethiopian administrative regions of Tigray, Wollo, Wollega, and Illubabor. The findings were reported in *Politics and the Ethiopian Famine*, authored by Bonnie Holcomb and myself. Subsequently, our findings were corroborated by a number of reports (e.g., Niggli, Steingraber, REST, OLF {Oromo Liberation Front}, MSF, WFP, numerous newspaper articles, and even reports from Ethiopia's RRC). Not one researcher in Sudan has found evidence to dispute the findings. Efforts at comparable, systematic research have been rejected in Ethiopia.

Cultural Survival's findings concerning resettlement can be summarized as follows:

• Participation in resettlement was, by and large, not voluntary.

• Families were separated, in many cases deliberately.

• Death rates were high in resettlement holding camps and sites—apparently far higher than in the feeding centers and famine-affected areas of the north.

- Resettlement became an important—perhaps the single most important—cause of mortality in Ethiopia in 1985.

- Resettlement was an expensive and risky "development" program, yet neither the Ethiopian government nor foreign donors evaluated the social or environmental costs of the program or compared its costs with alternative rehabilitation programs for the northern highlands.

- The rights of the previous residents in Wollega, Illubabor, and Keffa were ignored and resettlement uprooted tens of thousands.

- Resettlement caused famine in southwestern Ethiopia.

- Resettlement achieved at least two military objectives in the north: it enabled the government to remove young Muslim Oromos from Wollo, who were seen as potential recruits for the TPLF (Tigrayan People's Liberation Front), and to remove prosperous farmers from Tigray, who were suspected of supporting the TPLF.

- In the south, settlers were collectivized and used as security forces against local inhabitants, leading to a militarization of the areas around the resettlement sites.

Ethiopian estimates indicate that the resettlement program cost approximately E$5,000 (US$2,500) per settler. The USSR and its allies provided gasoline and some of the vehicles used for transporting the settlers. Other vehicles, which the West had donated for food transport, were instead used to move settlers. To date, the direct financial burden of resettlement has been borne by residents of the areas receiving settlers and by the WFP and the EEC.

The World Food Program and European Economic Commission provided much, if not most, of the food given to settlers. The Italian government funded resettlement sites directly, and the Canadian government gave just under one million dollars to the Irish agency Concern for its work in seven sites in Wollega. In addition, several Canadian and French NGOs and one German NGO have funded resettlement sites or channeled money to NGOs already working in them.

Prior to late 1984, the WFP had already been supplying food to Ethiopia for the resettlement program. The government not only continued but expanded this program from 1984 to 1986. In addition, the EEC gave considerable grain to the Ethiopian government intended for famine victims but failed to specify that it was not to be used in resettlement. Sixty to eighty percent of the EEC grain went to warehouses south of Addis Ababa and, apparently, was distributed in resettlement sites in southwestern Ethiopia (Roni Brauman, personal communication). According to an RRC food distribution coordinator stationed in Wollega, recipients of the EEC and WFP food in-cluded militia and members of the Sudan Peoples Liberation Army (SPLA), an Ethiopian-supported organization attempting to overthrow the Sudanese government.

Although it was severely rationed, some food given by the EEC and the WFP was used in the northern holding centers, where those to be resettled believed that food was withheld deliberately so that they would be too weak to escape. Although Westerners were generally prohibited from visiting the holding centers, a WFP food monitor who had performed spot checks at two holding centers indicated that death rates were so high that as many as 60,000 people could have died in the centers before being transported if other centers were similar.[18]

The government used western food assistance as bait to capture people for resettlement. Because agency personnel were forbidden to travel in the coun-tryside surrounding the feeding centers, many villagers headed for centers (many were told to go to them to get food by government officials) were cap-tured by the army or militia before they were even seen by the Western agency officials. In other instances, Western agencies (e.g., Save the Chil-dren-US in Shoa administrative region) were allowed to set up food distribu-tion programs only after local, government-set quotas for resettlement had been filled. Villagers were told that if quotas were not met their peasant asso-ciation would not be eligible to receive food and other assistance from West-ern agencies. Food provided by Western agencies, then, not only gave the government the power to coerce people to resettle, it also enabled local offi-cials to consolidate their own power by eliminating opponents or dissidents. In addition, thousands of people were taken forcibly from the Western-run feeding centers in which they had sought refuge. Some of these incidents, which involved such agencies as MSF, Save the Children, Oxfam, CRS and World Vision, were reported in the press.

In addition to resettlement, Ethiopia has pursued another policy, known as villagization. Through villagization, the government incorporates farmers into new villages in which agricultural production will eventually proceed cooperatively. Since 1978, these efforts to restructure rural life through vil-lagization have been most successful and intense during periods of social and economic chaos—events that act as smokescreens for the program [e.g., the aftermath of the war with Somalia (1979-1982) and the 1984-1986 famine]. At such times, the provision of Western assistance—first humanitarian and then development—aided the government's expansion of the villagization program (Clay, Steingraber, and Niggli, 1988; Clay, 1987, 1989).

In 1985 the government announced that it would intensify its villagization program so that in 10 years—i.e., by 1994—32 million peasants will have been gathered into central settlements that are to become producers' cooperatives. By 1988, 10 million people, some 25 percent of Ethiopia's rural population, had been moved into more than 10,000 new villages. More than 30,000 traditional villages were destroyed in the process (Clay, Steingraber, and Niggli, 1988; *New York Times*, 11 March 1987).

Western NGOs played only a marginal role in implementing the villagization program. Once villages have been established, however, agencies are invited to become key players. In fact, the government has stated that all development assistance in new areas must now go through these villages to make them more attractive to the people being moved into them. Agencies have been given the choice of funding through the producers' or service cooperatives or providing central water, social, or health services to new villages. To date, Oxfam-America/UK, Save the Children-US/UK, Lutheran World Federation, World Vision, and CARE are among those working in these villages.

In the new villages, agencies (e.g., CARE in Hararghe province) have been asked to provide food to people who produced surpluses in the last year but whose crops were taken from them and who now cannot, because of forced labor programs, devote enough time to cultivating their own crops. The government is asking Western agencies to fill the food shortages that it has created through its effort to control peasants and agricultural production.

Western agencies provide assistance (seed, tools, and oxen) to local organizations, which often use these inputs to produce crops for the state. Even when the inputs end up in the hands of individuals, during the creation of new villages the government nationalized crops and oxen from peasants (Clay, 1986b; Clay, Steingraber, and Niggli, 1988).

Although the villagization program is supposedly voluntary, a number of observers have openly questioned whether many would move without the threat of violence. Other forms of coercion have been used as well: some Western agency personnel have reported that in the eastern highlands of Hararghe new irrigation systems capture most of the water for the areas in which traditional villages were once located. Villagers then have the choice of remaining behind, where they will have no water to irrigate their crops, or moving to the plains, where evapotranspiration rates are so high that the water supplies are not sufficient for cultivation.

Ethiopia's official position on villagization, through its public pronouncements, internal directives, and even the record of an earlier version of the program in Bale administrative region from 1979-1984, clearly links the program with the creation of government-directed and -controlled communal systems of agricultural production, locally called producers' cooperatives (Clay, 1987; Clay, Steingraber, and Niggli, 1988).

The most complete documentation concerning villagization in Ethiopia can be found in Jason Clay, Sandra Steingraber, and Peter Niggli's, *The Spoils of Famine: Ethiopian Famine Policy and Peasant Agriculture*.[19] The authors trace the history of villagization in Ethiopia. Through interviews with refugees in Somalia and Sudan who fled their lands as a result of the program in the 1985 and 1986, they have also been able to document the program's systematic, coercive aspects. Villagization, which has been implemented in the major food surplus-producing regions of the country, is an attempt by the government to control agricultural production in these areas. Some villagized areas already have food shortages. However, the true impact of the program will only become clear in five to 10 or even 25 years, when intense cultivation will have reduced soil fertility in the fields nearest the villages and forced people to cultivate more distant fields; when irrigation without adequate supplies of water will have led to salinization of the soil, making it unfit for cultivation; when fuel wood near the villages will have been used up and the costs of cooking a meal will equal those of buying the food; and most important, when population increases will have strained the resources of new villages, where population growth will not have been taken into account (Clay, Steingraber, and Niggli, 1988; Cohen and Isaksson, 1987).

It is interesting to note in passing that three agencies working in villagized areas in eastern Ethiopia—Oxfam, Save the Children-UK, and CARE—were also working with Ethiopian refugees in Somalia who have fled the program. Yet after the flight of some 50,000 refugees in the second wave (December 1985 to April 1986) these agencies still had not bothered to have members interview those refugees in Somalia who had fled the program that the agencies supported across the border.

CONCLUSION

During the Ethiopian famine of 1984–1986, Western humanitarian agencies collaborated with the government, both actively and passively, in programs that both intensified the famine where it existed and extended it to new areas. The agencies' oft-stated and legitimate fears of expulsion for speaking out about problems in Ethiopia do not excuse their apparent willingness to take part in, even inadvertently, the orchestration of the famine. Ethiopia's intentions in this regard are a matter of public record. One can only conclude that in their attempts to save face about their role in these famine-producing systems, the agencies act as willing accomplices in this tragedy.

Is it possible to give nonpolitical, humanitarian assistance? In an absolute sense, probably not. However, the best way to remain neutral in such situations is to stay informed. This in no way implies that, given the same information, every agency would choose the same course of action. Each agency has its own agenda, goals, and, in some cases, constraints from local counterparts. Still, taking a rigorously informed position is the best way for an agency to achieve its goals *and* serve the victims.

Unfortunately, the agencies serving Ethiopia have instead taken a rather lofty, moral position, ignoring the political implications of their own actions. Furthermore, many have attempted to block researchers' efforts to uncover the intent of Ethiopia's programs, as well as their long-term impacts. In 1986, for example, I asked Save the Children-US to provide information concerning the location of their programs in Ethiopia and which of the sites were new villages. I wanted to test the hypothesis that in ethnically diverse areas, certain ethnic groups were being villagized before others. Save the Children refused to provide the information on the basis that it was too political. Also, clearly, the organization not only did not know the answers to the questions, but it was unaware of their significance as well. Similarly, Oxfam America has leaked internal documents only to those researchers favorably disposed to their programs. Such actions raise serious questions about these agencies; agencies raising funds from the American public—and, in some cases, from the US government—should willingly divulge such information. Their failure to do so could result in moves to regulate them or take away their tax-exempt status. Ultimately, however, the public must decide—through its donations—which actions are more appropriate.

Many Western relief and assistance agencies are setting themselves up for a fall. This fact, in and of itself, should not be our concern. However, it is inevitable that not only will famine continue in Ethiopia but that similar emergencies will develop elsewhere. The agencies' ability to meet these new demands will be impaired by the justifiable erosion of public trust stemming from their collective response, first in Cambodia, then in Ethiopia.

Will the agencies learn from their Ethiopian experiences so that they can better serve the victims—not just the governments that persecute their own people? It seems doubtful unless there is public pressure and, perhaps, even new regulations for humanitarian agencies. The Oromo, the largest single ethnic group in Ethiopia, have a saying that aptly describes the response of Western relief agencies to the political dimension of the recent famine in Ethiopia: "You can't wake a person who's pretending to be asleep."

ACKNOWLEDGMENTS

This essay is a shorter version of "Ethiopian Famine and Relief Agencies," a chapter in Bruce Nichols and Gil Loescher, eds., *The "Moral Nation": Hu-*

manitarianism and U.S. Foreign Policy Today, South Bend, Indiana: University of Notre Dame Press, 1989.

Since late 1984, researchers working for and with Cultural Survival have conducted more than one thousand interviews with Western government and humanitarian agency officials, former Ethiopian officials, journalists, and refugees from Ethiopia. Many agreed to be interviewed on the condition that they not be identified in any way. For that reason, individual sources of unwritten material are not cited.

In a number of instances, however, I have cited organizations for having undertaken certain types of programs or for having assisted the government, directly or indirectly, in its villagization and resettlement programs. These citations are included not because these agencies are more guilty than others but because Cultural Survival has received specific information about their activities. The organizations named are representative of—or, perhaps, even have better records in Ethiopia or elsewhere, than—many groups not cited here; that is why their actions in Ethiopia deserve close scrutiny. Future researchers will also find it easier to follow the lines of inquiry laid out in this article if they have more specific information about who did what and when.

NOTES

1. Many Ethiopians apparently hoped that the famine would force Mengistu Haile Mariam, Ethiopia's head of state, to open up to the West. " 'This famine is a blessing in disguise . . . ' I heard over and over again from articulate Ethiopians, many of them serving as officials. 'It forces Mengistu to open to the West . . . It demonstrates the pointlessness of trying to follow a Russian economic mode . . . It underscores Moscow's unwillingness to do anything to help Ethiopia' " (Henze, 1986:31).
2. See, for example, Ethiopia's RRC (Relief and Rehabilitation Commission) publications (1984a, 1984b, 1985) and Radio Addis Ababa 9 February 1985.
    According to Dawit Wolde-Giorgis, in an interview with the *New York Times*, the government's policies, as much as the drought, caused the famine of 1984–1985. "We called it a drought problem. Drought only complicated the situation. If there is no change in our policies, there will always be millions of hungry people in Ethiopia" (cited in *African Report* July/August 1986:49). The Ethiopian government also blamed the famine on the West (*New York Times,* 12 December 1984; *Washington Post,* 12 December 1984; *Boston Globe,* 13 December 1984 and *New York Times,* 11 July 1985).
3. The EPDA "has the appropriate right-wing credentials, but no military clout and virtually no following within Ethiopia," *Africa Report* July-August 1986:49.
4. In fact, Ethiopia, in an attempt to make the two appear similar in scale, consistently reported the food assistance from the USSR and its allies in 100 kg units while reporting that from the West in tons.
    During 1985 the percentage of foreign aid given through Ethiopia's RRC dropped from 75 to 25 percent (*New African,* March 1986: 43). Radio Addis Ababa (18 June 1986) reported that "It has been stated that 1.2 million metric tons of grain are required to satisfy the daily needs of a total of 6.4 million needy people in 1986. Donor organizations will contribute 70 percent of this amount while the Relief and Rehabilitation Commission

[RRC] will provide 30 percent through the assistance it will receive both from within the country and abroad."

5.   "Of a population of 7 m believed in danger of starvation early in 1985, relief was reaching only between 2.5 m and 3 m—and not all of these were getting full rations" (Korn, 1986:6). Later (in May 1985) the WFP estimated that the number of people reached with any assistance was 3.5 million (*New York Times*, 17 May 1985); one month later the figure was "adjusted" to 4.1 million (*New York Times*, 16 June 1985).

6.   Calculations concerning the inadvertent, overall contribution of Western assistance to the death of Ethiopian famine victims are difficult to make. It should be stated from the outset that statistics on deaths in general are hard to come by, particularly details concerning the circumstances under which the deaths occurred. Therefore, this calculation should be considered more an exercise than a precise measurement. Even as an exercise, however, the results are disconcerting.

If estimates of one million dead and if Fred Cuny's observation that the death rate had already started to decline before most Western assistance began to arrive around January 1985 are accurate, then I will assume in this calculation that more than half of the deaths occurred prior to the delivery of Western assistance. It follows, then, that most Western assistance was delivered when more than 500,000 people had died. Resettlement could not have been undertaken without the promise, at least, of Western assistance. Conservative estimates indicate that 100,000 people died in the resettlement sites by the summer of 1985. In addition to the estimates of high death rates in the resettlement sites made by Cultural Survival, MSF, and ICRC (International Committee of the Red Cross), in a 29 July 1985 letter from John A. Finucane, Concern's field director in Ethiopia, to Concern's main office in Ireland, Finucane estimated that "from the time they [colonists] were re-cruited for resettlement—to arrival—to 3 months stay I don't think it would be an exaggeration to assume that 25% died. Out of 1/2 million that is 125,000 people." Later Finucane was quoted in the (London) *Times* (24 October 1985) as estimating that more than 700,000 people had been moved by early October. Clearly Concern's calculation then, by January 1986, would be close to 800,000 resettled of which, by their calculation, 200,000 (25%) would have died.

The *Christian Science Monitor* (22 May 1986) reported that "A UN official confirmed that deaths have occurred among the 670,000 Ethiopians resettled from famine areas, but termed the 100,000 figure 'Astronomical.' 'I haven't seen their [MSF's] figure confirmed publicly by any other organization,' said Paul Mitchell, of the Rome-based World Food Program." The *Monitor* failed to ask Mr. Mitchell to speculate on what happened to the difference between the 670,000 people the UN admits were moved and the 545,000 the government claims are living in the sites. All these considerations aside, let us assume that only 125,000 died in the camps prior to 1987.

Internal memos of the WFP indicate that as many as 60,000 people could have died in the resettlement holding centers prior to transport.

Ethiopian officials indicate that 200,000 children were reunited with their parents in the resettlement sites. What happened to the remainder of the children? Cultural Survival's research indicates that as many as 400,000 may have been separated from their parents. It is likely that forced separation from their parents would cause the condition of already malnourished children to deteriorate rapidly.

MSF reported that 3,000 children died when the organization was prevented from caring for them because not enough parents had signed up for settlement. Was this "problem" unique to MSF?

Peasant associations in Wollo and Shoa were denied food assistance until they met their quotas for resettlement. How many people in all died while waiting for the assistance from the West?

How many refugees died trying to leave Ethiopia to receive assistance? How many died as refugees in Somalia or Sudan, choosing exile and possible death rather than Western assistance delivered under the auspices of the Ethiopian government?

If, as Cuny suggests, the death rate had peaked prior to the influx of Western assistance, then these figures suggest that most deaths in Ethiopia (or of Ethiopians in Sudan and Somalia) after late 1984 occurred as a result of government programs made possible by Western assistance.

7. Virtually every major newspaper in the West discussed man-made causes of the famine, as did various television programs on each of the major US public and private networks (Clay and Holcomb, 1986: 214-217).

8. See, for example, David Guyer, president of Save the Children-US, "Keeping the Aid to Ethiopia Coming," *Christian Science Monitor, 18 June 1986; John Hammock, "Aiding Peasant Production in Ethiopia," Oxfam America Special Report: Recovery in Africa, Winter 1986; and a mailing from Interfaith Hunger Appeal dated March 1987.*

9. Letter from Bob Cottingham, LWF program director for Africa, to Dr. Jason W. Clay, director of research at Cultural Survival, explaining why LWF could not fund Cultural Survival's research on the causes of famine in Ethiopia after three representatives of LWF had made commitments to the contrary. In 1987, LWF apparently decided to reverse this policy and is now undertaking a six-month research project with refugees in eastern Sudan about why they left Ethiopia. There are problems with research undertaken at this late date, however. Because most of the refugees left the country more than two years ago, it is likely that LWF will find considerably more homogeneity in their answers than the findings reported by Clay and Holcomb, 1986.

10. This research was a systematic investigation into the causes of famine. Although Cultural Survival was not allowed to work in Ethiopia, the team of three researchers did interview three types of refugees (1) those who fled to Sudan directly from famine-affected areas of Tigray, (2) those who were resettled from Wollo and Tigray and subsequently fled to southern Sudan, and (3) those residents of southwestern Ethiopia who were forced to leave their homes. The researchers hired independent translators and tape recorded and retranslated interviews to ensure accuracy. Each interviewer used the same basic questionnaire so that information collected simultaneously from different camps could be compared. interviews were randomly selected in each site to ensure that those interviewed represented the camp's population (see Clay and Holcomb, 1986, Chapter III, for a discussion of Cultural Survival's research methods).

11. Most of the US government and agency assistance was traced from the US to delivery to specific famine victims. This does not, however, illuminate the context in which the assistance was used. Carol Ashwood (an Oxfam-UK relief worker) said that Ethiopian authorities had deliberately denied Western grain to villagers in order to force them to move (Reuters, London, December 1985, No. 1828). Many humanitarian agencies apparently did not understand how their food was being used. For example, David Guyer, president of Save the Children-US, indicated in a 1986 interview on CBS's morning news program that he was not even aware that Save the Children was barred from working in peasant associations until a local quota for resettlement had been met. At this time, Save the Children, like all other Western agencies, cannot begin programs in new areas until the residents have been moved into new villages.

Europeans made few attempts to monitor the impact of their assistance. European governments and the EEC gave food to the RRC directly, which, in turn, sent most of it to the resettlement sites (Malhuret, 1985:42). thus, while most European governments did not approve of resettlement, their food added a key ingredient to the program.

12. Cultural Survival was asked by two agencies to discuss the kind of data they might be able to collect inside Ethiopia which could verify or reject the conditions reported by refugees in Sudan and Somalia. This included a discussion of specific questions that doctors and nurses could work into their discussions during routine examinations.

13. Population estimates in Ethiopia are more of an art than a science. Clay and Holcomb, (1986: 214-215) review the reports of the numbers affected. The *Christian Science Monitor* (November 2, 1984) reported that "The government has just escalated two estimates: It says Ethiopia's population has jumped to 42 million and that the number of people reg-

istering for emergency food has gone from 6.4 million to 7.3 million." An article written later stated that "The number of famine victims . . . is now officially estimated at 7.7 million . . . the new figure replaces the previous government estimate of 6.5 to 8 million, which was considered too vague" (*Boston Globe*, 4 December 1984). On 14 April 1985, US AID was reported to have estimated the number in need of assistance in northern Ethiopia at 2.3 million, while the government put the figure at 7.7 million (*Washington Post*). Mengistu even went so far as to claim in August 1986 that 16 million Ethiopians were affected by drought (*Der Spiegel, 18 August 1986: 140–145*).

14. The Tinker-Wise report (Tinker and Wise, 1986) has frequently been cited as a quasi-official assessment proving that Western assistance saved 6 million Ethiopians. There are a number of qualifications that should apply to the report, however. First, contrary to frequent citations, it was produced at the personal request of Senator Ted Kennedy, not the US Senate Judiciary Committee. Second, the two authors used Ethiopian government translators for interviews and did not tape-record the interviews. They spoke with very few victims, and quote only three in resettlement camps. They made no attempt to collect data in a replicable—i.e., reliable—way. Finally, their own qualifications and their interest in the issue are unclear. Jerry Tinker is a member of Senator Kennedy's staff, but appears to have no qualifications other than a brief visit in the fall of 1984. According to *Olsen's Agribusiness Report* [8(1) July 1986], John Wise is the export manager of ADM Milling Co. of Shawnee Mission, Kansas. This company exports food grain commodities from the US and handles some grain both in the US Food for Peace program and the PL-480 Program.

15. According to expatriates in Bale in 1983 and 1984, World Vision reportedly flew grain into a region that was accessible only by plane or military convoy. The grain was then turned over to the RRC, which distributed it. According to these observers, World Vision neither attempted to uncover the causes of starvation in the region or to monitor the RRC's actual distribution of grain. Since 1978, food has been used as a weapon in Bale: people have been systematically displaced by the military and then fed with internationally provided grain (see Clay, Steingraber, and Niggli, 1988). This was, in fact, how villagization first began in Ethiopia.

16. The *International Herald Tribune* carried a more complete version of the same story on orphans than did the *New York Times*, (5 March 1987). The *International Herald Tribune* article, in addition to indicating that orphans are taught the Amharic language and Coptic Christianity (although neither the language nor the religion was that of many of their parents), mentioned that the orphanage discussed in the piece is next to the local center at which political cadres are trained.

17. Mengistu also reported (Radio Addis Ababa, 2 September 1985) that in the resettlement sites alone 7.5 percent of Ethiopia's remaining forest would be cleared for planting in 1985-1986.

18. See John J. Mitchell, internal report (August/September 1985, dated 6 November 1985) to the WFP.

19. The best study of villagization conducted inside Ethiopia is by John M. Cohen and Nils-Ivar Isaksson (1987). Another report on villagization, Angela Roberts' "Report of Villagization in Oxfam America Assisted Project Areas in Hararghe Province, Ethiopia" (June 1986), appears to be made available only selectively by Oxfam.

REFERENCES

Clay, Jason W.
    1984 Help that Could Hurt. Boston Globe, 17 December.
    1985a The Politics of Famine in Ethiopia. Cultural Survival Quarterly 9(2): 36-37.

1985b Human Rights Abuses and Deliberate Politics of Starvation in Ethiopia. Statement: Committee on Foreign Affairs, US House of Representatives, October 16.

1986a Feeding the Hand That Bites. Cultural Survival Quarterly 10(2): 1.

1986b Ethiopian Refugees Flee Collectivization. Cultural Survival Quarterly 10(2): 60-65.

1986c Resettlement in Ethiopia. Prepared Statement, Foreign Relations Committee of the US Senate, 6 March.

1987 The West and the Ethiopian Famine—Implications for Humanitarian Assistance. Invited paper presented at the 1987 annual meetings of the American Anthropological Association, Chicago.

1988 Famine Returns to Ethiopia. Cultural Survival Quarterly 12(2): 48-50.

1989 Ethiopian Famine and Relief Agencies. In Bruce Nichols and Gil Loescher, eds., The "Moral Nation": Humanitarianism and US Foreign Policy Today. South Bend, IN: University of Notre Dame Press.

Clay, Jason W. and Bonnie Holcomb
1986 Politics and the Ethiopian Famine, 1984–1985. Cambridge, MA: Cultural Survival, Inc.

Clay, Jason W., Sandra Steingraber, and Peter Niggli
1988 The Spoils of Famine: Ethiopian Famine Policy and Peasant Agriculture. Cambridge, MA: Cultural Survival, Inc.

Choen, John and Nils-Ivar Isaksson
1987 Villagization in the Arsi Region of Ethiopia. Uppsala, Sweden: International Rural Development Center.

Doble, Jim
1986 Resettlement in Ethiopia. Unpublished manuscript.

Henze, Paul
1986 Behind the Ethiopian Famine—Anatomy of a Revolution (III). Encounter September/October.

Keleman, Paul
1985 The Politics of the Famine in Ethiopia and Eritrea. Manchester Sociology Occasional Papers No. 17

Korn, David A.
1986 Ethiopia: The Dilemma for the West. The World Today, January.

Malhuret, Claude
1985 Mass Deportations in Ethiopia. Paris: Médecins sans Frontiéres.

Niggli, Peter
1986 Ethiopia: Deportations and Forced Labor Camps—Doubtful Methods in the Struggle against Famine. Berlin: Berliner Missionswerk.

1988 On the Destruction of Peasant Agriculture, Famine Policy and "Development." In Jason Clay, Sandra Steingraber and Peter Niggli, The Spoils of Famine: Ethiopian Famine Policy and Peasant Agriculture. Cambridge, MA: Cultural Survival, Inc.

REST (Relief Society of Tigray)
1986 Report on Interviews Conducted in Damazine Camp in the Blue Nile Province of Sudan with Tigrayan Refugees Who Have Escaped from Resettlement Camps in Southwestern Ethiopia.

RRC [(Ethiopian) Relief and Rehabilitation Commission]
1984a Drought Situation in Ethiopia and Assistance Requirements. October. Addis Ababa: RRC.
1984b Review of the Current Drought Situation in Ethiopia. December. Addis Ababa: RRC.
1985 Review of Drought Relief and Rehabilitation Activities for the Period December 1984–August 1985 and 1986 Assistance Requirements. October. Addis Ababa: RRC.
Tinker, J. and J. Wise
1986 Ethiopia and Sudan One Year Later: Refugee and Famine Recovery Needs. Unpublished manuscript. April.
The World Bank
1984 An Economic Justification for Rural Afforestation: The Case of Ethiopia. Washington, DC: The World Bank.

CHAPTER 6

A Social History of Food, Famine, and Gender in Twentieth Century Sudan

Jay O'Brien
Ellen Gruenbaum

After escaping major famine in the droughts of the 1960s and 1970s, Sudan
became one of the African countries most severely hit by drought and famine
in the mid-1980s. The famine which devastated the Sahelian countries and
Ethiopia in the 1960s and 1970s seems to have left Sudan relatively untouched, despite the fact that the central agricultural zones of Sudan had poor
harvests due to low rainfall amounts comparable to those experienced in
most of the famine-stricken areas of the Sahel (Nicholson, 1976:186 ff.). Yet
hunger stress was not a serious problem in Sudan in those years.

It is our contention that the set of conditions which were responsible for
Sudan's good fortune during those years was derived from a pattern of agricultural development during the 1960s which was rare in Africa and indeed
in the entire Third World. This pattern of development was led by the expansion of capitalist food production supplying internal mass markets rather
than by export crop production. This internally articulated pattern of economic growth resulted in market conditions in Sudan which linked profits in
the leading sector of the economy—and the dynamics of capital accumulation generally—with the purchasing power of the working masses. It is only
a slight oversimplification to say that rural Sudanese escaped famine in the
droughts of the late 1960s and early 1970s because starvation would have
been bad for business. This represents a sharp contrast with the conditions of
internally disarticulated growth and capital accumulation prevalent elsewhere in the contemporary Third World (see de Janvry, 1981). In most primary export dependent countries, the dynamic linkage between wages as

source of demand for the products of the system and profitability within the system has been severed, creating conditions in which starvation is not necessarily bad for business since profits do not significantly depend on the ability to sell domestic products to wage earners or peasants.

By the early 1970s processes were underway in Sudan which would quickly vitiate the protection that their crucial role as consumers of commercially produced food had given rural Sudanese. By then, capitalist expansion had begun seriously to disrupt peasant and pastoral production systems, and a broad program to reorient Sudanese agriculture toward exports was being implemented. The resulting changes created conditions in Sudan which left its rural population marginalized as consumers from the markets of the leading sectors of the economy and increasingly vulnerable to the drought-induced famine which eventually did strike in the mid-1980s. By then their starvation was no longer necessarily bad for business. In fact, mass starvation in the rural areas had become one of the most profitable businesses in Sudan in the form of hoarding of and black marketeering in foodstuffs. This peculiar history makes Sudan an important case in the study of the dynamics of famine vulnerability.

PATTERNS OF ECONOMIC GROWTH
AND CAPITAL ACCUMULATION

Understanding the significance of the Sudanese case requires first of all situating it in comparison to the more usual patterns of agricultural development in the Third World and in the context of developments occurring in global economic structures since World War II. Following the successful trade union struggles of European workers in the nineteenth century, which increased real wage rates dramatically, European (and later U.S. and Japanese) capital sought cheaper sources of raw materials in the Third World. Cheap labor was the key. Labor could be kept cheap because capital's primary interest in it was in its productive capacity; since the products of that labor were to be exported to Europe, profitability did not depend in any significant way on the ability of workers to buy the products of the system. Thus, unlike the situation in the internally articulated markets of the industrial countries, where the importance of wages in generating demand for the products of the system mitigated the drive of capital to push wages down, in the Third World there was no economic interest restraining capital's single-minded preoccupation with keeping wages in the colonial export sector at rock-bottom.

The results in terms of structures of Third World labor forces varied, depending on the products sought, pre-existing social structures and forms of organization of work, patterns of resistance, etc. A relevant example for contrast with Sudan is French West Africa, where farmers were induced to expand their household plots and grow groundnuts for export in addition to growing as much of their own food as they could still manage. In any case, the successful development of a cheap primary export sector involved the formation of a wage or peasant work force which supplied most of its subsistence requirements directly while being paid wages or crop prices that covered little more than their tax obligations and individual subsistence needs while on the job. So long as there were enough of them to do the work required, there was no economic cost to capital in keeping their wages low.

De Janvry (1981) has characterized such primary export oriented structures in terms of disarticulated patterns of economic growth and capital accumulation. The spread of chronic hunger and political instability throughout most of the Third World in the 1960s and 1970s he attributes to a spreading and deepening crisis in structures of disarticulated growth as capital has expanded in most countries to a point at which further expansion can only occur at the expense of the subsistence sector, by absorbing its land and resources. Deprived of its resources, the work force has seen its ability to provision itself directly eroded and its ability to make up for these losses through consumer markets blocked by increasingly brutal military regimes.

The burden falls most brutally on women. Though there is much variety in gender roles in Sudan, generally Sudanese women share with women of many Third World countries a key role in reproducing the labor force. This goes beyond the reproductive labor itself (pregnancy, childbirth, and the care and feeding of young children), of course, to include their work in peasant production. As Beneria and Sen have observed, the line between domestic labor and other work is not as clearly drawn for Third World peasant populations as for urban industrial workers (1981:292). Here, women are involved not only in agricultural tasks but also in appropriating food and other resources directly from nature, food processing, manufacturing of household items, and other tasks necessary to meeting subsistence needs; such work shares with domestic labor the crucial economic function of contributing to the rest, recuperation, socialization, health care, and old age care of the workers made available to the economy from these areas. Thus their work is crucial to the social reproduction of communities which are able to meet many of their own needs but which are integrated through wage labor into the national economy.

As changes in the economy and ecology intensify that work and make it more difficult, and as women and children are increasingly drawn into wage labor or commodity production under conditions of the economic crisis, the double burden on women has increased. A number of forces conspire to increase pressures on women to maximize their fertility. Since most cash-earning activities are rigidly seasonal, the family that has the most members available to earn wages in season is best placed to maximize income. Women with enough small children to share household chores and work in the home plot are more likely to be able to fulfill their broadened responsibility. Of course, resulting population growth increases pressures on the shrinking, degraded land left to the subsistence sector, redoubling all the pressures in the long run.

AGRICULTURAL DEVELOPMENT AND
SEASONAL WAGE LABOR IN SUDAN

The peculiarity in the African context of Sudan's history begins long before the adoption of its unusual development polices in the 1960s. Sudan is Africa's largest country, situated at the same latitude as the Sahelian countries to the west. While its central zones, where commercial agriculture has been concentrated, share the same basic ecological conditions as those found in the Sahelian countries, the waters of the Nile system have made large-scale irrigation feasible in part of this region. This fact, combined with the British quest for the rare conditions suitable for the cultivation of long staple cotton at the time Britain conquered Sudan at the turn of the century, gave colonial agricultural development in Sudan a character unlike that of the Sahelian countries. A number of pump irrigation schemes were set up to produce cotton, but the centerpiece of this development was a massive irrigated cotton plantation, known as the Gezira Scheme, watered by the damming of the Blue Nile.

Despite the fact that the Gezira Scheme was divided for cultivation purposes among thousands of tenant farming families, it was centrally managed and depended upon the mobilization of a few hundred thousand wage-earning cotton pickers each year. Thus, the predominant mode of integration of Sudanese peasants and pastoralists into the colonial economy was through seasonal wage labor, rather than through peasant cash crop production, as in most of West Africa (see Franke and Chasin, 1980). Later colonial and postcolonial expansion of commercial agriculture in Sudan, both in the form of further irrigated cotton production in the hands of private Sudanese investors and in the form of government and private rainfed food production, took place on the basis of this same pattern of large-scale projects employing large numbers of seasonal wage workers.

Seasonal wage laborers have been drawn from a number of sources. The composition of this labor force has been influenced both by the nature of the demand for labor and by the socioeconomic and other characteristics of the communities from which the laborers are drawn (see O'Brien, 1988).

In some cases, for the earliest schemes, it was possible to draw on locally available labor, e.g., farmers with very small or no land holdings, socially isolated individuals, clients, and descendants of former slaves of wealthier families, etc. But as the demand for seasonal wage labor grew dramatically with the expansion of schemes, the supply of laborers had to be stimulated by British polices. One method used widely under colonialism was, of course, taxation. The British were reluctant to engage in heavy taxation in Sudan in the first two decades of the century, while "pacification" was not complete. But once the northern part of the country was securely under control, the labor needs for the Gezira Scheme during the 1920s led to changes in the British taxation policies: they began to levy head taxes or other types of taxes which were designed to stimulate the need for cash and consequently the population's interest in seasonal labor migration. Stimulation of consumer demand through the aggressive marketing of tea, coffee, sugar, and manufactured cloth was also employed to get people involved in the cash economy. The government found that when peasant harvests were good and few laborers came to pick cotton, supplies of these commodities could be manipulated through Gezira offices to induce workers to come (Ali and O'Brien, 1984:222).

Another major source of labor for the British was West African peoples. As early as the 1920s British policies sought to encourage additional settlement by immigrant West African families to fill the labor needs of the schemes. Large communities of mostly landless West Africans are now found throughout the Gezira Scheme. Because of the seasonality of the labor demand, a stable wage labor force large enough to do all the work in the schemes could not be settled there, for there were not enough other income generating activities in the schemes during the rest of the year. Additional labor had to be brought into the schemes for cotton picking each year. For this reason, other West African migrants were encouraged to settle in an area assigned to the Fulani sultan Mai Wurno southeast of Gezira, where they could cultivate for their families and then migrate for wage labor to the scheme seasonally (Duffield, 1981).

The majority of the needed seasonal labor had to be drawn from pastoral peoples and rainfall cultivators, who could provide for their own subsistence most of the year, but who were able to devote a portion of their energies to wage labor to meet cash needs. Communities drawn into regular wage labor migration did not all follow the same pattern, and the variations in incorporation, which are discussed in more detail in a subsequent section, are relevant to an understanding of what happened both to food production and to the gender division of labor later on. Particularly important are the differences between nomads (including both those who did some cultivation as part of their regular subsistence and recently settled former nomads), among whom women had taken prominent roles in pastoral work and agricultural production, and members of certain groups in which women were excluded from most agricultural labor. Among the former, women and children as well as men became involved in seasonal labor migration, whole family groups migrating together to pick cotton, while among the latter only men migrated, leaving the women and children at home.

In both cases, it was possible for the incorporation into the agricultural wage labor force to take place without necessitating any profound transformation of existing production systems. What happened was that the potential for increasing production in the precolonial systems was tapped through either expanded or intensified production within the village or indirectly by drawing off surplus labor for work outside the village. Thus, the colonial capitalist penetration proceeded on the basis of absolute, rather than relative, surplus value. Since these large supplies of labor were needed only seasonally, it was important to the British to allow communities to participate in wage labor in ways that were compatible with maintaining the pastoral and peasant production systems where this labor was socially reproduced. The system that resulted allowed the ethnic and other variations which influenced the gender division of labor to be preserved; indeed, its successful operation required them. This ethnic segmentation of the agricultural labor force pivoted around gender divisions of labor and wide variations in them from community to community. The maintenance of the community and its moral identity was crucial, and women who stood at the heart of reproducing this moral. When a young man is asked to work hard away from home to earn cash on behalf of his extended family, he needs an explanation of why he cannot at least enjoy the company of his family while working and have them, including women and children, share in the work when he sees his counterparts from the next village operating this way. Similarly, a woman who is asked to go along with her husband to pick cotton while pregnant or tending small children, may well want to know why she cannot stay home like her counterpart in the next village. Reproduction of the family and larger community depend upon general acceptance of these assigned roles. We examine these roles and the structure of village life in more detail in a later section.

THE EXPANSION OF CAPITALIST FOOD PRODUCTION

Already by independence in 1956 a small agrarian bourgeoisie had formed on the basis of cotton-producing, pump-irrigated agriculture, which had served as the source of the initial private accumulation of capital. This class consisted primarily of leaders of the Islamic Ansar sect and its affiliated Umma Party, who had been granted concessions by the colonial administration in recognition of their loyalty in World War I and the nationalist agitation which followed (Ali, 1982). During the transition to independence this class managed to build an alliance of fractions of different classes on the basis of a type of fundamentalist Islamic appeal and to gain control over the government.

The power and wealth thus achieved came under immediate threat as the profitability of cotton production weakened in the years immediately following independence. The recession in world cotton prices which set in during the late 1950s threw into sharp relief the disadvantages of having large amounts of capital tied up in the infrastructure of irrigated agriculture. In this context agrarian capitalists began to search for more favorable investment opportunities. Partially mechanized sorghum production in the central rainlands provided an ideal opportunity. Rapid post-independence expansion of capitalist agriculture on the basis of the colonial pattern of large-scale projects employing many seasonal workers boosted internal demand for commercial food crops to feed this labor force, which was paid partly in kind. Thus capitalist production of sorghum enjoyed a buoyant internal market for its product.

To support this pattern of investment, which began to emerge in the late 1950s, the agrarian bourgeoisie and its allies in power used the facilities of the state. This power bloc used the state to give priority in the provision of fuel, in imports of machinery and spare parts, etc., to private capitalist agriculture, often at the expense of the export sector. The result was that by the mid-1960s private rainfed farming dominated capitalist growth in Sudan (Ali, 1982; O'Brien, 1983).

The effects on the export sector were severe. Government expenditure on servicing the economy declined drastically between the early 1960s and the early 1970s. Overall development expenditure also fell: although it rose from a ratio of 35 percent of current expenditure in 1955-56 to a higher level in 1963-64 (when several large new projects reached completion), the downward trend left it at only 18 percent in 1972-73. In the 1960s and early 1970s, according to the International Labour Office, "development finance [was] treated more as a 'residual' after growing current expenditure needs were met . . . The level and pattern of the Government's development expenditure has in fact been influenced more by the availability of external project assistance than by the availability of domestic resources" (1976:467). Starved of resources, the export sector declined drastically. By 1960 Sudan's export revenues began to stagnate, and by 1970 to decline (World Bank, 1978b:86). Neglect of the irrigation infrastructure in Gezira and other cotton schemes led to massive deterioration and to declines in yields (World Bank, 1978a: Annex 9,24).

The export sector experienced other problems as well. As export revenues declined, the central government sought to make up for them by increased taxation of foreign trade, which accounted for 45 percent of all central government revenues by the mid-1970s (International Labour Office, 1976:468). Tax revenues grew in relation to such non-tax revenues as freight-charges for shipping cotton (and other goods) by the government-run railway and the government's share of the proceeds of cotton sales deriving from its role in production. As a result of such policies, the total implicit rate of taxation on cotton (produced for export) rose to more than double than on sorghum (produced for the home market). This had further negative effects on export performance by reducing producers' incentives to grow export crops. Clearly, the export sector was being made to bear the burden of sustaining the state in an era of private capital accumulation in rainfed agriculture.

Even so, the hegemonic power bloc pursuing these policies took no significant steps to resolve the contradiction of the switch to a pattern of internally oriented growth from a structure of acute export dependency. Growth continued to depend on export revenues to finance imports of agricultural machinery, fuel, and luxury consumption goods, and Sudan's import bill soared (increasing by an average of 7.8 percent each year between 1970 and 1976) as export revenues declined by 9 percent annually (World Bank, 1978b:86). The balance of trade and payments deteriorated rapidly, financed primarily by foreign borrowing. The external public debt rose from $308 million (15.3 percent of GNP) in 1970 to $3,097 million (37.2 percent of GNP) by 1980 (World Bank, 1982:138). Foreign reserves were insufficient to pay for even half a month's imports. By 1979 debt service had risen from the 1970 figure of 10.7 percent of export revenues to 33 percent, and by the time Nimeiri was overthrown in April 1985, current export earnings were insufficient to service Sudan's foreign debt—which had increased to about $12 billion. Even internally, the government could not always meet its payroll or pay its other bills due to declining revenues coupled with inflation induced by balance-of-payments difficulties. This paved the way for a crisis of massive proportions.

For a period of about 15 years from the late 1950s to the early 1970s, however, this strategy resulted in a pattern of growth which differed sharply from the export-led growth pattern which has dominated in Africa and other Third World economies since colonial times. It was this difference which was responsible for Sudan's escape from famine in the Sahelian drought. In fact, in a study of the agricultural production performance in 35 sub-Saharan Afri-

can countries between 1961-65 and 1976-80, Hinderink and Sterkenburg
(1983:2) found that only Sudan and Botswana showed a substantial growth
in per capita food production at the expense of export crop production. In
both these countries, per capita food production rose from an index of 100 to
112 while overall per capita agricultural output was virtually stagnant. Only
five other countries in the study showed significant growth in per capita food
production, and among them only Ivory Coast showed greater increase in
food production than in export production. Four other countries showed stagnation in food production as well as in overall agricultural output per capita,
while output in the remaining 23 countries failed dismally to keep pace with
population growth.

Sudan's pattern of internally articulated growth and capital accumulation
did more than simply increase food production to protect its population from
the effects of drought. We examine the consequences for rural populations in
later section.

ECONOMIC "STABILIZATION" POLICIES

Beginning about 1972, the World Bank became more insistent in pressing its
arguments about Sudan's "comparative advantage" lying in cotton production for export and against the polices which the government had pursued
toward diversifying production in the irrigated schemes. In 1978 the World
Bank halted its support for further expansion of this type of agriculture and
initiated a rehabilitation program for Sudan's export sector.

The IMF imposed an austere "stabilization plan" on Sudan in 1978, involving drastic currency devaluations, removal of government subsidies on
food and other consumption items, a moratorium on new development projects, and other draconian measures. The value of the Sudanese pound declined from $2.87 in 1978 to more than twelve to the dollar by 1989, and
living standards of urban workers as well as rural producers declined sharply.

Foreign Arab capital, following the October War of 1973, began to promote Sudan as the potential "breadbasket" of the Arab world. Arab oil
exporters agreed to provide key recovery assistance—guarantees to Sudan's
creditors on its mounting debts, short-term balance-of-payments support and
development aid—in return for Sudan's acceptance of the stringent terms of
the IMF "stabilization plan" and Arab access to Sudan's agricultural resources for direct private investment. Arab capital took over further expansion of rainfed mechanized farming with the aim of using the sorghum and
other products to feed livestock and poultry for export to oil-producer
markets.

These foreign influences played an important role, but the reorientation of Sudanese agriculture during the 1970s and 1980s was not simply imposed on the Sudanese. The combined crises brought about intense internal struggle among the fractions of the Sudanese bourgeoisie and their allied power blocs. Foreign intervention gave a decisive advantage in these struggles to the import-export oriented commercial bourgeoisie, which dominated the class alliance that captured control of the state by 1972 as junior partners of big foreign Arab capital. Many observers have missed the significance of these struggles, since the rival blocs have organized and expressed themselves through competing Islamic sects and their corresponding religious ideologies and prestigious leaders. Concealed behind these ideologies, however, stand complex and shifting alliances of fractions of different classes subordinated to distinct segments of capital. The links are varied. They include kinship ties, as, for example, between the educated, civil servants, police, etc. and the religious and/or tribal leaders through whose patronage their families gained access to schooling or jobs. Other links are based on common economic and political interests, such as those which join Native Administration sheikhs to the Umma Party on the other hand in opposition to merchants on the other, who have tended to be in competition for the surpluses produced by the sheikhs' followers and who, on the whole, support the abolition of Native Administration. In general, fractions of the pretty bourgeoisie whose incomes are linked to the profits of one fraction of the bourgeoisie have tended to ally with that group politically as well. Nevertheless, political struggles in Sudan are generally portrayed as essentially religious in character, and the competing material interests of the dominant groups within each go unnoticed. The fact the Nimeiri's regime survived the struggle of the early 1970s and remained in power until 1985 has further mystified analysts, who have tended to view the rightward drift of Nimeiri's policies consequent on the change in hegemonic power blocs in personal terms.

THE EFFECTS OF DISARTICULATED GROWTH

Recent patterns of disarticulated growth stand in stark contrast to earlier patterns of growth based on expanding internal markets, because the welfare—or lack of it—of the producing population has little direct impact on the profitability of export production, which does not depend in a significant way on the purchasing power of the domestic work force. Wages figure only as a cost of production which can be kept as low as prevailing social and political conditions allow without damaging profitability in marketing the products. And as long as subsistence production is not destroyed entirely, the wages offered need not approximate the true costs of sustaining, much less reproducing, the labor force, but can be kept artificially low, at least in the short term. The resulting pressures on the environment and on the increased workloads of all members of the rural communities from which labor is drawn may be quite drastic, of course, as wages come to provide for less and less of a family's needs, forcing greater reliance on subsistence production and/or bringing more members of the family into wage labor and thereby increasing the subsistence and other domestic workloads of the others.

Policies adopted by the Sudanese government since the mid-1970s which are nonsensical from a strict cost/benefit standpoint, such as the mechanization of cotton picking for several years, do make sense in terms of the logic of disarticulated accumulation. Such measures represent components of a program aimed at halting the rising tide of agricultural wage rates that characterized the mid-1970s and at resisting the efforts of rural workers to integrate themselves into consumer markets to make up for their losses in subsistence production.

Faced with rising prices for a widening array of necessary consumption items for which they must pay cash, but unable to increase their wage incomes sufficiently to meet these needs, rural producers made adjustments which exacerbated their difficulties in the long term. Increasingly in direct competition with capital for land, peasants and pastoralists adopted ecologically damaging practices, which further reduced their abilities to provide for their own needs directly. As their crop yields declined and they came to buy a growing proportion of their food, they lost the ability to maintain food reserves—whether in the form of grain or livestock. As they further alter their crop selection to maximize cash returns rather than direct consumption requirements, they incur greater risks of crop failure in times of unfavorable rains and, in the long run, further impoverish their soil. With the loss of forests and scrub lands, important reserves of natural food sources which could be used in times of shortage are no longer available.

IMPACT ON RURAL POPULATIONS

Until the mid-1970s the overall structure of Sudan's rural economy led peasants to become oriented toward the production of food crops on their own plots, supplemented by seasonal wage labor, rather than toward the direct production of export crops as happened in the savanna zones of West Africa. Some peasants did produce export crops, especially sesame, but generally within a framework which did not involve large-scale dependency on high-risk hybrids, but which was dominated by the criterion of self-sufficiency in grain. This situation protected Sudanese peasants and pastoralists from famine in several ways, despite unfavorable rainfall and poor or failed crops during the period of the Sahelian drought. Limited development of rural market-orientation inhibited social differentiation from developing to the extent of undermining the ability of most people to produce substantial proportions of their subsistence requirements directly. This went significantly beyond simple food production to include—through maintenance of bush and forest fallow and so forth—the ability to provide other consumption needs, such as fuel and building materials, directly from the environment rather than through the market. When all else failed, there were plenty of opportunities to find wage labor, which usually included payment in the form of food—thus insulating seasonal laborers from some of the impact of price inflation. In addition, many cultivators produced sufficient grain surpluses in good years to maintain reserves, relatively easily stored for as long as several years in pits in the ground. Such reserves were a regular aim of production in many communities and helped peasants to survive the frequent low yields due to fluctuations in rainfall.

These conditions can be attributed to the orientation of the most dynamic sector of the economy to the internal mass market and the overall dominance of agricultural development by large-scale projects employing seasonal wage labor rather than by peasant cash crop producers, as in most of the areas in West Africa hit hard by the famine. It was also important that there was considerable room for expansion before the point was reached that capitalist agriculture and peasant agriculture came into direct competition over land. Many pastoralists were displaced from their pastures by the rapid expansion of the 1960s and 1970s, but either found open land to cultivate or maintained smaller herding units by undertaking seasonal wage labor to supplement herding incomes.

The growing reliance of rural communities on seasonal wage labor took a variety of forms, some of which had a greater impact than others on the gender division of labor and social reproduction. Two villages with distinctly different patterns of incorporation into wage labor where we conducted research in the late 1970s illustrate this variation: Um Fila, in Blue Nile Province, and El 'Igayla in central Kordofan. In the former, the productive autonomy allowed people to avoid the necessity of regular migration, resulting in irregular migration of adult males only; in El 'Igayla, however, whole family groups migrated regularly to engage in cotton picking in Gezira.

Um Fila: marginal incorporation. The people of Um Fila are members of a strongly patriarchal Zabarma clan who came to Sudan from West Africa in the last century. Coming from an area which had been subjected to taxation and tribute-taking, this ethnic group was accustomed to disciplined peasant agriculture and exploitation.

The seclusion of women in the mid-1970s was significantly more marked here than in other areas, even in neighboring villages (such as Hallali, mentioned below) of other ethnic identifications: women were careful to avoid encountering men when moving outside the extended family's fenced compounds to fetch water, visit neighbors and kin, etc., and they generally specialized in work that could be done inside of courtyards, such as pounding and grinding grain, manufacturing household items, child care, and other domestic tasks. Although married women sometimes cultivated small plots in or next to the fenced compounds, they did not work in the main agricultural fields, which were some distance from the village.

Large patrilineal extended families were the common production and consumption units of the village. Men and boys of an extended family worked together in the agricultural fields under the control of the senior male. Fathers controlled their sons' ability to marry through their control of the family treasury, but fathers' control over their married sons and their families was based on the mutual benefit of maintaining the larger production unit (to provide a viable age and sex mix of the various types of workers needed in the production unit), buttressed by ideological supports, such as respect for elders. The ability to maintain a large and well-off production unit depended in part on luck—in fathering enough sons spaced appropriately—and on being able to marry second and possibly later wives as each approached the end of her childbearing years, while at the same time keeping married sons satisfied with their income and influence in decision-making so that they did not decide to split off and form independent production/consumption units (*see* Gruenbaum, 1979; O'Brien, 1980, 1987; Ali and O'Brien, 1984).

The rainfall cultivation of sorghum, millet, and some vegetables for consumption and sesame for sale provided adequate amounts of food in most years on the relatively abundant agricultural land. Riverbank and river bottom cultivation of additional vegetables and the herding of goats, sheep, or sometimes cattle (for milk, meat, and hides) could be carried out if the production unit was large enough. Thus, large families could expect to have somewhat better diets year-round than small units or nuclear families.

For the people of Um Fila, resorting to wage labor migration was not a regular necessity, occurring only when crops were poor or in order to meet extra expenses like marriages. Only adult males migrated to work, and it was usually the young and those with small production units (e.g., a family with only young children or one which had a disproportionate number of daughters) who had to migrate most frequently. Migrating without families, these men tried to earn as much as possible, working long hours at piece-rate tasks and seeking out higher paying tasks even if they were more arduous. When opportunities later became available for higher-paying sorghum harvesting and threshing on nearby schemes, these were the jobs Um Fila men most often sought.

El 'Igayla: disarticulated production. Most of the inhabitants of El 'Igayla, located to the west of the central scheme areas along the rail line in central Kordofan, are the Joama' ethnic group. In the first decades of the twentieth century they cultivated millet primarily and some cotton for local use, using long-fallow shifting cultivation of plots in a woodland savanna region.

During the 1920s, the east-west rail line came through a few miles from the village, and when the Gezira Scheme opened in 1925 large numbers of migrants from the west began passing through the area looking for places to settle as well as for wage labor opportunities. The British were at this point beginning to pursue taxation in rural areas more vigorously and had begun to make attractive consumer goods like manufactured cloth available in local markets. While new cash needs arose, the village was hit hard by drought in 1925-26, so the people of El 'Igayla responded to colonial recruitment efforts and went to the Gezira to pick cotton. With no cultural prohibitions on female participation in agricultural work, and because cotton picking is relatively light work in which children can easily participate, whole family groups migrated together.

Some of the cash earned began to be invested in hiring migrant labor circulating in the area during the rest of the year to clear forests and cultivate additional fields near the village. As this process developed, production decisions began to be made increasingly on the basis of returns to labor and investments, rather than household production needs. Landowning farmers often chose to reduce the area devoted to household food crops and to grow large cash crops, particularly sesame, and eventually peanuts, instead. These farmers then purchased more of their food, including grain as well as meat, from local sources and small amounts of processed foods from outside the region.

Since the available cultivable land was claimed and cleared by the original settlers, other migrants were encouraged to settle in the area as wage laborers and share-croppers. After the local harvest they would go to the Gezira to pick cotton.

There are clear differences in the respective histories of the capitalist penetration of Um Fila and El 'Igayla: while the people of Um Fila found ways to insulate themselves from full incorporation into markets and managed to maintain the semblance of a self-sufficient subsistence community in spite of limited commodity production and wage labor, El 'Igayla lost, at a very early stage, all real internal economic integration as even much direct production of food became commoditized. Nevertheless, in the very different patterns of development of both Um Fila and El 'Igayla, substantial local food production continued and many subsistence needs (e.g., for fuel, building materials, etc.) continued to be met, at least in part, outside of markets.

CHANGES AFTER THE MID-1970S

The effects of incorporation of rural populations into the wage labor force and the growing encroachment on their lands by spreading capitalist agriculture began by the mid-1970s seriously to inhibit the ability of the rural masses to meet their subsistence needs through their own direct production. Forest and scrub rapidly began to disappear as new schemes were cleared, commercial charcoal-making expanded to meet growing urban demand for fuel, and people displaced by the schemes sought new land on which to settle. Capitalist agriculture expended by at least five millions acres in the 1960s and 1970s, and most of the land taken had previously been prime seasonal pasture of nomadic herds. The displaced herders sought new pastures in areas already used by other pastoralists or small-scale cultivators or shifted to increasingly marginal ecological zones (El Medani, 1978; O'Brien, 1980). Pastoralists thus often became the direct agents of the depletion of fallow and scrub and generally receive the lion's share of official blame for Sudan's current rate of desertificaiton. As conflict rather than cooperation has come to dominate relations between settled and nomadic communities, herds have at times been barred from agricultural fields, which thereby lose the fertilizing benefits of their manure (cf. Franke and Chasin, 1980: 46).

Cash needs began to increase rapidly as more and more people came to depend on markets to supply their needs for building materials, cooking fuel, and other important items of consumption previously taken directly from bush and forest. As cash needs rose and rural producers felt increasing pressures to maximize cash returns to their labor time, ecologically important fallow and crop rotation practices came to be abandoned or attenuated (*see below*), even where fallow land continued to be available.

Still, it is pastoralists who tend to be most vulnerable and first blamed. As the economic viability of herding units was undermined and urban markets for meat expanded, herding practices changed in ecologically damaging ways. Where most herds were previously composed of at least two or three different species of livestock which made complementary and undamaging demands on grazing lands, single-species herds—especially of sheep or goats, which yield the greatest cash returns—have recently come to predominate. This can become a problem, for example, when sheep, well-known for grazing very close to the grass roots, tend to remain in a pasture until there is nothing left for them to eat, instead of being forced to keep pace with the browsing of camels, as they would have in a mixed herd. As a result the best grasses began to disappear (see Sørbø, 1977).

Cultivators also became participants in the process of destroying delicate ecological balances. A vivid example was provided by the village of Um Fila. Located in woodland savanna, this village had depended on surrounding forest and scrub for convenient sources of firewood and building materials. In 1975, urban merchants had begun to truck wage labor into the area to make charcoal, setting up tree cutting and charcoal firing operations less than 200 meters from the houses of the village. As the villagers saw the forest visibly retreat from their homes and began to have to walk farther afield for their daily firewood supplies, they decided that since they were powerless to prevent the destruction of the forest they might as well get some of the profit from it, and they began to make charcoal for sale on their own account. Elsewhere in Sudan we have learned of the deforestation of whole regions which had already taken place under similar pressures of competition for resources, as occurred over large areas of central Kordofan, including El'Igayla, in the 1920s and 1930s when most forest cover was cleared for agriculture (O'Brien, 1980; Ali and O'Brien, 1984: 230).

As the surrounding forest and scrub recede, people also lose vital natural sources of food that they used to fall back on in times of shortage. One illustration of the importance of such resources is evident from interviews of Nuer women done by Gruenbaum in 1976. The Nuer are a pastoral Nilotic group in southern Sudan who also rely heavily on the cultivation of sorghum. The Nuer women referred to one year of widespread crop failure due to floods as the Year of the Lalob, since they had to gather large quantities of these fruits (often called wild dates) from the forest for food. Even in good years, Nuer women gathered several varieties of nuts, greens, and wild fruits to provide themselves with oil seeds, variety in the diet, and in some cases additional cash income from marketing such forest products in the towns. Thus, although we tend to assume that foraging as a way of life has been supplanted by pastoralism and agriculture, in actuality both gathering and to a lesser extent hunting are subsistence activities which have continued to contribute to rural people's survival, particularly in bad years when droughts, floods, or diseases result in food shortages (cf. Waller, 1988).

Expansion of cash needs has also led to basic changes in crop selection, with farmers dropping some crops important to ecologically sound rotation practices. In Blue Nile Province, as an example, long-standing cropping patterns involved a primary alternation of sorghum and sesame, supplemented by small amounts of millet, which was cultivated primarily because of the protection it afforded to sorghum against the parasitic weed striga. As a crop millet was too labor-demanding (in terms of field labor, which for some vil-

lages meant mostly male labor) and vulnerable to birds to cultivate exten-
sively when decisions were being made on the basis of returns to labor time
under conditions of market integration. The greater processing effort, primarily female labor, necessary for sorghum as compared with millet, could
be absorbed by the women of villages like Um Fila where women were not
migrating or engaging in significant field labor. The people in some villages
(for example the Kenana of Hallali) had not bothered with it, cultivating only
the bare minimum of sorghum needed to feed themselves between periods of
wage employment, when they were fed by employers. But in the 1970s, other
farmers who had included millet in their rotations—both the most prosperous and the poorest—were dropping it altogether. For the rich, a crop from
which they derived no profit came to be of no interest, since there were more
profitable ways to invest their resources (e.g., in trade) and since they could
afford to hire tractors to clear new lands when yields fell. For the poor, all
labor had to be devoted to producing food for their families to eat immediately, and the returns form sorghum cultivation were much better than from
millet. Yields have consequently declined drastically, forcing even greater
dependence on markets, both to generate income and to meet consumption
needs.

Such rotation changes were typically decided year by year. As the need to
spend more and more months of the year in wage labor or to send more members of the household to do wage labor expanded, farmers found themselves
working very long work days in their fields to get their crops harvested and
threshed for their families' food supply before leaving for wage labor migration. To meet their cash needs they often had to stay longer than they would
have liked at wage labor sites, returning home too late to devote time to millet
or to the expansion of their fields. For some of the farmers of Um Fila there
was not even enough time to cultivate sesame. When they were unable to
afford tractor plowing (which people preferred to do every few years at
least), the ground also tended to get compacted, resulting both in increasing
labor demands for hand turning of soil, weeding, etc., and in lower yields.

It is significant that part of the variation noted in the strategies of adapting
to increased cash needs was due to constraints of gender expectations, which
differ among the ethnic groups represented. For the Zabarma of Um Fila, as
we have noted, the seclusion of women was culturally valued, and female
involvement in agriculture or wage labor was considered extremely undesir-
able. Although women contributed long hours of work in water carrying
(from river and wells), grain processing, manufacturing of household items,
and other domestic work that could be carried out in the private, fenced
courtyards of their families, labor in the fields was considered highly inappropriate for women. Children's labor in the fields, however, was both ac-

ceptable and extremely important to family well-being, and that additional impetus to high rates of child-bearing meant that significant amounts of women's energies were being devoted to reproductive and child care functions, as well as to their other non-agricultural work (*see* O'Brien, 1987). In response to cash shortages and increasing labor needs, Um Fila's male farmers preferred to work longer days and drop millet from the rotation rather than ask women to work in the distant fields, where they might encounter strangers and have their family's honor compromised, and to migrate to wage labor sites where people of various ethnic groups mingle. For the Zabarma, then, while they still practiced rainfall cultivation in Um Fila before many of them moved into the Rahad Scheme, changes in cropping and rotation were in a sense the last line of defense against the use of women's labor in agriculture.

The Kenana of neighboring Hallali village, however, did not maintain a strict seclusion of women, to the extent that they did not bother fencing courtyards for privacy. Although Hallali women, like the Um Fila women, did wear traditional Sudanese veils, which provide head to ankle coverage but no face veiling, they were otherwise quite visible, visiting neighboring villages, working in agricultural fields, and migrating with their husbands and children to pick cotton on the agricultural schemes.

IMPLICATIONS FOR THE GENDER DIVISION OF LABOR

The impact of the changes we have discussed for the gender division of labor and the participation of women in the political economy can be summarized in terms of changes in female participation in wage labor, changes in subsistence tasks in social reproduction, and influences on child-bearing.

As more operations in the capitalist farms are mechanized, the main demand for seasonal labor is increasingly concentrated in a short peak season, increasing wage-competition among workers and reducing their ability to compensate for village crop failure through agricultural wage incomes. This process has also contributed to the breakdown of ethnic group segmentation of the agricultural labor market and the reduction in recruitment activities (*see* O'Brien, 1988:148–151). The impact on the gender division of labor has taken several forms.

For many families, one important development has been that children, particularly sons, are able to find opportunities for earning wage incomes at an early age. This was particularly noted in El 'Igayla, where local wage labor opportunities were so well established that old systems of cooperative labor had largely been replaced by the hiring of labor—including one's neighbors who were also farmers—when needed, and children over the age of twelve could often demand the going wage from their own parents. In terms of labor migration of family groups for cotton picking, it has in such cases become increasingly difficult for parents to get their older children to work with them or to contribute all of their income to the household. To meet cash needs, then, it is necessary for contributing family members to work longer and more intensely during these periods of wage-earning or to seek higher-paying work. One trend has been for male members of such families to seek work in sorghum harvesting while the rest of the family picks cotton. During the period when wages had been rising in cotton picking (in response to the competition from alternative work in sorghum and sesame harvesting), there was an incentive for greater participation of more family members in this work, despite traditional divisions of labor and female seclusion practices.

Wage rate differentials between sorghum and sesame harvesting on the one hand and cotton-picking on the other are likely to remain, reflecting the differences in physical effort. The higher-paying work does attract some women, but since they must be unencumbered by small children, not nearly as many women as men seek this work. The labor force for cotton-picking, however, has increasingly become preponderantly female (Aricanli, 1983a, 1983b).

As we have discussed, changes in the environment (loss of forest and fallow lands, particularly, which have led to shortages of fuel and building materials and declining productivity in peasant agriculture) have made rural communities increasingly dependent on markets. Women or children supervised by women who had supplied some of these needs for their families can no longer do so and cash must be obtained to buy them. In many areas certain key household tasks done by women have been commercialized: mechanical flour mills, government deep bore wells (which charge for water), and commercial water delivery are welcomed as relatively cheap substitutes for two of the most ardous and time-consuming tasks which are usually done by women. As a result women are both more available for and more in need of wage labor opportunities.

Yet, as we have mentioned, there are increasing pressures on women for child-bearing, as many communities find they need more young family members to participate in both food production—in order to maintain yields in the face of losses due to changes of rotation and loss of fallow—and wage labor. Also, as economic pressures have led to the break-up of the traditional large extended family production units, not only are more children needed, but also there are fewer women in the household to share the burdens of tasks which cannot be done by a woman during periods of physical and social incapacity (such as the forty days following childbirth, when she cannot fetch water or perform other vital tasks for her family). Thus biological reproduction and child-rearing become a greater burden on individual women (*see* O'Brien, 1987).

Considering these changes together, it is clear that nothing less than a disruption of traditional divisions of labor and the destruction of autonomous systems of social reproduction has taken place. In Sudan's rural areas a clear tendency is emerging toward the nuclearization of production units, which are able to provide only a narrow range of goods and services and thus face increasing economic individualization. Transformed in these ways, with their social reproduction increasingly coming to serve the needs of a national labor market rather than their own autonomy, peasant and pastoral units in rural Sudan can be said to have been subsumed in a process of expanded reproduction of labor power and capital.

Hints of the sorts of ideological shifts necessitated by these realties could be gleaned from fieldwork observations. Even among the Zabarma of Um Fila, for whom women's work in agriculture was considered *haram* (forbidden, sinful) during our first field trip, shifts had occurred within a year of the opening of the Rahad irrigated schemes, to which a several families had moved. By then men expressed a more pragmatic reason why it was better for women not to work in the fields: because there would be "no hot meal waiting" when the men returned. Thus, although Zabarma women were still not fully integrated into agricultural work, they were sometimes observed returning from fields, and a weakening of the old prohibitions was clearly in progress. This trend had run its course by the time we visited the scheme in 1989. By then, most women, unless they were newlyweds or had small children, regularly participated in at least certain tasks in their families' fields.

While it may be tempting to conclude that such individualization and nuclearization of production units as is occurring might thus lead to emancipation for women—as their domestic work is commercialized and their employment in wage labor offers the possibility of greater individual autonomy from husbands and fathers—there are significant forces inhibiting such an outcome. Women share with men the loss of community autonomy and self-sufficiency; although their greater dependency on uncertain employment opportunities (with built-in instability due to the economic fluctuations, etc.) may be compensated somewhat when they are fortunate enough to become scheme tenants and live near schools and other social services, for most the loss of the safety net of independent production of storable surpluses combined with the resources of surrounding forests leaves them in what is in many ways a less secure position than that of their grandmothers. Further, since nearly all tenancies are formally registered to males, women are economically dependent on husbands, who may choose to use their income to marry a second wife rather than to improve the family's standard of living. It should also be noted that moving to scheme areas has at times also eroded the personal autonomy of women, particularly when the move has placed women who had previously been involved in field or pastoral labor in communities of kin into a new situation where they were living side-by-side with strangers of other ethnic groups. Ideological pressures concerning family honor may lead to greater seclusion of women in such circumstances if resources and employable laborers are available to compensate for the loss of women's labor (Sørbø, 1977). This has become a social class issue in some areas, such as the Gezira Scheme, where long-term scheme tenant families who have adequate resources prefer to take women and children out of agricultural labor, sending the children to school (which has successfully promoted intergenerational upward mobility), and bringing the women home to specialize in homemaking. Most families, however, cannot afford to seclude women in this way.

THE 1984–86 FAMINE AND ITS AFTERMATH

It was the consequence of agricultural growth on the basis of the pattern of disarticulated accumulation that made rural producers in Sudan dangerously vulnerable to starvation when the inevitable drought finally came. Sudanese peasants and pastoralists contributed to the process of increasing their vulnerability, but under circumstances in which they had no options. Roughly half of Sudan's population suffered acute hunger during the peak of the famine in 1985 and 1986. Analysis which simply lists contributing factors compounds the tragedy by blaming the victims of famine for having struggled to survive impossible conditions not of their own making.

Beginning in 1980, the northern provinces suffered renewed drought. Already pushed to the limit by the destruction of the surrounding bush and fallow and the resulting declines in the fertility of agricultural lands, rural people lived off their stored surpluses and meager wages until, by 1984, these were exhausted. Meanwhile, exports of sorghum rose during the years of drought, peaking at over 412 thousand metric tons in 1982 (Shepherd, 1988:63). People began to starve, especially among pastoralists, particularly in the far west. Others still had some cash—or assets they could exchange for it—which they took to merchants to purchase grain. In Gedaref and el Obeid, angry mobs rioted and invaded the full granaries of merchants who refused to sell them sorghum while anticipating further rises in price. The merchants hired armed guards to prevent the same thing from happening again, and went on hoarding their grain.

With the introduction of Islamic law in 1983, the government had taken over responsibility for collecting a zakat tax to be distributed as alms to the poor, but without first having devised a program for its distribution. Zakat on crops was assessed in kind, and by the time people started starving, thousands of tons of grain were in government storage awaiting a decision on how it should be distributed—a decision never made during the famine, despite the fact that zakat continued to be collected. Faisal Islamic bank bought up sorghum and became the leading exporter, and Saudi Arabia provided subsidies for sorghum shipments from Sudan to feed livestock and poultry.

It was a tragic irony that the people of the richest agricultural regions were among the hardest hit. But it was in the far west, particularly Darfur, where the suffering was most widespread and enduring. Many pastoralists lost their entire herds and destroyed much vegetation in their failed efforts to keep their animals alive. Many of the people who fled the area in search of food have remained in squatter settlements around Khartoum—where people displaced from the west and from the war and famine in the south have doubled the population to over four million. In addition, thousands of small boys, sent to Khartoum by families that could not feed them, roam the streets picking through the trash of the more fortunate for their food and begging for handouts.

The urban population was not immune to the effects of the famine. As these effects became severe and were combined with the repression of Nimeiri's use of Islamic law and the dislocations of the deepening civil war which broke out in the South in 1983, opposition coalesced under the leadership of professional and trade union leaders in the capital. The resulting movement culminated in a comprehensive general strike in March 1985 which brought the national economy and the apparatuses of government to a complete standstill. Finally, on 6 April 1985, the top brass of the military deposed Nimeiri. The striking populace refused to return to work until the generals agreed to freeze the harshest Islamic laws, restore basic civil rights, and allow political parties to organize above ground for the first time since 1969 and prepare for elections, which were held about a year after the Intifada (uprising).

In these elections, however, there was a new and important factor in the form of the National Islamic Front, the party formed by the Muslim Brotherhood—funded by Saudi money and the Faisal Islamic Bank (FIB)—to contest the elections. With nearly a fifth of the seats in the Assembly (though only just over a tenth of the popular vote) the NIF was in a position to exert some muscle through influence over the more fundamentalist MPs in the two larger parties.

In the meantime, the ruling parties began to scramble to catch up with the vast wealth accumulated by Nimeiri's small band of cronies and began the wholesale looting of the state. Cabinet ministers, provincial governors, and other high officials sold food aid, government licenses and contracts, urban real estate, and other favors to the highest bidders. The public sector has been substantially privatized, with the assets of government corporations going to leading supporters of the major parties (and, in some cases, to their foreign Arab sponsors) at bargain prices. With so much of the foreign and domestic revenues of the government going into private pockets, the ability of the government to function has been severely compromised. Inflation, conservatively estimated at 60% in early 1989, rapidly eats up the few salaries that are actually paid.

This blatant corruption takes place in the context of acute economic crisis precipitated by the crisis of subsistence in the rural areas and the declining profitability of agricultural investment. In addition, a new and voraciously aggressive fraction of capital has come into existence under the sponsorship of a marginalized faction of the Saudi royal family and primarily through the FIB (founded in 1979), which has thrown the old contest between the agrarian bourgeoisie and the commercial bourgeoisie into chaos. What has been going on since the Intifada—against the backdrop of famine, civil war, and rural anarchy—is a full-scale scramble for the realignment of capital, economically, institutionally, and politically. The scale of accumulation required to be a player has taken a quantum leap from that of the 1970s, and the productive base of the long-dominant agrarian fraction of capital has been eroded (see O'Brien, 1989).

At the center of this scramble are the Islamic banks—the first and strongest of which is the FIB—and their subsidiary enterprises. In the last few years, the two older fractions of capital have each established an Islamic bank in efforts to compete with the NIF for dominance by shifting their economic base into finance. When the FIB first opened it doors, its Islamic legitimacy—its avoidance of the interest payment—and the prestige of its Saudi connection attracted large deposits. Depositors are "partners" who earn a share of the bank's annual profits in proportion to their deposits. Phenomenal profits in the FIB's first few years attracted still more depositors and "partners" (borrowers).

Keys to the success of FIB and the other Islamic financial institutions in Sudan are their legal status as religious institutions exempt from all taxation and central bank oversight and their favored access to government licenses, export credits, and the like. This position also makes their accounts private and unavailable for inspection by government, "partners," or employees.

Conditions of economic instability and high rates of inflation make efforts to corner the markets for various consumption items and urban real estate the favored activities of these banks. FIB controls a large share of the sorghum market, including about a third of sorghum exports (*see* Shepherd, 1988). The buying up and hoarding of basic commodities, of course, fuels the spiraling inflation and the chaos of shortages.

In the context of economic chaos, in which the formal organs of the state are increasingly impotent onlookers without budgets or resources, a power vacuum has been created at the center. In this vacuum have emerged parallel state structures within each of the three main parties. While police officers and soldiers have a strict ration of bullets checked out to them for use in their often antiquated guns when they go on duty and checked back in at the end of a shift, well-equipped private militias bristle with AK-47s and all the ammunition they can use.

Many of the militia units in Southern Darfur and Southern Kordofan Provinces and southern parts of Blue Nile Province were initially armed by the armed forces or the Umma Party (representing the former agrarian bourgeoisie) in the hopes that they could be used as auxiliaries in the war against the Sudanese Peoples Liberation Army in the neighboring areas of the Southern Region. Instead, these mainly pastoral tribal groupings have used automatic weapons to make up for their crippling losses in the famine at the expense of their sedentary, non-Arab neighbors. Heavily armed bands attack villages, steal livestock, and kill or drive off the inhabitants. Sometimes women and children are captured and put to working herds, tilling fields, etc., or are sold to other groups experiencing labor shortages as the result of the deaths of many children in the drought. Captured women are also valued as breeders of more children to accelerate the tribe's recovery.

Large areas of Darfur and Southern Kordofan have been carved up into the domains of local warlords who control all movement in their territories, preying upon southerners fleeing the devastation in the South (where hunger and relief supplies of food have cynically been used as weapons of war), looting relief columns trying to get to the South or to the camps for the displaced across the border in the North, and organizing raids on various communities. There is no effective government presence in these areas. With automatic weapons so widely distributed, local and personal disputes often erupt into deadly violence within communities.

In 1988 Sudan reaped its best harvest in at least a decade, yet as many as half a million people may have starved to death. Most of these people were victims of the warfare and corruption in the relief effort in the south and the bloody anarchy in the west. Many people in riverain Sudan suffered crop failure or were made homeless by heavy floods in August 1988.

Even if the civil war is ended soon, there would be massive problems to contend with before Sudan's crisis abates. Not all the killing would stop with an end to the war. The basic conditions of subsistence crisis responsible for the chaos and slaughter in the west would remain; what would be needed is a coordinated shift to a pattern of articulated growth and environmental rehabilitation. It is not easy to see how communities locked in life-and-death struggles over shrunken and damaged resources can quickly patch up their differences and resume living amicably again as neighbors, even assuming their resources are somewhat restored. The apparatuses of the state have been stripped of their capacity to deliver resources and services to the people; the military rulers who came to power in a coup in June 1989 have shown no sign of being able to restore these functions or end the war. It is indeed a tragedy that a country endowed with abundant land and water, inhabited by hard-working people, must languish under the economic deformities and the political instability caused by the bitter struggles for control of wealth among tiny privileged groups.

ACKNOWLEDGMENTS

Jay O'Brien's research in Sudan was funded by the Manpower Research Project of the Faculty of Economic and Social Studies, University of Khartoum, the Economic and Social Research Council (Sudan) and the National Endowment for the Humanities (U.S.A.). The analysis in this chapter draws heavily on O'Brien 1985. Ellen Gruenbaum's research was sponsored by the Economic and Social Research Council (Sudan), the Ministry of Social Affairs (Sudan), and a fellowship from California State University, San Bernardino.

REFERENCES

Ali, Taisier
    1982 The Cultivation of Hunger: Towards the Political Economy of Agricultural
        Development in Sudan 1956-1964. Ph.D., University of Toronto.
Ali, Taisier and Jay O'Brien
    1984 Labor, Community and Protest in Sudanese Agriculture. In J. Barker (ed.),
        The Politics of Agriculture in Tropical Africa. Beverly Hills: Sage Publica-
        tions, pp. 205-238.
Aricanli, Ali Tosun
    1983a The Second Report on the Findings of a Research Project on Gezira
        Scheme Village Census of Demographic, Occupational, and Health Status.
        Unpublished ms.
    1983b Sources and Changes of Agricultural Labour Force in the Sudan. Unpub-
        lished ms.

Beneria, Lourdes and Gita Sen
    1981 Accumulation, Reproduction, and Women's Role in Economic Develop-
          ment: Boserup Revisited. Signs: Journal of Women in Culture and Society
          7 (2): 279-298.
de Janvry, Alain
    1981 The Agrarian Question and Reformism in Latin America. Baltimore: Johns
          Hopkins University Press.
Duffield, Mark
    1981 Maiurno: Capitalism and Rural Life in Sudan. London: Ithaca Press.
El Medani, Khalil Abdalla
    1978 The Impact of Economic Development on the Ethnic Groups Inhabiting
          Al-Renk Region of the Upper Nile Province. M.Sc. thesis, University of
          Khartoum.
Franke, Richard and Barbara Chasin
    1980 Seeds of Famine: Ecological Destruction and the Development Dilemma
          in the West African Sahel. Montclair, N.J.: Rowman & Allanheld.
Gruenbaum, Ellen
    1979 Patterns of Family Lining: A Case Study of Two Villages in the Rahad
          Area (Sudan). Monograph 12. Khartoum: Development Studies Research
          Centre.
Hinderink, J. and J. Sterkenburg
    1983 Agricultural Policy and Production in Africa: The Aims, the Methods and
          the Means. Journal of Modern African Studies 21,1.
International Labour Office
    1976 Growth, Employment and Equity: A Comprehensive Strategy for the Su-
          dan. Geneva: I.L.O.
Nicholson, Sharon
    1976 A Climatic Geography for Africa: Synthesis of Biological, Historical and
          Geographical Information and Data. Ph.D., University of Wisconsin.
O'Brien, Jay
    1980 Agricultural Labor and Development in Sudan. Ph.D., University of Con-
          necticut.
    1983 The Political Economy of Capitalist Agriculture in the Central Rainlands
          of Sudan. Labour, Capital and Society 16 (1): 8-32.
    1985 Sowing the Seeds of Famine: The Political Economy of Food Deficits in
          Sudan. Review of African Political Economy 33: 23-32.
    1987 Differential High Fertility and Demographic Transitions under Peripheral
          Capitalism in Sudan. In African Population and Capitalism: Historical Per-
          spectives, edited by Dennis Cordell and Joel Gregory. Boulder: Westview
          Press, pp. 173-186.
    1988 The Formation and Transformation of the Agricultural Labour Force in
          Sudan. In Economy and Class in Sudan, edited by Norman O'Neill and Jay
          O'Brien. Aldershot, U.K.: Avebury Press, pp. 137-156.
    1989 Depredation and Terror in Sudan. Middle East Report, no. 161.
Shepherd, Andrew
    1988 Case Studies of Famine: Sudan. In Preventing Famine: Policies and Pros-
          pects for Africa, by Donald Curtis, Michael Hubbard and Andrew Shep-
          herd. New York: Routledge, pp. 28-72.

Sørbø, Gunnar
    1977 Nomads on the Scheme: A Study of Irrigation Agriculture and Pastoralism in Eastern Sudan. In P. O'Keefe, ed., Land and Development in Africa, London: International African Institute.
Waller, Richard
    1988 Emutai: Crisis and Response in Maasailand 1883-1902. In The Ecology of Survival, edited by Douglas Johnson and David Anderson. London: Lester Crook, pp. 73-112.
World Bank
    1978a Sudan Agricultural Sector Review. Report No. 1836a-SU, 10 August.
    1978b World Development Report, 1978. Washington, D.C.: World Bank.
    1982 World Development Report, 1982. Washington, D.C.: World Bank.

CHAPTER 7

Labor, Economic Power, and Gender: Coping with Food Shortage in Guinea-Bissau

Ursula Funk

Famine is the final stage of a complex set of ecological, economic, social and political processes. To understand famine, it is not only necessary to analyze the historical processes, but the current macro-economic and political influences on food supplies, as well as the micro-dynamics of the impact of the response to food scarcity. This chapter focuses on the social and cultural complexity of the micro-level responses and the relationship to macro-level developments. The objective is to analyze changes in labor input, income, and wealth, and their influence on gender and other social inequalities.

After presenting a brief background of the national food situation, I will discuss the coping strategies used by different socioeconomic groups in the urban areas. Subsequently, I will give examples of how rural dwellers deal with food shortages, compare the responses of two ethnic groups, and analyze the differential impact of these shortages on men and women.

THE NATIONAL CONTEXT

People have been plagued with the threat of famine in Guinea-Bissau not only because of the tremendous variation in rainfall and frequent droughts, but because of historical pressures, such as the trans-Atlantic slave trade, colonialism, and the protracted anti-colonial war from 1963–1974, which devastated local economies and disrupted social relations.

Although Guinea-Bissau borders on the Sahelian zone, the precipitation—ranging from 1,250 mm in the north to 2,750 mm in the south—is high enough, despite fluctuations, to allow for the production of sufficient food for national consumption if grains are redistributed. Rather than drought or overpopulation, it is the process of underdevelopment promoted by historical forces such as colonialism (Bigman, 1989) and manifested in the lack of infrastructure, scarcity of trained human resources, poor management capacity, dysfunctional transportation and marketing systems, and inappropriate macro-economic policies, that has created the conditions of scarcity and potential famine in Guinea-Bissau. Since independence, it remains one of the poorest countries in the world, suffering from a lack of foreign currency concomitant with a severe shortage of all basic commodities and foodstuffs in the national market.

After independence, the PAIGP (Partido Africano da Independência de Guiné Portuguesa), who led the nationalist struggle against Portugal, established a government with a socialist-oriented development policy. Agriculture and rural development were to be given priority. However, the centralization of the party established during the struggle was maintained during independence, giving the majority of the population little influence in decision-making. Thus the state, in its attempt to control the economy, established a market monopoly of primary products and fixed prices. As a result, the new marketing structures showed considerable resemblance to the colonial ones (Galli and Jones, 1987). Low farmgate prices resulted in an indirect taxation of rural producers, who increasingly resisted the state policies. Galli (1987:19) argues that the resistance of food and export crop producers to commercial, fiscal, and exchange rate policies has been the main reason for the decline in agriculture production and trade. National production declined not because farmers reduced their efforts, but because many Guineans emigrated to produce peanuts in Senegal or Gambia for a currency with more buying power in markets offering a wealth of items unavailable in Guinea-Bissau. Peanut production also decreased because farmers occasionally shifted from export to subsistence crops. Moreover, they increasingly sold goods through clandestine networks at higher prices, or took them to Senegal because they could not find many inputs and consumer items for sale in local currency. As a result, chronic food shortages developed in urban areas.

Agricultural, fishing, and forestry products provide most of the export earnings for the state, but these cover less than half the cost of imports. The external financing of imports led to an alarming increase in the national debt. In response to the trade deficit and the shortage of foreign currency, the government curtailed the importation of basic production and consumption items. Shortages were especially pronounced in the rural areas, "because of the manipulation of the market by state officials in their own rather than in the interests of the producers" (Galli, 1987:25).

Facing a very difficult economic situation, the government appealed to the international community for aid. Many donors responded with short-term food aid and long-term development program aid. However, Luís Cabral, the first President, was more interested in industry than agriculture, despite a tremendous lack of raw materials, foreign currency, and trained personnel. Continued shortages of food and consumer goods led to a coup d'état in November 1980. The new government under President Bernardino Vieira and the party congress criticized the failed attempts at industrialization and asserted that the country's first priority was to attain national food self-sufficiency by supporting the agricultural sector and fisheries, and subsequently to increase export production with the promotion of cotton and cashew nut production in addition to peanuts and palm kernels. However, while there were chronic shortages of basic food items such as oil, Guinea-Bissau continued to export peanuts, palm oil, and seafood.[3] Moreover, the national commerce was poorly managed, so that rice from the surplus production areas in the south did not reach the regions with a grain deficit in the north and east or the stores in Bissau.

At the same time the government lacked sufficient foreign currency to buy grains on the international market, and as a result food shipments were largely dependent on international aid. Food aid provided some relief in times of hunger, but it created a dangerous level of government dependence on foreign donors. The regular supply of food aid enabled the government to sell grains at low prices, benefiting principally urban dwellers. The low prices, however, diminished the incentive of peasant farmers to sell their crops on the national market. Trade and price policies have been changed in the last few years, but it remains to be seen whether rural men and women have gained control over marketing and benefit from the changes.

In order to decrease the dependence on food aid, development projects have been initiated to increase agricultural production, but they pay insufficient attention to women as the major providers of food. Although some development planners have designed projects to train women, for example as extension agents, they continue to downplay women's role as economic actors. Planners tend to allocate such benefits as irrigated perimeters, technology, training, and credit to men, who are presumed to be the heads of households. Special programs for women are often geared to their domestic roles or supplementary productive activities. Moreover, the government, despite its stated commitment to the promotion of the equality of women, has not questioned the prevailing gender divisions of labor in which women in all ethnic groups work more hours per day than men.

Despite the severe national economic crisis, rural and many urban dwellers have been able to avert famine by maintaining a high degree of self-sufficiency by farming and gardening. Aaby et al. (1981) conclude that malnutrition is mild to moderate rather than severe by WHO categories. About 82 percent of all Guineans live in the rural areas, working as "family"[4] or smallholder farmers, and as artisans and traders on the side. There are a few state and commercial farms, but they employ only a small or temporary labor force and contribute insignificantly to national food production. There is still sufficient arable land,[5] and free access to land in unsettled areas is guaranteed either by indigenous systems of land tenure or by government decree (Funk, 1988). An important part of male and female farming and resource use is for subsistence, especially in times of crisis. Peasant farmers practice a broad range of preventive measures to minimize the risks of crop failure and hunger, such as intercropping, crop and field diversification, and planting fruit-bearing trees. Moreover, they have developed various strategies to cope with an impending food shortage.

Most farming is manual, the predominant tools being axes, machetes, hoes, and knives. The introduction of new technologies, such as fertilizers, improved seeds, pump irrigation systems, ox plows, and tractors,[6] has been limited and they rarely benefit women producers. Yet female farmers exceed the number of male farmers[7] and they provide more than half the food used for home consumption. In all ethnic groups, women devote more hours to the provision of food than men expend on subsistence activities. Men's input varies by ethnic group, and is strongly influenced by whether or not they produce peanuts for cash. Despite capital and technological constraints, the rural population is not only able to feed itself, but also produces a surplus for sale.

Coping Strategies in the Urban Areas

Urban dwellers by contrast are largely dependent on the market for food supplies. Until 1986 they regularly faced virtually empty stores. On the rare occasions that rice, oil, bread, milk, or sugar were available, usually from food aid shipments, long queues formed immediately, and the quantities were often rationed. Crowds, predominantly women, waited for hours to get their share, and food riots broke out more than once. Being accustomed to shortages, people bought excessively when goods were not rationed, intending either to store them or to resell them profitably. As a result, supplies were depleted rapidly. Petty traders who hoarded goods were often women trying to make a living. They became the scapegoats of the national economic crisis, and were accused of causing the food shortages. Knowledge of clandestine trade networks where one could get bread, palm oil, eggs, meat, and imported items became essential for the survival of urban dwellers.

Government agencies organized the distribution of rations to state employees, including the police and military, so that they would not waste their time standing in line to get food aid. Everyone consequently tried to get a job with the government or a state enterprise, or tried to take advantage of kin or friendship relationships with an official who had access to this distribution network. Holding a government job became the basis of socioeconomic differentiation. Of course, even among government employees there is considerable stratification, with the few people in the upper echelon enjoying significant additional privileges.

The few people with access to a car regularly drive to the countryside during the weekend increasingly in pursuit of food instead of leisure. Petty traders, mainly women, take their goods from their settlements to the roadside of the major thoroughfares from the capital. Thus, if rural producers are not willing or able to go sell in the markets of Bissau, the urban elite customers meet them half-way, which allows them not only to buy chicken, fish, yams, and other scarce foodstuffs, but to pay less than in Bissau.

The majority of the inhabitants of Bissau and the small regional towns belong to the lower socioeconomic strata. They have limited possibilities of finding employment in the large public or small private sector, owing to the scarcity of jobs and because they lack the educational prerequisites. Many people who had not received any education during colonial times migrated to the urban areas during the war to escape the bombing. Fewer unskilled jobs are available to women, not only because of occupational segregation, but because the competition among men is considerable, such that newly migrated young men with primary education are also standing in line. Facing unemployment and chronic shortages in the market, many urban dwellers, especially women, still grow their own food. Around most houses in Bissau and other towns they plant small gardens with vegetables, cassava, and fruit trees. To be able to plant rice during the rainy season, women and occasionally men attempt to get a plot on the peripheries of the towns. During the dry season, the more enterprising women try to get access to plots nearby to plant irrigated vegetables, not only for domestic consumption, but for sale. However, their ability to produce in the urban areas is restricted by the scarcity of unoccupied land near the towns. The primary hazard of planting in the periurban areas is the theft of crops, because fields not located near the houses are more difficult to protect.

Another way to make a living for women and men is to take a *candonga* (bush taxi) to the rural areas in order to buy goods to trade in the urban markets and to have some food for the "family." However, before the economic restructuring in 1986, it was rather difficult to live on petty trade. The government monopoly of peanuts and palm oil for export made even the sale of

roasted peanuts illegal. Moreover, the state fixed the prices of meat, fish, tomatoes, palm wine, etc. Authority to enforce these rules was given to the police, who not only fined the traders, but confiscated the goods, often for their
own consumption. The message the producers and traders received was that
the state was against rather than for them, and many of them were no longer
willing to trade in the open markets. This increased the food shortage in the
urban areas.

Many urban residents still have relatives in the rural areas. When food crises become acute, unemployed women and men go to stay with their rural kin
during the rainy season to plant and harvest food for their families.

Despite the resistance of peasant farmers to the trade policy, they supply a
good part of the urban population with food. Urban dwellers who are employed or not willing to farm travel to the southern rice surplus areas to buy
food when the shortage becomes acute in Bissau. In 1983 large numbers of
people went to the south on trucks or ships to procure rice this way. The more
fortunate ones were able to rely on kin networks; the others had to go to the
communities and plead with the farmers to sell them their preferred staple,
rice.

In sum, the majority of women and some men in the urban areas have to
find ways outside the wage economy and state marketing network to provide
food for themselves and their children. However, the choices available to
them are limited and can bring them in conflict with the authorities. In their
struggle to cope with food shortages, they often find themselves accused of
illegal activities or blamed for the scarcities in the market.

Growing food and engaging in petty trade allow a woman to provide for
herself and her children if the wage-earning husband does not give her sufficient means to live. Even if men intend to contribute income to provide for
the "family," they may not be able to buy the necessary goods, such as rice,
fish, and oil, because the stores are empty, and they may drink[8] more to deal
with this frustration. Scarcity can thus lead to an increase in domestic conflicts, a stressful family environment, or even divorce. Marrying more than
one wife becomes problematic for an urban man. Especially women with little economic capacity run a risk of being abandoned with their children.
Women and children, therefore, often suffer more from the national economic crisis and gender antagonisms are increased by macro-level processes.

Coping Strategies in the Rural Areas

In the context of the national economic crisis, rural dwellers have had to rely
largely on themselves to deal with food shortages. To cope with scarcity,
peasant farmers use various strategies. I will compare and contrast the spe-

cific measures taken by two ethnic groups, the Bejáa (Balanta-Mané) and the
Brassa (Balanta).[9] Farming systems differ greatly by ecological zone and
type of land use in Guinea-Bissau. The Bejáa and Brassa represent the two
principal production systems, land-extensive upland rainfed agriculture and
land-intensive lowland wet rice production respectively. They live in scattered compounds of patrilineages who control the land. Wives, who have to
move to the compound of their husbands, generally gain access to land
through them. The Bejáa and Brassa socioeconomic systems differ, but they
both have only limited sociopolitical hierarchies; there are no chiefs, only
village committees. Every able-bodied man and woman has to participate in
food production; they cannot simply live off the labor of others.

   Most of the examples of coping strategies are from Oio, a region located in
the northern, drier area of Guinea-Bissau, where the Bejáa and many of the
Brassa live. In Oio surpluses are limited, and people are more severely af-
fected by drought. In the northern part of the region which borders on
Senegal, Aaby et al. (1981) found the highest rates of malnutrition among the
Muslim Mandinga, who have a farming system that is similar to that of the
Bejáa.[10]

THE BEJÁA

The Bejáa have a land-extensive hoe farming system in rainfed upland areas.
They are best known for men's shifting cultivation of peanuts for export and
the exploitation of palm wine for cash. Less well known is women's unusual
role in slash and burn[11] cultivation of dry rice, in which they themselves cut
the forest, clear, and hoe plots. Thus, men and women usually plant different
crops on separate fields. Women also broadcast swamp rice in hydromorphic
depressions, plant fonio (*Digitaria exilis*), sometimes called "hungry rice,"
and vegetables. Men practice shifting cultivation of upland crops, such as
finger millet (*Pennisetum glaucum*), corn, and beans, mainly for subsistence.
Having more than one wife allows a man to spend less time in food production and increase the cultivation of peanuts. Men also plant mango, banana,
cashew, and citrus trees. The division of labor in agriculture, as well as in all
other work spheres, is predominantly sex-segregated. The Bejáa do not have
households, but compounds composed of separate men's and women's
houses with the latter divided into several matricentric *fugon* (hearths). Co-
wives who reside together assert their autonomy by splitting up into separate
production and consumption units, while close kinsmen, or the men of an
entire compound produce and eat together.

In the following section I will discuss the coping strategies that are employed by rural dwellers in general, and give examples of the specific responses of the Bejáa to food crises.

Dry Season Coping Strategies

Following a bad harvest,[12] Guinean farmers, in anticipation of a shortage of food supplies, start precautionary measures early to ensure that the food in their granaries lasts until the next harvest. To limit the depletion of stored grains, they restrict the sale or exchange of the harvest, procure additional food sources, reduce the daily consumption of grain, and postpone social ceremonies, like initiations or weddings, which require large amounts of rice and the slaughter of animals. They begin these measures in the dry season after the harvest, when their farm work requirements are minimal.

To obtain additional food, people forage the natural resources of the forest under community control. They also procure free food aid or use savings to purchase food on the national market or from other smallholder farmers. However, these latter options were not viable in Guinea-Bissau before 1986. Free food aid was almost never available to rural producers, and there was a perennial shortage of grains and other basic food supplies at official prices in the stores or, at much higher prices, in the parallel markets. Moreover, peasant farmers with a surplus of grains had little interest in selling food for local currency; they would only exchange them for livestock. For these reasons, rural producers most commonly resorted to foraging.

Gathered food—roots, wild vegetables, and fruit—are the main source of supplementary foods. Hunting and fishing provide occasional sources of protein. Under the prevailing gender division of labor in all the ethnic groups, women do most of the gathering and some fishing. Children mainly gather fruits and nuts. This organization of work implies that in times of anticipated scarcity, women are the first to intensify their search for additional sources of food. Women also plant and irrigate such vegetables as tomatoes, okra, *jagatú* (*Solanum indicum*) (bitter pepper), *baguiche* (*Hibiscus sabdarifa*), and they dry vegetables, cassava, and fish for use in the "hungry season," when the crops are not yet ready to be harvested. If they fear a food crisis, women sell less or none of their crops, and reduce the time spent at income-generating activities.

One precautionary measure Bejáa women take is to modify the meal plan to save rice and millet for the planting season. In men's low-activity months preceding the rainy season, women often prepare only one meal based on grain products a day instead of two; they cook wild yams for the other meal. They go frequently to the forest to gather yams, despite other demands on their time. Since women normally sell some of their wild yams, the domestic consumption means the loss of an important source of income during times of food scarcity.

The only activity of Bejáa men that falls under the category of gathering is the tapping of palm wine and the cutting of palm fruit. Palm wine provides an important source of income for men, besides its nutritional, social, and ritual use. Nutritionally men benefit more, because they drink palm wine every day, while women only infrequently receive any. I did not observe any change in the pattern of palm wine consumption during "hungry periods." Men continue to sell palm wine in times of scarcity, and thus do not forego this source of income, although drought may diminish the quantity of wine tapped. They occasionally exchange palm wine for fonio, but only when other households have a grain surplus.

During a food crisis, men cut more palm fruit while they are tapping, but this does not significantly increase their work. Palm fruit sauce and oil provide valued supplements to the diet, but there are not sufficient palm groves in the Bejáa area for palm fruit to provide a major additional food source in times of scarcity. Bejáa women cook and pound the palm fruits to separate the flesh from the kernels, then press it by hand and sieve it, either to make a sauce for immediate consumption, or to cook it again to extract the oil. Because Bejáa men climb the palm trees to cut the fruit, they claim ownership of the oil, despite women's labor-intensive work to extract it. Women keep the palm kernels, which they usually sell for export. Men generally sell most of this highly valued oil, which fetches a good price in Senegal, but in times of food shortage they keep more for domestic consumption or use the proceeds of the oil, extracted with women's labor, to buy rice.

For protein, some of the men hunt, and they distribute part of the meat to the members of their compound and extended family. However, they usually sell the good parts of a deer, at least to recover the high cost of ammunition. Other meat is only consumed when livestock is slaughtered on ritual and ceremonial occasions, which they postpone if possible during crisis years. Meat provides a nutritious and welcome addition to the diet. Its consumption is qualitatively but not quantitatively significant. Boys get more protein when they catch small animals with traps, roast them over an open fire, and gorge themselves in the forest. Fishing is not a viable option during a drought year because the swamp ponds in the Bejáa area tend to dry up. Men assert that they are expected to provide the ingredients for the daily *mafe* (sauce/ stew), such as palm fruit, fish, or meat. For this reason they occasionally buy fish, but more often the sauce only consists of women's vegetables.

Bejáa women's food reserves are further taxed because of male labor migration. Many young men migrate to Senegal during the rainy season to plant peanuts to sell for F CFA (Senegalese currency) to buy bicycles, radios, and clothes for bride prestations,[13] while other young men migrate to Bissau to look for jobs. During the dry season some of these men return, and other young men come from Senegal in pursuit of brides. They all stay with and are fed by their kin. Although they sometimes bring rice with them from Senegal, it does not cover their consumption needs. In times of food shortage, more consumers pose an added threat to the meager granary reserves and increase the demand on women's rice stores and domestic labor time.

Moreover, in all ethnic groups women's duty of fetching water becomes more difficult as the wells dry up during drought periods since they have to walk farther to find water. Wells with hand pumps have been introduced by development projects in many villages to provide a closer water source. However, during my stay many pumps broke down, several during the dry season, and the peasant farmers did not have the spare parts, equipment, or training to repair them. It often took months for them to be repaired by the state maintenance crew. In the meantime, women had to return to unmaintained old wells further away.

All rural Guinea-Bissau women work more hours per day than men. In addition to farming, gathering, and other food-related activities, women do most of the domestic work and child care with the help of older children. The examples show that after a scant harvest, women are the first to shift the allocation of their labor to cope with a food shortage. In the prevailing social relations of work, most of women's time is already allocated to subsistence activities, especially among the Bejáa and other ethnic groups, such as the Mandinga and Fula, with similar farming systems and gender division of labor (Hochet, 1983). An increase in women's work in food procurement can only take place at the expense of time women would normally spend in income-generating activities. This increase then, means not only more work for women, but a loss of income. Consequently, one bad harvest amplifies the economic inequalities inherent in the preexisting structural inequality in the gender division of labor.

Even though the dry season coping strategies have an insignificant impact on men's labor burden, men do participate in other precautionary measures following a bad harvest. Lacking a surplus, both men and women forsake the sale of some of their crops. For example, if the harvest has been good, Bejáa men may sell some of their millet, but not in times of food shortage. Thus, men experience a cut in income, but because they have several sources of income, this cut is proportionally small.

For additional income, Bejáa men produce peanuts. If possible they invite a cooperative labor group to hoe the fields. Goat or bush meat with palm oil sauce over rice served with palm wine is the standard meal given to the invited group. A man who has two or more wives may be better able to hire labor groups, because he may have easier access to rice from his wives. He also needs women willing to take time off their planting activities to pound extra rice and cook for the group. Men only give a small part of the peanuts to the women to cook, even though this would provide a much appreciated supplement of protein and oil to the diet. Even as a precautionary measure men do not keep peanuts for consumption (after two bad rainy seasons I still observed men selling their peanuts), but their income is diminished after a scant harvest. In the nineteenth century the colonists pressured the farmers to produce peanuts for export, and they continue to be perceived as a cash crop. They are not thought of as a major food source, and are not used to replenish food reserves, despite their important nutritional value. Since the introduction of peanuts, men spend less time producing cereal crops, and women have to use more of their crops for subsistence.

Bejáa women, who are the recognized producers and owners of rice, do not sell any during periods of food shortage. If a mother sold rice when food was scarce, she would be accused of neglecting her children. Consequently, during periods of scarcity women earn less money from rice and yams, which is significant because of the few sources of income they have. The fact that Bejáa women are criticized if they sell their rice in times of shortage highlights the cultural expectation that mothers should provide for their children. I did not hear criticisms of men who sold their peanuts, deer meat, or palm wine. Indeed, they are perceived as supplementary rather than staple food items. However, as long as Bejáa men put a lot of time into the production of peanuts, women are forced to use most of their crops to feed the "family," and thus have to relinquish the income from their sale.

Until 1985 rice or millet was rarely available at official prices. After a bad harvest, the Bejáa in the compounds researched were interested in buying grains, but because they lived at a distance of ten or more miles from the nearest market town, they only heard about the availability of grain in the stores two or three days later. By that time the supplies had often run out, unless the peasant farmers had a patron merchant who guarded rice for them in return for exclusive buying rights of their peanuts. If the men, who went there on foot or bicycle, arrived in time, they usually had to wait in line for hours to be able to get their ration of 10–25 kg of rice. Bejáa men paid for this rice, becuase women had little money left after employing their precautionary measures. Men would have liked to buy more rice, especially for ceremonies, but this was rarely possible. Thus, Bejáa gender inequalities are exacerbated not because of men's increased attempts to exploit women, but because of the local reverberations of the national economic crisis. Since men's principal coping strategies involve the purchase of food, in the absence of this possibility, the burden falls increasingly on women.

As is common with the practice of polygyny in many parts of Africa, Bejáa spouses have separate control of their incomes. This contributes to women's economic autonomy. However, men usually spend more of their money on personal needs and on arranging marriages for themselves or their male kin. They only contribute to domestic expenses at their own discretion, and if goods are available. As we have seen, Bejáa men have significantly more income than women, but because they alone decide how to use it, wives rarely benefit from their husband's greater income. Therefore, even though Bejáa women structurally enjoy budgetary autonomy, their limited earnings and lack of access to men's money ultimately leaves them with little financial means. In sum, during the dry season after a bad harvest, both Bejáa women and men experience a cut in income, but in contrast to men's relatively small loss, women's is more significant.

Rainy Season Coping Strategies

If the precautionary measures taken during the dry season are successful in preserving sufficient grain until the beginning of the next harvest, then, with the start of the new agricultural cycle in May, the peasant farmers can concentrate their efforts on cultivation. However, if food reserves are beginning to run low, rural producers have to employ other coping strategies that interfere as little as possible with their agricultural labor demands. For example, they resort to their social networks for help, or they exchange livestock for rice or millet. Although the Bejáa rarely own cattle, both men and women keep small livestock, such as pigs, sheep, and goats which predominantly belong to women.

Bejáa women, who have separate granaries and hearths, may ask other women in the compound to help out, or they may visit their kin and ask if they can give them some grain. Because all the men of one compound eat together, they share the calabashes of food that women from each hearth bring to the men's eating house. This redistribution within and between compounds is only a solution as long as the crisis has not reached all the communities.

Bejáa women not only work more and give up income and livestock in their attempt to deal with a food shortage, they also take ritual measures when the rains are not sufficient. In August 1983, when the rainfall was low for the second year in a row, women organized a ritual for which a woman from each hearth sacrificed a chicken. They were cooked and served with rice in a ritual meal, shared by everyone, as an appeal to the divine powers for more rain. Women usually raise chickens for cash and to offer them to healers in return for treatment. That all the hearths of several compounds participated in this ritual and material sacrifice shows women's ability to organize and take social action in the face of a crisis.

When grain reserves were near depletion and rice was not available in Guinea-Bissau, men went to buy rice in the well supplied stores in Senegal. This option was expensive because of the limited purchasing power of the Guinean Peso, which had only a fraction of its official value in Senegal. However, the parallel market was the only place where farmers could get access to F CFA. The other option was to take animals to Senegal and sell them for F CFA. This strategy is risky, because the animals may be confiscated by the border guards. It is unclear how many of the goats exchanged belonged to women, but given that women owned the majority of them, it is likely that a significant number of the goats sold came from them. This meant a loss of wealth for both women and men. among Bejáa number of the goats sold came from them. This meant a loss of wealth for both women and men. Among Bejáa men, who are economically more stratified, these options are restricted to those with sufficient income or livestock, but common meals among men in the compound have a levelling effect.

Although men make more efforts to procure grains during the rainy season when there is a food shortage, this does not result in a significant increase in their work time. The measures taken at this point result in losses of income and wealth for both men and women. Moreover, the food crisis begins to have a negative impact on health as consumption is reduced. Thus, men do make sacrifices during a food crisis, but only after the food shortage has been prolonged and other measures, many taken by women, have not been sufficient to alleviate the problem.

If at the end of the rainy season the harvests are good, people can return to a normal way of life. Women can again spend more time in commercial activities and social ceremonies can be held in the dry season. However, the losses incurred during the previous year cannot be recovered with just one year of good harvests. Bejáa women, who have less income-earning capacity, will take much longer to recoup their losses. It takes more than a year to accumulate a sufficient surplus to reconstitute savings and such wealth as livestock. The Bejáa still have not been able to build up new herds of cattle to replace the ones that were stolen or killed by the Portuguese army during the liberation war.

Therefore, even a food crisis every other year will progressively undermine local self-sufficiency, slowly deteriorate the economy of an area, erode women's economic power, and increase gender inequality among the Bejáa. If the food shortage reaches national proportions, it can lead to a major crisis and widespread hunger. This scenario is more devastating when harvests are bad for two or more years in a row.

Coping Strategies After Second Bad Harvest

During the dry season after a second bad harvest peasant farmers repeat the precautionary measures taken in the previous dry season. This means another increase in women's labor input for gathering and processing food, a further loss of income for both women and men as they consume, instead of sell, their produce, and an additional reduction in savings when they buy food.

The measures taken during the dry season may not be sufficient, because food reserves from previous years have been depleted. As a consequence, in the following rainy season they repeat the measures taken in the second stage, such as the sale of livestock, and enact some novel strategies to cope with the food crisis.

For example, even though Bejáa and Mandinga men did not give up the sale of peanuts for consumption, in 1981 after two years of bad harvests and hunger, some men decided to abandon the production of peanuts for cash, and decided to plant more millet instead. This resulted in a significant loss of income for them, and a lack of seeds for the following year, unless they could get seeds from the kin, neighbors, or the state.

Thus, when a food crisis is prolonged, men's losses become more severe, and both women and men experience a major loss of wealth. In particular the sale or exchange of livestock for food has long-term consequences, because domestic animals constitute an important basis of food security and their sale makes the rural dwellers more vulnerable to famine.

Many of the strategies the Brassa use are similar to those of the Bejáa, but given the differences in their economic system, gender division of labor, and cultural practices, the impact on men's and women's work load and economic power is not necessarily the same.

THE BRASSA

The Brassa practice land- and labor-intensive wet rice agriculture. They have developed a technically sophisticated farming system using special long hoes to make high ridges and dikes in permanently cultivated *bolanha* (swamp paddies). Brassa men invest a major portion of their time in the preparation of the fields and contribute significantly to subsistence, thus sharing the burden of food production with women. Rice and cattle are the mainstay of the Brassa economic and ritual system. In the southern regions of Guinea-Bissau, large surpluses of rice are not uncommon. However, the Brassa who currently live in the northern regions, where swamp lands are limited and rainfall is erratic, supplement wet rice with upland crops, such as millet, corn, fonio, cassava, and beans.

In contrast to the Bejáa, the Brassa do have domestic units that can be categorized as households. A married Brassa man shares a house with his wife/ wives and children, and occasionally his mother or other relatives. This residential unit is at the same time the production and consumption unit. To get a wife, a Brassa man has to fulfill a number of obligations, such as bringing palm wine or rum to his future parents-in-law, but getting married has been less costly in the past than for the Bejáa. However, in the present situation of scarcity and with inflation, the costs of marriage are rising.

Brassa social relations of agricultural labor differ considerably from those of the Bejáa. Gender and age are important organizing principles. Several age grades of boys and uninitiated men[14] form the basis of cooperative male labor groups. The gender division of tasks in agriculture is complementary. Men prepare the fields for planting, do some weeding, and often invite a cooperative labor group to hoe, harvest, or thresh the rice in return for a good meal, drinks, and occasionally a pig or other compensation. Women transplant rice, help weed millet and beans, and carry the harvest home. In contrast to the Bejáa, Brassa men own the rice and other crops from their fields, but use the majority of the harvest for domestic consumption. Rice is the preferred staple, and it is also used in rituals and ceremonies. Men determine at harvest time what part of the rice to store for consumption, how much to sell, and whether to exchange some rice for livestock[15]. Depending on the quantity of the harvest, the husband gives his wife/wives one or more baskets to sell so they can buy some pieces of cloth for themselves. Rice is one of only a few sources of income for men.

Because Brassa men contribute a considerable amount of labor to food production, under normal circumstances women's time is not entirely taken up by field work, food processing, and domestic work. Indeed, Brassa women pursue many commercial activities. One is to plant a personal field of rice with the help of daughters or foster daughters. Women can sell the rice, but they often use it to host a male labor group to ridge a field the following year so that they can plant peanuts. Because Brassa men and women have separate budgets, as do the Bejáa, a woman controls the income from the sale of this crop. Women also plant and sell yams, taro, vegetables, and spices. they fish, collect crabs, raise chicken, and produce salt, palm oil, cashew wine, and lemon juice vinegar for consumption and sale. In addition they engage in trade, and produce soap, pottery, and charcoal.

The Brassa are less vulnerable to a food crisis, and women carry a lesser burden in the provision of food than Bejáa women, because men work predominantly in food production. Although the Brassa gender division of labor in agriculture is complementary, in other work spheres the division of labor is sex-segregated like that of the Bejáa, and with the gender-typing of tasks and spheres, the work load tends to be unequally distributed. Especially in food processing and domestic work, women's responsibilities are much more extensive than men's, as indeed is true in all of Africa. In what follows I will give examples of Brassa coping strategies and contrast their impact on men's and women's labor burden and economic assets with the situation of the Bejáa.

Brassa Dry Season Coping Strategies

To limit the depletion of grains, Brassa women gather *manganasse* [*Icacina senegalensis*], fruit, leaves, and other forest products. Boys and men help in the harvesting of tree crops, such as the seed pods of the *faroba* [*Parkia biglobosa*], baobab, and mango. After a poor harvest, women spend more time gathering and processing *manganasse* and other wild food to avoid the threat of hunger.

Much of the gathered food requires extensive processing to be edible, and this is exclusively women's work. *Faroba* must be shelled, soaked to ferment, and pounded before cooking. *Manganasse* requires drying, then soaking in water for a week, a second drying, then cooking and pounding to be edible. If incorrectly prepared, *Manganasse* can be fatal. In one village in 1981, fifteen people died of poisoning because they ate *manganasse* too soon. Green mangoes are preserved by peeling, cutting, and drying them; cooked, they taste like potatoes. With the increased consumption of wild foods, women's labor burden increases significantly.

Brassa women, instead of Brassa men, are culturally expected to procure the ingredients for the *mafe* (sauce/stew) that is served on rice or millet. The sauce can include sea food, peanuts, baobab, or milk, all of which provide important nutritional supplements. During a period of scarcity women intensify their fishing and collecting of oysters and crabs for consumption, and they sell less of the rice, peanuts, and other goods they usually collect or produce to earn money. Thus, as they spend more time trying to find food for the family, they also take a reduction in income. However, this loss is less dramatic than for Bejáa women because Brassa women have more sources of income.

During the dry season young Brassa men and women like to migrate to commercial farms, plantations, or urban areas to earn money to supplement their limited incomes from agricultural production. In contrast to the Bejáa, the Brassa strongly discourage migration during the rainy season, because a shortage of male labor can have a very negative impact on the production to

food crops. Given the Brassa gender division of labor, it is necessary to intensify both men's work in field preparation and women's tasks of transplanting
and weeding, in which they are occasionally helped by men, in order to be
able to extend the planting areas of crops and increase the yields. Thus, social
pressures are applied to discourage male migration during the rainy season,
especially during periods of scarcity. Moreover, both male and female kin in
the urban areas are encouraged to return temporarily to help cultivate.

After a bad harvest, men may only sell as much rice as is absolutely necessary for them to pay taxes, and women may not receive any to sell. Thus, as a
result of a food shortage both women and men have less money. Given that
Brassa men have fewer sources of income than Bejáa men, this cut in income
is more significant for them.

If despite these measures grain reserves are running low, men attempt to
get rice by travelling to rice surplus areas in the south during the dry season.
Many Brassa have relatives in the south and can sometimes get rice from
them. For those people without extended kin networks, this option is limited.
Until 1986 it was difficult to find peasant farmers who were willing to sell
rice, because there was virtually nothing for them to buy with local currency.
Moreover, they would not sell at the low farm-gate prices, so the cost of this
rice including the transport by bush taxi was quite high. If men do not have
financial reserves, women have to defray these costs (Hochet, 1983).

As we have seen above, there are some commonalties and differences in
the impact of the precautionary measures on the Bejáa and Brassa. Women in
both societies have similar domestic obligations, but Bejáa women carry a
heavier burden in producing food for subsistence, and as a result they have
less time for income-earning activities than Brassa women. During the dry
season after a bad harvest, all women spend more time than men gathering
and processing food, and consequently they have less time to pursue commercial activities. In contrast, men of both ethnic groups do not experience
much increase in work in the first phase of a food shortage. Women and men
both take a cut in income during this period. This loss is most dramatic for
Bejáa women who already have little income, and relatively important for
Brassa men who forego the sale of rice, one of their few sources of cash, but
less drastic for Brassa women or Bejáa men. In sum, while everyone experiences some loss in income, for women a food crisis additionally translates
into an important increase in their labor burden.

Brassa Rainy Season Coping Strategies

If the depletion of grains becomes imminent before the ripening of the new
crops at the end of the rainy season, the Brassa search for ways to ward off

famine that do not interfere with their planting activities. They try to get help from people in other households or compounds. Brassa men say they would be ashamed to have their wives go ask their kin for food, because they are expected to provide the grains to the "family," which they do with the help of female labor. Women may still resort to their own kin networks to try to get food if the shortage becomes acute and their kin still have reserves.

Brassa men say that because of the cultural expectation that they supply the grains to the "family," they are forced to sell or exchange their goats or cattle for rice or millet when other strategies have not been sufficient to alleviate the food shortage. Women also own some cattle and small livestock, which may be exchanged when the crisis becomes more severe. There are individual differences in the amount of ownership of livestock, but they are downplayed in Brassa society. One mode of forced redistribution is the raiding of cattle. The Brassa say they go on cattle raids when they are hungry, and young men who are successful are admired for their courage and shrewdness. Cattle raiding or an attempt to exchange cattle in Senegal often brings the Brassa in conflict with the authorities, and they end up paying heavy fines or see all their cattle confiscated. All these activities lead to a decrease in livestock, and therefore a diminution of men's and women's wealth.

One bad harvest can negatively influence production the following year. During a period of food shortage people are exposed to more health risks as they start to reduce caloric intake or consume potentially hazardous foods. For example, during the hungry season more cattle die of such diseases as anthrax (splenic fever),[16] and people eat the infected meat because of the scant food supplies. Hunger leads to weight loss, making individuals more vulnerable to illness, and reduces their productive capacity during the planting season. The Guineans say *saku limpu ka ta firma,* "an empty bag does not stand up," meaning that a hungry person cannot work.

If the food shortage continues for a second year, the Brassa repeat the coping strategies. First, woman increase gathering, and later men and women exchange more livestock. Once the livestock is decimated, it cannot be reconstituted rapidly. Thus, the depletion of livestock is a sign of considerable distress in the system.

In contrast to the Bejáa, among the Brassa gender inequalities in economic power are not necessarily aggravated when people respond to food shortages. Although women suffer more from an increase in the work load, men may have to relinquish relatively more income and livestock when the food crisis becomes more severe. Thus, depending on the structure and relations of the pre-existing gendered political economy, and the duration of the crisis, the impact of food shortages on men and women varies.

CONCLUSION

Without the work of peasant farmers, urban cultivators, and traders, widespread famine would have been a reality in Guinea-Bissau. Facing a severe national economic crisis and unfavorable market conditions, people of all lower socioeconomic strata have to cope with recurrent food shortages on their own. International food aid benefits predominantly the government employees. The success of development projects oriented toward increasing food production is limited because of managerial, technical, and sociopolitical problems.

In the urban areas, socioeconomic or class status determines how an individual is affected by a food crisis. The small group of people who belong to the elite have regular access to imported foodstuffs as well as to cars, which allow them to buy goods in the rural areas. Although women are usually responsible for the household, elite women have domestic servants who shop and queue for them. For the majority of urban dwellers, access to food is restricted by scarcities in the market, low salaries, and inflationary prices, which limit their buying power on the parallel market. Moreover, only few people are able to get salaried employment and women have less chance at it because of gender stratification in education. However, with the "tradition" of separate spousal budgets, men are reluctant to hand over their salaries to their wives for family expenses. The national economic crisis is keenly felt at the household level, and conflicts over the allocation of scarce income, especially in polygynous unions, increasingly result in domestic tensions or divorce. To survive economically, married women and single mothers have to take greater responsibility for producing or procuring food. Poor women and men who try to cope with food shortages through petty trade often find themselves in conflict with state policies. Thus, food shortages create tensions between authorities and the masses, exacerbate socioeconomic inequalities, and aggravate domestic conflicts.

For the "family" farmers, in the absence of well-supplied markets and irrigation systems, food shortages are strongly related to fluctuations in rainfall. Given the common pattern of one year of drought, followed by one or more years of sufficient rainfall, dry season coping strategies are employed most often. Frequent enactment of these strategies leaves women with an inordinate amount of the increased labor burden, because non-monetary measures, such as gathering, and food processing, are culturally constructed as female. Therefore, it is not the availability of labor of an individual that determines who will cope, but the gender division of labor. The pre-existing gender inequality in the division of tasks and responsibilities in the rural areas is exacerbated with repeated years of food crisis. So far the government, despite its ideological commitment to gender equality, has not recognized the central role of the unequal gender division of labor in the perpetuation of the exploitation of women.

The gender division of labor in agriculture and some of the coping strategies vary culturally. The Bejáa and Brassa men and women may use similar coping strategies, but they are affected differently. Among the Brassa, who have a complementary gender division of labor in agriculture, men contribute significantly to staple food production, and as a consequence gender inequalities in coping are less pronounced. While women start with measures that increase their work load, men forego income, so their initial sacrifices are comparable.

Among the Bejáa, men's involvement in the production of export crops has forced women to take on much greater responsibility in providing food, and consequently they have less time to earn an income. Because of the feminization of food production following the colonial promotion of cash crops, Bejáa women suffer the greatest loss in economic power with recurring food shortages. In contrast, Bejáa men, who are more strongly linked to the monetary economy, have considerable financial reserves. Cultural expectations reflect the ethnic differences in the gender division of labor in agriculture, and give ideological justification for the exploitation of women, as when Bejáa women are accused of neglecting their children when they sell their rice or yams.

Prolonged food shortages require an increasing sacrifice of savings and livestock. Unlike the earlier stage, where Bejáa gender inequalities are exacerbated, when the crisis becomes more severe, men are more seriously affected, and their losses are more comparable to those of women. Similarly, among the Brassa, where gender inequalities are fewer at the early stages, in the later ones it is the men, in particular those with large herds, who lose more. Thus the exchange or loss of livestock due to raids may decrease Brassa economic inequalities associated with gender and social status. As poorer members of the communities exhaust their resources, they become entirely dependent on their kin and friends for survival. Thus the process of immiseration brought about by the threat of famine eventually affects everyone seriously, although in a gendered and culturally complex manner. As both rural and many urban dwellers are driven to poverty or even starvation, they may try to rely on a government already deeply indebted, which will have to rely on the international community and become more dependent. The option more frequently taken by people is emigration to Senegal.

To prevent famine it is necessary to study the course of this complex process. This chapter has traced some of its gender, ethnic, socioeconomic, and rural/urban complexity. National economic policies should not only aim to strengthen the capacity for national self-sufficiency, but be sensitive to the sociopolitical and cultural aspects of the relations of production and distribution. Policies that bring producers in conflict with the authorities will do little to promote an increase in food production and domestic trade. Finally, polices that do not question gender inequalities in the social relations of work undermine the important role women play in production and trade.

NOTES

1. The article is based on research carried out during summer 1979 and from 1981-1985, generously funded by the Department of Anthropology, the Center for Research in International Studies, and the African Studies Committee (FLAS),all at Stanford University, and the Directorate of Development Cooperation and Humanitarian Aid, Switzerland. I am grateful to the people of Guinea-Bissau for their help. This paper has benefited from the comments of Jane Collier, Leonel Galvâo, Charles Hale, Nickie Irvine, Wunyabari Maloba, Deborah Rubin, and Felix Sigrist.

2. Economic power here refers to the control of goods, income, and wealth, such as in livestock, which not only increases an individual's economic autonomy, but puts her/him in a better bargaining position in decision-making, and gives him/her more social and political influence.

3. Most of the fishing areas are exploited by industrial ships that rarely even come into the ports of Bissau. The government lacked the capacity to control large-scale fishing, and with the chronic scarcity of fish in the local market people benefit little from the rich fishing grounds.

4. Because the social and economic organization varies considerably by ethnic group and the social units often do not fit the customary definition of a family or household, these terms are put in quotes.

5. Sugar cane, cashew, and other plantations occupy a very small part of the total arable land area.

6. This is not to imply that all these technologies are appropriate and viable options for Guinea-Bissau.

7. It is reasonable to deduce from the census that there are ca. 159,000 male farmers and ca. 240,000 female farmers, despite the fact that women in the census were mistakenly listed as *domesticas* (housewives) under the category "inactive population" (MICEP, 1980: 158-160). All healthy women in the rural areas, and many women in the urban areas, farm.

8. Palm wine, cashew wine, sugar cane rum, beer, and imported alcohol were more regularly available than basic foodstuffs.

9. The Portuguese called the Bejáa and the Brassa Balanta-Mané and Balanta respectively. The people call themselves Bejáa and Brassa, and in due respect to them, I am using the indigenous names (plural form).

10. Unlike the Bejáa, the Mandinga, as well as the Fula (both Islamic) and the Manjaco, have historically been socially and politically stratified, with chiefs and occupational castes.

11. The terms "slash and burn" and "shifting" cultivation refer to different processes here. While in the former case the forest is cut and then burned, in the latter there is a rotation of fields with a short fallow period of 2-3 years, so that only the clearing of small bushes before planting is required.

12. The rainy season begins late May/early June and ends in October; the dry season lasts from November until May. The harvest begins with the first crop in September and ends with the last crop in December/January.

13. A groom has to give several sets of clothes and other things to the bride and offer palm wine, tobacco, and cloth to her family.
14. Brassa political structure is also based on age grades. Men can only assume positions of authority in the council of elders after an initiation ceremony in their thirties. Elder women can participate in council meetings, especially if they have displayed outstanding wisdom and eloquence.
15. They raise goats, sheep, pigs, and cattle.
16. This illness is transmitted by encapsulated cysts that can survive a long time. To break the cycle of transmission, meat from cattle that die of this illness should be burned and not eaten.

REFERENCES

Aaby, P., Bukh, J., Smits, A., and I. Lisse
  1981 Child Mortality in Guinea-Bissau: Malnutrition or Overcrowding? Copenhagen: Institute of Anthropology.
Bigman, Laura Ellen
  1988 The Political Economy of the Food Question in Lusophone West Africa. Ph.D. dissertation, Howard University.
Funk, Ursula
  1988 Land Tenure, Agriculture, and Gender in Guinea-Bissau. In Agriculture, Women, and Land: The African Experience. J. Davison, ed. pp. 33–58. Boulder, CO: Westview Press.
Galli, Rosemary E.
  1987 The Food Crisis and the Socialist State in Lusophone Africa. African Studies Review, 30(1): 19–44.
Galli, Rosemary E. And Jocelyn Jones
  1987 Guinea-Bissau: Politics, Economics and Society. Boulder: Lynne Rienner.
Hochet, Anne-Marie
  1983. Paysanneries en attente: Guinée-Bissau. Dakar: ENDA.
MICEP (Ministry of Economic Coordination and Planning, Guinea-Bissau)
  1981 Recenseamento Geral da Popluaçâo e da Habitaçâo. Resultados Provisorios Fase II. Bissau: MICEP.

CHAPTER 8

Food Traders and Food Security in Ghana

Gracia Clark

The importance of African traders to their food systems has been more directly acknowledged recently as policymakers shift their focus to food security rather than simply food production. Amartya Sen (1981) first highlighted the concept of food entitlement in discussing causes of mass as well as individual starvation. Even when food production rises, individuals, social groups, or nations face hunger if they lack the finances or the social and physical infrastructure for steady access to food supplies.

In current African famines, financial, political, and transport crises compound the effects of drought and declining crop yields. In response, the Food and Agriculture Organisation of the United Nations (FAO) has stressed the need for "physical and economic access" to food supplies available at national or global levels (FAO 1983). This FAO report elaborates "three specific aims: ensuring production of adequate food supplies; maximizing stability in the flow of food supplies; securing access to available supplies on the part of those who need them."

This paper evaluates the actions of Ghanaian market women, specifically foodstuffs traders based in Kumasi Central Market, the largest single market in Ghana, in terms of their effect on those three aims. It pinpoints aspects of trading relations that strengthen or weaken food security by affecting prices and incomes, the available food supply, the physical flow of goods, and food production levels. The potential degree and direction of traders' influence on these aspects of food security are determined by their capacity for storage, credit and price fixing, the direction and stability of commodity flows and price incentives, and employment and income distribution through trading. Gender enters as a critical intervening variable here, because of its role in constructing both men's and women's access to capital, labor, income, and essential physical and social facilities in historically and culturally specific patterns. Kumasi traders' recent short and long-term responses to food shortages and non-traders' reactions to their actions demonstrate mainly positive effects on food security, but some negative effects as well. The strategies and conditions identified here as promoting or undermining food security in this case may well have similar effects when found elsewhere in Africa, but in different proportions according to their importance in those specific contexts.

Generalizations of this kind appear more useful for constructive policy recommendations than the more common conclusion that one or another kind of trading system is most or least effective for the whole of sub-Saharan Africa. Even a highly sophisticated analysis of specific complex national and regional situations concludes with such general statements (Bates 1981). Parastatals, transnational corporations, and indigenous traders have each found their defenders in the sometimes hot debates over African food marketing involving both scholars and policymakers. Advocates seem convinced that all the most serious abuses or inefficiencies can be avoided and dependable access to food supplies and adequate incentives to food farmers assured by allowing their favored system to operate without interference. However, identifying positive and negative aspects that may be found within a variety of food distribution systems facilitates the selection of trading policies appropriate to specific local conditions. Such an analysis would suggest effective improvements to existing trading institutions as well as suggest strategies to increase the chances of effective operation of proposed new institutions.

Concrete analyses of food commercialization processes confirm the significance of such locally specific factors for the performance of distribution systems when food security is threatened. In Guyer's introduction to a volume of historical studies of African urban food supply systems, she joins many other analysts in calling for respectful attention to local variations within Africa in analyses of social institutions, farming systems, and the like (Guyer 1987). Smith's analysis of Guatemalan regions shows how fruitful such attention can be. Her mapping of local variations in the role of traders and craft producers reveals significant aspects of the complex historical process of articulation with the international economy. Their aggregate actions helped negotiate the balance of power between the directly and indirectly controlled sectors of the economy (Smith 1984).

Comparing examples from different parts of the African continent enables Guyer to select flexibility as an aspect of distributive systems that contributes consistently to long-term food security (Guyer 1987). Rigidities in trading relations that keep trade tightly held in groups defined in ethnic, class, gender, or geographic terms lead to a less reliable urban food supply and more severe and frequent famines in the long run. More flexible systems can respond to dramatic changes in personnel and sources of foodstuffs to keep the level of food supply relatively stable. The studies she collected also confirm how influential trading relations are in ensuring steady food supplies. Dynamic trading networks stimulate commercial production in both nearby and distant regions, creating the reserve capacity needed to respond to droughts or rapidly expanding urban populations.

When the flexibility and relative economic power of specific groups of traders become an issue, the traders' gender emerges as an important determinant of their capabilities in ways arising from by their indigenous heritage and their experience of colonial rule. Vaughan's study of a colonial-era famine in Malawi draws attention to the effect of gendered aspects of food distribution and entitlement systems on vulnerability to famine (Vaughan 1987). She shows how the pattern of socially-constructed responses to seasonal shortages and non-catastrophic bad years stretched and broke, in many cases, during 1950 famine conditions. In an accepted dry-season strategy, men left on labor migration and trading trips from food-deficit districts to find food. Weak local commercial networks presented little grain for purchase and few income alternatives. The severe drought Vaughan studied required longer absences, and too often neither the food nor the men returned to their wives and families. Colonial regional authorities responded to poor harvests by further restricting inter-district trade. This policy only accelerated the famine by preventing those left at home from marketing craft products, earning other income or even finding food to buy with money sent home or saved.

In southern Ghana, much more highly commercialized than colonial Malawi, even subsistence production is intimately linked to small-holder production of export crops and commercial food crops, imports of consumer and producer goods, and industrial agriculture and manufacturing. A well-integrated marketplace system distributes the local foodstuffs, produced mainly by small-scale, female farmers, that make up most of the local diet. Traders manage the physical flow of goods and bargain the prices at which consumers have access to food. They stimulate farm production for sale by providing dependable retail and wholesale outlets at consistent prices. As breadwinners, both urban and rural women traders secure financial access to food for themselves and their families. This pivotal position makes market women essential actors in all three aspects of food security, with the potential for either the negative or positive effects seen in comparative examples.

Tensions raised by current conditions of both chronic and acute food shortage make the question of African traders' contribution to food security especially controversial. In Ghana, debates over market traders' responsibility for high food prices and shortages have been intense from colonial time to the present day (Danquah 1947; Lawson 1966; Bentwi-Enchill 1979; Robertson 1983). Allegations of hoarding, price-fixing and debt manipulation have affected national commercial policies, not to mention their effect on individual traders' fortunes and personal safety, by triggering confiscations and beatings.[1]

This paper aims to contribute constructively to food security debates on both the Ghanaian national and the African continental levels by identifying characteristics of one influential trading system that have both positive and negative effects on local food security. It considers the responses to short-term and long-term food shortages shown by traders in Kumasi Central Market, a large urban market operating as a central node in the Ghanaian food distribution network. Located in the moist forest zone, Kumasi lies in the midst of a key food-producing region. It is the capital of Ashanti Region, and administrative unit roughly corresponding to the territory controlled and inhabited by the Asante kingdom and ethnic group before colonial rule, but which now contains many non-Asante residents. Kumasi's commercial hinterland reaches into the neighboring savannah and coastal zones, to the north and south respectively.

Kumasi traders responded with cyclical, temporary, and permanent changes in commercial practices, since they faced all these types of crisis at once. Seasonal shortages, severe drought years, and political events interrupting food distribution, including a total currency exchange, price-control enforcement episodes, coups and attempted coups, all occurred during fieldwork periods from 1978 to 1984.[2] The same years saw long-term deterioration in food security through falling yields and growing import dependence, conditions familiar throughout the continent (Chazan and Shaw, 1988).

Considering a wide range of the problems traders confront highlights the interplay between society-wide crises, labelled as abnormal or unusual by the use of such terms as famine, and more normal or predictable conditions which may nonetheless present themselves as crises to individual traders. Resources and strategies are tested and kept viable in response to the usual vicissitudes of commercial life under local conditions, ranging from pre-harvest shortages, to childbirth, to heavy school fees, to official corruptibility. These resources and strategies proved to be highly relevant indicators of traders' capacity to respond positively or negatively to the unexpected or infrequent events that threatened, and occasionally succeeded, substantially to disrupt the food distribution system. Responses to famine conditions are consequently presented in the context of accommodations to chronic, expected food shortages and other supply problems.

FACING NORMAL PROBLEMS

Seasonal Strategies

The strategies which make seasonal shortages manageable demonstrate both strengths and weaknesses within the food system that are very relevant to making droughts and other more serious food shortages manageable. This existing repertoire of strategies can be readily put into practice, and so local citizens usually resort to them first when trying to avoid as well as survive major famines. The resources and relations utilized also indicate the structure of relative advantage which famine is likely to intensify. Traders' seasonal strategies therefore suggest strongly how they will respond more or less constructively to more serious and unexpected food system dislocations. The potentially positive or negative effect food traders can have on food security depends on their ability to smooth out or conversely to exaggerate seasonal fluctuation in supply, and consequently in price.

Ashanti Region faces sharp enough seasonal variations in the availability of the most popular foodstuffs that traders and consumers must exercise some significant responses. Fruits and vegetables have relatively short harvest seasons and spoil quickly. Plaintains, roots, and tubers, the main starchy staples grown in the forest zone, have a longer harvest period, but very a limited storage life. Grains and beans, imported from the savannah zone, suffer high losses from insects and mold in this moist area as the year progresses.

While such perishable goods cannot be effectively stored with readily available techniques, other popular items have a significant storage life. Processed foods, such as dried fish, *gari* (toasted cassava meal) and edible oils, can be stored up to one year, much longer than the raw materials. They are produced partly in order to even out income variations, but still show seasonal peaks of supply and price reflecting the availability of their raw materials and the time needed to process them. Seasonal fluctuations for potentially storable items show that the physical facilities and capital required are not available for long-term storage. Overall shortages demand the use of such resources for more pressing needs, namely housing and immediate income from rapid turnover, as the next section discusses in some detail.

Non-storage strategies offer the most effective relief from seasonal supply variations under these circumstances. Ashanti forest-zone farmers (men and women) can plant a variety of crops with different harvest seasons, spreading out the available food supply. Consumers commonly vary their diet on an annual cycle, to take advantage of the foodstuffs currently in season and relatively inexpensive.

Traders in foodstuffs also vary their diets, but must take other measures to stabilize their incomes as supplies of their trading commodities dwindle. The first response is to intensify their search for supplies. Garden egg buyers, for example, spend longer hours in their supply villages as the season ends, visiting more locations on each buying trip. They extend their search to less accessible villages which produces smaller amounts for the market. They are willing to buy lower quality garden eggs (aged, lumpy, and worm-infested) and to buy in smaller, irregular amounts that they would not bother with in season.

The search effort absorbs more persons as well as more labor hours. Small-scale sellers who have been buying their supplies inside the market, from travellers or local wholesalers, must now go looking for their own supplies or sit idle, as travellers return less frequently. Occasional traders become more significant as professional channels shrink. Rural dwellers visiting town bring small amounts of goods with them, and non-traders contact a few supply area connections, since escalating prices make their efforts worthwhile. The higher labor input expended per unit of food in the system also means higher price differentials between farm and consumer.

Instead of traders establishing relations with farmers that would intensify seasonal shortages and raise prices further, the relations they actually establish extend the boundaries of the harvest season as far as possible in order to catch the higher prices. Traders cultivate familiarity with a regular annual circuit of supply areas, aiming to provide themselves with a steady flow of deliveries. Local climate variations in specific districts make some people harvest consistently earlier or later than average, as, for example, those specializing in yams and oranges. Incidentally, these sequencing practices reduce price peaks by stimulating off-season supplies from favored districts.

Farm districts or individuals specialize heavily in food crops in which they have this kind of seasonal advantage. For example, early-season premium prices for tomatoes (a high-value, highly perishable crop) justify the backbreaking labor of hand irrigation to give plants a head start. This has become a local specialty in certain districts where streams are available.

This kind of local and personal specialization creates food farmers who depend on their cash earnings and local markets to buy other foodstuffs throughout the year. Village markets draw in produce through the nearest town from other districts with different seasons or crop specialties. This may provide a more even year-round supply in rural areas than subsistence planting alone would furnish. However, the urban shopper faces the smallest seasonal price and supply fluctuations, since she has more equal access to the full array of supply areas.

Small scale traders unwilling to travel seasonally to maintain supplies can sometimes increase their labor input to compensate for reduced turnover with a higher markup. Orange retailers spend more time peeling oranges, and egg-sellers prefer to fry or hard-boil their eggs for sale as snacks. Rural-based traders also turn to food processing when supplies dwindle. Rural cassava traders with insufficient supplies to justify a trip to Kumasi will make *gari* until they accumulate enough. These practices not only maintain daily incomes and food budgets, but reduce the spoilage and damage of scarce goods in transfer and transport.

Many traders cannot compensate sufficiently with such strategies, and must shift commodity lines to bridge the supply gap. The ideal secondary commodity has an exactly opposite season, and supplies the same consumer need. In several such popular commodity pairs, substantial numbers of the Kumasi traders in the primary commodity switched over en masse. For example, off-season orange sellers furnish most of the pineapple traders, and yam sellers and consumers both turn to water yams before the early yam harvest. This allows traders to use the same colleague and customer relations, although they need separate supply contacts for their secondary commodities. Other women have habitual non-trading occupations for the off season, turning to sewing or other crafts. Those who can afford to do without income for a time visit family or attend to house-building.

Trading itself is an important off-season occupation for farmers. In Northern districts with an extended dry season, trading by both men and women can contribute a sizable part of the family income. The marketplace system not only provides employment directly, but services rural craft and processing industries that produce small, dispersed amounts of goods. Weaving or making mats, shea butter, or fermented bean paste in small-scale, individual enterprises can be an important element in survival between harvests, whether annual or delayed. As a contrast, inadequate commercial channels and demand for basketry in Malawi frustrated local women's efforts to expand this dry season activity to provide daily income during the 1950 famine (Vaughan 1987).

Price incentives are essential to maintain or restore production in drought-prone districts in both the short and long run. They also increase production in favorable areas which can supply drought-affected districts and cities. The price must not only be high, but farmers must reliably find buyers at that price and also find needed farm inputs and consumer goods to buy. Any marketing practice or condition that lowers effective producer prices discourages commercial food production. This includes the hoarding, price-fixing, or debt manipulation that would require trader oligopoly, but also simple market inefficiencies such as lack of transport, spoilage losses, or even poor judgment. Farmers have less incentive to produce more food, and also fewer resources with which to do so.

The seasonal trading strategies clearly have the effect of increasing the total amount of food in the distribution system. In the short term, they flush out every scrap of food at times of scarcity. As part of a predictable seasonal cycle, they encourage production of off-season supplies, in remote or marginal areas as well as major supply areas. Seasonal commodity switching encourages production of minor crops valuable mainly because they stabilise the flow of food supplies. It provides a cheaper infrastructure for their distribution, by sharing the burden of supporting a year-round trading labor force.

Storage Constraints

Hoarding and other monopolistic practices that make food access more unequal and erratic depend on traders' ability to store large quantities of foodstuffs or keep them off the market by controlling them on the farms. Traders could only intensify overall shortages of food and raise prices (whether during an annual lean season or a famine) if they could keep control of a sufficient proportion of the total available goods to reduce supplies significantly, either locally or nationally. Such practices, if successful, would also tend to concentrate access to food further on a class basis by increasing income differentials and raising prices. This would lower overall food security. Effective storage by traders without such monopolization of supplies would actually raise off-season supply levels and reduce price peaks.

Classic hoarding by Kumasi traders through storage is conspicuous in its absence. Perishability alone makes the vast majority of forest-zone foodstuffs completely unsuitable for storage in anticipation of price rises. Traders in fact go to considerable lengths to have effective ownership of staple like cassava for as short a period as possible, to minimize their responsibility for spoilage losses.

Storage in other locations, under other ownership, is preferred. Cassava harvesting can be delayed until the money is needed. Yams, which deteriorate in a matter of days in the market or town, are stored for some months by farmers in the field, before or after harvest. Supposed non-perishables, including rice, corn, and beans, also suffer rapidly from mildew and insect damage in Kumasi. Wealthy traders with extra capital that might be employed in building up stocks for the off season loan money to farmers rather than assume the risks and losses of storage themselves. By contrast, in the drier savannah climate, grain purchase at low post-harvest prices for seasonal storage is a major source of income for the larger-scale grain traders. Saul and McCorkle describe this central dynamic for adjacent Burkina Faso, and Watts presents historical depth for Northern Nigeria (Saul 1988, McCorkle 1988, Watts 1987).

Kumasi market traders lack the space or physical facilities needed for significant hoarding of comparatively bulky foodstuffs. Their market stalls, like those throughout southern Ghana, are tiny compared to storefronts outside the market, with only enough room for stocks that will turn over in a week or a month. The open design of foodstuffs sheds makes it impossible to conceal stored goods, as required for market manipulation, or to protect them adequately from the elements that accelerate spoilage. Northern men who wholesale grain in Kumasi operate from storefronts outside the market.

Traders have little access to other storage facilities outside the market. Very few attain the basic index of Asante middle-class status, building one's own house. With the acute housing shortage in Kumasi, both self-built and inherited houses have every room filled with relatives or renters. Ordinary traders rent or live with relatives, and have only one or two rooms for themselves, their children and dependents. Lack of private, secure space prevents them from buying in quantity for their own consumption, let alone hoarding. They do not have access to the suburban garages, closed-off apartments, or government back rooms featured in the examples of hoarded goods photographed for newspapers in 1979.

In addition, most foodstuff traders (along with most non-food traders) cannot afford to tie up any of their capital long enough to enjoy the delayed profits of hoarding or storage, however high and assured. With little capital, they must turn it all over as frequently as possible, even if at lower rates of profit. Small-scale traders need the income from their daily, or at least weekly, turnover to meet family consumption needs. They show great anxiety if unable to sell, even when prices are rising. Kumasi traders could not store to take advantage of predictable seasonal price variations or ensure supplies during erratic political shortages, much less attempt to corner the market and create artificial shortages.

Even relatively prosperous traders, such as Ga fish smokers along the coast, prefer to keep their money turning over. Seasonal price variations in smoked fish are high and relatively predictable, because fish catches drop off sharply in the rainy season. Although storage-linked profits would be reliable, these women rarely holds stocks if buyers are available. They complain bitterly if forced to hold stocks for a few days because of oversupply. Even groups with access to low-interest, year-term loans invested the money in buying more fresh fish to sell immediately, rather than in storing smoked fish for the off-season.

Another indication that Kumasi traders cannot effectively manipulate shortages is the absence of an expressed preference for shortage conditions. This undermines the unspoken assumption that traders are motivated to try to create such conditions, either seasonally or occasionally. Foodstuffs traders did not have the kind of privileged access to producers that would enable them to benefit consistently from low supply conditions and manipulate prices. In response to questions about whether they made more money when goods were short or plentiful, they most often asserted that you made money equally in both cases, if you knew the right prices to buy and sell, and you could lose heavily in either case as well.

Market traders usually expressed an overall preference for conditions of abundance, since they suffered during shortages as workers and consumers. Very low supply conditions meant that many had nothing to sell, leaving them essentially unemployed. High food prices reduced real income dramatically for the ordinary trader with little capital, who spends most of her income on food. Profit margins could not rise enough to compensate fully for the decline because of her poor customers' low buying power.

Credit and Debt

One potential way of monopolizing access to marketed food without assuming the risks of storage or cultivation is through establishing rights to the future crop through moneylending. In other continents, notably India, pre-harvest loans can force farmers to sell at below market prices to loansharks immediately after harvest, thus creating widespread long-term debt dependency. The system of credit between traders and farmers sending food to Kumasi therefore deserves detailed attention, if only as a negative instance.

As seasonal shortages set in, capital flows towards the rural areas in association with the increases in overall search time already discussed. Retailers take their capital with them on longer trips to the supply area, or advance it to buyers who promise to deliver them goods. These buyers expect immediate cash payment, whereas they might advance goods on credit during the harvest season. If supplies dry up to the point that trade is impractical, traders send their capital further back up the food chain to the farmer. Traders with enough capital not to require daily or weekly turnover for meals (a small percentage of Kumasi traders) lend money to farmers in the months just before harvest. Loans are used to hire labor for the last weeding or harvesting. In return, the lender has the right to buy the crop at the price prevailing when it is sold.

One reason why chronic indebtedness does not arise around Kumasi-based food trading is that the size of the loans traders extend to farmers is relatively small. Those reported were for less than 10% of the total value of the crop to be harvested. Also, the future sale price is not fixed at the time of the loan, but bargained for when the crop is transferred.

The trader has little leverage for demanding exorbitant price concessions, as she does not control the farmer's access to the market. A farmer can sell elsewhere and repay the loan without destroying his or her general credit reputation, especially if the price offered by the creditor does not compare closely to current offers by other traders. Traders also depend on credit extended by farmers in the glut season, in the form of advances of goods, so they cannot afford to alienate the debtor or his neighbors. For both sides, the primary sanction is that others will consider you an unreasonable or unprofitable business partner.

Farmgate buyers face effective competition from other traders from their own and other urban markets, and from other sales outlets. In most villages, farmers have access to more than on trader, as well as the option to transport goods to the nearest market center, or to become traders themselves. Access to transport, rather than debt or lack of debt, was shown to be the critical variable in price bargaining power in a systematic study of the Koforidua hinterland, adjacent to Kumasi (Gore 1978). The transport shortage only gives traders a monopoly position in the relatively rare and transitory condition where the road is bad enough that farmers cannot convince a truck to travel it but is still good enough that a trader can.

Traders are willing to make farm loans without interest or substantial price discounts for the right to negotiate over the date of delivery of the goods. This chance to even out their personal supplies means more for crops like yams, that can be held on the farm for a significant period of time. The dispersed geographical structure of yam trading also concentrates the long-distance trade in fewer hands, yielding more farmgate buyers with enough capital to consider loans. A highly perishable vegetable crop like tomatoes leaves little discretion for either party. They can only agree to postpone the debt cancellation sale until later, when more become ripe for harvest. Creditors do not gain an absolute right to demand the crop when they wish. Those observed exchange a series of messages with debtor farmers requesting early or late delivery.

Traders did not apparently try to manipulate delivery times to hoard goods when they were scarce. Several cases observed showed traders trying to buy at high price levels, early in the season, so they would have something to sell. Far from demanding sales at low prices when supplies are abundant, the trader will attempt to save her promised goods for a rainy day by pointing out that prices are now low. The farmer will reap the major price benefit from delaying sale. Traders also pressed for delivery on specific supply trips when they needed to make up a full truckload in a hurry. If necessary, they agreed to take from the farmer selling them little or nothing more than the amount to cover the debt, renouncing their option on further amounts.

Farmers questioned about why they sold at low prices immediately after harvest did not mention debt or pressure from traders. Yam farmers interviewed said most of them held onto all or part of their main harvest to await higher prices later, selling in three or four sizable transactions. Since they can store yams fairly effectively on the farm, they sold only to meet immediate needs. The urgent need for sales for family medical expenses or school fees (the examples given by them) was created by poverty, when no savings existed. A farmer desperate to sell may have to extend the goods on credit or even on commission (accepting all the price risk), whether to a creditor or another familiar trader.

Ghana's Northern and Upper Region farmers, most at risk for drought, famine, and chronic food deficit, have little direct interaction with Kumasi-based traders. These districts primarily grow grain, which Kumasi market women do not buy directly from Northern farmers. They purchase wholesale quantities of grain by the bag from male, predominantly Moslem, middlemen in Northern towns or border markets, such as Techiman and Ejura. Linked middlemen sell bags and smaller quantities in Kumasi, but outside the marketplace itself. Any debt dependency would presumably focus on these middlemen, although no evidence of it was found.

Chronic indebtedness seems to be rare in this region, although the evidence comes from adjacent locations with overlapping ethnic groups. Several studies of grain marketing in Mossi areas just north of Ghana's border with Burkina Faso either specifically deny its presence or do not mention the subject (Sherman 1984, Saul 1988, McCorkle 1988). Both the Mossi ethnic group and the grain trading networks described extend across the border, so one would expect these findings to be relevant at least to the extreme north of Ghana, the Upper Region, the area most affected by chronic drought and famine. Poor households did more often sell grain soon after harvest, but not because of dependence on traders. Like the yam farmers just discussed on the forest fringes, their choices were constrained by lack of alternative income possibilities at harvest time to supply daily cash needs, rather than debt obligations.

Women as Farmers and Traders

Women predominate in the labor force of both trading and food farming in Ghana, suggesting direct competition for their labor between the sectors. The rapid expansion of employment in marketplace trading throughout the twentieth century, accelerating to the present, has been proposed as a major factor in declining food production during the same period. Ghanaian women traders were exhorted by official radio and newspaper editorials in 1979 to return to the farm and contribute to national food self-sufficiency. In this argument, the lure of supposedly easy cash through trading diverts rural labor that otherwise be invested in food farming, reducing total yields in both good years and bad.

Women are the mainstay of rural food production in the Ashanti Region surrounding Kumasi, as in most parts of Sub-Saharan Africa, even though Asante men are also active farmers. As mothers, women assume responsibility for providing food supplies for themselves and their children, in kind or by purchase. In rural areas, the mixed plantings intended for family consumption can be found mainly on women's farms. A woman owns these crops and can sell the surplus freely, but her family's subsistence has the first claim on them. Men may be planting some of the same food crops, but expect to sell the bulk of the crop without necessarily reserving much of it or the proceeds for family meals. Their lesser subsistence obligations also enable men to plant crops raised for export more often and in greater quantities.

While a mass exodus of rural women from farming would be grounds for concern, the official denunciations of greedy traders focus on urban-based traders, to whom this proposed dynamic does not apply. Demographic data on Kumasi Central Market traders suggest, on the contrary, that urban trading feeds many who could not realistically farm. Urban-born or urban-raised Asante women predominate among these traders, an overrepresentation compared to the general city population (Clark 1984). These women spent their childhood years in a city, and would not know how to farm well enough to make a living at it, either through subsistence or cash production. Although Kumasi residents often send or bring children frequently to visit rural relatives, such visits do not train fully competent farmers.

Land access is also problematic for those who have grown up in Kumasi, especially as the second generation, since they will not have close links to specific tracts of farmland. Although Asante lineages retain residual rights to much of the land in Ashanti Region, the closest descendant of the previous farmer or the descendant assisting in the cultivation of that plot normally inherits rights to cultivation. In relatively densely occupied parts of Ashanti near Kumasi, the shortage of farmland has become acute. Would-be farmers migrate to more remote parts of Ashanti and adjacent Brong-Ahafo Regions, where land can be obtained through forms of rent or purchase. Some traders' original villages have been completely engulfed by the recent expansion of Kumasi or other towns, owning valuable real estate but no farmland. Interviews in rural areas, however, indicate that a large and possibly increasing number of experienced women farmers are indeed turning to trading, devoting significant amounts of their labor time and proportionately reducing their potential farm production. Interviews with Asante and closely related Akan village women revealed many who were successful farmers, but chose to diversify into trading and food processing rather than expand their farms. They were discouraged from setting up commercial food farms on the same scale as male family members by disadvantages in access to good land, in access to unpaid family labor or the capital to hire labor, and in retaining control of the crop produced. These are the same issues shown to restrict Akan women's production of export crops such as cocoa (Okali 1976, Vellenga 1981, Mikell 1985). These structural problems deserve concern, but undermine the assumption that these women would be able to expand food production proportionately if they did not trade.

Although the matrilineal Asante kinship organization entitles women to claim land allocations from their lineage resources, they consistently have less access than their brothers and uncles. Lineage land is distributed by male elders who give priority to male members, rural women report, especially for the large tracts of relatively fertile land needed for accumulation purposes. Mikell's historical analysis of farm foundations in Brong-Ahafo Region shows that women only received significant amounts of land when economic conditions made it difficult for most men to claim land (Mikell 1985). Even lineage members often need to make payments for permission to plant the lucrative permanent tree crops, such as cocoa, oil palm, and coconut trees, because they preempt later reallocation. In more developed districts, much of the available land has already been bought up in large blocks, leaving little for distribution under the lineage system. Purchased or producing lands are inherited by a successor of the same sex chosen by lineage elders, preserving the male bias.

Women's lesser access to financial capital also hinders their food crop production. Planting large acreages requires payments: for land rights, for wage laborers, and for supplemental food until the produce is ready for sale. Village women traders interviewed had not stopped farming, but said they lacked money to expand their farms. Instead, they diversified into trading and food processing, which apparently required less capital. Savings from previous wage labor provide a significant source of capital for the larger-scale male farmers, while few women worked for wages. Money from family loans and inheritance is also more available to men. Among city traders, for example, the men reported inheriting and borrowing capital from both male and female relatives, while women rarely received money from male relatives. Men not surprisingly average much higher capital levels. The same gendered sources of capital also result in men monopolizing transport ownership.

Male farmers also can rely on greater control of their own and other's unpaid labor. A women farmer must honor legitimate claims from her husband for domestic labor, which shortens her work day, and for labor on his own farm, which shortens her work week. When a husband performs male farm tasks on his wife's plot, he gets rights to the crop. Domestic work is even an essential part of the rural wage labor system. Farm laborers require meals that inflation has made a large part of their compensation. Married men can call on their wives' unpaid labor for food preparation and food supplies, making it much easier and cheaper for them to hire labor. Women hiring laborers find it difficult to supervise them and cook simultaneously.

Judging the effect of trading on individual or family food security requires comparison of income levels, control of income, and investment opportunities for women as traders and farmers. Trading requires less money to enter, gives a woman unambiguous control of the proceeds, and incidentally removes her physically from the village, where her husband can call on her unpaid labor. Even if trading is inherently less productive, it could result in more disposable food income if farm production were substantially diverted away from the female farmer's food budget. This happens when female farmers honor claims to work on their husband's export crops or cash crops, generating income used for his non-food purposes but spending less time generating food income.

By increasing the income over which women have absolute control, trading increases the income available for food provision. A higher percentage of women's income than men's goes towards food, which is especially important for children's food security. The urban poor, a category disproportionately female, spend most of their budget on food and have more precarious access to both income and food. Large numbers of both urban and rural poor, especially women, depend on trading for income to buy food. The small daily or weekly income typical of traders and producer-traders can provide a more even family food supply than annual crop sales or harvests.

Since women are also the major rural food producers, and retain rights to the surplus from their own farms, stimulation of food production through effective trading also tends to put more money in rural women's pockets. Guyer (1984) shows how access to urban food markets markedly raised the independent income under women's control in Cameroon farming districts. Villagers trade seasonally in the non-farming months and as a stopgap measure when drought suspends the farming cycle, not only as an alternative to farming. Vigorous local markets may improve the long-term survival capacity of the agricultural system by diversifying the rural economy.

RESPONDING TO ACUTE CRISES

Political Events: 1979–80

The food shortages arising from political events, including price control enforcement episodes, coups, and attempted coups, differed from seasonal
shortages in several ways. They were less predictable, although frequent
enough that the ability to cope with them was a significant contributor to
food security levels. Unlike harvest cycles and drought, these crises interrupted the process of distribution more directly than that of production.

Unlike contemporary Ethiopia or Angola, Ghana did not reach a level of
political unrest that interfered with farming directly through conscription or
bombardment. Peaks in customs enforcement and foreign exchange shortages had a considerable impact by shrinking the supplies of legal and smug-
gled farm inputs, especially cutlasses, fertilizer, and diesel fuel. Direct
intervention and physical danger focused on towns like Kumasi, main roads,
and officially recognised markets. Urban traders' proximity to political centers and transport, normally a great advantage, became a disadvantage. Their
conspicuous, accessible location gave them less room to maneuver than
farmers in adjusting to and compensating for these particular shortages.

Seasonal timing affects the depth of these politically-triggered shortages,
because farmers can hold crops off the market more easily at certain times of
the year than others. During a dry season price control enforcement episode
in 1980, after the inauguration of Limann's government, traders and farmers
simply abandoned the attempt to get the remaining scarce and scattered food
supplies onto the market. The AFRC government of Rawlings came to power
on June 4, 1979, under more favorable conditions. Soup vegetable crops had
already entered their harvest period, and other perishables that had to be sold
or abandoned matured shortly thereafter.

The events of June 4 itself, which included minimal violence in Kumasi,
affected food sales only slightly. Supplies dropped for a few days because
people minimised travel in general until the situation stabilised, but food
availability soon recovered to near normal seasonal levels, with fresh vegetables plentiful in their harvest period. Price control operations on imports and
manufactures were in full swing. Many foodstuffs traders, like other urban
workers, took some time off work to seek bargains on goods being sold off
from downtown stores. Neither they nor consumers seriously expected price
control extension to local food crops, despite some rumors. Indeed, many
former traders of cloth and other imports had moved into foodstuff sales to
avoid the stress and cost of price controls.

The government extended price control activities to foodstuffs so gingerly
as to suggest concern to avoid affecting supply levels. They began on a na-

tional holiday, when wholesale yards were closed and few traders in the market. Local female police officers, rather than the male soldiers used in imports and manufactures enforcement, carried out the first operations. The compelled retailers to sell off displayed goods at lower prices, but did not collect the money themselves of confiscate any goods. They used methods of crowd control appropriate to women, such as throwing buckets of water, to control lines of customers. Male police in those days used their belts and, occasionally, nightsticks to control male and female lines for goods at downtown stores.

In the ensuing days and weeks, however, levels of violence increased and discipline broke down. Soldiers and police entered the market daily to sell goods at arbitrary low prices and confiscate stocks. Both retailers and wholesalers of all foodstuffs and craft products like pottery were approached, although no official prices had been established for these goods. Foodstuffs en route to Kumasi were also confiscated from freight or mixed passenger/ freight trucks at police roadblocks or "hijacked" by soldiers on major roads that passed near large barracks. Public sales at such remote spots were impractical, providing the rationale for confiscation. Goods owners were supposed to be entitled to collect compensation later at the relevant police station or military barracks for the "control" price of their goods, set by the confiscators. Owners without substantial police connections feared beatings or prosecution if they appeared, however, and stayed away.

The immediate effect on Kumasi's food supply was catastrophic. Perishable vegetables such as tomatoes, cassava, and plantains, normally renewed daily, were completely unavailable. For the first few days, traders were still selling off their stocks of grains, beans, and other non-perishable items like onions. When these were exhausted, real famine set in. Most Kumasi families were unable to secure even a minimal diet for several weeks. Traders alleged that soldiers were continuing the confiscations simply to obtain food for themselves and their families.

Suspension of food supplies partly reflected farmers' and traders' fear of generalized violence, especially on the roads. People remained afraid to travel certain roads that had seen especially frequent attacks, or passed beside large barracks. Casual travellers to Kumasi no longer brought in small amounts for sale, since casual travel had stopped. Traders who dared to visit their usual periodic markets in villages near Kumasi reported back that villagers were afraid to attend them, so there was little point in taking the risk. Such markets are important for collecting small amounts from marginal areas and from non-specialist producers.

Many farming areas retained enough subsistence production on the family or village level to avoid actual food shortages. Non-specialist producers simply ate more of their own produce, especially since the other foodstuffs they might have bought with the proceeds were not available anyway. Reports from very remote areas indicated considerable resort to barter exchanges among villagers isolated from their usual markets by interruption in trade and the severe gasoline shortage. Interviews later in highly crop specialized farm villages uncovered some hardship when farmers depended on the market for a balanced diet. Hospital expenses or school fees also presented crises when farmers could not sell as expected, although institutions like these also closed for lack of food supplies for inmates.

The way shortage levels in Kumasi varied between different food crops clearly shows that it was farmers' rather than traders' actions that determined the degree of urban shortage. Highly perishable vegetables recovered most quickly, because farmers had to sell them when ripe or lose them entirely. It was peak harvest time for tomatoes and greens, and after a few days their supply was only slightly below seasonal expectations. Low seasonal prices reduced the apparent need for price control. Soldiers confiscated or sold off produce less often, and reduced prices less from the lowered market levels when they did.

Squashy vegetables are also considerably less convenient and attractive for confiscation than, for example, yams or cooking oil. Soldiers did not have facilities to dispose of large quantities of vegetables quickly enough, so profits would be low. Sellers likewise had more trouble establishing clandestine trading networks, since speed of disposal was imperative. By contrast, the popularity, high value, and relative storability of yams both made them highly vulnerable to confiscation in transit, and motivated the clandestine sales arrangements observed.

When farmers had the option, they consistently chose to delay harvest and sale. This reduced immediate supplies by removing significant foods from their place in the annual cycle. For example, yam farmers normally harvest a few tubers from each plant in July, with the earliest earning high prices. They carefully recover the plant's roots to produce larger tubers for the main harvest several months later. The new yams, a favorite and ritually significant Asante food, become the dominant street food for a few weeks amid a holiday atmosphere.

In 1979 there were no new yams seen in Kumasi. Even after the normal time for the main harvest, farmers left their yams in the ground. They only harvested them as they needed to begin preparing their fields for the next year's planting, and even then they could and did store large amounts in pits on the farm. This reduced supplies throughout 1979, but it eventually raised supplies above the usual level in the very late season (early 1980), since yams cannot be stored indefinitely without near-total losses.

Corn growers also chose to delay harvesting. Some corn, especially from areas more accessible to urban markets, is usually picked at a stage when it can be boiled and eaten on the cob. This "green corn" is the first starchy staple to be harvested each year, and helps bridge the gap until the new yam time. In 1979 farmers left their corn on the stalk to become fully mature, dry, and suitable for grinding or storage. Even then, stocks reached the market only gradually. Farmers held off marketing until they needed the money or until conditions improved. Dried and green corn are sold in standard sacks, relatively easy to confiscate and to price, so they were very risky to market. Processed corn products were also subject to price intervention, reducing total demand for corn. Sellers of *kenkey*, a common street food, faced harassment and regulation over the size of *kenkey* balls, especially in Accra, where it is a major staple.

Cassava can be left in the ground for months without much deterioration, although after harvest it lasts for only two or three days. Unlike plantains, which ripen and eventually rot, fresh cassava did not reappear on the market until the danger of confiscation had virtually passed. Farmers harvested only when they feared the hard dry-season ground would later make harvest impractical. Some villagers also reported processing more fresh cassava than usual into *gari*, which they sold after conditions improved.

Politics and Food Security

Political turmoil seriously threatens the food security of urban dwellers, even at these moderate levels. Prices rise during shortages and overall supply is reduced, producing inadequate consumption levels even among relatively wealthy consumers. The impact of the price control episode contrasts with the March 1979 currency exchange exercise, also aimed partly at wealthy traders, which in fact hit farmers in remote villages the hardest. During the acute shortages of 1979, as in the 1982–3 drought, even the wealthiest consumer found little to buy, although the traders among them may have had more food-related connections than most non-traders.

The majority of traders, however, faced as severe problems in June and July 1979 as other poor urban workers and consumers. Their modest capital was soon exhausted at high price levels, and the interruption in trade made them unemployed as well as hungry. Alternative occupations, such as food traders turn to during seasonal shortage periods, were not available. The off-season foodstuffs they usually sold were equally affected, and craft and other non-trading occupations were thoroughly disrupted. Pathetically high numbers of traders turned to selling ice water as the ultimate inoffensive, low-profit commodity, only to face soldiers offering them obsolete, nearly valueless coins and smashing their containers. In Kumasi, the level of general economic paralysis that interrupted income for all but wage workers in large enterprises eventually put something of a ceiling on food prices. Even though food remained scarce, sellers could not sell at the highest prices because so few townspeople had money left to spend.

The effects of price control enforcement increased the disparity in food security between wealthier and poorer traders, and also broadened the gap between traders with and without official or military connections. Well-connected traders not only avoided arrest or collected compensation, but might gain access to confiscated supplies for resale. A similar differentiation process had previously driven many long-time traders out of business in imports and manufactures.

The nature of the disruption also destroyed or reversed some economies of scale. Truckloads or obviously commercial quantities of goods, as well as recognized village or roadside markets, were conspicuous targets for an exercise deliberately aimed at traders. Trade was diverted to back roads and more dispersed roadside and clandestine locations. These strategies reduced efficiency and increased losses from spoilage, although they did keep some food trickling towards the cities.

A serious reduction in the amount of labor and capital available for employment in trade inhibited the recovery of food supplies after price enforcement loosened. The danger associated with travel significantly reduced the search for goods. Many traders had simply lost their capital, through confiscation or through consumption during idle periods, and could not resume their previous levels of trade. Those with capital remaining employed as little of it as absolutely necessary to provide daily food for their families due to persistent fears. Efficiency remained low as economies of scale were lost.

Capital loss affected commercial farmers both directly and indirectly. Farmers lost capital directly if they had advanced confiscated goods on credit or had been unable to sell perishable goods. Seasonal reinvestment of traders' capital into rural areas during the late farming season also shrank when traders lost capital. Both farm acreage and ability to pay for optimal labor and inputs suffered as a result.

The accumulated experience of price control, currency exchange, gasoline shortage, and other crises linked to politics contributed to a growing lack of confidence among farmers in food marketing, legal or illegal, as a reliable outlet for their produce. They reduced commercial production (plantings intended specifically for sale), with serious effects on overall food security in the medium term. Villages on the margins of trading networks lost effective market contact altogether and simply returned to subsistence production. Accessible areas withdrew more acreage and labor from commercial production and planted more subsistence mixes, as an insurance against future unpredictable disruptions. This withdrawal was not permanent, however, because the high food prices of the 1982–3 drought stimulated a rapid expansion in commercial food planting the year after.

Such subsistence-oriented planting strategies arguably raised or preserved rural food security in Ashanti Region or other forested areas, even if temporarily. Farmers there could plant enough different species to fill in most of the hungry months, although self-sufficiency left them more vulnerable than before to local climate variations. The return to subsistence production in marginal supply areas more clearly decreased urban dwellers' food security, since they depended on a smaller number of localities.

The effect on the northern fringes of Kumasi Central Market's hinterland was probably also negative, although the evidence is very thin. Asante commercial farmers make extensive use of wage laborers, including migrants from Northern districts with chronic food deficits and low, erratic rainfall. Reducing these employment possibilities reduced Northerners' ability to send money home to relatives for buying food. Less marketed food from moister areas was also available for purchase.

The 1982–83 Drought

When food shortages throughout the commercial system are created primarily by drought itself, trading relations are less critical to the relative distribution of suffering. Food production is disrupted directly and immediately, rather than through the delayed effects of pricing and instability. Trading can merely exacerbate or ameliorate existing shortages, in either rural or in urban areas.

At first, trading patterns respond to a drought as they do to a normal dry season. To some extent, a drought appears as simply an extension of the current dry season, because the rains are further and further delayed. When food supplies run low, traders intensify their search for supplies, spending longer in the rural areas and visiting more remote villages. Hopes of late but adequate rains prolong the perception that shortages will be normal, or at least manageable.

The great unsatisfied demand for food during the 1982–3 drought naturally led to an intense search for food supplies for the market throughout Ghana. Since both urban and rural areas were seriously short of food and the drought was widespread, these strategies were less successful than usual. Traders could not bring food from neighboring areas of surplus to fill local shortages, as in localized famines.

The efficiency and energy of traders' search under drought conditions, even more than in normal dry seasons, tend to raise effective farmgate demand and prices. This raises rural incomes, and certainly ensured the harvesting and processing of every last dwarfish grain, tuber, or tomato in 1983. By raising prices in less drought-affected areas in the south, it motivated them to sell more food, such as *gari*, and send it to the north, where prices were even higher. Increasing the amount of food marketed should logically lower urban food prices, decreasing the rural/urban gap, if only marginally. In 1983, the overall shortages dwarfed any such effect.

Intensive trading can present a danger to rural food security if the total food supply tends to move towards wealthier urban consumers from poor farming districts already short of food. This is especially likely when debt constrains the average farmer to sell, whether on an annual basis or in time of famine. Such urban bias could easily increase in times of famine or other food system stress.

The relative availability of food in Ghana's cities and villages during shortages provides the best evidence on this question. In 1983, food supplies in the Ghanaian countryside apparently remained consistently higher in the city, as they had during the political crises in 1979. Urban families in both years sent or considered sending their children to stay with rural relatives, because the food supply was better there. This suggests that urban demand, at least within Ashanti Region, was not succeeding in draining off food supplies actually needed for rural subsistence.

The physical movement of goods through an active marketplace system contributes to food security when famine threatens if it makes excess production more easily available to food-short districts. To take advantage of such existing distribution channels, UNICEF proposed using the trading network to overcome transport constraints in Ethiopia, distributing cash to isolated villagers and assuming that the money would induce private traders to bring grain to them (UNICEF 1985). The 1950 Malawi famine displayed a weak distribution network that could not perform this function under the pressure of famine (Vaughan 1987). Inadequate physical availability of grain locally, despite surpluses in other districts, forced men willing to buy grain to travel in search of it, whence they were tempted not to return.

With respect to the Ghana savannah districts with the highest food deficits, net flow and relative vulnerability were less clear. Food did travel from the North, where shortages were extreme, into the southern cities, but it was replaced at least partly by return flows. Millets and sorghums grown primarily in the North continued to be available in small quantities at high prices in Accra, on the coast. Debt burdens from normal years probably were not sufficient to force farmers to sell regardless of the availability of replacement foodstuffs on the market, if conditions resembled those in adjacent Ashanti Region or Burkina Faso. Anecdotal reports certainly indicate that many more farmers in the Northern and Upper Regions found themselves with nothing to sell and were hence unable to buy, a situation that market reforms would not have corrected.

According to accounts from Damongo, in the Northern region, local people did get significant access to foodstuffs from southern production centers less severely affected by drought. Damongo informants, who were cassava producers, said that the harvest of maize, millet, and sorghum were a near-total loss in much of the north, including Damongo. People harvesting small amounts sold it to traders at extremely high prices, who sold it to urban elites who could pay. With the money, Northerners could buy larger amounts of less preferred foods, principally *gari*, made from drought-resistant cassava. These informants claimed that general consumer acceptance of *gari* in the North dates from that year. While *gari* gives less nutrition than the same weight of grain, the exchange provided more calories for the families involved. Most of the *gari* was imported from southern districts, although Damongo *gari* makers also expanded production.

The experience of Damongo shows a drought-stricken area becoming more dependent on foodstuff markets during the crisis period. Maintaining cash income was even more essential than usual to maintaining steady food access. Transfer of family members' labor to non-farm enterprises and to local and southern cities through migration was a key strategy in reducing suffering. Secondary occupations and labor migration are always important here in bridging the long dry season. In a dry year more people participate, and for more months. Men more often migrate south, while women more often rely on local enterprises.

Personal accounts from near Damongo indicate that these secondary occupations became primary in 1983, among both townsfolk and very remote villagers. Many women intensified the collection and processing of wild foods, especially shea nut. Normally a dry season, part-time sideline, making shea butter offered a realistic refuge occupation due to good market demand. Farmers who had planted grain and vegetables saw their plants die off that year with no rain in sight. Released at least from the burden of weeding, women devoted all their energy to gathering shea nuts. They went to more distant groves of wild trees that they normally neglected in the press of farm work, and they began to process the nuts immediately instead of waiting until after the harvest. Income from sales of shea butter helped to feed their families throughout the following year.

Damongo women's processing strategy echoes the adaptation Maclachlan reports for a drought-prone Indian district (Maclachlan 1983). These farmers complemented subsistence grain production with dry season irrigated vegetable gardens in normal years. When a drought decimated their grain yields for several years running, they came to rely almost entirely on the irrigated gardens for year-round income generation. Such intense specialization, particularly in perishable vegetables, depends on a highly reliable marketing system serving urban demand.

The ability to exchange scarce, expensive grains or vegetables for larger amounts of cheaper foodstuffs brings higher food security for drought-prone areas, although absolute shortages were also reported as common in Ghana's Northern and Upper Regions. The same year saw poor urban residents in southern Ghana eating dangerous, inedible items like coconut husks, which makes the substitution of *gari* for cereals seem mild. Donated supplies of exotic foodstuffs like wheat-soy grits eventually joined *gari* as less desirable cereal substitutes. They were aimed specifically at those facing an absolute shortage through lack of income or other entitlements to food, but some recipients sold them to buy more preferred foods. Trading networks proved effective in distributing them to a much wider public than entitled to them or reachable through official channels.

Within cities like Kumasi, traders were apparently unable to preserve their own food security at the expense of ordinary urban consumers. Traders interviewed were as desperate for food supplies during 1983 as other urban residents. They joined in expeditions to comb towns and villages for unsuspected food. Little concrete evidence of hoarding by traders was ever produced, although their professional search skills and networks may have given their families better access to food supplies than the non-trading urban family. Those without capital to spend lost weight, as did other urban residents.

Traders' access to food was further threatened by the breakdown of the trading system that employed them. There was not enough food in circulation to sustain normal marketing networks. Traders stopped trying to work, and took off searching for food for their families. Even when a trader found some commercial supplies, they were sold outside normal channels. One oil seller was afraid to display several kerosene tins of oil, for example, not for fear of arrest, but because she expected a stampede when shoppers saw them.

Traders' food situation compared closely with that of other urban residents employed of self-employed in small enterprises. Most occupations ground to a halt as both producers and consumers concentrated on finding food. Waged workers in larger factories or agencies had two major advantages: they continued to collect wages, and many received small food distributions at their workplaces.

CONCLUSION

The behavior of traders in this case confirms the initial premise that systemic strengths and vulnerabilities revealed in famine response are not distinct from those present in the everyday food system and exercised on seasonal shortages and individual or family income crises. Kumasi traders' potential for increasing or threatening food security during famines or long-term crises had the same limits as their influence on food security under "normal" conditions. Strengthening everyday capabilities within the food system therefore seems an effective way of building diverse capacities to withstand famine.

Flexibility in the Kumasi market system enabled it to soften seasonal fluctuations and political shocks. Capital and personnel shifted dramatically towards the farm during times of shortage and towards the city at harvest. Traders invested in farming during the pre-harvest period; farmers effectively subsidized trading through credit when marketing resources were strained. Easy entry into trading and transfer between different trading roles was important to permitting rapid intensification of search and preservation efforts during shortage periods. It is also reduced the personnel cost of keeping a large variety of staple foodstuffs in active circulation. Duplicate marketing channels that also might appear inefficient actually maintained alternative channels ready for quick response to changing conditions.

This rapid response depends not only on the autonomy and financial independence of traders and potential traders, but on the inability of specific sets of traders to consolidate control of the distributive system at the expense of farmers, urban consumers, or other traders. The same conditions that restricted traders' ability to contribute substantially to food security, especially their lack of facilities and capital for significant long-term storage, also restricted their ability to create negative food flows during times of scarcity. Disproportionate control at one point in the distribution system slows responses to problems in another location, whether the control is located in an individual enterprise, a cartel, or a government agency. Highly concentrated storage and capital facilities, such as the State Fishing Corporation complex at Tema, can intervene more directly in the overall availability level of foodstuffs, but present commensurate opportunities for abuse.

Expansion of full or part-time market trading reduces the farm workforce fairly directly when, as in Ghana, the two occupations recruit from labor pools that largely overlap. Without proportionate productivity increases, this leads to a substantial weakening of food production in the short run. The cause and effect relationship is not entirely clear, however. Ghanaian farmers' own statements suggest that such exoduses take place during times when returns from farming are reduced (as by drought), or from social groups, including women, with restricted returns due to resource constraints. Removing these social or ecological constraints would restore the availability of farming personnel more effectively than direct restraints on trading. During acute attacks on Kumasi traders, for example, large numbers of women did stop trading but resumed as soon as possible because of the lack of viable alternatives. Asante men, on the other hand, left trading in large numbers in the early twentieth century in favor of cocoa farming, then quite lucrative (Hill 1963).

The mixed influence of traders on food security partly arises from the mixed effect of commercialization itself, since their trading efforts stimulate and reproduce commercialization. Market institutions provide networks for short-term, local distribution of food and capital needed to smooth over local fluctuations in harvest or supply, increasing the contribution of resources under local control to food security. These positive potentials are particularly well realized in a system like that centered on Kumasi, which offers farmers several alternative routes of access to urban demand and offers urban centers several alternative sources of supply.

Compared to other systems of integration into the world system, a balanced marketplace system leaves farmers with some autonomy. It stimulates and sustains a diversified rural economy specializing for demand within the country and region as well as overseas. The marketplace network delivers to small-scale commercial farmers their immediate reproductive needs as farmers, whether from other farming regions or international sources. These locally-oriented producers retain some degree of capacity for withdrawal when their reproductive needs fail to be offered. Ashanti farmers' ability to withdraw at fairly short notice from the national food distribution system may have harmed urban food security, but it demonstrated their own.

Expansion of commercial demand often stimulates surplus food production in the short run, but this hyperactivity can reduce food production in the long run by undermining its resource base. The effect of Ghana's high 1983 corn prices was certainly apparent the next year, when corn plantings increased dramatically and harvest prices fell below cost. High national demand for food crops like rice, corn, and cassava encourages the expansion of acreage planted, but pressure to plant marginal or recently rotated plots damages soils and social relations fundamental to food security. Large-scale commercial plantations like those for irrigated rice in Northern Ghana have seriously disrupted local farming systems without producing the anticipated bumper crops (Goody 1980).

Traders share with farmers and other urban consumers the long-term vulnerability of dependence on commercial prices and supply and demand levels. Ever more remote farmers come to rely on trading connections that harness them to the needs of production for the world market and the urban consumer. Kumasi women market traders apparently lack an economic or political basis for establishing control over farmers that would enable them to manipulate supply or price levels to their own lasting advantage. Their linking position gives them enough flexibility to achieve relative security and occasionally individual prosperity, but not the ability to transform the terms and conditions of trade beyond the upper or lower limits of local buying power set by other aspects of the international economy.

The structure of marketplace systems themselves leads one not to expect simple duplication of Kumasi traders' actions and capabilities in other West African markets or even across Ghana. One rather expects trading practices and relations to vary with the structural location of specific markets within a regional market system, and between systems with relatively distinct historical and cultural processes. Evidence of different and similar conditions in other markets constitutes additional rather than supportive or contradictory data.[3] Even within my own field experience, substantial differences in commercial conditions and practices appeared between town and village markets and between different city markets in Ghana and other West African countries. Since many of Kumasi food traders' actions respond to conditions widely reported elsewhere, an investigation of the distribution of similar or different reactions would be valuable.

Consequently, direct imitation of Kumasi market features, even those that promote food security in Kumasi or another specific location, seems likely to prove unproductive. Such features would be difficult to establish firmly, and might have quite opposite effects on food security in the new context. It seems more realistic to suggest the incorporation of such positive characteristics as flexibility between alternative marketing channels, by removing obstacles specific to local conditions for the social groups involved in trade and by encouraging or innovating forms consistent with the local commercial context.

NOTES

1. For a full summary of the dynamics of Ghanaian agricultural policy, see Kraus (1988). The introduction to Clark (1988) discusses the mediating position of informal sector trade between local and international or national/state demands, with ambiguity and frustration arising at both ends. My chapter there gives much more detail on events during 1979.
2. The initial fieldwork period from 1978 to 1980 included price control enforcement episodes under three successive governments. 1979 was particularly eventful, with the currency exchange in March, the June 4 Revolution, a gasoline and foreign exchange crisis, and national elections. During a second residence from 1982 to 1984, severe drought was

compounded by political conflicts. Although the forest zone has not been destroyed ecologically by drought in the same way as the Sahel zone, Kumasi's surrounding Ashanti Region did suffer a substantial crop failure in 1982-3. Rainfall proved inadequate for the crops planted and uncontrolled bush fires destroyed significant food crop acreage in early 1983. Tense relations between Ghana and potential donor nations and the sudden arrival of Ghanaian migrants expelled from Nigeria exacerbated food shortages throughout 1983.

Responsibilities in a development project prevented systematic data collection from 1982-4, but the project did provide opportunities for gathering anecdotal material from a wider range of locations throughout Ghana on local responses that included shifts in commercial as well as producing and consuming patterns. Relating that material to the 1978-80 analysis of market trading relations makes it more informative on the balance of power between farmers and traders.

3.   Studies of other market systems in Southern Ghana partly confirm and partly contrast to the conditions found in Kumasi Central Market. Particularly full information is provided for Accra by Robertson (1984), for Koforidua by McCall (1956) and Gore (1978), and for Suhum by Schwimmer (1976).

REFERENCES

Bates, Robert H.
  1981   Markets and States in Tropical Africa. Berkeley: University of California Press.
Bentwi-Enchill, Nii K.
  1979   Losing Illusions at Makola Market. West Africa (Sept. 3, 1979) p. 1590.
Chazan, Naomi and Timothy Shaw, eds.
  1988   Coping with Africa's Food Crisis. Boulder: Lynn Rienner.
Clark, Gracia
  1984   The Position of Asante Market Women in Kumasi Central Market, Ghana. Phd thesis, U. of Cambridge.
  1988   ed., Traders Vs. the State. Boulder: Westview.
Danquah, J. B.
  1947   Irregularities in Import Control, motion by Hon. Dr. J. B. Danquah, 26/3/47. (Joint Provincial Councils) Ghana National Archives, Accra, No. 0028 SF8.
Food Agriculture Organisation (UN)
  1983   Director-General's Report on World Food Security: A Reappraisal of the Concepts and Approaches. Committee on World Food Security, 13-20 April 1983.
Goody, J. R.
  1980   Rice Burning and the Green Revolution in Ghana. Journal of Development Studies 16(2): 136-55.
Gore, Charles
  1978   Food Marketing and Rural Development: a study of an urban supply system in Ghana. PhD thesis, Pennsylvania State University.
Guyer, Jane
  1984   Family and Farm in Southern Cameroon. Boston University African Studies Center, African Research Studies No. 15.
  1987   ed., Feeding African Cities. Manchester: International African Institute.

Hill, Polly
  1963 Migrant Cocoa Farmers of Southern Ghana. Cambridge University Press.
Kraus, Jon
  1988 The Political Economy of Food in Ghana. In Coping With Africa's Food
        Crisis. Naomi Chazan and Timothy M. Shaw, eds. Boulder: Lynne Rien-
        ner.
Lawson, Rowena
  1966 Inflation in the Consumer Market in Ghana—Its Cause and Cure. Eco-
        nomic Bulletin of Ghana X, no. 1
Maclachlan, Morgan
  1983 Why They Did Not Starve. Philadelphia: ISHI.
McCall, Daniel
  1956 The Effect on Family Structure of Changing Economic Activities of
        Women in a Gold Coast Town. PhD thesis, Columbia University.
McCorkle, Constance
  1988 "You Can't Eat Cotton": Cash Crops and the Cereal Code of Honor in
        Burkina Faso. In J. Bennett and J. Bowen, eds., Production and Autonomy:
        Anthropological Studies and Critiques of Development. Monographs in
        Economic Anthropology, No. 5., Lanham, MD: University Press of Amer-
        ica.
Mikell, Gwendolyn
  1985 Expansion and Contraction in Economic Access for Rural Women in
        Ghana. Rural Africana 21:13.
Okali, Christine
  1976 The Importance of non-economic variables in the development of the
        Ghana cocoa industry: a field study of cocoa farming among the Akan.
        PhD thesis, U. Ghana, Legon.
Robertson, Claire
  1983 The Death of Makola and Other Tragedies. Canadian Journal of African
        Studies 17:469-95.
  1984 Sharing the Same Bowl. Bloomington: Indiana University Press.
Saul, Mahir
  1988 The Efficiency of Private Channels in the Distribution of Cereals in
        Burkina Faso. In J. Bennett and J. Bowen, eds., Production and Autonomy:
        Anthropological Studies and Critiques of Development. Monographs in
        Economic Anthropology, No. 5., Lanham, MD: University Press of Amer-
        ica.
Schwimmer, Brian
  1976 The Social Organization of Marketing in a Southern Ghanaian Town. PhD
        thesis, Stanford University.
Sen, Amartya
  1981 Poverty and Famines: an Essay in Entitlement and Deprivation. NY; Ox-
        ford University Press.
Sherman, Jacqueline
  1984 Grain Marketing Decisions of Subsistence Farmers in Burkina Faso.
        CRED Discussion Paper No. 111, U. of Michigan, Ann Arbor.

Smith, Carol
    1984 Local History in Global Context: Social and Economic Transitions in
          Western Guatemala. Comparative Studies in Society and History
          26:193-228.
UNICEF
    1985 Within Human Reach: A future for Africa's children. NY.
Vaughan, Megan
    1987 The Story of an African Famine. Cambridge University Press.
Vellenga, Dorothy Dee
    1981 Matriliny, Patriliny and Class Formation Among Women Cocoa Farmers
          in Two Rural Areas of Ghana. Presented at African Studies Association
          meetings, Bloomington, Indiana, October, 1981.
Watts, Michael
    1987 Brittle trade: a political economy of food supply in Kano. In Jane Guyer,
          ed. Feeding African Cities. Manchester: International African Institute.

CHAPTER 9

Gender, Hunger, and Crisis in Tanzania

Donna O. Kerner
Kristy Cook

This chapter examines Tanzanian women's strategies for coping with food shortages and basic household consumption needs during a period of crisis caused by both political/economic and natural causes. Our case study is drawn from the experience of Chagga peasants, who inhabit one of the relatively well-developed areas of the country.[1]

We will advance three related arguments: one, that long-term patterns of socio-economic change occurring in Kilimanjaro have affected the ability of Chagga women of different strata to cope with short-term crises; two, that women's short-term coping strategies necessitated by severe conditions both accentuate and potentially alter longer term directions of change toward increasing differentiation between households; and three, that commercial activities of Chagga women, particularly beer brewing, are both the result of the household's ability to generate a certain standard of agricultural income and an important factor in the expansion of the household into more diversified farm and non-activities. The control over income from such commercial activities represents a contested domain between men and women, both between husbands and wives in the domestic realm and collectively in the arena of village politics.

KILIMANJARO AND ECONOMIC CRISIS IN TANZANIA

Kilimanjaro, one of the United Republic of Tanzania's twenty regions, is located in the northeast corner of the country bordering on Kenya. It has an area of 13,200 sq. km and a population of 902,000, approximately 5.3% of the country's total population (United Republic of Tanzania, 1982a). Most of the region's inhabitants, the Chagga people, live on the slopes of Mt. Kilimanjaro and the Pare Mountains at altitudes between 800 and 2,000 meters, where population density is the highest in Tanzania.[2] The intensive cropping system of the Chagga has been fairly stable for about a century (Fernandez et al., 1985), but is beginning to experience the effects of severe population pressure, diminishing land resources, and changes in dietary habits.

The primary export crop of Kilimanjaro is coffee, which averages 31% of the country's total foreign exchange earnings (United Republic of Tanzania, 1982 b). Coffee and the staple crop, bananas, are interplanted in *kihamba* ("home") gardens on the middle and upper slopes of the mountain and watered through a traditional irrigation system of furrows which capture run-off water from the melting snowcap. Vegetable gardens and livestock are also raised in homestead *kihamba*. Annual food crops, such as maize, finger millet, and beans, are grown both for home consumption and sale ten to sixteen kilometers away on the drier plains below the southern and eastern slopes in fields called *kishamba*. Here cultivation is rainfed and mainly unmechanized.

Productive farmers in Kilimanjaro have contributed to Tanzania's national economy through sales of coffee, maize, and other crops. These farmers also suffered from the debilitating effects of economic crisis in Tanzania in the early 1980s. Several warning signals of impending national economic trouble had been sounded earlier by those watching the progress of this African nation, renowned for its commitment to socialist rural development policies. Long term declining trends in agricultural production, with accompanying low export earnings, had restricted the availability of foreign exchange, which contributed to balance of payments problems (Ellis, 1980; Lofchie, 1978). The public sector continued to expand during the 1970s without gaining in efficiency or contributing directly to production.[3] Major changes in political and economic institutions (the resettlement of some five million villagers into nucleated settlements, the decentralization of the Party and government bureaucracy, and establishment of marketing boards) disrupted rural economic and social patterns (McHenry, 1979; Von Freyhold, 1979). In addition, during the late 1970s the country became increasingly dependent on external aid for domestic capital formation.

Several external events in the late 1970s contributed to the macro-economic problems of the country: the dissolution of the East African community, the war with Idi Amin's regime in Uganda, and declining world market prices for major export crops, along with rising oil prices. The confluence of domestic policies and external shocks resulted in quite severe economic deterioration throughout the country in the early 1980s.

The main economic base of Kilimanjaro region is agricultural production, and the stagnation of coffee production, accompanied by contracted government budget transfers, has reduced net financial inflows for the entire region. Kilimanjaro is relatively well integrated into Tanzania's economic system. Strong communication and transport linkages connecting Moshi (the regional capital) and Dar es Salaam (the country's largest city and most important port and business center), large commodity transfers in and out of the region, and a more developed infrastructure in terms of roads, electricity, hospitals, and schools have perhaps reduced the absolute impact of the crisis, but have also contributed to the perception among local inhabitants that the current crisis is particularly acute.

Kilimanjaro residents in 1984 were experiencing not only the severe economic crisis prevalent throughout the country, but the effects of three successive years of drought. In the next section we argue that short-term strategies employed by women and men against the increasing threat of *njaa* (hunger) both vary according to the class position of the household and reflect longer term changes in the production and exchange relations among men and women.

SOCIAL CHANGE, GENDER RELATIONS, AND COPING STRATEGIES

Kilimanjaro is one of the most highly stratified regions in Tanzania. Land on the mountain is intensively cultivated and in short supply. Processes beginning in the nineteenth century have fragmented some family plots, while consolidating others. Increasingly, farmers of all strata depend on non-farm sources of income to meet basic social reproduction needs of the household. However, even the wealthiest inhabitants, who work as self-employed entrepreneurs and in white collar occupations, maintain their farms as a form of security and as a status symbol.

Our survey material from a middle highland village in Moshi Rural District indicated that there are three main divisions between households in highland Kilimanjaro villages. The small peasant household is devoted exclusively to farming and raises food crops mainly for subsistence, though some is for sale, and coffee. Land-holdings tend to be smaller (one acre or less) in these households, which may not even possess *kishamba* land on the plains. Such households have no off-farm income, live in traditional mud and wattle homes, own few tools and no major consumer items, and potentially hire-out to wealthier farmers and government coffee estates. Although superficially such households appear to have limited involvement in the exchange economy, the fact that they are engaged in agricultural wage labor and are as actively engaged as middle and large peasants in parallel market activities, suggests that their "exit" options are limited.[4] In the face of economic crisis, such households are forced to sell assets, such as livestock, to balance the increased sale of wage labor against the continued viability of the household labor pool, and draw increasingly upon non-familial kin for the loan of tools, livestock, and agricultural inputs.

At the second tier are middle peasant farming households with more acreage to farm in the highland and lowland areas and substantial non-farm income. Many possess permanent or semi-permanent houses and one or more major consumer items (exclusive of vehicles). In middle peasant households the division of labor in the 1980s can be described in the following way. Men are responsible for the cultivation and sale of coffee and control the assets of cattle and goats. They are expected to plough (or arrange tractor rental to plough) the fields for food crops, aid in harvesting food crops (or supply cash to hire day laborers), contribute to communal village labor projects organized by the government, and maintain the irrigation system. Major house and tool repairs are also their responsibility. Women cultivate the cereal and legume crops on the plains, cultivate and market bananas and garden vegetables, brew and sell beer, milk cows and control the milk sales, and raise chickens for sale. The labor of young girls is employed in a range of domestic and child-caring tasks which are the exclusive domain of women and are also employed in cutting and head-loading grass from the plains to feed cattle, which are kept in stalls in the homestead.

Theoretically, women are expected to provide for the subsistence needs of the household from their cultivation of food crops and marketing activities. Women in these households were more actively engaged in regular or seasonal non-farm work, particularly in commercial beer brewing, than those in small farming households. Men, who control the cash income from coffee and livestock, are expected to provide for such regular expenses as clothing, house repair, and agricultural inputs and additional major expenses, such as school and medical fees. In reality, the control over family assets (in land and livestock) and income from the sale of food crops and beer constitute a domain of struggle between men and women, a point to which we will return.

Households in the middle category have a larger resource base to draw from, but are faced with the choice of lowering investment and even reducing existing assets during crisis periods. Additionally they may attempt to increase non-farm income through the sale of beer or increased output in artisanal trade. Finally, they intensify demands on children in the form of direct remittances from those living outside the region or on the labor input of those residing at home. Contrary to a more general trend towards the reduction of major household expenditures, interview data indicated that investment in children's education remains stable or is even intensified during such periods of economic retrenchment.

At the third and wealthiest level are households engaged in major off-farm business (transport, construction, mining). Such households may grow limited crops for home consumption and some coffee, or may have used income from non-farm businesses to expand their land under cultivation for the sale of food crops. These non-farm business households can employ the labor of poor peasants to cultivate their fields and domestic labor in their homes, while husbands, and increasingly, wives, pursue white collar or business occupations in the nearby regional capital, Moshi Town. The wealthiest of these farmers possess tractors, improved inputs, and lorries to transport their crops to markets where they will fetch the highest prices. As one might expect, economic crisis conditions have considerably less direct impact on households at these levels. Their activities are far more diversified and they have access to a range of different markets though secure access to transport. They may even be in a position to take advantage of trading opportunities unavailable to lower and middle income households and to purchase assets of impoverished families. On the other hand, they are subject to intensified demands from poorer relatives and are also increasingly visible to local government scrutiny of their activities.

However, even this brief sketch presents a somewhat artificial picture of Kilimanjaro's demography. In the area where research was concentrated, the majority of our sample households were comprised of late-middle aged to elderly couples residing with younger children and grandchildren. Extreme land pressure, combined with educational and occupational opportunities outside the region, forced the majority of young men and women into the towns. Delayed marriage, due to the economic hardship imposed on young men by the tradition of having to obtain land and build a house on the mountain prior to marriage and inflationary bridewealth payments, has increased illegitimate birth rates. Many couples choose to enter premarital liaisons while working outside the region for several years to raise bridewealth payments. For young Chagga women residing in the towns or the capital, Dar es Salaam, compulsory paid maternity leave and the extraction of child support from the child's father represent a viable alternative to conjugal attachment. Young Chagga women between the ages of 16–24 were overrepresented in Swantz and Bryceson's 1974 survey of minimum wage-earners in the capital (Swantz and Bryceson, 1976). Illegitimate children from such unions are often left in the village for the grandparents to raise while the daughter sends home cash and commodity remittances.

262   D. O. KERNER, K. COOK

Thus many Chagga women bear the burden of providing for the basic food
needs of not one generation of children but two. They do so amidst the constraints of reduced labor contributions by husbands and older children to
food production,[5] unfavorable weather conditions, rising market prices for
staples, and opposition from their husbands regarding the disposal of their
non-agricultural income.

A five-village study conducted by the German Development Institute
(Schneider-Barthold et al., 1983) provides a comparative context for our
sample data. Two general strategies are outlined in this report: farmers either
attempt to produce items whose prices have kept pace with inflation, such as
new crops which are unregulated, or they attempt to sell crops on parallel
markets, where prices are higher. Acreage under coffee has not necessarily
fallen,[6] but cultivation practices have lapsed and the labor has been reallo-
cated to activities with higher returns. Household census data from our own
sample support the hypothesis that non-agricultural income is the differenti-
ating factor among the households. We will suggest that women's contribution to the household income from commercial activities has the potential to
raise the family's class position, although the redistributive benefits in terms
of increased food security for the woman and her children may in fact
diminish.[7]

THE COMMERCIALIZATION OF FARMING
AND CHANGING GENDER RELATIONS

An historical view indicates that while periodic scarcity and differentiation
among households is not a new development, increasing involvement in the
exchange economy has exacerbated both processes. Fragmentation of labor
relations and subsequent conflict over redistribution of the fruits of labor
have been the result. The commercialization of agriculture in Kilimanjaro,
which began with increased food crop production for the Arab coastal trade
during the nineteenth century and intensified during the colonial period with
the introduction of the export crop coffee, increased differentiation within
and between households. This in turn weakened the cooperation within
larger lineage units and undermined the complementarity of conjugal roles.
One development that reflects this dual process is the decline of male cooperative labor patterns and its connection to commercial beer brewing by
women.

Male informants in the 1980s bemoaned the fact that male cooperative agricultural labor was a thing of the past. They attributed the disintegration of
traditional male solidarity to the atomization of the minimal lineage homestead resulting from the commoditization of labor. In the past, Chagga men

had the ability to command their wives' labor in the cultivation of banana and finger millet and the production of beer for public male ceremonial redistribution. Cooperative farming is one such occasion that requires the provision of large quantities of local beer (*mbege*), yet nowadays it must be purchased at a cost far in excess of that of contract labor, although the cost of beer production was calculated to be roughly equal to the cost of contract labor. The fact that the production of beer has now become a commercial endeavor controlled by women—the wives of most of these male informants produced local beer of banana and finger millet for sale—is the outcome of the commercialization of agriculture in general and an attempt by women to overcome an increasing dependency on their husbands' income and their loss of security in land and livestock.

How did this increasing dependency come about? The Chagga are patrilineal and virilocal. Each contiguously located minimal lineage segment occupies a homestead consisting of sleeping quarters, granaries, cooking houses, and cattle stalls. The homestead is surrounded by coffee and banana groves, laced by irrigation furrows, and fenced in by dracaena hedges.

Today the great majority of Chagga households are at least nominally Christian and monogamous. In the past, each wife in a polygynous union was accorded her own homestead, with her own fields and a share of her husband's livestock. While women did not inherit either land or livestock, they normally brought with them cattle and goats as part of the initiation and marriage gifts from their lineage, and the livestock put under a woman's control by her husband could not be disposed of without her permission. Her security after his death was insured by levirate marriage and the patrilineal inheritance rule of rewarding the youngest son with the house and property and surrounding banana groves (Dundas, 1924; Johnston, 1946). Uncultivated land on the mountain and on the plains was held by the chief to dispose of as he wished.

In precolonial times the domestic and political economy were highly intertwined and ideologically symbolized by a cosmology which highlighted the discrete and complementary forces of male and female powers of sexuality and reproduction. The mystical combination of food production, eating, and sacrifice was inextricably linked to the life of people and their ancestors in harmony with their environment. Both male "milk" (semen) and female menstrual blood were seen to combine to produce new life. According to Moore and Puritt (1977) sharing milk from the same breast signified siblingship, while sharing beer from the same container symbolized comradeship. Bananas, a staple food and primary ingredient in beer, came from the "milk tree," which was so named because of its milky sap. Boys were circumcised sitting on a banana stem. While men owned banana groves and handed them on to their sons, women tended the groves and produced the beer from which male solidarity flowed. The manure of cows (tended by women) brought fertility to the bananas and was therefore magically linked to fertility. Cow manure and male feces were essential ingredients in male and female initiation rites. Husbands and wives were buried in the banana groves and ancestral propitiation was performed there. That beer and meat were essential features of Chagga social life provides evidence of precolonial production for surplus (Kjerkshus, 1977). Meat slaughtering distribution groups were coterminous with maximal lineage units and roasted meat and beer accompanied all sacrificial and political obligations. Women's contribution to male public redistribution was offset by the labor contributions of their husbands and children in food production and in their secure access to land and livestock products. Thus, male and female roles were symbolically and in reality complementary.

The introduction of coffee farming and formal education by missionaries in the late nineteenth century had far-reaching effects on the social status of Chagga women. Mission education for women, when it was provided, concentrated on conversion of the female population to Christianity and also to the Victorian ideal of the model housewife and mother, rather than on the attainment of literacy and skills which would have facilitated their entry into the wage sector of the economy. The missions and colonial administration excluded women from extension services, marketing opportunities, and the income generated by coffee. Increasing amounts of land were given over to coffee cultivation, and this drew off the labor contributions to food crop production of younger lineage members. Communal grazing pastures shrank and cattle declined in number and grew in price. Land speculation fragmented family holdings, which created classes of middle and land-poor peasants, and control over inherited land became increasingly a matter of bitter dispute.

In this scenario, commercial beer brewing has been one response by uneducated women to offset the loss of power within the domestic economy and their unequal access to the exchange economy. Income from beer brewing and marketing projects represents both a long- and short-term accumulation strategy for Chagga women. In the short term such income may be used to cover basic household expenses, which are still regarded as a wife's responsibility. In the long run savings from beer brewing are directed toward the education of children, particularly daughters, whose remittances are viewed as a form of retirement fund.

WOMEN'S COLLECTIVE ACTION DURING
DROUGHT AND FOOD SHORTAGE

Long-term investment strategies from beer sales gave way to short-term subsistence needs during the economic crisis of the 1980s. Women, who perceived such income as necessary for the basic social reproduction needs of
the household, found their right to control this income hotly contested by
men, both in the domestic and public realm. In the domestic arena, Chagga
husbands almost always represented their wives' income from beer sales as
part of the general household fund which they controlled. Women viewed
this income as their own. In the public domain, village court cases for this
period indicate a large number of grievances between female brewers and
male beer shop owners. In one such case the local branch of the women's
organization (UWT) brought suit against the male-run village cooperative
beer shop. The women's organization had lent a substantial sum for start-up
costs of the shop in the hopes of securing a regular outlet for their product,
only to find that their money had been squandered during the initial weeks by
the male village leadership, who were unwilling or unable to repay the loan.

The women's organization struggled valiantly to provide adult education
and vocational training programs to uneducated peasant women to enable
them to increase their economic independence through crafts production and
the development of cottage industries. Such schemes were curtailed sharply
during the drought, when, as the male village leaders put it, "Hunger has
driven everyone to look for food." This is worthy of deconstruction. The men
of this village were in regular attendance at village meetings and engaged in
village projects. Their wives could not attend meetings, they said, because
they were responsible for preparing the afternoon meal. Those "looking for
food" during the drought were overwhelmingly women. The search for food
during that period entailed far more than engagement in farm activities for
Chagga women, who dominate the regional market structure. Forced to purchase food and other commodities at black market prices, they were also
forced to sell their produce at inflated rates and many combined their market
activities with smuggling across the nearby Kenyan border.

Parallel market activities were tragically extended as well to the distribution of so-called "free" emergency hunger maize shipped from the United
States. Maize prices had quadrupled between 1983–84. Government stocks
were depleted, as few farmers would sell their produce at the low farm-gate
price to the National Milling Corporation. This meant that women who had
sold much of their grain stock and needed to purchase maize before the next
harvest season were unable to purchase grain at the low government-subsi-

dized price. Prices on the parallel market fluctuated between four and five times the subsidized rate.

Within this century maize has gradually supplanted bananas as the staple food in Chagga households, as coffee cultivation has superseded banana growing at the upper altitudes. The compromise struck was to expand the cultivation of food crops on the plains, which are more vulnerable to drought. Although we do not have the data to support it, impressionistically it appears that banana cultivation has become increasingly specialized, with a concentration on those varieties used for beer brewing at the expense of cooking varieties. This impression is supported by evidence of peasant women seeking to purchase cooking bananas at inflated parallel market prices during the pre-harvest season.

Hunger maize was theoretically supposed to be available to poor farmers free of charge. Village chairmen were supposed to draw up lists of the poorest farmers who qualified to receive supplies. Transport breakdowns and delays caused a shortfall in the expected supply. Farmers who were able to afford it were asked to contribute the standard government subsidized sale price toward the shipping expenses. First priority for food aid was to be given to lowland villages, whose dependence on rainfed agriculture left them in straitened circumstances.

Chagga women in the highland village complained bitterly that they had never been given the opportunity to add their names to any list and were forced to purchase the hunger maize in the regional market at the black market rate. At one heated meeting of the women's organization, sixty women took the time away from the preparation of their husbands' afternoon meal to accuse the village leadership of having appropriated the emergency grain supplies to make a killing on the black market. The village chairman, seeking to pacify the organization, claimed that he had received a permit from the area commissioner for them to travel to a distant regional market center, where they would be able to purchase maize at a price below the rate obtaining in their own market, but three times the subsidized price. The meeting was disbanded as the women continued to protest that they could not afford either the compromise price or the transport time and cost of travel to this distant market.

CONCLUSIONS

The two cases described above illustrate the interrelated trends of long-term patterns of socio-economic change and short-term coping strategies presented at the beginning of this chapter. In summary, Chagga women cope differently with short-term crisis according to their class position. This is an outcome of historical processes of commercialization in which fragmenta-tion of land holdings, changing labor relations, and shifting patterns of in-vestment have accentuated the unequal allocation of resources both within and between households. Under severe conditions of crisis, women, particu-larly from middle-income households, exhibit short-term coping strategies which potentially alter longer term directions of change. Finally, the ability of women from this middle-income group to implement a viable set of cop-ing strategies in the face of economic crisis may be an important factor in the expansion of households into more diversified farm and non-farm activities.

Our case material in this chapter is drawn almost exclusively from the em-pirical study of women from middle-income peasant households. While we observed variations in women's strategies for income generation and the ex-tent to which such income was pooled into the larger household budget among different classes, further documentation of these variations is an im-portant area for future research.

Our observations suggest that at lower and higher income levels there is less tendency to pool incomes for investment between husbands and wives. In poor peasant households few funds exist for investment. In wealthier households income generating activities for men and women constitute sepa-rate domains. Men in these wealthier households are not dependent upon their wives' income to sustain or expand agricultural activities or to support their ceremonial redistribution in the prestige sphere. Our case material from middle-income peasant households indicates the opposite trend. Women in this peasant stratum operate within a sphere of restricted autonomy. Under normal conditions, these women are freed from basic survival pressures and attempts to pursue various entrepreneurial activities. Under conditions of economic crisis, income from these activities activates a realm of contention between spouses (and other family members). During crises, a woman's con-tribution to the general household budget may be necessary to sustain the survival level of the household, but the ideology of conjugal and/or age/authority relations may mitigate against a woman's ability to determine how household resources should be allocated.

The cross-cultural literature on women's collective action[8] indicates that otherwise politically quiescent women will organize publicly when their right to a basic household subsistence income is threatened. The two focal points of women's political action in our research area in 1984 were (1) the right of women to a secure income from beer brewing and (2) their right to a share in the distribution of emergency grain supplies. We believe that the two issues are linked in the following way.

Women from middle income Chagga households have come to rely on the sale of beer to supplement the family budget. This is made possible by the devotion of more land and labor toward the production of finger millet and certain varieties of banana. At the best of times women can use such income to cover not only basic subsistence needs for themselves and their children, but also to invest in education and other income-generating projects. Their ability to raise income from commercial beer brewing offsets their insecure access to their husbands' income from cash cropping and livestock sale and their husbands' overconsumption of beer and meat at the expense of their dependents.[9] In times of shortage, loss of beer brewing income threatens the survival of a woman and her children. On the domestic front, a woman's desire to manage her income from beer sales may conflict with her husband's desire to expand cash crop or non-farm production and/or his own consumption/redistribution needs. We reach the tentative conclusion that income from women's commercial activities tends to be pooled into a general household fund directed toward the husbands' agenda. In the political arena as well, women's attempt to gain secure income from beer sales is lost to the redistribution desire of male leaders, but under protest.

The conflict between women's right to basic subsistence and male redistribution practices is also highlighted by the women's public charges of corruption in the distribution of hunger maize. In this case, the desires of wealthy male leaders won out over the basic needs of poor peasant women, a public reflection of domestic gender inequality.

A comparative case from Tanzania's impoverished Dodoma region (Thiele, 1986) is illuminating. During a famine crisis, male village authorities tried to prohibit female commercial beer brewing activities with the rationalization that necessary grain would be wasted in alcohol consumption. Female beer brewers protested that these sales formed their survival income. Clearly Dodoma women did not anticipate receiving an adequate share in the food crop they produced or in income from its sale.

A number of researchers (Bryceson, 1985; Geiger, 1982; Muro, 1979; Swantz et al., 1975) are drawn to the conclusion that the ideology of gender and inequality continues to mask the real subsumption of female labor to male control. Swantz (1977:559), for example, states,

> The woman gives her labour as part of family obligation without having a share in the planning of the use of it nor in the monetary benefit ensuing from it. The woman herself has not come to a full realization of the implications of her position and submits herself to it because of the ideas inculcated in her by social norms belonging to a mode of production left behind.

Without romanticizing the very real struggles of Chagga women, we want to suggest that such a conclusion fails to recognize the dynamic quality of the social construction of gender relations.[10] Gender ideology, which reflects and supports structures of cooperation and competition between women and men over access to resources, the management of the production process, and entitlement to shares in the end product, cannot be taken as a fixed or static set of ideas. Male informants may attempt to represent them as such, but women's behavior, particularly in periods of severe economic crisis, is indicative of the degree to which the social reproduction of gender organization is an arena of struggle which requires continuous re-definition in reaction to changing political and economic realities.

ACKNOWLEDGEMENTS

The research upon which this paper was based was conducted by Donna Kerner in Kilimanjaro region in 1983–84 under a Research Assistantship and the Andrew Silk Dissertation Fellowship from the Graduate Center of the City University of New York. Donna Kerner was affiliated with the Department of Education at the University of Dar es Salaam and the Tanzania National Scientific Research Council as a Research Associate from 1982– 84. Kristy Cook was a Rotary Fellow in Tanzania, affiliated with the Department of Economics, University of Dar es Salaam from 1982–84. We gratefully acknowledge the support of these institutions. We also wish to thank Patience Boyd and Teresa Leavitt for their assistance in coding the survey material. An earlier draft of this paper was presented at the 1987 American Anthropological Association meetings in Chicago, IL and published under the title, "Gender and Food Shortage in Tanzania," in *Feminist Issues* 9:1:57–72 (1989). We would like to thank the participants of the symposium, "Gender and Famine in sub-Saharan Africa" for their comments and the editors of *Feminist Issues*, Mary Jo Lakeland and Susan Ellis Wolf, for permission to use material published in the article for this chapter.

NOTES

1. Thirty households in a village located in the Mamba South Division of Moshi Rural District were surveyed between December 1983 and June 1984. A single intensive survey was made of each household and was complemented by formal and informal interviews with a range of village members (total village population: 830 families, 3337 individuals) and participant observation. The survey was conducted primarily to relate attitudes towards education to socio-economic status. Therefore, questions about household assets, cropping patterns, labor allocations, and educational levels were asked. The sample was selected by identification of differentiated households by village representatives.
2. Using figures from the 1978 population census (United Republic of Tanzania, 1982a), there were 3.62 acres/person in the region, but only 0.54 acres/person of cultivated agricultural land.
3. Ellis (1980) notes that there were 20 parastatals in 1968 and 380 in 1986. Nellis (1986) shows 400 in 1981.

4. G. Hyden is the main proponent of the argument that peasants have an "exit option" of withdrawal from market transactions in the Tanzanian case (Hyden, 1980). This retreat to subsistence phenomenon has been contested and a counter hypothesis is that even though farmers move out of cash crop production, they do not withdraw from the market and instead attempt different strategies to gain access to scarce goods. D. Rubin (1986) presents strong evidence against Hyden's "exit option" thesis.
5. See Mbilinyi (1986) concerning changing labor patterns in agricultural production.
6. A variety of explanations is offered by researchers: (1) by law, farmers are not allowed to uproot coffee trees, (2) coffee provides a slow, but steady income, (3) coffee cultivation represents a considerable labor/time investment and, (4) for wealthier landowners, coffee continues to maintain a mystique of traditional prestige.
7. Howard (1980) cites alcoholism and overconsumption of meat by the father as contributing factors to child malnutrition. See also studies by Attems et al. (1969), Kreysler (1973), and Swantz et al. (1975), which discuss the apparent contradiction between the relatively high level of regional development in Kilimanjaro and relatively high levels of malnutrition with differential effects by age and gender.
8. Brusco (1986) provides an instructive summary and suggests that we need to expand our analysis of women's collective action to the domestic arena. Her research in Colombia demonstrates how women actively work to transform gender relations (particularly the male conjugal role) as a means of redirecting income away from public male consumption back into the domestic economy.
9. Geiger (1982) reports that women in neighboring Majengo, Arusha region, attempted to control beer sales through their own UWT cooperative shop in order to compete with illegal establishments and control the quantity and hours of male drinking.
10. Marjorie Mbilinyi, Professor at the Institute for Development Studies, University of Dar es Salaam and her colleagues in the Women's Resources and Documentation Project have made a most significant contribution in creating a context for the analysis of the social role of Tanzanian women (see Mascarenhas and Mbilinyi, 1983). In one of her earlier articles Mbilinyi (1972) reminds us that the role of women is socially constructed in the labor process and is exceedingly complex. Social identity cannot be abstracted merely from "traditional" norms/ideologies, but is highly dependent on situational context.

REFERENCES

Attems, M. C. et al.
    1969   Investigations in Northeast Tanzania, in H. Kraut and H. D. Cremer, Investigations into Health and Nutrition in East Africa. Munich: Weltforum. Abstract cited in O. Mascarenhas and M. Mbilinyi, Women in Tanzania: An Analytical Bibliography. Uppsala: Scandinavian Institute of African Studies, 1983.
Brusco, E.
    1986   Colombian Evangelicalism as a Strategic Form of Women's Collective Action, Feminist Issues, 6:2.
Bryceson, D. F.
    1985   Women's Proletarianization and the Family Wage in Tanzania, in H. Afshar (ed.) Women, Work and Ideology in the Third World. London: Tavistock Publications.
Coffee Authority of Tanzania
    1984   Coffee Production Metric Tonnes Clean Coffee 1962–1984, Northern Zone Statistics, Moshi, Tanzania.

Dundas, C.
1924 Kilimanjaro and its People. London: Frank Case & Co.

Ellis F.
1980 Agricultural Marketing and Peasant-State Transfers in Tanzania, Journal of Peasant Studies, 10:4.

Fernandez, E. C. M., A. Oktingati, and J. Maghembe
1985 The Chagga Home Gardens: A Multi-storeyed Agro-Forestry Cropping System on Mt. Kilimanjaro, Northern Tanzania, Agroforestry Systems, 1:3.

Geiger S.
1982 Umoja Wa Wanawaka Wa Tanzania and the Needs of the Rural Poor, African Studies Review, 25:2-3.

Howard, M. T.
1980 Kwashiorkor on Kilimanjaro: The Social Handling of Malnutrition, unpublished Ph.D. dissertation, Michigan State University.

Hyden. G.
1980 Beyond Ujamaa in Tanzania. Underdevelopment and an Uncaptured Peasantry. London: Heinemann.

Johnston, P. H.
1946 Some Notes on Land Tenure on Kilimanjaro and the Vihamba of the Wachagga, Tanganyika Notes and Records, 21.

Kjerkshus, H.
1977 Ecology Control and Economic Development in East African History. London: Heinemann.

Kreysler, T. V.
1973 An Analysis of Survey Data Pertaining to Prevalence of Protein Energy Malnutrition, in The Young Child in Tanzania. Dar es Salaam: UNICEF.

Lofchie, M.
1978 African Crisis and Economic Liberalization in Tanzania, Journal of Modern African Studies. 16:3.

Mascarenhas, O. and M. Mbilinyi
1983 Women in Tanzania: An Analytical Bibliography. Uppsala: Institute of African Studies.

Mbilinyi, M.
1972 The 'New Woman' and Traditional Norms in Tanzania, Journal of Modern African Studies, 10:1.
1986 Agribusiness and Casual Labor in Tanzania, African Ethnohistory, 15.

McHenry, D.
1979 Tanzania's Ujamaa Villages. Berkeley: University of California Press, Institute of International Studies.

Moore, S. F. and P. Puritt
1977 The Chagga and the Meru of Tanzania.The small peasant households in highland Kilimanjaro villages. London: The International African Institute.

Muro, A.
1979 The study of Woman's Position in Peasant Production and Their Education and Training. A Case Study of Diozile I Village in Bagamoyo District, unpublished M. A. thesis, Education, University of Dar es Salaam.

Nellis, J.
   1986 Public Enterprises in sub-Saharan Africa, World Bank Discussion Paper
         No. 1, Washington, D.C.: World Bank Publications.
Rubin, D.
   1986 People of Good Heart: Rural Response to Economic Crisis in Tanzania,
         unpublished Ph.D. dissertation, Johns Hopkins University.
Schneider-Barthold, W., N. Boschmann, S. Gruchmann, W. Hehn, W. Leidig, and
         M. Plesch
   1983 Farmers' Reactions to the Present Economic Situation in Tanzania with
         Respect to Production and Marketing. A Case Study of Five Villages in the
         Kilimanjaro Region, Berlin: The German Development Institute.
Swantz, M.
   1977 The Strain and Strength Among Peasant Women in Tanganyika, Research
         Paper No. 49, Bureau of Resource Assessment and Land Use Planning,
         University of Dar es Salaam.
Swantz, M. and D. F. Bryceson
   1976 Women Workers in Dar es Salaam: 1973/74 Survey of Minimum Wage
         Earners and Self-employed, Research Paper No. 43, Bureau of Resource
         Assessment and Land Use Planning, University of Dar es Salaam.
Swantz, M., U. Henricson, and M. Zolla
   1975 Socio-economic Causes of Malnutrition in Moshi District. Research Paper
         No. 38, Bureau of Resource Assessment and Land Use Planning, Univer-
         sity of Dar es Salaam.
Thiele, G.
   1986 The State and Rural Development in Tanzania: The Village Administra-
         tion as Political Field, Journal of Development Studies, 22:3.
United Republic of Tanzania
   1982a 1978 Population Census, Dar es Salaam: Government Printer.
   1982b The Tanzania National Agricultural Policy (Final Report). Dar es Salaam:
         Government Printer.
Von Freyhold, M.
   1979 Ujamaa Villages in Tanzania: Analysis of a Socialist Experiment. New
         York: Monthly Review Press.

CHAPTER 10

Ideology, Gender, and Change: Social Relations of Production and Reproduction in Nso, Cameroon

Miriam Goheen

"...What else could a woman want but to have sons who would give her a decent burial?"
Nnu Ego, in *The Joys of Motherhood*

INTRODUCTION: GENDER IDEOLOGY, HUNGER, AND CHANGING RELATIONS OF PRODUCTION

In her novel, *The Joys of Motherhood*, Buchi Emecheta (1979) poignantly reveals the contradictions between the ideology of motherhood as a symbol of female power and the actual power relations the reality of motherhood creates in urban colonial Nigeria. Precolonial ideologies regarding women in much of West Africa were not free of contradiction, but they afforded most women a clearly defined sphere in which they had acknowledged status and power. The cultural categories of gender in Nso in western Cameroon today, as in the past, link farming-female-food as a gender marker. The designation of women as primary food farmers and providers has sometimes been problematic,[1] but it has effectively encouraged a relative equality and complementarity between male and female qualities. With changing material conditions, which are increasingly determined by the political economy of the marketplace and commoditization, the complementary roles played by men and women have become much less equal. Like Emecheta's heroine, Ngu Ego, women in Nso are discovering ironically that the very qualities which had given them status and power are those which have been under-

273

mined and subverted by the marketplace and the differential valuation of male and female work. The contradictions in women's role as primary food farmers have deepened, and a "feminization of poverty" has taken place—a poverty that is exacerbated by a growing social stratification in rural as well as urban Cameroon.

Changes in the status of women's roles have resulted partly from the changing meaning of the limits set on women's access to and control over productive resources—including land and education—as well as from a simultaneous increase in the demands on female labor and income. In Nso people are not starving, but some are hungry and malnourished, and almost half the population of rural villages has a minimally adequate and sufficient diet.[2] As a group, women and children are at risk in ways that men are not. The demands on women's time and labor as well as their obligation to grow the bulk of the food supply preclude most women from engaging in wage and salaried jobs. Access to paid work for most Nso people means migration out to larger towns and cities. Nso men often leave the village for wage and salaried jobs, but few women, especially married women with children and family obligations, are able to do so.

The weakening of women's access to various entitlements[4] such as land, labor, and credit potentially threatens the nutritional level not only of the rural household but of a large proportion of the national population.[4] In Cameroon women grow the bulk of the food consumed both locally and nationally.[5] Nso is an important source of the national food supply, particularly of corn, beans, and Irish potatoes.[6] The region's relevance to national nutritional levels becomes more apparent when we note that nationally, food self-sufficiency is on a decline.[7]

Until the mid-eighties Cameroon was almost entirely self-sufficient in food production. However, by 1984–85 the percentage was under 90% and food imports rose in that year by nearly 8% for a total of 40 billion FCFA.[8] This trend has continued to the present, increasing—in rhetoric at least—a national emphasis on agricultural development and commercialized agriculture in the Grassfields region, including Nso.[9] National policies have encouraged land speculation by a growing rural elite who file for large amounts of land for "development projects" which more often than not develop their personal fortunes rather than the national food supply.[10] While individual households have to date been able to retain access to enough land to satisfy subsistence requirements, some are having difficulty doing so, and many women trek long distances to farm far out in the countryside.[11] Land for farming, even in outlying villages, is becoming scarce and often expensive, much to the dismay of most Nso farmers, who consider access to land to be a right of citizenship.[12]

The social relations of production in Nso and the struggles over their changing meaning have created a discourse in which feminine voices, which should be at the center of these conversations, are instead muted and often silent. Changing material conditions have exacerbated inherent contradictions in the division of labor, especially where these involve gender roles.

I will argue in this paper that an important key to a comprehension of these contradictions and their relevance to a sufficient food supply is an understanding of Nso gender ideology, which emphasizes women's obligation to farm food crops while denying them ownership of the fields. The problem of women's access to various entitlements needs to be seen in relation to household, and ultimately to national, nutrition needs. I will explore several facets of Nso economy and gender relations, concentrating on the role of gender ideology and the cultural norms and practices in which it is embedded in the production and reproduction of inequalities.

I will argue four points in this connection:

(1)   that gender is a necessary and crucial variable in the political economy of production and consumption (and thus nutrition)—that women's labor is the critical factor in the social reproduction of Nso society;

(2)   while gender is perhaps the factor most critical to an understanding of household production and consumption it is not always sufficient: it must be understood in the context of increasing rural stratification;

(3)   perhaps the most crucial factor in this increasing rural stratification is unequal access to resources, the most important of which are education and land—a differential access related primarily to knowledge of and access to the national bureaucracy, and

(4)   if we are to understand (1)-(3) we must first understand gender ideology in Nso and the contradictions this ideology, which emphasizes women's responsibility to provide food while denying them firm control over critical productive resources, has created for women in the context of a rapidly commercializing economy.

BACKGROUND AND SUMMARY OF
THE NUTRITIONAL SURVEY

The quantitative data on which much of the following discussion is based were obtained from a survey of 72 households in eight Nso villages in 1981. The information is supplemented by observations and interviews with Nso farmers and bureaucrats over a two year period (1979-81) of fieldwork in Nso and from two months of fieldwork in the summer of 1988.

The survey included information on land access, nutrition, marketing opportunity, and production choice. Although we found that the average caloric and protein intake were above the MDRs, (minimum daily requirements) twenty eight percent of households surveyed had per capita intakes substantially below the MDR. Estimated consumption elasticities indicate a net decrease in household consumption as a result of higher prices for marketed food crops. Increased cash in the rural household budget is not invested in more food and better nutrition. Price elasticities of food consumption indicate that when people earn more by selling their crops rather than eating them, the money earned is not invested in nutrition but rather in "prestige foods" like sugar, tea, beer, and white bread, or in non-consumables such as radios, cloth, soap and kerosene.[13] It was estimated that an increase of 18 percent in food prices would result in over half of Nso households falling below 100 percent MDR.[14] If real income were to decline, as we believe it is likely to do in the context of the current national economic situation, nutrition levels could become even more precarious. Given the current economic crisis in Cameroon it is courting disaster for rural households to lose their subsistence base.[15]

While nutrition levels are not yet critical, clearly some households are at risk and a large percentage are increasingly vulnerable in the social context of a process of commoditization and the further development of markets among differentiated rural producers. Land issues loom large since guaranteed access to land is essential to the ability of rural subsistence farmers (who are overwhelmingly female) to continue to feed the household at even a marginally acceptable nutritional level. And land *is* increasingly scarce and expensive—especially arable land within reasonable trekking distance from rural villages. I have argued elsewhere[16] that land is becoming concentrated in the hands of a new rural elite—"modern big men," who by and large use the land they obtain as surety and for speculation rather than for commercial agricultural production. I will not recapitulate the entire argument, but some factors are of significance to the present discussion.

Throughout Nso there is an underlying uneasiness that the commoditization of land and escalating land prices will lead to the marginalization if not outright disenfranchisement of small rural producers from their land. A crucial aspect of this potential disenfranchisement is the fact that the majority of the small rural food producers are women. Both the changing pattern of the land tenure system and the allocation of new land through government development projects not only discriminate against women but often directly exclude them from participation.

If we just look at national statistics these rumors and apprehensions appear unfounded, and consequently land tenure issues until very recently have been largely ignored in national and international development schemes.[17] But national statistics, where available, do not really allow us an adequate reading of the situation, and clearly do not give an adequate picture of regional patterns. Cameroon is an extremely diverse country, both culturally and ecologically. Land tenure patterns vary substantially from one region to the next, as do farm size and population densities.

The picture is further blurred by a growing political sensitivity to land issues as national bureaucrats and others in positions of local and regional leadership and power use their influence to manipulate the national land ordinances to further their individual positions—both by acquiring substantial amounts of land themselves and by helping others to do so in return for personal favors. While everyone "knows" that "some people" have differential access to large tracts of land, names and figures are elusive. Fingers are pointed and rumors abound, but the actual facts do not appear to be a matter of public record.[18].

In Cameroon as a whole, land scarcity and land distribution are not yet national issues, but in the more densely populated rural areas like the Northwest Province, including Nso, they are becoming local issues.[19] These conflicts are reflected in the increasing confrontations between farmers and herders and in the growing number of court cases involving land disputes. The issues are complicated further by a prevailing ideology which emphasizes the fact that farm land is free (if not freely available). Changing patterns of land use and land access in and around Nso appear on first reading to be national-local and male-female conflicts over control of the distribution and use of land, but these are deceptively simplistic readings of a complex situation. The processes which have created the current conflicts over land in Nso and the potential consequences of these processes involve a complex set of issues. In order to understand these processes and their consequences we need to understand the political economy of land within the regional context, and gender relations within the household economy in Nso, as well as Nso cultural symbols and gender categories and the ways in which these interrelate in the current social, economic, and ecological context.

THE REGIONAL CONTEXT:
POLITICAL ECONOMY OF LAND

Historically the Nso Chiefdom has been the largest and most powerful chiefdom in the Bamenda Grassfields in what is today the Northwest Province (NWP) of Cameroon. The Northwest Province is one of two anglophone provinces in a largely francophone country. Land area in the province is 1,730,000 hectares—approximately 3.8 percent of the national territory.

With a population of over one million, the NWP is one of the most densely settled areas in the country, with an average of 53 persons/km². Over 85 percent of the population lives in rural areas, compared to 72 percent nationwide. In Bui Division, whose boundaries follow the boundaries of the Nso Chiefdom, population is approximately 200,000, with a density of over 65/km², most of whom are designated as rural dwellers. Even in Kumbo, which as capital of the Nso Chiefdom and seat of Divisional government is officially designated as urban, most households produce their own food, with women often travelling 15–20 km for more land to farm.[20]. While land is not scarce in absolute terms, in fact good arable farmland with even marginally adequate transport access is in scarce supply—a situation which has been exacerbated by both population growth and commercialization of agriculture.

Blessed with a healthy climate and diverse ecological zones, the region has long been a rich agricultural area and center of long distance trade. Given the extent and diversity of agricultural production in the NWP, the area is viewed as a potential breadbasket to feed the rapidly growing urban populations and alleviate future urban deficits, which are expected to be quite substantial by the year 2000.[21] The national government obviously has a keen interest in developing commercial agriculture in the NWP. This goal, however, is more easily envisioned that accomplished. Although this region is ecologically diverse and agriculturally rich, it is also an area of steep escarpments cut by low-lying valleys. Poor roads, high transport costs, and consequent low farm gate prices have discouraged the commercially-oriented production of foodstuffs in the Province. Farmers receive less than one-third of retail prices; transport costs account for two-thirds of the mark-up and are the main cost factor in the difference between farm gate and market price.[22] Transport costs have been a crucial stumbling block to increased production. But access to other resources—most importantly to land and credit for capital (technological and labor) inputs—is also a critical factor. The government in Yaounde, while dragging its feet in regard to improving the roads, has attempted to increase production by instituting a number of land ordinances in 1974 aimed ostensibly at privatization, land reform, and opening up new areas for production.[23] Although these ordinances were expressly instituted to clarify land use rights and give small farmers surety of tenure so as to encourage expansion, they have, by virtue of their ambiguous content and relationship to customary tenure, created a situation of increasing stratification between the uneducated small village farmers, who cannot take advantage of them, and the better educated rich farmers, who can and do. Since customary tenure arrangements are an integral part of traditional subsistence agriculture, the State promoted economic development of agriculture and privatization of land titles have created complex changes in tenure relationships and arrangements. At the same time, customary tenure has remained the primary mode of access to farmland for most people in Nso—for virtually all women—and the ideology that farmland should be free and available to all Nso citizens remains a salient theme in local politics.

In Nso, rights over land have become a critical issue and a source of controversy. Farmer-herder competition for land and population growth are only the tip of the iceberg. There are two particularly pivotal conflicts which are changing the meaning of the social relations of land control. The first stems from competition over land for commercial vs. subsistence use. This often appears on first reading to be a gender conflict. The second problem concerns the ambiguous relationship between customary tenure arrangements and national land policy. This may be at first interpreted as a national-local conflict.

But to reduce this problem to a two-factor formula is a reductionist explanation for a complicated set of issues. These conflicts are actually the expression of an increasingly obvious rural economic stratification; that is, they are the result of a growing number of new rural elites who file for national land allocation and in doing so both limit the amount of farmland available to smallholders and raise the price of land in and around larger villages. I have referred to these men as "modern big men"[24] to distinguish them from traditional lineage heads, but traditional-modern is a false dichotomy. These new elites, these "modern big men" buy offices in secret societies, hang out at the *fon's* palace (*fon* is the name by which Grassfield chiefs are known), and are actively involved in traditional politics. They have, in effect, become the new lineage leaders.[25]

How, one might ask, does this relate to the political economy of land? Due to increases in population (both human and animal), to urban expansion, and to commercialization of agriculture, land in Nso is becoming both privatized and scarce. There is a developing tendency for land to become concentrated in the hands of this new elite—who are almost exclusively male. At the same time, these modern big men play local (i.e., traditional) politics and assume the symbols of traditional office and title to symbolize and legitimate their new leadership role. There is thus a high degree of collaboration between traditional chiefs and the new elite.[26] This has resulted in the emergence of a regional elite that is both rooted in local tradition and has access to the State. This collaboration has facilitated the acquisition of land by these new elites through national land allocation grants, which must be approved by both national and traditional authorities. Although they are not precluded from participation by law, this collaboration has effectively kept women from filing for national land grants, since in local belief and practice women own only the crops, not the fields.[27] The expressed purpose for these grants is to further agricultural development; however, to date little of the land acquired in this way has been brought into production. Instead it is used for speculation and as surety on loans and investments in commercial ventures and urban properties, which bring more assured and immediate returns.[28] The practices of these new elites not only reduce the amount of land available to smallholders, but importantly also limit the amount of capital invested in food production.

The emerging rural stratification in Nso isn't a question of traditional/modern, or local/national or simply male/female: it is a question of differential access to resources through knowledge of how to manipulate both national laws and local institutions to further individual personal careers in the local context. The modern big men have been able to take advantage of the ambiguous situation which has emerged with the juxtaposition of national land ordinances with customary tenure arrangements. We cannot view the national context and the local context as discrete units nor as directly opposed. But the goals of national policy may ultimately be at odds with local needs and with local values stressing freely available land and a self-sufficient subsistence base. Nor are struggles over land for subsistence as opposed to cash crops simply a gender issue. It is important to understand stratification between households as well as gender, and necessary to understand both of these in relation to ability to control land use. Given that access to land is crucial to the rural standard of living—indeed to the ability of most households to grow enough food to get enough to eat—it is important to look very briefly at production patterns within the household economy, and at the ways in which these are reproduced by cultural symbols and gender categories.

THE HOUSEHOLD ECONOMY

If we are to understand the seriousness of women's marginalization in terms of access to land, we need to understand the domestic economy, which relies so heavily on women's labor and their contribution to household subsistence.

The household is the basic unit of production. Over 90 percent of food consumed is homegrown and 85 percent of all income is produced within the household economy—that is, through sale of agricultural products rather than wages or salary. Women's production is primarily subsistence oriented. They till, plant, weed, and harvest virtually all food crops—activities which, in combination, require year-round, almost daily attention.

Women's labor is thus allocated to food production and to reproducing household subsistence; men's labor is allocated to growing cash crops and to investment in capital-intensive and often status-oriented activities. Men and women most often work in different sectors of the economy and do not necessarily combine or allocate their time and resources to maximize the commodity output of the household as a unit.[30] Men and women have different networks and obligations within and between households. Demands on both male and female incomes have risen substantially over the last thirty years as the demands of the market economy have expanded exponentially the amount of cash needed to reproduce the household.

Of the total household income in cash value, men contribute on the average 58 percent and women 42 percent.[31] The major part of a woman's contribution comes from the market value of her subsistence crops, while a man's income is most often evenly divided between marketed crops and off-farm income. Women's expenditures are dominated by supplements to the household food supply in the form of condiments, palm oil, and salt. Women contribute over 90 percent of the food consumed as well as twenty-five percent of additional household expenditures. Characteristically women and men keep their incomes separate. Women spend their cash on household items and children's education, while men divide their expenditures between capital intensive items within the household such as roofing, furniture, school and medical fees and items largely outside the household, including gifts to relatives and friends and payments to men's fraternal organizations, where they wine and dine—mostly wine—their compatriots.

From one perspective we can see the household in Nso as the principal place where commodity and non-commodity relations come together. Women's production is oriented toward the production of subsistence (use value) while men's is oriented to creating capital—both material and symbolic. Women's income is invested almost entirely in maintaining the household subsistence level. Men's income is invested in expanding predominately individual material and symbolic capital. As primary food producers, women's labor underwrites and supports men's activities outside the household. Thus women produce, provision, reproduce, and underwrite the reproduction of social relations, not only within the household but within Nso society as a whole.[32] Clearly it is crucial that women maintain access to land if they are to continue to underwrite the reproduction of social relations in general and of the nutritional adequacy of rural households in particular.

CULTURAL SYMBOLS AND GENDER CATEGORIES

Farming—food—female have remained linked in Nso gender ideology. When a man is going to be married, he says he is "going to eat porridge." The interrelationships between female sexuality and food is reinforced by arrangements in polygynous households—the wife who cooks for her husband is the one who also sleeps with him. Farming is viewed as a female occupation, one in which men feel they have neither the competence nor the inclina-

tion to intervene.[33] Today, as in the past, women in Nso derive a good deal of
their status and sense of self from their position as primary food producers.
Indeed, a woman without a farm is suspect as lazy, a bad citizen, even immoral—clearly not capable of fulfilling the obligations of an adult Nso
woman. Women grow over 90 percent of the food consumed in the household and contribute over 25 percent of additional household expenditures.
They derive their income almost exclusively from the sale of produce, and
use it predominately to buy supplements to the household food supply.
Women's high income is positively correlated with high nutritional levels,
while men's income bears little relationship to the adequacy of household
nutrition.[34]

Women's role ad primary farmers has remained essentially the same since
Phyllis Kaberry wrote her classic study *Women of the Grassfields* (Kaberry
1952) over three decades ago, when she called them the "backbone of the
country." Nonetheless, women are excluded from full participation in public
life. "Women," I was told (by men), should go to the farm, the market, and to
church, and otherwise should remain close to the compound. Too much going around always brings trouble." While farming-female-food remain
linked in Nso gender ideology, so too does the axiom that "men own the
fields, women own the crops."

Women's work has remained essential to the social reproduction of Nso
society. Over the past thirty years, however, women's workload has increased substantially as have the cash demands on their incomes. Women are
cultivating twice as much land today in order to fulfill their responsibility to
reproduce the adequacy of the household diet, and are travelling longer distances to farm as arable land close to villages becomes scarce and expensive.
While thirty years ago women seldom sold their produce, today they sell an
average thirty percent of what they grow in order to keep up with new cash
demands. They often travel long distances to market carrying headloads av-
eraging over seventeen kilos.

In spite of the fact that women are working longer and harder, their access
to and control over such resources as land, labor, and capital have decreased
in relation to men's control over such resources. State policies regarding land
allocation and agricultural credit for development programs widen the gap
between male/female access to crucial assets, while local norms and ideology perpetuate static ideals of male-female roles and spheres of influence.
Women's work is perceived ideologically as demeaning to men and therefore is assigned a lesser value.[35] Women continue to cultivate food crops
while men grow cash crops—the most important of which is coffee—and
engage in a number of entrepreneurial activities. As food prices rise relative
to coffee prices (as they have over the past decade and a half) it becomes

crucial that the rural household retain its capacity to grow its own food. The weakening of women's access to and control over land, in particular, has negative—even foreboding—implications for future food production and nutritional levels.[36]

IDEOLOGY, GENDER, AND CLASS

Social conditions and the cultural categories which inform them do not change at the same rate. As Rabinow (1975) has argued, symbolic formulations, which are the vehicles of meaning, change much less rapidly than the material conditions. This seems to be the case with symbolic representations of male and female in relation to the changing material conditions of production and distribution in Nso today. Gender ideologies assert the fundamental differences between male and female qualities; these are realized in concrete terms in the differences in tools used, crops grown, plots cultivated, and the division of labor.[37] Nso gender ideology links farming-food-female as qualities defining women's gender identification, while at the same time asserting that "men own the fields, women own the crops." Social categories of women as producers, provisioners, and caretakers (of food and children) and men as "hunters and warriors and big men"—as protectors, status seekers, and authority figures—are reproduced in the division between male and female in production and in the reproduction of the domestic economy.

To understand the hierarchy of gender relations in Nso we need to inquire into the political and economic implications of gender discourse, and into the material preconditions which make such discourse possible and authoritative. As is the case with all power relations, gender relations are doubly determined by everyday life[38]—an everyday life in which women's work is assigned no real value; an everyday life where, although women produce most of the crops, they are denied ownership of the fields; an everyday life where women are assigned the longest, hardest, most tedious tasks—tasks whose definition as "women's work" involves a downgrading of status and value; an everyday life in which the definition of male and female qualities has remained static while material conditions have changed; and one in which the complementarity and equality once denoted by gender categories have been lost with the changing material conditions, which are increasingly determined by the political economy of the marketplace and commoditization. A woman's everyday life in Nso today is experienced as one in which male/female cultural categories and qualities guarantee inequality.

As central as gender is as a determining factor in the political economy of entitlements, it must be understood in the context of growing rural stratification. If we look at the spread of household income in our survey sample, we see an extreme range from a high of 7 million FCFA (US $35,000) to a low of 14,500 (US $72.50). Average annual household income was 447,270 FCFA (US $2236) with a standard deviation of 427,980 FCFA (US $2136), indicating a high level of income stratification. Farm size and nutrition levels, too, are unequally distributed. Since credit access often depends on farm size and cash crop production levels, small farmers—male and female alike—have little access to credit. Jua (1988) comments that it is telling that no small farmers have been given FONADER agricultural loans.

In the context of rather rapid commoditization of land and a deepening of market relations, access to capital for hired labor, for transport, and for farm expansion becomes critical. while all households in Nso have been able to retain access to enough land more or less adequately to fulfill subsistence needs, in the poorer households women trek further to farm. They leave land in fallow for shorter periods of time, decreasing its fertility and yield. They contribute a higher percentage of cash income to the household budget, and pay a higher percentage of "male" expenses, such as medical and school fees. The poorest households are those with no male adult in residence.

Wealthier households are those in which men have off-farm wage or salaried employment. These tend to be men who are "school leavers"—men who have finished at least seven years of primary school. Their wives tend to also have more education, and to have income from petty trading as well as from selling part of their crops. Often women in these households borrow money from their husbands to help establish themselves in trade. Importantly, these households have enough income to educate both male and female offspring.

To understand the dynamics of local agricultural production and rural self-sufficiency we need to concentrate on both the internal and external relations of production. We need to understand both farm women and "big men." Differential access to critical entitlements—land, labor, credit, and education—is central to this understanding. It can be argued that there is an on-going "feminization of poverty," even in rural areas like Nso. But gender itself is not a homogeneous, undifferentiated category. The importance of gender should not blind us to exploring other unequal dimensions of resource entitlement systems. These include education, access to wage and salaried jobs, access to capital, and perhaps most critically, knowledge of and access to the national bureaucracy.[39]

CONCLUSIONS

As Sen (1981) has pointed out, it is crucial that we understand entitlement systems in order to determine food distribution between various sectors of the community. Sen is talking primarily about households when he talks of entitlements. In Africa we must pay especially close attention to gender in determining access to entitlements, since men and women combine neither their income nor their labor to reproduce the household, but rather have separate networks and responsibilities which extend outwards in different directions. Husbands and wives keep separate budgets and each spouse is expected to meet personal, production, and specific family expenses from his or her own earnings.

I have argued here that gender is a—if not *the*—critical factor to an understanding of the political economy of entitlements in Nso: women grow the bulk of the food crops both for local consumption and for export out of the region to national urban centers. Women's labor and capital are almost exclusively invested in reproducing the household, thus freeing men to invest in capital intensive—both material and symbolic—enterprises. Yet although women in effect underwrite the social reproduction of Nso society, they are essentially excluded from ownership and real control of land both by the current structure of customary tenure and by national land and development policies. As a group, women also have less access to other crucial resources.

But gender in and of itself is not sufficient to our understanding; gender must be understood within the context of a rapidly growing rural stratification—a stratification indicated by differentials in income and farm size, in education and access to credit, in employment opportunities, and importantly, by unequal access to the national bureaucracy. What Vaughn (1987:131) notes regarding women's access to entitlements in Malawi is pertinent here: "the gender dimension does not always override that of class and employment, but the fact that it sometimes does is nevertheless of interest."

Finally, I have argued that gender in this context cannot be interpreted without a comprehension of Nso gender categories and qualities. Gender categories assign to "male" the qualities of hunters and warriors—protectors, status seekers, and authority figures, and to "female" the qualities of producers, reproducers, and provisioners of both food and children. These qualities are reflected in patterns of income, expenditure, and investment, as well as by tools used, crops produced, land farmed and the division of labor, and are doubly determined and reproduced by daily practices—what Bourdieu (1979) calls "the mundane workings of everyday life." Farming-food-female are linked as gender qualities, although women's role as farmers is limited by the fact that they are precluded from owning the fields. This ideology has been central to women's exclusion from control over critical resources, especially but not exclusively, from national land and development projects.

It is outside the scope of this chapter and the competence of its author to discuss the overall consequences of the Cameroonian government's policy in encouraging commercialization of agriculture in Nso. Excellent and some-

times ardent arguments have been made both for the large-scale commercialization of agriculture in Africa (Hart (1982), Hyden (1985), Cohen
(1988)) and against it (Watts (1983), van Appledoorn (1981), Raikes
(1988)). But it should be kept in mind that the overall production and availability of food are not finally as important as an individual's or a group's
entitlement to enough to eat. Famines can ravage areas where there is no deficit in food availabilities.[40]

Within the context of the commercialization of agriculture in Nso, women
have remained socially responsible for producing the household food supply
and reproducing adequate nutritional levels. Indeed, women's labor underwrites the adequacy of the national food supply in Cameroon. It is important
that if the connection between farming-food-female is to be reproduced in a
way that does not ultimately marginalize women's labor and put women (and
those who depend on them) at risk, the "farming" in the equation must include ownership of the fields as well as the crops. Otherwise, women in Nso,
like Nnu Ego, could find themselves destroyed by the contradictions in the
very roles which once gave them status and power.

NOTES

1. See Kaberry (1950 and 1952).
2. See Ariza-Nino, *et al.* (1982).
3. I am using "entitlements" here following Sen's (1981) terminology. Here he points out (p.
    154) that "A person's ability to command food—indeed to command any commodity he/
    she wishes to acquire or retain—depends on the entitlement relations that govern posses-
    sion and use in that society." It is a person's entitlement relations that in total govern
    whether he/she will have the ability to acquire enough food to avoid starvation during a
    famine.
4. See Jane Guyer (1987) and Polly Hill (1986), Chapter 12. Hill argues that it is entirely
    possible that women in rural West Africa are actually responsible for a larger proportion
    of the gross domestic product than men. She attributes this to several factors, including the
    large proportionate value added to raw food crops by elaborate processing most often
    done by women, the large contribution made by women to food farming, women's role in
    transporting food from farm to market, and the predominant role of women traders outside
    the Muslim north. Megan Vaughn (1987) points out that in the 1949 famine in Malawi it
    was the old, the young, and the pregnant who suffered most—were the most vulnerable to
    famine—and that women as a group experienced more hardship than did men, who were
    both more mobile and more apt to have access to wage employment.
5. See Guyer (1987) and Meilink (1988). According to a 1981 report of the Ministry of Eco-
    nomic Affairs, Cameroon, food production comes mainly from two sources: 1) the "tradi-
    tional" smallholder section and 2) agricultural projects in the modern sector. The former
    is by far the most important, accounting for 90% of total grain production (millet, sor-
    ghum, and maize), almost 100% of starchy leguminous plants, and 90% of fruits and
    vegetables (quoted in Meilink 1988:3). The "traditional" smallholder sector is over-
    whelmingly female.
6. See Scott and Mahaffey (1980). The Northwest Province of Cameroon grows approxi-
    mately one-third of the national food supply of corn, beans, and Irish potatoes. Kumbo,

the capital of Nso, is a major market in the Northwest Province, second only to Bamenda as an assembly point for foodstuffs shipped out to major urban centers.

7. See Franke and Chasin (1980) for a telling analysis of the relationship between dependence on food imports and famine in Africa.

8. Joseph Ngu (1988). Ngu argues that Cameroon's dependence on oil while it pays lip service to agricultural development accounts for a good deal of the current economic crisis. He claims that export instability is both undermining the legitimacy of the State and exacerbating the current crisis: "...in the first half of 1987 the Cameroon economy became a victim of not only the depreciation of the American dollar (the currency in which Cameroon chose to store its oil revenues) and the fall in the price of oil, but also a victim of a fall in the price of its agricultural export crops including coffee, cocoa, rubber, bananas and palm oil...[the economy] is experiencing major sectoral shocks and dislocations which are manifested in rapid urban growth and overcrowding, un-and underemployment, high food prices and potential shortages, and the increasing wave of criminal activities in its cities."

9. In much of the literature the "Cameroon Grassfields" refers to the highlands of the Northwest and Quest Provinces. It lies directly north of the tropical forest zone and ranges in altitude between 2000 and 6000 feet above sea level. The Bamenda Plateau lies within the southwestern part of the area and is defined by a series of escarpments which lead down into the lowland forest zone of the Upper Cross River Valley to the southwest and Mentchum Valley to the north. "Grassfields" as used in this chapter refers to the Bamenda Plateau of the former Bamenda Province of Southern Cameroon and does not include Bamoun or Foumban.

10. Goheen (1988). Speculation in agricultural land ("suburban land") has to date not greatly increased agricultural production in the area. In the summer of 1988 rural food prices were quite high and a lack of rainfall in parts of Nso—especially in the western side near Oku—had people worried about the sufficiency of the harvest for home consumption.

11. Goheen (1984 and 1988b).

12. During the summer of 1988 I conducted preliminary research for a longitudinal study of land tenure to be undertaken in 1990-91. At that time farmland, even in small outlying villages like Nseh, had become commoditized, with one-half hectare plots costing 140,000 FCFA ($460 US), while cash incomes were on the decline.

13. Women's income was established by the local market value of their crops as well as cash income earned. If women have easier market access (lower transport costs, proximity, etc.) they tend to sell a larger percentage of what they grow. With this money they buy mainly condiments (salt, ginger, tomato paste), soap, kerosene, etc. When men can market the few food items they grow (plantains, bananas, avocados) they buy for the household, if anything, "prestige foods" like tea, sugar, and sometimes white bread. Cash income is, therefore, not spend on nutrition; as market access increases, women (and men) will sell food they might otherwise have fed into the family diet without increasing the nutritional level of family food intake. There is probably an upper limit for women whereby they can keep enough for a sufficient diet and get enough cash from what they sell to meet their obligations, but we didn't see it for most of our sample.

14. See Ariza-Nino et al. (1982).

15. This was in 1981. In the summer of 1988 it was my impression that food prices in the urban areas of Cameroon had increased substantially, especially for staple crops such as corn and beans. In Nso, too, food prices have gone up, although not as rapidly as prices in urban areas. A good deal of the farmgate to market price differential is due to high transport costs. But prices in Kumbo market in Nso were higher, while the CFA had declined in value in relation to the US dollar (from $190 US in 1979 to $300 US in 1988). Rumors are that the oil revenues in Cameroon have been almost depleted and that the World Bank in the next year and a half will "restructure" the Cameroon economy. Chances are that the FCFA will be devalued within the year; therefore it is critical at this point for Cameroon to retain a high level of food self-sufficiency to avoid high food import costs (personal com-

munication). On the economic crisis see Ngu (1988). For elaboration of the nutrition survey, see Ariza-Nino *et al.* (1982).
16. Goheen (1988b).
17. With the exception of some early pioneering work, land tenure until recently has also been ignored as a theoretical issue in African studies. The growing concentration and commoditization of land in many African countries has focused attention on land issues. See Davison (1988) and Downs and Reyna (1988). I am told by a reliable source that the World Bank and USAID have recently become interested in land tenure issues.
18. See Goheen (1988b) and Jua (1988). Jua concludes here that "...it cannot be postulated that Cameroon's land legislation is designed to promote social justice for all its citizens."
19. In the Quest Province as well, land tenure issues have been a point of much controversy. See den Ouden (1981).
20. Scott and Mahaffey (1980); Goheen-Fjellman and Matt (1981).
21. A USAID-Yaoundé study and report (1981) predicted substantial deficits in food in the major urban centers if production does not increase substantially. Large deficits are predicted for corn (40–60 tons), beans (8–15 million tons), Irish potatoes (5–10 million tons). Deficits are also predicted in palm oil, banana, plantain, rice, groundnuts, vegetables, wheat, cassava, and sweet potatoes. Meilink (1988) records declining per capita food production beginning in the early 1980. The two major cities in Cameroon, Douala and Yaoundé, are experiencing annual growth rates of 6–7%. By 1986, population was estimated at 1.5 million for Douala and 450,000 for Yaoundé (*Le Cameroun en Chiffres, June* 1986, Direction de la Statistique et de la Comptabilité Nationale, Yaoundé, p. 8). Quoted in Ngu (1988)). The future of food self-sufficiency does not look bright.
22. Scott and Mahaffey (1980).
23. United Republic of Cameroon (1974); Goheen (1984).
24. Goheen (1988b and forthcoming).
25. For a discussion of these modern bigmen and Nso politics, see Goheen (forthcoming).
26. See Goheen (forthcoming).
27. When I was in Nso, I questioned the District Officer as to why women had not been granted land within the Young Farmer Resettlement Program since they are obviously the main farmers, the District Officer replied, "well, you see, this program is designed to keep young families in the countryside and of course no self-respecting man would want to move to his wife's farm." whether or not this is true is an empirical question, but ideologically it has served to keep women from owning land. Another example: I was giving an earlier version of this paper at an international conference on Cameroon. One of the Cameroonian participants, a well-educated man with an important government position, questioned me as to what I meant when I asserted that women were often discriminated against in national development programs. I pointed out women had great difficulty getting access to land and therefore were precluded from participation in the Young Farmer's Resettlement Program. He looked at me in astonishment and said, "Oh, well *land*—of course you cannot give a woman land—it would destroy our whole social system." Enough said.
28. See Jua (1988) and Goheen (1984). Jua writes in part "...the petty bourgeoisie-qua-State instituted the national Fund for Rural Development (FONADER) in 1973 to accord agricultural loans...FONADER was also supposed to help catalyze the transition from primitive to expanded accumulation...the avid petty bourgeoisie has not refrained from seeking to obtain loans from this institution. And loans are not a common good." This practice is not peculiar to Cameroon. Haugerud (1989) writes regarding land as an investment rather than for production, that more than one-half the people in her study sample had left over two-thirds of the land they claimed uncultivated.
29. This is an attenuated discussion. For a more detailed and complete discussion of the Nso domestic economy see Goheen (1988a and 1984).
30. This is, of course, a common pattern in sub-Saharan Africa. See Guyer (1988, 1984, 1980).

31. Raikes (1988) notes that women's incomes are often overestimated from monetization of subsistence activities by ignoring associated losses (of time when they could be engaged in wage-earning activities), so that women's earnings are inflated while their loss of time to earn cash income subsidizes men's income activities outside the household and the reproduction of the household. This is especially important in African households like those in Nso, where men and women keep their incomes and their responsibilities separate. Thus these numbers represent almost the totality of women's income being reinvested in the household, while men only invest a proportion of their income in household expenditures, keeping a large part for extra-household investments.

32. This is a common pattern in much of Africa, especially where women grow a bulk of the food while men are engaged in the capitalist sector. Cf. Meillassoux (1981).

33. Although when men are asked their occupation in an official survey they will most often say they are "farmers" (even if they have only a few coffee stems) they continually deny knowledge of food farming and say "it is only the women who know]about farming]—it is they who are being the farmers." Unofficially they claim they cannot work on the farm because they are not women—they are hunters and warriors. When I questioned one young man about why his mother worked long hours in the fields while his father did no farm work, he looked at me as if I had lost my senses and said, "of course my mother goes to the farm—that is her work. If my father went to the farm, who would tap his mimbo [palm wine]? Who would go to the palace? Who indeed!

34. See Goheen (1988a) and Ariza-Nino, E. et al. (1982). This relationship was found in a nutrition survey of eight Nso villages over a three month period during "hungry season" (May–July, the months when much of the food supply from the previous harvest was depleted and the new crops were not yet ready to be harvested).

35. Over a two year period while travelling frequently to outlying farms and villages in Nso I saw one man working in the fields farming food crops. He was pointed out to me as an anomaly—the subject of barely suppressed laughter and pointed fingers—as a "wonderful" sight ("wonderful" in pidgin English can mean "astounding"). A hoe is seen as a woman's tool and carries much symbolic significance as such. I was told by a friend who worked in another part of Cameroon that a man and woman there were accused of witchcraft by a jealous neighbor when the man helped his wife with the food crops—they were accused of "stealing" their neighbor's crops through the use of sorcery of men working food crops, using a hoe, and breaking a taboo. Around Bamenda, the provincial capital, men often work as wage laborers on food farms, but these are most often young men who are migrant workers—and working for a wage is different from working for household production, which is women's responsibility.

36. See Vaughn (1987:46) regarding land in the Malawi famine of 1949. She writes, "As land shortages grew this was of particular significance to women as a group, because it meant that the resources over which they had control were becoming less central to the reproduction of society." In "Africa's Worst Year of Famine," Derrick (1984) writes that "...the impact of all factors encouraging growing rural inequality depends on the land tenure system."

37. Berry (1989), in an article on investing in institutions, places gender ideology as a primary focus in elucidating historical processes embedded in changes in the wider economy and in the transformation of social relations.

38. Gender relations, like all power relations, are organized by the dominant power relations and played out in reproducing everyday life so as to appear self-evident or "natural"—as the only way of organizing the world or as, in Bourdieu's terms, both orthodoxy and orthopraxis (Bourdieu, 1979).

39. This is hardly a novel situation. Access to the State has been given by virtually all authors writing on related topics as the most important mechanism for personal wealth and advancement in African countries. See especially Hart (1982), Jua (1988), Kennedy (1988), Lubeck (1987) and Nafziger (1988).

40. Sen (1981:154) discusses this at length. In many famines complaints have been heard that while the famine was raging food was being exported out of the famine-stricken region. This was a major political issue in the 1840s, as large quantities of food were exported from Ireland to England while the Irish were dying of starvation—and the memory of this is of no small consequence in Irish-Anglo politics today. For a history of the Irish famine, see Cecil Woodham-Smith (1962).

REFERENCES

Ariza-Nino, E., M. Goheen-Fjellman, L. Matt, and R. Rice
    1982 Consumption Effects of Agricultural Policies: Cameroon and Senegal. CRED. University of Michigan, Ann Arbor.
Berry, Sara
    1989 Investing in Institutions. Africa, 59(5).
Bourdieu, P.
    1979 Outline of a Theory of Prejudice. Cambridge: Cambridge University Press.
Cohen, Ronald (ed.)
    1988 Satisfying America's Food Needs. Boulder, CO: Lynne Rienner Publishers.
Davison, Jean (ed.)
    1988 Women, Land, and Agriculture: The African Experience. Westview Press.
Den Ouden, W.
    1981 Changes in Land Tenure and Land Use in Bamileke Chiefdom. In Essays in Honour of R. A. J. van Lier, pp. 171-263. Wageningen: Department of Rural Sociology of the Tropics.
Derrick, Jonathan
    1984 West Africa's Worst Year of Famine. African Affairs, 83(332):281-300.
Downs, R. E. and S. P. Reyna (eds.)
    1988 Land and Society in Contemporary Africa. University of New England Press.
Emecheta, Buchi
    1979 The Joys of Motherhood. New York: George Brazziler.
Franke, R. and B. Chasin
    1980 Seeds of Famine. Totowa, NJ: Rowman and Allanheld.
Goheen, M.
    1984 Ideology and Political Symbols: The Commoditization of Land, Labor and Symbolic Capital in Nso, Cameroon. Ph.D. Dissertation, Harvard University.
    1988a Land and the Household Economy. In Davison, op cit.
    1988b Land Accumulation and Local Control: The Manipulations of Symbols and Power in Nso, Cameroon. In Downs and Reyna, op. cit., pp. 280-308.
    forthcoming Buying Legitimacy: Secret Societies, Titles and the Modern Big Men of Nso. In Guyer, Jane (ed.), African Transformations. University of Wisconsin Press.
Goheen-Fjellman, M. and L. Matt
    1981 Effects of Demand Aspect on Production and Nutrition. Yaoundé: USAID.

Guyer, Jane
  1980   Female Farming and the Evolution of Food Production Patterns among the Beti of South Central Cameroon. Africa, 50:341-356.
  1988   The Multiplication of Labor: Gender and Agricultural Change in Modern Africa. Current Anthropology, 29(Q2).
Guyer, Jane (ed.)
  1987   Feeding African Cities. International African Institute, Manchester University Press.
Guyer, Jane and Pauline Peters (eds.)
  1987   Conceptualizing the Household. Journal of Development and Change, Special Issue.
Hart, Keith
  1982   The Political Economy of West African Agriculture. Cambridge: Cambridge University Press.
Haugerud, Angelique
  1989   Land Tenure and Agrarian Change. Africa, 59(5).
Hill, Polly
  1986   Development Economics on Trial: The Anthropological Case for a Prosecution. Cambridge: Cambridge University Press.
Hyden, Goran
  1980   Beyond Ujamaa in Tanzania: Underdevelopment and an Uncaptured Peasantry. London: Heinemann and Los Angeles and Berkeley: University of California Press.
  1985   Urban Growth and Rural Development. In G. Carter and P. O'Meara (eds.), African Independence: The First 25 Years, pp. 188-217. Bloomington: Indiana University Press.
Jua, Nantang
  1988   The Petty Boyurgeoisie and the Politics of Social Justice in Cameroon. Paper presented at the Conference on the Political Economy of Cameroon. African Studies Center, Leiden.
Kaberry, Phyllis
  1950   Land Tenure among the Nsaw of the British Cameroons. Africa, 20:307-323.
  1952   Women of the Grassfields. London: H. M. Royal Stationery Office.
Kennedy, Paul
  1988   African Capitalism: The Struggle for Ascendency. Cambridge: Cambridge University Press.
Lubeck, P. M. (ed.)
  1987   The African Bourgeoisie. Boulder, CO: Lynne Rienner.
Meilink, H. A.
  1988   Food Price Policy and Food Production in Cameroon. Paper presented at the Conference on the Political Economy of Cameroon, African Studies Center, Leiden.
Meillassoux, Claude
  1981   Maidens, Meals, and Money. Cambridge: Cambridge University Press.
Nafziger, E. Wayne
  1988   Inequality in Africa: Political Elites, Proletariat, Peasants and the Poor. Cambridge: Cambridge University Press.

Ngu, Joseph N.
1988   The Political Economy of Oil in Cameroon. Paper presented at the Confer-
       ence on the Political Economy of Cameroon, African Studies Center,
       Leiden.
Rabinow, Paul
1975   Symbolic Domination. Chicago: University of Chicago Press.
Raikes, Paul
1988   Modernizing Hunger. Catholic Institute for International Relations and
       Heinemann, Portsmouth, NH.
Scott, W. and M. Mahaffey (Goheen)
1980   Agricultural Marketing in the Northwest Province. Cameroon, Executive
       Summary. Yaoundé, USAID.
Sen, Amartya
1981   Poverty and Famines: An Essay on Entitlement and Deprivation. Oxford:
       Clarendon Press.
United Republic of Cameroon
1974   Land Tenure and State Lands: Ordinances No. 74-1, 74-2, 74-3, of 6th July
       1974. Extract of OGURC. No. 1 Supplementary of 5th August 1974.
       Yaoundé.
1986   Le Cameroon en Chiffres. Direction de la Statisque et de la Comptabilité
       Nationale. Yaoundé.
USAID, Yaoundé
1981   Plan Alimentaire à Long Terme. Report by USAID (mimeo). Yaoundé:
       USAID.
Van Appledoorn, G.
1981   Perspectives on Drought and Famine in Nigeria. London: Allen and Un-
       win.
Vaughn, Megan
1987   The Story of an African Famine: Gender and Famine in 20th Century
       Malawi. Cambridge: Cambridge University Press.
Watts, Michael
1983   Silent Violence: Food, Famine and Peasantry in Northern Nigeria.
       Berkeley, CA: University of California Press.
Woodham-Smith, Cecil
1962   The Great Hunger: Ireland 1845–49. London: Hamish Hamilton (repub-
       lished by New English Library, 1975).

CHAPTER 11

Sex and Starvation: Famine in Three Chadian Societies

Ellen Patterson Brown

Chad, one of the poorest of the Sahelian countries, has over the years been doubly cursed: first, by drought in the 1970s and '80s and, secondly, by civil turbulence and external interventions which have waxed or waned from 1965 to the present. Drought and disorder have sown famine and disaster in practically all regions of the country at one time or another and the harvest of suffering has been rich indeed. Foreign countries and non-governmental organizations have made efforts to stem starvation through food distributions and disaster assistance, but it has been the ways in which men and women have coped with famine independently of external assistance which, in many cases, have determined whether they survived or succumbed (Brown, 1987). In three Chadian societies, all afflicted by recent food deficits, it appears that when men and women in their traditional social context have learned economically useful skills and have access to a variety of resources they are better able to cope with famine and to survive. The way in which these three traditional societies, Kanembou, Maba, and Sara, have reacted to famine bears witness to this.[1]

The patrilineal Kanembou in Kanem and the Lake, in the west of Chad, and the matrilineal Maba in Wadday, in the east, are two agropastoral societies which grow rainfed millet as their staple crop. The richer among them also herd cattle, sheep, goats, and some horses and camels. Both Kanem and Wadday have long and illustrious histories as feudal empires with powerful pagan, then Muslim, rulers and complex social systems. Although some men migrate to town for dry season employment before they marry and feudal sharecropping is said still to exist in some places, the vast majority are rural agropastoralists, not landless farm laborers, urban wage earners, or cash crop farmers dependent on export markets. The Sara,[2] egalitarian agriculturists, live in the Sudano-Guinean zone of southern Chad, where they cultivate rainfed millet and sorghum and, as a cash crop, cotton. The income from cotton is enough to pay for clothes, tea, bridewealth, and taxes, but not much else. They raise chickens, dwarf goats, and a few horses. Introduced in the 1960s and still rare, plow oxen are the only cattle the Sara keep. As all three societies still have essentially subsistence economies and are what Hay in his description of a typical food system calls "self-provisioning societies" (1982), when faced with famine most households have some direct control over material resources they can exploit to lessen its effects.

THE GENDER DIVISION OF LABOR AND RESOURCES: RIGHTS AND REALITY

The Kanembou and Maba make far more distinctions about the division of labor and rights to resources than do the Sara. The most pronounced distinctions are those by class/wealth and, secondly, by sex. On the whole, class membership among the Maba and Kanembou corresponds to the distribution of wealth in these two groups: at the top are the sultan and nobles, relatively well-to-do and wealthy agropastoralists in the middle, and rural farmers at the bottom. The Kanembou are divided into two castes[3] as well: the true Kanembou and the Duu (or Haddad). The Duu, who form a socially inferior endogamous group are, in principle, hunters and smiths. Though very few Duu still practice these crafts, they tend to be economically less well-off than other Kanembou, so that caste membership reflects class wealth. But in some regions of the Lake, Duu seek the same or similarly valued goods and goals (property, means of production, power, privilege, wealth, symbols of prestige) and are in most respects the social equals of other Kanembou, until their heritage is remembered. Generally, noble, wealthy, and well-to-do Maba and Kanembou control more productive resources than do the poor and lower class or caste. Among the Kanembou, for example, cattle and other livestock, polder and wadi fields, and date trees are concentrated in the hands of the nobles, who hold ultimate control of the land, and the rich, who have the money to purchase usufructory rights to these valuable productive resources.

Many studies of the political economy of famine have related vulnerability to poverty (Sen, 1981; Pariser in Carter, 1982; Mellor and Gavian, 1987; O'Keefe and Watts in Torry, 1979). According to O'Keefe, "the poorest classes generally suffer the most. Vulnerability to disaster is essentially a class concept." Watts considers that in famines "the poor suffer and the rich gain." Among the Maba and Kanembou it is clear that wealth and class have a major impact on how people cope with famine. In Wadday, the rich in Abéché were lightly touched by the famine except when someone collapsed or died on their doorstep. In these societies the two factors of wealth and class affect the kinds and numbers of assets people can dispose of, the skills and social contacts they can call upon, and their willingness to employ "unseemly" or "undignified" coping mechanisms in order to get food.

But another factor, definition of gender,[4] has a manifest and important effect on how Chadians deal with famine. Legal control of most resources, for example, is restricted to men in Kanembou and Maba societies, where women do not control nor have effective access to nearly as many economic resources as among the Sara. Sanday (1973) and Blumberg (1978) have linked lesser control of resources with fewer contributions to agricultural production and, indeed, Maba and Kanembou women do not engage as much in agricultural production as Sara women. Many Kanembou women claim to participate in agricultural activities only a little or not at all (67% of sampled wadi farmers' wives so reported, for example) and to spend most of their time solely on domestic tasks (44% of wadi farmers' wives), unlike Sara women. Well-to-do Kanembou and Maba women spend most of their time on domestic, not agricultural production, including treating the milk from their families' ample herds. An emphasis on domesticity was found by Burton and White (1984) to show that the importance of domesticated animals was a good predictor of female agricultural contributions; in societies where domesticated animals were important, women spent more time caring for the animals and relatively less on subsistence agriculture. An emphasis on domestic work, lesser contributions to subsistence agriculture from women, more sexual segregation and lower status are, according to Ember (1983), tied to intensive agriculture, all of which holds true for the Kanembou, who practice slightly intensified farming, manuring millet fields, and farming in wadis and naturally irrigated polders.

Highly polarized definitions of manhood and womanhood have also been linked to class-divided societies (Fernandez Kelly, 1988). Both Kanembou and Maba exhibit many differences between the two sexes' participation in productive activities such as farming, livestock herding, and household maintenance. These societies value sexual segregation, as well. This is a vivid contrast to the economically and socially homogeneous Sara, who practice extensive slash and burn agriculture and who keep only a few small animals. There, men and women, ideology aside, hold similar rights and resources and labor at similar tasks in the fields. Sara women do the housekeeping and socialize mainly among themselves, but they are neither enjoined from engaging in agricultural production of subsistence or cash crops nor from owning the same kinds of resources as men. They appear in public and conduct their own economic business just as men do.

Gender distinctions in all three societies are supported by their religions, which hold significant religious concepts about the differences between men and women: women are seen, and see themselves, as easily corrupted sexually and as dangerous to the social order and tranquility which men struggle constantly to maintain. While these religious ideas strongly permeate the symbols and everyday behavior of the Sara, they do not have as many legal and economic consequences as they do among the Kanembou and Maba. One behavioral concomitant of these beliefs for the latter is sequestration: men and women are separated for the good of all. Among the Sara, women eat apart but otherwise mix with men in social and economic activities except once a year, during the annual funeral celebrations (*badi*), when women and children confine themselves indoors every time men bring the rhombus, representing death, into the village. But, as Muslims, Kanembou and Maba believe in sequestering their womenfolk as much as possible.

Distinctions in male and female behavior bear heavy economic and social overtones for Kanembou and Maba. Among the Kanembou sequestration takes on strong economic and political as well as religious meaning. A man's standing rests on the degree to which he can keep his women cloistered. It demonstrates his economic capacity to dispense with their services in the fields and to pay others to fetch water and firewood. Even Kanembou wadi farmers, who are said to have been among the poorest Kanembou before the drought and therefore conceivably in need of their womenfolk's aid in farming, are embarrassed to admit that their wives do agricultural work. The author's observations support wadi farmers' claims that most of their wives do not participate much in wadi or polder farming[5] and only to a limited point in rainfed agriculture. Cloistering women takes on even more importance because only lower caste (Haddad/Duu) women are supposed to engage in trade. Having women who walk openly to and from the fields or market towns lowers a man's social standing.

Ethnographic materials on the Maba are limited, but there appears to be less emphasis on women's seclusion. This may be because patrilateral parallel cousin marriage is highly favored and intra-village marriages among kin are said to be frequent, hence there are fewer unrelated males from whom women need to be sheltered. Among the Kanembou, however, only 10% of marriages are village endogamous (Conte, 1983). Village endogamy can be helpful to Maba and Kanembou wives in times of famine, since they are more likely to have kin in the same village to look after them than women married into strange villages.

There is a large economic and legal gap between the sexes among the Kanembou. Women do not own or inherit land. A Kanembou father passes on in equal parts some of his dune fields and precious polder and wadi fields to his sons *inter vivos*, whereas women are entitled to and get access to land or the food grown on it only through men. Widows and the large number of divorced women over forty farm their husbands' or sons' land or depend on their own male relatives. The extent to which Kanembou women depend on males for subsistence is highlighted by the far-fetched relationship one divorcée in an economic survey had called on: she had sought the protection in another village of her classificatory son by a former co-wife.

A Kanembou man not only owns the land but he alone is entitled to what he and his wife produce. Nevertheless, both of them manage the household budget in common. As a marriage endures, many wives come to handle all but the most expensive household affairs. In recognition of his wife's aid a man is obligated to make her presents: gold or costume jewelry, according to his means; pots and pans; perfumes and pomades; and perhaps a goat or donkey, all of which belong to her. These gifts and what her kin give her are her only personal property.

The rules governing transmission of land among the matrilineal Maba remain to be elucidated; however, women farm with their husbands, husbands' kin, or own male relatives and depend on them for food or access to land when widowed or divorced. Husbands control the household income and should make their wives presents in recognition of their household services. Women in both societies can inherit movable goods such as livestock, but, when the deceased's property includes cattle, women get not the valuable chattels but the goats, sheep, and donkeys instead. Usually women own only a donkey or two and perhaps some goats that they themselves have purchased, inherited, or received as gifts from their husbands or kin.

Among the Sara, legal rights to material goods are similar for men and women. Men and women effectively own the same kinds of productive resources despite the fact that the distinction between the sexes is preserved in the transmission of movable property from a man to his brothers and sons and from a woman to her sisters and daughters. By the end of the year-long funeral proceedings, however, there remains precious little to pass on, and consequently such inheritances are of little consequence. Inherited land is also of little importance; both men and women can and usually do clear new fields in virgin bush or in long-fallow fields. Because women can have their own fields, raise their own food, sell their produce in the markets and keep the income, widows, divorcées, and women with absent husbands are not dependent on males for their subsistence.

Sara women's ideal behavior remains just that—an ideal. Under the ideal division of labor, according to the Sara, a wife should work for her husband in fields, kitchen, and bed. In exchange he will provide her and her children with food and clothing. A Sara woman is supposed to work alongside her husband in his fields. Unlike the Kanembou or Maba, a Sara man gains kudos for having a wife who helps him farm every day, not for letting her sit at home cooking and taking care of children. In principle the husband clears and works the ground, the woman sows, and both weed and harvest. He owns the food they product together and he controls and doles out the grain. But it is rare for any but a young married couple to live up to this ideal. As women grow older they wish to free themselves from their husbands and what they see as the burden of sex, cooking, and caring for small children. Wanting to take a rest (*ta ko sey*), they clear and plant their own fields, usually with subsistence crops which they can eat and sell for money for themselves and their dependents. Some set up separate households away from their husbands. In a 1973 survey, of 201 male household heads (both married and unmarried), 50% had resident wives who had their own fields; 11% had resident wives with whom they made absolutely no economic exchanges (this does not preclude exchanges of sexual and domestic services); and 23% of the men had no wives residing with them even though they were married (Brown, 1975).

A crucial event in distinguishing males from females in Sara culture is the male initiation, during which boys are irrevocably separated from their mothers and sisters. Boys, with their mix of childlike and ambiguous male/female behavior, are transformed into real men. (The girls' initiations remove the male aspects of a child's body and character, but these initiations are much less momentous.) After initiation Sara men would never do women's jobs such as cooking or fetching water. As a result, marriage consists of one negotiation after another seeking to balance the services each partner needs and the other is willing to provide. Many men find that their wives perform minimal or no services and that they must eat with their brothers or ask a variety of "sisters," "mothers," and "daughters" to cook and get water for them.

Both "brothers" and "sisters" turn, above all, to their siblings of either sex in times of trouble. In the sibling bond an individual finds the security and reassurance he seeks. Through a never-ending series of small gifts of grain, alcohol, cooked foods, and invitations to dinner, individuals bind their siblings and other kin in a web of transactions which must always be reciprocated. This flow of food and services provides men with a safety net when their wives cut out services to protest their husbands' parsimony. Women turn to their brothers and other relatives when their husbands go on strike and refuse grain, money, or clothing to protest lack of services from their wives

(Brown, 1981 and 1983). These networks are also of use in other times of trouble, such as famine.

In the abstract, the Sara's definition of gender imagines a division of household and farm labor between men and women that is almost as pronounced as it is among the Maba and Kanembou. Sara men hold themselves strictly to their male roles as defined, but not women. Most women adopt behavior which Sara culture defines as male—farming, providing money for household expenses, and acting as head of household (indeed a woman who acts this way for many years is called "*tel-dingam*," changed into a man). Such behavior is accepted as normal and to be expected from women. A married woman who does not adhere to the ideal is in no way punished for her deviations.[6] In reality most Sara women perform the same sorts of jobs as men plus their own jobs as well.

GENDER DIFFERENCES AND DIFFERENCES IN RISK AVOIDANCE AND FAMINE COPING

In all three societies cultural definitions of gender have limited and defined men's and women's entitlements to food and resources, their rights and obligations to others, the skills they can depend on to help them out in a famine, and the readiness with which they have used certain of their culture's famine coping mechanisms. Men and women who have considerable flexibility in using different skills and in finding different entitlements and resources to substitute for their usual sources of food have fared better than others. Their flexibility has been determined in part by their wealth, but the definition of gender has played a large part in addition to wealth or poverty in shaping individuals' economic and social reactions to famine. For when a society makes pronounced gender distinctions and grants men and women very different resources, it restricts the activities and resources open to each sex and limits the flexibility crucial to finding some way to get through a food deficit.[7]

The "coping mechanisms," "adaptations," "buffering systems," or "coping behaviors" that individuals in these three societies have employed to deal with famine are numerous and varied, but most steps people have taken to deal with drought and famine are "not independent behaviors which come into existence during times of crisis, rather are activities which are available continuously but assume greater importance during food deficits" (Campbell, 1986). Instead of developing new behaviors specifically for the critical circumstances of a food deficit, people depend on activities already known to them, the resources to which they are entitled, their rights in other people, behaviors previously learned, observed or heard about,[8] and on the options already available to them in their culture, most of which are gender-specific.

Entitlement to food or other resources is established by legal, economic, political and social characteristics (Sen, 1981). Since many social character-istics are determined in whole or in part by gender, the social definition of gender affects entitlement. Discovering what a person owns, what exchange possibilities are offered to him or her, what is given to him or her, and what is taken away (Sen, 1981), helps us to understand a man's or woman's entitle-ment to food and his or her ability or inability to command food during a famine. Kanembou women, for example, cannot take out loans from mer-chants with future crops as collateral, since even when women help grow the crop men are the proprietors and only they can pledge the harvest.

How a society views gender affects skills as well as entitlement. In addi-tion to legal, economic, and political rights to resources and over people,[9] ability, knowledge, and training enter into surviving famine. Famine victims select different ways to cope with hunger depending on their knowledge and past experiences. When the author asked a Kanembou woman why she had chosen to migrate to town when food got scarce instead of substituting fam-ine foods as her neighbor, just interviewed, had done, she replied haughtily that although she knew about famine foods, she had never been taught how to prepare them (because of her higher caste). Among the Sara, when family members out in the bush find themselves near the moist, low-lying spots where certain lilies (*ger*) sprout, conscientious parents take the opportunity to point them out to their children (and ignorant anthropologists) and remind them of how, since they grow in humid areas, they can be found in a drought long after other wild fruits and vegetables are gone. According to Sara, how-ever, lily roots require painstaking preparations to render them edible. Every year Sara women spend two or three days gathering lily roots and preparing a special pudding as the *pièce de résistance* of the family's celebration of the moon festival.[10] So all Sara learn the value of lily roots in a famine, but only women, as the cooks, learn how to prepare them. In 1984-5 lack of food forced many Sara to turn to wild foods, including lily roots. In the area for which the author has information, more deaths occurred from food poisoning than from starvation or other diseases induced by malnutrition. Unfortu-nately, many men and young children, driven by hunger and separated from their families by fighting, did not know how to prepare lily roots, and ate toxic famine foods just as they found them in the bush (Dr. David Seymour, personal communication).

Famine can come on slowly, as harvests fail, food stocks dwindle and live-stock die off, or suddenly, when armed forces carry off or destroy an area's food, or floods or other natural disasters wipe out the food supply. Two of the groups studied here, the Kanembou and Maba, were slowly squeezed by hunger. Two, the Maba and the Sara, were also plunged into famine by pillage and destruction. Lower than normal precipitation year after year in the early 1980s diminished Sahel pasture land and drew down food stocks in Wadday, Kanem, and the Lake. The Sara, in both the 1970s' and 1980s' droughts, were not badly touched by the lack of rainfall. But fighting between conflicting political factions and with Libya worsened the effect of the 1980s' drought on the Maba and also on the Sara (where some political factions had Libyan arms and support), since their crops and livestock were often destroyed or appropriated. These military actions limited people's options for coping with the food deficit. Where granaries had been plundered, people could not fall back on grain stored in previous years. Where armed marauders drove off animals, the owners could no longer sell them in the market to buy grain. Some towns where Maba or Sara migrated to find grain in the markets, and work or charity to buy it, were unfortunately threatened by fighting, and both townsfolk and displaced people alike fled. But by the height of the famine in 1984, the incumbent government of President Hissène Habré had gained the upper hand, and disorder affected relief efforts only in the south. The government and donors adopted a policy at the end of 1984 of staving off the formation of large camps of displaced persons. They created resettlement areas where they made Food For Work distributions and special wet feedings for the children most at risk. Displaced persons, including Maba and Kanembou, were given materials and training in irrigated agriculture so that they could earn Food For Work and money from the sale of what they grew in order to reestablish themselves. To avoid further dislocations the government and donors made general food distributions in the Sahelian provinces they could reach, but the amount of food distributed in this way was insufficient and late, so people also used other methods to cope with famine. In the south, because of the dangerous military situation, only a few areas were reached and food distributions were made only to groups particularly at-risk. Most areas of the south had to deal with famine without any outside assistance at all. This history shows how external events can pare away some of the options people could use to cope or can offer new choices for escaping starvation. Of course, gender concepts of both donors and recipients can affect even outside relief efforts. Are food distributions made only to male heads of households? Are women given equal access to training and materials, etc.?

As famine grew in the 1970s and again in the 1980s all three societies went through similar stages in their reaction to starvation. A number of authors have related coping behavior to degree of stress (Campbell, 1984; Mellor and Gavian, 1987). Some have sketched the chronological order in which coping mechanisms are used and have discussed stages of famine either in sociological terms (Brown, 1987, Cutler, 1986, Tobert, 1985) or as social and biological reactions (Dirks, 1980). A recent study of famine early warning systems (DEVRES, 1987) mentions Corbett (1987) as having, in unpublished material, developed an economic framework for coping behaviors. Her three stages are highly descriptive yet concise: "asset preserving," followed by "asset stripping," and finally "destitution," to which this author would add a fourth stage: reconstruction.[11] These early, middle, and late stages of famine correspond essentially to Dirks' (after Selye, 1956) three phases of "alarm," "resistance," and "exhaustion," terms more evocative of physical than social conditions.

   The order in which Maba, Kanembou, and Sara victims turned to various behaviors to cope with hunger supports Corbett's stages. In the early stages families tried to conserve resources and increase production to meet the food shortages, either by intensifying productive activities or by substituting similar activities for the usual ones which had failed.[12] When asset preservation was no longer sufficient to ward off hunger, people started divesting themselves of their belongings in order to purchase food. First they sold off discretionary, then essential property, stripping themselves of their assets, not to mention their clothes. When there was no relief from the famine some found themselves destitute except for their own labor power, which they could substitute to earn food. What individuals chose to do in this third stage probably relates in large measure to their physical condition. Did they still have the strength to seek food or had they so exhausted themselves that they had arrived at the state described by Dirks (1980), where humans remained passively social to the end, huddled together in listless groups?

   In Wadday in 1984 relief supplies could not reach the main city as long as the seasonal rains, which had finally ended the drought, had cut the road. One famine victim described how, in the final stage of destitution, too exhausted to work any longer for food, she made her way to the courtyard before the Sultan's palace and sat. The square was packed with people like her, waiting either for some charity from the Sultan or for death.[13] This was the last step of many to which she had resorted as hunger's grip had tightened over her family.

   This woman's experiences illustrate how poor Maba survived at first: by conserving, then striping assets, by intensifying productive activities, and substituting their own labor for agricultural output. 1982 was the last year this woman and her husband reaped any of the millet they had sown and resown each time it looked like rain. After that the family ate grain stored earlier. Her husband (her patrilateral parallel cousin from the same village) was not particularly wealthy; with only two cows and several goats he did not bother to move them to distant but greener pastures. Instead the family stayed together and the livestock died off. Into 1983 she and her husband were able to earn enough money to buy grain by taking donkey-loads of firewood into Abéché, the main city, to sell every few days. Her husband would accompany her and look for any day labor he could find—delivering loads of firewood, making bricks, and so forth. Firewood was selling for a very low price,[14] but they were able to earn enough for grain to make into gruel for their children, whom they left at home. At that point they had already begun eating the leaves of a tree, *Balanites aegyptica*, as a famine food. Her mother had shown her the tree and how to prepare its leaves while she was yet a child. In 1983 the donkey died and she and her husband were too weak to carry wood constantly into the city. In 1984 the whole family moved to Abéché. By now people in their village, some adults, some children, were beginning to die; in all, ten perished during the famine in a village of no more than 200. She herself lost a two and a half year old child to illness complicated by starvation. In Abéché father and mother got whatever jobs they could to earn money. She would pound millet; he would carry water. A 50 kilo sack of millet, usually 6,000fCFA, was selling then for 30,000fCFA. By selling off her jewelry and with both of them working, they were able to buy a kilo of millet from time to time. When jewelry, hoes, knives, pots, and clothes were gone, the parents could no longer buy food for their children. On days when she was fortunate she might get a job where she would be fed in exchange for her labor. She left her children in the streets in the hope that someone would take pity on them and give them food as alms. She and her husband each went their own way in search of work and food. Eventually she was too weak to do any work at all, so she turned to the Sultan as her final recourse. There before his palace she awaited her fate. Fortunately, a few food distributions from the World Food Program (WFP) allowed the family to come together again, but the distributions were erratic because of the difficulties in provisioning the city. So they returned to their village after the 1985 rain to eat famine foods, especially wild millet ('*krep*' or *Cenchrus prieuri*) which had sprung up. Although they discussed going to Sudan, where more relief and jobs were available, they decided to stay in place in their village, since the WFP was able to make small grain distributions from time to time which they supplemented with famine foods. At the beginning of 1986 both husband and wife had enrolled in a Food For Work irrigated agriculture training project which was being used to assist famine victims. Their involvement in this program and the WFP distributions were the only non-Maba coping mechanisms they used. She gardened in the project and stayed at home with her children and relatives. Her husband would walk with construction wood to sell in Abéché to earn money for the seed, hoes, etc. they would need to begin millet farming again.

This woman's story is typical of some options poorer Maba families with little livestock chose. Like some poor Maba, this family stayed together at the beginning. During the first stage of famine they conserved their assets and intensified their exploitation of the resources at their disposal. In the second stage they increased their use of bush products both for sale and for home consumption and sold off their assets. Men used their time to hunt for construction wood and gum arabic instead of farming. Women hunted more firewood and used more wild items in sauces and substituted famine foods for what they had once grown. Eventually, exploiting bush resources and selling off property were not enough and many were forced to move to towns to find grain in the markets and money to buy it with. Those who got some food could stay in the city and work; those who did not get food grew too weak to work. Of these, those who had enough strength returned to their own villages to live off famine foods if they could. Those without the energy to return were trapped in the city, waiting for charity, food relief, or death.

Other poor Maba families did not stay together. Poor men sought to substitute their labor as migrant workers for their usual agricultural activities. Women stayed behind and intensified their usual productive activities. Working as migrant labor is a normal activity for many poor Maba. To maintain their families, young men, especially, become migrant workers. Some go to Sudan and Saudi Arabia for long term jobs and send back money. Married men with families tend to go to towns in the dry season and return with the first rains to cultivate. Those who had gone as usual in 1980 did not come back in '81, since they heard there was no rain. In 1982-3 village men who did not usually look for jobs started to migrate as their resources shrank. Among these poorer males the amount of money at their disposal affected how they could deal with famine. The better-off were more fortunate. Those who could pay their way on a truck got to Sudan or N'Djamena, the capital of Chad, fast and got jobs. Those without money to pay transport went slowly on foot and had less chance of finding employment. Of those who got work, many could barely earn enough to feed themselves, much less to help out their relatives. By the beginning of 1986 many of their families had not heard from these migrants for over three years and had no idea if they were alive or dead. But not all men abandoned their families for the duration of the famine. One worker in Sudan found he could not earn enough to send home so he returned, thinking it was better that he earned 100f here and there to help out his family than to stay where he was and eat what he earned.

Wealthy men,[15] those with cattle, sheep and goats, camels, and horses, mostly sought to preserve their assets by finding alternate pastures, following their usual dry season pattern. In normal years these semi-sedentary cattle-keepers move their cattle to dry season pastures, leaving the women, children, the elderly, and the sick behind to farm with their own relatives or their kin by marriage when the first rains come. One typical group of Maba left at home as usual in 1981 consisted of seven women, two old men, numerous children, and five milk cows to provide for their needs. However, the men did not return with their cattle as they would have if rain had fallen as usual, crops had been planted, and grass had sprung up. They kept their animals in the lusher south. Some wealthy stockowners had the misfortune to have many or all of their animals taken by armed men; meanwhile at home in their villages marauding soldiers robbed many of what few animals they had and much of their stored grain.

The population that remained in rural Wadday was at risk: women, children, the old, and the sick. The composition of Maba villages in 1981-2, in the first stages of famine, appears to have been, basically, entire families with only a few animals, richer men's wives and kin left behind to take care of themselves with a few goats and milk cows, and poor young migrant men's wives left to depend on relatives for access to land, money, and help in farming and caring for animals. By 1982-3 even more men had left to look for jobs.

Wealthy and poor women left in their villages used different assets and had different abilities and training that they used for survival. The people left behind were able to survive at first on stocks of food which relatives shared with them, by eating more wild foods, and by selling an animal or two here and there as in normal years. By late 1983/early 1984, asset preservation was not enough. Women and poor families were selling property as well as intensifying productive activities to buy food. Late in '84 poor families had nothing left to sell and started moving, as we have seen, to towns. The old, sick, and women with young children were, however, unable to leave. One man, for example, had gone to the capital city in 1981 for a job; he stopped sending money in 1983 to his wife and nine children. She had no one to help her except an ill maternal uncle and no transport. They were stuck. After all their assets were gone she left her children behind "to beg and eat leaves," as she put it, and walked to Abéché to earn food for them. After two months she had barely fed herself much less earned extra food, so she went back home to help her children. Wealthier women and their families lasted in the villages until early 1985 by selling off whatever jewelry their husbands had given them in acknowledgment of their household services. Till then they had tried to sell the animals they owned in their milking herds; one woman was able to sell two out of eight cows, one for 2,000fCFA and one for 500fCFA, rather than at the normal price of 60,000fCFA. The other cows died. These women did not substitute their own labor to earn money as their poorer neighbors did. If these women still had donkeys they headed south with those of their family they could transport, because they had heard that food relief was being distributed there. A number of women who made this trip reported that once they arrived they did not receive relief aid because they were not inscribed on the provincial rolls at their destination. To survive, some earned money by carrying water, but most did nothing; many died. Once the rains returned, women who still had transport headed home. Those who had survived but had lost their donkeys found themselves far from home and unable to return.

All Maba, male or female, rich or poor, faced the same problem if they were destitute when the drought ended: how to get enough food for the next year? After the rains in 1985 had broken the drought, people began to return home. First, they had to obtain clothes and pots for their household and seeds and tools to farm; second, some were so weakened by famine that they could not farm as much land as before. Where a big family might have farmed 5-10 ha., now they could only do half that many, and the weakest less than one ha. To survive they still had to supplement their diet with famine foods. Many people noted that, unfortunately, the quantity of famine foods was diminishing because they had been over-used during the last few years: wild millet was gathered rather than left to reseed itself and trees had fewer leaves because they were so stressed by the drought and harvesting by hungry people. Some areas had relief-cum-development projects sponsored by voluntary organizations, which helped people regain their livelihood using non-traditional means. In other areas those few who had stayed behind and were able to plant supported their returning relatives. In one village fifteen families had returned; to get food they offered their help in harvesting to the two families who had stayed behind and sown crops—one basket of millet for each day's work. In January/February of 1986 in one village enough people had returned for 70-100 families more or less to reconstitute themselves. Many herdsmen had not yet returned; they were waiting in lusher pastures to hear that the '86 harvest and grasslands could support them.

Kanembou experiences with famine were similar to those of the Maba, but nature offered some Kanembou a way out. The drought in Kanem and the Lake has endured for many years. Some areas of Kanem had not harvested rainfed millet in the ten years preceding the 1985 rains; some tracts in the Lake have not born mature grain from the late '70s to 1988. But the Kanembou are geographically more favored than the Maba and nature presents them with more options than are available in Wadday. Lake Chad offers evergreen pasture and water, even when surrounding areas have grown brown and sere. On its borders farmers can grow crops in naturally moist or lightly irrigated fields. Dotted throughout the Lake and Kanem provinces are oases, known as wadis, which can be cultivated year-round with the simple irrigation technology of the shadoof. With these additional options many men did not find it necessary to leave home and family to cope with the famine. It is, however, men rather than women who normally own or rent and exploit these resources, usually without the aid of their wives.

Men who own or rent polders leave their families and go there for one to two weeks at a time from February to April to plant, weed, and harvest maize. Polder farmers are frequently better off than others since they are practically guaranteed a bumper polder crop in the dry season to supplement the usual rainfed millet harvest. In keeping with their husbands' prosperity it is rare for women to accompany them on these polder trips. They stay at home and tend house and children. Likewise, when men drive their cattle south in the dry season, few women go along. They stay behind with a small milk herd and a few goats. Women are the sedentary part of this semi-sedentary society.

Although wadi farmers can plant up to three crop rotations per year—grain in the cold season, vegetables and highly profitable onions for sale in the other two—they used to be among the poorer Kanembou. Wadi farming is hard work with no respite, and in many areas it is done by the lower caste. Men do most of the farming with the aid of their boys and girls age four and up. Wives, when they work in the wadi, usually harvest and sometimes work the shadoof. But many wives have experience in wadi farming because they helped as children; when widowed or divorced, such women may cultivate their late husband's or some male relative's wadi field with their children or grandchildren. Access to the field may be through males, but their skills are their own. Female cultivators, however, tend to be among the most impoverished wadi farmers. On the whole, though, wadi farmers are no longer among the poorest Kanembou. Not only was the drought a great leveler but these farmers own and exploit what is now one of the few productive resources in the region.16

Thanks to these geographical conditions, as the drought continued many Kanembou were able to get along simply by tightening their belts to conserve assets and intensifying polder or wadi production. In one village of 300 with a wadi to farm, not a single person left to earn money or find food elsewhere. Many of the polder and wadi farming families interviewed never reached the stage of stripping themselves of their assets.

Other poor Kanembou were not so lucky. Without a wadi parcel or polder plot wet enough to cultivate, people economically squeezed by the food deficit had to look elsewhere for some substitute for rainfed millet. As in normal years, poor men supplemented their household income with any number of dry season activities. Single men and young husbands would sometimes migrate to the nation's capital to earn money as street hawkers or to nearby towns as construction workers. Others would go as far as Nigeria, Cameroon, and Saudi Arabia. Men of any age could become regional traders in salt, onions, sugar, etc., either buying their own stock or acting as salesmen on commission. Working as salesmen on market days has also long been the way young boys and hard-strapped men earn a little extra cash.

In the first and second stages of the famine poor men also intensified their gathering and selling of bush products, such as dum palm cord and leaves and construction wood. They exercised considerable ingenuity in using products and skills which had not yet flooded the market. One old man sold the pods of a locust-like bean used for medicating camels, another the pounded seeds of some wild tree used to cure bloated animals. Poor women also stepped up their money-making activities. Like the men they relied more and more on bush products to earn a bit extra, using skills appropriate to their sex: mat-and basket-making, collecting firewood, gathering dum palm and jujube fruits, sometimes making them into flour to sell in the market. One husband picked dum leaves in the bush which he rolled into cord and which his wife and sister wove into mats or used for repairing worn ones, and so they earned enough to eat twice a week.

For some, intensifying production was not enough. By 1983 low-income Kanembou were divesting themselves of their assets—a cow or two, jewelry, then goats and household items. Men who did not usually migrate in the dry season nevertheless moved to town to find jobs. One man left his wife and six children (two of whom died during the famine) behind and worked making bricks. The pay was 500f/day, of which he had to spend 200f for food and lodging. Since his village was not far, he tried to take his family food every 3-6 days. At the price of millet in 1983 he was probably able to buy them six *coro* (local measure equal to 2.5 kg) of grain/month, versus the fifteen *coro/*month (1/2 *coro*/day) which Kanembou consider is the minimum of grain for a family of this size in normal times. Despite this enormous drop in food consumption to about 80 grams of cereal/day, which would provide about 250-300 calories/day, or about 1/5th of the WHO recommended daily requirement, his wife remained at home caring for the children and house. Her productive capacity was not used to help cope with the famine because of her position as a cloistered female.

Well-to-do cattlemen faced different problems in the first stage of famine, just as among the Maba. They had substantial assets to preserve. Those with small herds tried to sell them off or watched them die. Big owners confided their animals to relatives, or to Kanouri or Arab pastoralists, or took them to the Lake themselves. Though in normal years they would return from dry season pastures, now the grass never greened up near home and they were stuck in the south trying to conserve their capital assets. Their wives and families, who normally stay behind with a small milk herd, were left on their own for a much more protracted time, just as among the Maba. Women used to a prosperous and sheltered existence as dairy maids and conspicuous consumers reflecting their spouses' power and influence found themselves in changed circumstances. As long as the small herd left for their use produced milk, these families got along. But by the end of 1983 or the beginning of '84 they had to sell off for food their personal assets and the few small animals and donkeys they had inherited or been given by relatives. They had no right to dispose of their husbands' cows. In any case there was little to be gained from their sale; the price of cattle had plunged as local Kanembou, Arab, Kreda, and Daza pastoralists sold off their animals. Nigeria, the major cattle market for this region, sealed its border with Chad for the duration of the drought for political reasons and also devalued the Naira. Chadian cattle owners were left without an important outlet for their animals and with useless wads of paper Naira which no one would accept for food. The only people who profited in these circumstances were the smugglers, whose business prospered.

Wealthier women had to get by on their personal property, whereas poor and lower caste women had the power to generate income. Women whose husbands had migrated to earn money in the famine had probably been selling family farm and bush produce all along, even before the drought, since their households could not afford to do without their economic contributions in normal years. In addition, some of these women had savings of their own; women, who by thrifty management keep down household expenses, pocket the small difference between purchases and income from the sale of the family's weekly produce instead of handing it over to their husbands. They hoard it to invest in goats or more items to trade and so acquire some modicum of personal property which they are entitled to sell when they need cash. Well-off women, who only get personal property as gifts from their husbands or other relatives, do not have this avenue to savings and investment, since Kanembou consider it unsuitable for them to do more than make purchases in the market. Although their property may be more valuable than a peasant woman's, they lack the latter's earning power. They have no experience in repairing torn mats or gathering firewood or any other of the skills poor women employ to get money.

Women, whatever their economic status, were entitled to few of the resources their husbands cashed in to subsist on during the second phase of the famine. Except for the gifts a man gives his wife, all forms of savings, as well as fields and crops, belong to the male household head. Men were entitled to pledge future crops as collateral for credit from merchants, rent out polder fields, sell off cattle, camels, and horses and, in large towns, their real estate.

In contrast, women were more or less able, depending on their economic and social status and their freedom to move, to engage in market transactions and to earn money with their own labor power. Women whose husbands had left home could monetize none of their husbands' assets. By 1983-4 many of these women had divested themselves of their jewelry and other personal property and started moving to towns to stay with kin, to send their children to schools with free cafeterias, some to beg, and a very few to find work. Like once well-off Maba women they tended not to use their own labor or turn to money-earning bush resources as did poorer Maba and Kanembou women, less susceptible to their societies' gender and class distinctions. In comparison with men these women had a limited variety of resources for survival.

By mid-1984 life had become very difficult for numbers of these women and for many poor families, who were now impoverished and clustered in towns. Agricultural training relief projects in Kanem helped many people avoid the third stage of destitution and physical exhaustion. Several voluntary organizations that had agricultural development projects in the area converted them into Food For Work disaster assistance and training projects to help the destitute. In one case, in November 1984, an informant, who had seen his animals die off and his family's belongings slip away, moved to town to live with a relative and get a job. He found seven other male relatives already there. He received Food For Work, which he split, one half going to the relative with whom he was living and one half back home to his family of twenty. The amount of monthly Food For Work distributed was: two 50 kg. sacks of millet, 1 liter oil, and 1 kg. powdered milk. His family members thus received 166 grams of cereal/day or 550 calories, which is adequate if the ration is supposed to be supplementary. Another project centered on training in wadi irrigation and allowed women as well as men full access to plots, material, Food For Work, etc. Displaced female heads of household, some of whom were Kanembou and some of whom were nomadic Tubu refugees fleeing fighting in the north, proved to be among the hardest workers. Nevertheless they still faced restrictions because of their gender. Merchants who were eagerly buying up men's standing irrigated crops refused to issue women credit for equivalent production.

If Kanembou were saved from destitution by their geographical situation, the Sara were plunged into destitution by their political situation. The drought of the 1970s touched the Sara only slightly; peanuts did not mature for lack of rain and the late sorghum harvest was destroyed by fires in the tinder-dry bush. Sara short on grain coped by pruning the list of neighbors and friends invited to share a meal and by calling on their networks of gift-giving kin.[17] Further retrenchment, such as simplifying or cutting out ceremonies to cope with the food deficit (Torry, 1979), was not necessary. The male initiation, which demands large amounts of food, went ahead as planned. Ironically, in the following year of adequate rainfall, an initiation staged for the "Cultural Revolution" led to a cut-back in agricultural activity and to a food shortage more extensive than that caused by the drought. President Tombalbaye, seeking to maintain his grip on power, involved Chadians from diverse social and religious backgrounds in a pseudo-Sara initiation. Men spent their time in initiation camps, not the fields. Women's farming activities undoubtedly lessened the severity of the shortage that year for the Sara. With the end of Tombalbaye's regime and the return of near-normal rainfall in this region Sara quickly restored themselves to a more prosperous state. Even families which had gone through the first asset-conserving stage and had begun to divest themselves of their animals had not lost enough assets to hamper renewed farming. With equal economic and farming opportunities for both sexes, male and female-headed households recuperated equally. What natural reproduction did not replace men and women could purchase, thanks to their usual money-making activities: for men the sale of cotton, alcohol (made by wives or sisters for a share of the profits), grain, and grass fencing and for women the sale of grain, alcohol or beer, dried fish, and wild sauce ingredients. It should be noted that the major money-making activities hinge on a good rainfall; when precipitation is poor Sara have a much more limited business repertoire.

The 1980s famine in the south was provoked, in the main, by combat among numerous political factions, some with Libyan support. In the fighting, markets were disrupted, granaries and corrals plundered, fields burned, and people killed. Villagers were often caught in an impossible situation. One faction would make an example of a village which did not fully cooperate by killing some men and destroying property. An opposing faction would then pounce upon the remaining villagers to punish them for cooperating with the enemy. Citizens fled to live in the bush just as they had heard, in stories still vividly recounted, that their parents and grandparents had done to escape press gangs and slavers. Thus people who one day ate their fill sometimes found themselves the next day without food.

Gender distinctions limited only a few of the options Sara used to cope with this famine. Nor was their "buffering system" trammeled by the differences in wealth and status-making behavior that typified the other two societies. Both men and women were able to turn to their "brothers" or "sisters" with whom they had carefully fostered ties of food exchange in the past. For some the food, materials, and shelter they received were enough for them to recover with careful conservation. But as fighting persisted the number of people afflicted increased and fewer people in food exchange networks remained untouched. With their safety nets in shreds people had to find yet other ways to cope. Men and women were equally entitled to monetize any private property, such as livestock, hoes, and plows that they had been able to save from the fighting. Men and women had an equal right to engage in commercial activity, such as selling property or bush produce. So men and women entered the second stage of famine equally entitled to make the best of a bad situation. Unfortunately, selling one's own labor power was not much of an option for them. In this region there is little demand for men's labor, and since all women do the household chores of fetching water, pounding millet, and collecting firewood there was little demand for these services.

Some escaped the fighting by going south to the Central African Republic. But the main means of coping in the second stage of famine was using bush resources. The Sudano-Guinean bush is a rich source of many wild foods and other exploitable commodities. Anyone, man or woman, is entitled to use things growing in uncultivated bush or wild in another person's cultivated field. In the 1970s men and women caught fish as a major source of food, but by the 1980s persistent low water levels had enormously reduced the number of fish. Gender did limit some of the ways in which each sex exploited wild resources. Certain activities, such as cutting construction wood, weaving mats, and making cord, are viewed as men's work and gathering firewood and sauce ingredients as women's work. But, since fighting was destroying both food and housing in this period, there was a market for both men's and women's produce.

There was, however, one fatal gender difference. Recurrent battles in some area stripped almost everyone involved in kin networks of their assets. Unable to turn to relatives for food and with only a few goods salvaged from the fighting, with markets and economic and agricultural activities disrupted, some destitute people were quickly faced with starvation. Men, women and children went their separate ways seeking food, just as among the Maba. Ignorant of how to prepare famine foods, and without a woman to prepare them, in their hunger some men and children ate the toxic famine foods anyway and died.

CONCLUSION

When a culture like that of the Kanembou or Maba defines men as very different from women in their behavior and rights to resources it is saying that one sex cannot behave in certain ways or have access to certain items because they belong to and are appropriate only for the opposite sex. Their gender definitions affect both the ideal and actual control of resources, household labor contributions, and economic production and exchange. Entitlements to food are a prerequisite to getting food (without turning to theft, looting, or pillage), but in a famine such entitlement is worth only the amount of real food it provides. Therefore not just legal, economic, and political rights *in res* and *in personam*, but behavior, ability, knowledge, and training must be considered in understanding different reactions to famine. Pronounced differences in the definition of gender, like those among the Maba and Kanembou, deny one sex the flexibility of using the behaviors or resources which belong to the other sex. In a society like that of the Sara, where men and women behave in many similar ways and where most resources are accessible to both sexes, men and women have a wider range of coping mechanisms to choose from and perhaps a better chance for survival.

The most crucial factors in coping with a food deficit are the possession of some economically productive skills and the right to use and dispose of a large variety of resources on which an individual can depend for existence. Attitudinal factors are important, too: how has the society defined what is proper, correct, conceivable, or possible for an individual (e.g., for a sequestered woman to take a job such as hewing wood or hauling water)? A person's readiness to resort to certain actions and behave in certain ways depends on how strongly one's culture has defined these as appropriate for one group (sex, caste, class, age group, etc.) and not another (e.g., how quickly a sequestered woman will seek a job outside the home when her absent husband cannot provide for her family). The definition of gender also affects the skill with which an individual uses certain coping mechanisms; when masculine activities are fixed as very different from feminine, one sex will have very little knowledge, training, or practice in the skills the opposite sex uses to cope with famine (e.g., preparing hunger foods). In all these ways the definition of gender helps determine the outcome of a famine.

The skills and resources an individual at first employs to deal with famine are necessarily those which that individual already possesses. People start with what they know best and what they can do easily to cope with a food deficit. As famine continues and these options are canceled by a degenerating environment, depleted assets, physical decline, and changes in social context, individuals turn to other possibilities: ideas, examples, and practices already existing in their culture and available to those who know about them. People choose what their culture and their present environment offer and their intelligence, skills, physical state, and social condition (e.g., parent of small children, ownership of resources) allow. In the famine rural Maba women started out doing what they knew best, gathering firewood as they had always done for their families or for occasional sale, but now taking it to sell several times a week. When they grew too weak, they had to try things they had less practice doing, for example emigrating to Abéché in order to find enough people who would pay them to perform tasks they were skilled at, such as pounding millet.

It should not be surprising that most coping mechanisms are not new or original but already exist in the culture. If one looks at famine in biological as well as social terms, it would be unlikely that, with all the physiological changes concomitant with famine, such as the body becoming more conservative of energy (Dirks 1980), one would become particularly imaginative or creative as one reached the stage of exhaustion. At this point Maba simply sought to cope in whatever way they were still strong enough to do so. Some too weak to work still had the energy to return home and forage for famine foods again. Others could make it to the sultan's palace. These solutions for coping with hunger are also used at other times—one eats famine foods when one cannot get enough regular food at the beginning of the rainy season; the sultan by noblesse oblige takes care of his people. Large numbers of destitute people sitting together in front of the sultan of Wadday's palace (or before the Alifa Mao's palace in Kanem) is a cultural expression of what Turnbull (1972), Dirks (1980), and others describe from a physiological point of view: sitting for long hours in one another's company—to all appearances dead.

Gender must be considered as a factor which may enter into the political economy of famine. The way a society defines gender restricts people in some behavioral and legal fashion. These restrictions may make some people more likely to suffer from famine than others. Definition of gender determines entitlements in just the same way as economic or political status does. Gender is a factor which cannot be ignored in any attempt to understand social reactions to famine and to assess at-risk groups. Indeed, the ways in which gender left some people susceptible to famine in Kanem and Wadday raises questions about the exact link between poverty and famine. Where richer women are sequestered, do not learn, and are not allowed to practice economically useful skills, they are less able to manage economically, once their resources are gone, than are poorer women. The data on Maba and Kanembou women also shed light on the men in these societies and other semi-sedentary groups in Chad. In Kanem and elsewhere wealthy owners of large herds sent their animals away to find large patches of grazing and wells not too deep to render watering animals too taxing. Thus their herds escaped decimation. But relatively well-to-do cattle owners with smaller herds were not forced to act as quickly and their animals were sometimes caught in areas of reduced food and water. As a result, they lost most of their investment when their livestock died or when the price of cattle plummeted as herders tried to cash in on their dying cows and get money to buy food. Farmers with polder fields left high and dry by the recession of Lake Chad lost not only their rainfed millet crops during the drought but considerable irrigation in-

Table 1   Stages of 1981–85 Famine and Its Effects in Chad

Stage	Characteristics	Remedies
Asset Preserving		
1	Food will not last till next harvest; married men leave for urban jobs to get food; women sell goods, services, jewelry, household effects	In situ Food For Work
	Pastoralists take herds farther afield; milk production stops	Wells and boreholes for pastoralists
Asset Stripping		
2	Malnourishment begins, especially among poor and pastoralists; people sell goods, services, last of possessions	In situ feeding Food For Work
	Pastoralists move family and dwindling herds south or abroad	Resettle pastoralists in better areas
3	Rich remain in villages; urban areas flooded by severely malnourished, displaced persons, beggars; camps spring up	Resettlement schemes Food For Work Targeted feeding for worse off
Destitution		
4	Advanced aggravated malnourishment; camps with more disadvantaged and vulnerable groups; those who can leave towns for famine foods in rural areas	Resettlement Food For Work Feeding centers General distribution Seeds, tools, etc.
Reconstruction		
5	Rains return; wealthy have means to cultivate and reestablish herds; many stuck in camps and urban areas; poor are destitute; unable to begin again without help	Targeted feeding and Food For Work Seeds, tools, etc. Resettlement or transport home

Although these stages appear to be linked with the years of the famine, in fact they are tied to amount of rainfall, the ecology of each area, the social constitution and condition of the populations, etc.

316 E. P. BROWN

come. They were left with dry plots of earth for which they had laid out large sums of money to purchase or rent. These losses may or may not have forced the better-off to the brink of poverty and starvation, but, if the example of Kanembou and Maba women is instructive, one cannot assume that the well-to-do are protected better or longer than the poor from the irreversible losses of assets necessary for existence or that they do not suffer destitution at the same time or to the same extent as some of the poor. Victims' verbal accounts of their reactions to famine suggest strongly that some wealthy women had it easy in the early stage of famine but encountered trouble more quickly than the poor. The author lacks enough data to come up with some sort of "misery index" showing, for example, that wealthy women suffered as much or more than poor women. To conclude which groups were most at-risk one needs numerical data indicating: the stages of famine at which different kinds of households and economic levels began to suffer; how quickly they passed from one stage to another; how many households of each kind experienced the misery of asset stripping, destitution, and, perhaps, death. But the lessons to learn from these three Chadian societies are that: 1) one needs to consider all the factors governing access to resources and acquisition of skills; 2) poverty is not in itself an infallible indicator of at-risk groups; and 3) one needs to look at reactions to famine in the framework of stages of famine in order to determine which groups are most at-risk and when.

ACKNOWLEDGMENTS

The research on which this paper is based was conducted from 1969–1973 with the aid of the Wyse Studentship in Anthropology, Trinity College, Cambridge. Research in 1986 was funded by the Bureau for Peace and Voluntary Assistance of the Agency for International Development, from 1986 to 1988 by the Agency for International Development in conjunction with the Organization for Rehabilitation and Training, and in 1988 by the FAO and World Bank. I did not observe early reactions to famine in the Wadday, Kanem and Lake firsthand. I observed in person the Sara reaction to the food deficit in the 1970s; my information on the 1980s famine there is derived from numerous conversations with Sara, medical personnel, and written reports.

NOTES

1. Chad has probably been on the margin of economic stress for hundreds of years because of its geography and history. The region that today is Chad has not known peace as far back as we can discover. Recorded and oral history recount the attacks of one feudal state

on another and the devastation of capital and countryside as well as raids on the pagan peoples, such as the Sara, on their borders. On dry season slaving expeditions these states pillaged their victims' grain and animals for food. Those who were not taken slave were often left destitute. All three societies had ways of coping with these human and climatological disruptions, some no longer applicable in today's circumstances (e.g., the Sara practice of pawning children) and others which are still in use (e.g., Sara scattered and hid in thorn thickets and treetops to escape both slavers in the past and political partisans in the 1980s and lived off wild bush foods because they could not return to their villages without being caught).

In the last famine in Chad, production of sorghum and millet, the staple foods, dropped by 77%, from 277,000 metric tons to 64,000 MT in the Sahelian zone in the years from 1976 to 1984; livestock, whose milk is another staple, dropped by 10% from 1984 to 1985 alone (USAID/Chad 1985, FAO 1985).

2. "Sara" is the name used by outsiders and in anthropological literature to refer to a group of tribes in southeastern and south central Chad, all of whom speak mutually intelligible dialects. The tribes are distinct geographic, political, and endogamous entities. Each tribe calls itself and other tribes by their own proper names, but in conversation with outsiders they use the commonly accepted designations of "Sara," "Sara Madjingaye" (the best Sara), "Sara Noh" (the Sara over there) and "Sara Noo" (far away Sara). The Sara Madjingaye of southeastern Chad refer to themselves as "Sar" (plural "Sarge"). To their west the Sara Noh form a separate political and geographic entity from the Madjingaye, but refer to themselves as "Sar." The Sara Noo of south central Chad divide themselves into "Nar," "Pen," and "Gor." The Nar and Pen participate in male initiation with the Sar (Sara Madjingaye and Sara Noh); the potent value of the male initiation creates a cultural unity, especially between the "Sara Madjingaye" and "Sara Noh." The Nar, Pen, and Gor consider themselves, despite the communal initiation, as distinct from each other and the Sar. The author deals in this paper only with what she refers to in other publications as the "Sara Nar" and the "Sara Noh" or "Sara Koumra," since these two groups were the main Sara victims of the 1980s famine. For ease of exposition she refers to them here as "Sara."

3. The author uses caste in the sense given by the Encyclopedia of Anthropology (Hunter and Whitten, 1976): "hereditary, endogamous group of people or a collection of such groups, bearing a common name and having the same traditional occupation."

4. A society's definitions of "man" and "woman," "male" and "female" set up differences and similarities in their basic human natures, define what behaviors are appropriate to each sex, and establish the rights men and women have in other people and in things. Kanembou, Maba, and Sara all conceive of men and women as antithetical, as opposed to one another in their moral qualities, their interests, and their abilities. But among the Kanembou and Maba there is a far greater gap between the kinds of behavior acceptable from men and from women than among the Sara. Likewise, the rights Sara men and women have to resources and in people are rather similar, whereas they are quite different among the Kanembou and Maba.

5. Polders are fingers of water along the edges of Lake Chad which are either naturally or artificially closed off at their narrowest point. As the water in the polder is evaporated and reduced over the years, more and more rich, moist, and fertile land becomes available for farming during the dry season. Wadis are oases, depressions in the dune-like terrain, where the water table is close to the surface. They, too, are rich and cultivable in the dry season, either because the soil is naturally moist or because simple irrigation equipment (the shadoof) can provide enough water.

6. A married woman may be brought before a court of law ("saria") by her husband when she ceases to provide one or another of an ideal wife's services. The court case is meant to identify what has provoked her into changing her behavior. Has she decided to divorce her husband by moving in with another man or returning to her father? If so, the father or new husband must pay the ex-husband the entire sum of the woman's original bridewealth. If it is to protest some lapse on her husband's part, the couple may decide either to rectify the

misunderstanding or to continue the marriage at this lower level of services. A woman may also call her husband up before the law in order to find out why he has ceased to provide some service. If he wishes to divorce her he forfeits her bridewealth; if he is protesting some lapse on her part they may agree either to remedy the situation or to continue as is, with reduced services. The extent to which a maiden approximates the feminine ideal in character, comportment and looks, does, however, determine in part the size of the bridewealth asked for her.

7. Torry (1979) has noted that flexibility is important in resisting famine, though he discusses this in reference to hunter-gatherers. Flexible resource management and elasticity of movement allow them to make opportunistic utilization of productive tracts of land. Similar adaptations are important for these three agricultural or agropastoral societies as well.

8. Dirks (1980) refers to preservation of the idea of famine and famine coping mechanisms in semantic categories, folklore, history, and myth. In the case of the Sara, women preserve the knowledge and get repeated practice in preparing the main famine food in an annual ritual.

9. Rights *in personam* as well as *in res* should be considered; Sara said it was common practice, before the French presence became too widespread, to pawn one's most obstreperous child in a distant village in exchange for food.

10. Another important famine food for the Sara is *duy*, a category including both *strychnos spinosa* and *strychnos densiflora*. Sweet and enjoyable in small quantities, these fruits induce vomiting and illness if eaten in large quantities.

11. The characteristics of a fourth stage of reconstruction need to be explored. If everyone does not perish, what happens to them? How does reconstruction come about? Does the society go on as before the disaster. It is clear that among the Kanembou there has been a change in the distribution of wealth. How permanent is the change? Has there also been a change in the way gender is constructed? What explanations can be found for any changes which occur? Reconstruction is also related to other problems of social change. If most coping mechanisms are not new to the culture, although some are new to individuals, and if social turmoil and revolution are less likely as people grow weaker (Dirks 1980), does change occur—and how—during the drastic experiences of a disaster? Are cultures "homeostatic" and in equilibrium, or does change occur in a "developmental" fashion (Torry 1979). (For example, the irrigation technology projects which became Food For Work/resettlement programs among the Maba and Kanembou were accepted by many more people than is likely had there been no famine.) Are the ways in which a society's options are limited by gender, class, etc., determinants of the direction in which social change will occur?

12. Coping mechanisms seem to have in common an element of either intensification or substitution. In the drought of 1982–4 and again in 1987, when rain fell only twice in some areas of the Lake and Kanem, many Kanembou farmers, as time for planting came and passed, sowed their fields not just once or twice, but three times, and carefully covered the grains with moist dirt, intensifying or repeating their usual agricultural activities. Kanembou also increased young men's temporary or long-term migration for wage labor, increased ritual prayers for rain, etc. This intensification is analogous to what Dirks, analyzing both the biological and social conditions of famine, calls "recursive" or recurrent changes in the first, "alarm" phase and the second, "resistance" phase of a three-phase general adaptation syndrome. In these phases reactions involve general hyperactivation, intensified interaction, and abnormal excitement (Dirks, 1980). Campbell depicts intensification, too, when he writes of activities which have existed all along but which assume greater importance during a food deficit (1986).

13. In Kanem the same thing happened. Over 200 people a day were fed in the sultan's palace.

14. Pastoralists are not the only ones to suffer low prices in a flooded market during the famine.

15. By "wealthy" the author does not refer to the super rich in any of these three societies, e.g.,

those with government jobs or large businesses. She is concerned with those people who are a bit better off, i.e., those who have not just 1 or 2 cows but a sizeable herd, those who can afford to buy a piece of real gold once in a while, not just costume jewelry.

16. The waters of Lake Chad receded in the 1970s and '80s, with continued low rainfall. The major port of Bol was 17 km. from the water's edge in 1988. Many polder owners found themselves left high and dry and the land they owned was no longer humid enough to be used for dry season agriculture. Such polder owners had to rent fields along the lake shore just as did the common man.

17. Except for invitations to close relatives and next-door neighbors, men issue invitations to eat as a political maneuver to gain status and influence. Cutting back on such invitations does not conflict with Dirk's (1980), Schacter's (1959), and others' findings of gregariousness and altruistic sharing in the first stage of famine. At this stage Sara men put their political ambitions on the back burner and instead share their food with the kin and neighbors to whom they are linked in food exchanges.

Friedl (1978) notes that where men control significant goods exchanged outside the family it is the men, even when women produce the goods, who receive recognition, since it is the act of giving that creates obligations and alliances. Thus, although a Kanembou woman's most time-consuming activity is preparing food, she has no control over the food; it is her husband who invites people to partake and he who garners the guests' respect, even more respect if he has a wife who is a good cook. Among the Sara a man tries to achieve two goals by giving food that he and his wife have jointly produced and prepared: 1) political influence through generous dinner invitations; 2) widespread networks of kin in food exchanges. But Sara women also produce food by themselves, control it themselves, and use it to create important obligations to exchange food and provide support within their own network of kin.

REFERENCES

Blumberg, R. L.
  1978 Stratification: Socioeconomic and Sexual Inequality. Dubuque: Wm. C. Brown.
Bose, C., R. Felberg, and N. Sokoloff, eds.
  1987 Hidden Aspects of Woman's Work. New York: Praeger.
Brown, E. C. P.
  1975 Family and Village Structure of the Sara Nar. Ph.D. dissertation, University of Cambridge.
  1981 The Ultimate Withdrawal: Suicide among the Sara Nar. European Journal of Sociology XXII: 199-228.
  1983 Nourrir les Gens, Nourrir les Haines. Etudes et Documents Tchadiens, 8. Paris: Société d'Ethnographie.
  1987 The Social Impact of Famine in Chad, 1981-86. An Evaluation of the African Emergency Food Assistance Program 1984-85, Chad. Washington: AID Evaluation Special Study #48.
Burton, M. L. and D. White
  1984 Sexual Division of Labor in Agriculture. American Anthropologist 86(3):568-583.
Campbell, D. J.
  1984 Responses to Drought among Farmers and Herders in Southern Kajiado District Kenya. Human Ecology 12(1):35-64.

1986   Coping Strategies as Indicators of Food Shortage in African Villages. Paper: American Anthropological Association Meeting 1986.

Carter, J. P., ed.
1982   Famine in Africa. Oxford: Pergamon Press.

Conte, E.
1983   Marriage Patterns, Political Change and the Perpetuation of Inequality in South Kanem (Chad). Paris: ORSTOM.

Corbett, J.
1987   Household Food Security when Famine Threatens: How do Households Cope?, draft. Food Studies Group, Oxford. Since published as Famine and Household Coping Strategies, World Development 16, No. 9 (1988): 1099-1112.

Cutler, P.
1986   The Responses to Drought of Beja Famine Refugees in Sudan. Disasters 10(3):181-188.

DEVRES
1987   Report on the Role of Coping Mechanisms as Socioeconomic Indicators in Famine Early Warning Systems: A Literature Review and a Framework for Identification, Interpretation and Use. USAID PDC-1096-I-00-4162-00. Washington: DEVRES.

Dirks, R.
1980   Social Responses during Severe Food Shortages and Famine. Current Anthropology 21(1):21-44.

Ember, C.
1983   The Relative Decline in Women's Contributions to Agriculture with Intensification. American Anthropologist 85(2):285-304.

FAO
1985   Evaluation de la Situation de l'Agriculture et de l'Elevage au Tchad. OSRO 03/85/F. Rome: FAO.

Fernandez Kelly, M. P.
1988   Women in the Economy, review of Bose, Feldberg and Sokoloff, Hidden Aspects of Woman's Work. Science 240(27 May):1208-9.

Friedl, E.
1978   Society and Sex Roles. Human Nature 1(4):68-75.

Hay, R.
1982   Description of a Typical Food System. In J. P. Carter, ed., Famine in Africa, p. 5-6.

Hunter, D. E. and P. Whitten
1976   Encyclopedia of Anthropology. New York: Harper and Row.

Mellor, J. W. and S. Gavian
1987   Famine: Causes, Prevention and Relief. Science 235(30 Jan):539-545.

O'Keefe, P.
1979   Comment on W. I. Torry. Current Anthropology 20(3):517-540.

Pariser, R.
1982   Food Losses During Storage. In J. P. Carter, ed., Famine in Africa, p. 25.

Sanday, P. R.
1973   Towards a Theory of the Status of Women. American Anthropologist 75(5):1682-1700.

Schacter, S.
  1959 The Psychology of Affiliation: Experimental Studies in the Sources of
        Gregariousness. Stanford: Stanford University Press.
Selye, H.
  1956 The Stress of Life. New York: McGraw-Hill.
Sen, A.
  1981 Poverty and Famines, An Essay on Entitlement and Deprivation. Oxford:
        Clarendon Press.
Tobert, N.
  1985 The Effect of Drought among the Zaghawa in Northern Darfur. Disasters
        9(3):213-223.
Torry, W. I.
  1979 Anthropological Studies in Hazardous Environments: Past Trends and
        New Horizons. Current Anthropology 20(3):517-540.
Turnbull, C.
  1972 The Mountain People. New York: Simon and Schuster.
USAID
  1986 The U.S. Response to the African Famine, 1984-86: an Evaluation of the
        Emergency Food Assistance Program: Synthesis Report. Vol. 1, A.I.D.
        Program Evaluation Report no. 16, Washington: USAID.
USAID/Chad
  1985 Basic Agricultural Information for Chad. NDjamena: USAID/Chad.
Watts, M.
  1979 Comment on W. I. Torry. Current Anthropology 20(3):517-540.

PART D

Prospects for the Future

CHAPTER 12

New Crop Varieties in a Green Revolution for Africa[1]: Implication for Sustainability and Equity

David A. Cleveland

THE PROGRAM AND THE ASSUMPTIONS

The green revolution began after World War II in Mexico and the Philippines as the large-scale application of industrial agriculture from the First World to the Third World. At its center are new crop varieties created by plant breeders which produce much higher yields in the optimal and stable environments created by irrigation, chemical fertilizers, and pesticides, and often mechanization. The green revolution has been widely adopted in Asia and parts of Latin America, and has led to some dramatic increases in production. It has not fared so well in Africa.

Many observers see the growing agricultural crisis in Africa as largely a consequence of the failure of the green revolution to take hold there. As a result there are increasing calls to adapt the green revolution to Africa's unique environmental and socioeconomic conditions. This means strategies that will work on poorer soils with less water management (Christensen et al., 1981:105-107; Lal, 1987; Mellor et al., 1987:361) and that place the small-scale farmer at the center, with scarce resources prioritized to achieve maximum production results (Mellor et al., 1987:356-357, 359).

Adapting the green revolution in Africa is part of a broader response of the international development establishment to experiences with the green revolution in Asia and other areas of the world. Proponents have realized that in the future the green revolution will not produce the quantum leaps in production that characterized its early years. Expansion to less optimal environments, increasing cost of inputs, increasing resistance of pests, social disruption, increasing economic inequity, and resistance of consumers to new varieties have led to plant breeding programs placing more emphasis on traits such as taste, cooking, and storage qualities. Emphasis has also increased on drought tolerance and disease resistance that adapt crops to less optimal conditions of poorer farmers on more marginal land, and which demand less expenditure on inputs.

Changes in the green revolution and in its adaptation to Africa are also part of profound developments in industrial agriculture in the First World (Cleveland, 1991). These changes are the result of two major factors: first, the decreasing profits and increasing consumer and environmental pressures that are leading to calls for a more "sustainable" agriculture; and second, the growth of the new agricultural biotechnologies like genetic engineering that promise the creation of dramatically new crop varieties.

In summary, the new green revolution in Africa has the stated goal of increasing production, while at the same time promoting both environmentally sustainable agriculture to assure that future generations will not pay the cost of present production, and social equity so that the poor will not pay the cost of national and global growth.

However, to understand what this new green revolution means, it is necessary to move beyond the platitudes and wishful thinking which fill the international agricultural development project proposals and newsletters, and to examine the assumptions about agricultural development on which it is based. Two of the most important assumptions are the unilineal evolution of world culture and agriculture following an idealized Western model, and the necessity of unlimited economic growth, along with the availability of the resources to support it, on which that evolution is based (for examples see Harrison, 1987:113,333; Lal, 1987; Todaro, 1985:304–310).

These assumptions are ethnocentric and constrain intellectual inquiry, resulting in analysis of and solutions for Africa's food and agricultural crisis which are inappropriate, and likely to fail. For example, the cause of the crisis is seen to be within the continent, and the solution is massive investments "To *give* Africa the tools to meet her food needs," including biotechnology to accelerate the development of drought tolerant and disease resistant varieties (Brady, 1985, emphasis added). "Biological science research" and the "dynamic institutions of modernization" will comprise the green revolution for Africa, leading to "major increases" in productivity (Mellor et al., 1987: 363). This means increasing integration with the world economic and agricultural system, with the ultimate aim of transforming small-scale, "inefficient" African agriculture into a replica of large-scale, capital intensive industrial agriculture. The ultimate goal is the total replacement of indigenous agriculture, since it is "incapable of feeding rapidly growing urban and rural populations" (Plucknett et al., 1987:174-175; see also Lal, 1987). There is no alternative to industrial agriculture: its "the only game in town, and in the countryside too" (Lipton and Longhurst, 1985:15).

Large-scale, high input, commercial agriculture will in turn fuel the rise of urban industrialism (La-Anyane, 1985:28; Mellor and Gavian, 1987; World Bank, 1984:36). The "transformation from an agrarian to an industrial society must proceed through the development of the agricultural sector....Agricultural commercialization generates incomes and surpluses necessary to absorb occasional disruption" and liberates "resources for industrial expansion" (Mellor and Gavian, 1987:543). The farmer will move to the city, find a job in industry, and, being no longer dependent on her/his children, will curb her/his fertility to replacement levels (Mellor and Gavian, 1987).

Thus, the assumptions preclude consideration of the possibility that the cause of Africa's food crisis lies primarily in the disruption of African agriculture and society under colonialism, the imposition of inappropriate production models, and the dependence of African economic development on the Western economic system. Sustainability and equity are defined in ways that make them subservient to production economics, and indigenous agriculture is not considered at all. "Sustainable" has become the ubiquitous buzz word in agricultural development (CGIAR, 1987; Holden, 1987; Jahnke et al., 1987). However, the time scale of economists is much shorter than that of ecologists (Goldsmith, 1987), and in the words of one ecologist, "economic analysis is utterly incapable of coping" with sustainability (Ehrenfeld, 1987:7). In fact, sustainable agriculture is being totally transmogrified by the development establishment from its ecological sense to fit the assumptions of industrial production dominated agriculture and the green revolution (*see* Orr, 1988).

The concept of equity also takes on a special meaning in the context of an inevitable evolution toward industrial, large-scale agriculture. "Small-scale farmers" and "low input" agriculture are relative terms, and geographical areas and farmers with the most potential to make a rapid return to the required investments will continue to be targeted (Flinn and Denning, 1982:10-11; Mellor et al., 1987; World Bank, 1981:52). In light of their underlying assumptions it is not surprising for proponents of the new green revolution for Africa to state that "the low-input systems now recommended in Africa as an intermediate measure may be obsolete by the year 2000," replaced by "commercial enterprise" with "high inputs of agrochemicals and water management" (Lal, 1987:1075; *see also* Harrison, 1987:323, 332- 333).

Many of the critics of the green revolution in Africa emphasize the social relations of production as encouraged by the Western capitalist system as the primary cause of increased inequity (e.g., Lawrence, 1988; Clough and Williams, 1987). Unlike the development establishment, the cause of Africa's agricultural crisis for them is to be found outside the continent in the industrial world. Yet they often assume that if small farmers could have access to the green revolution technology, it would be to their long-term benefit. In doing so they, to, seem to adopt a unilineal model of cultural evolution. Like the establishment, these critics do not appreciate the need for a long term, ecological view of agricultural development.

My purpose in this chapter is to analyze the assumptions on which proposals for a green revolution are based in order to help encourage more open discussion of alternatives for agricultural development in Africa. Most anthropologist have rejected unilineal evolutionist models of cultural and biological evolution since Franz Boas stood up to the racist eugenics movement at the beginning of this century. Then as now, when the ratio of data to social importance is low, science too easily falls into the tautological trap, and produces results which do little "but validate a social preference (Gould, S.J., 1981:22-23). Yet in agricultural development these unilineal evolutionist models are not challenged often enough or vigorously enough by anthropologists and other social scientists.

Admittedly this will be difficult, as it has been only recently in the United States that the accumulation of environmental, economic, social, and health problems resulting from industrial agriculture has created sufficient awareness and pressure to allow discussion at the national level of alternative systems of food production (Cleveland, 1991). The success of the green revolution in Africa will depend on many factors, including the markets and infrastructure necessary to deliver inputs to the farm and export produce from the farm. I will focus here on the crops themselves, suggesting that the green revolution approach of the development establishment is not ecologically sustainable or socially equitable. First, the development of new crop varieties for Africa is controlled by the Western dominated international development establishment, and this control will increase to the extent that the green revolution becomes more dependent on the new agricultural biotechnologies. Second, the high yielding varieties themselves lead to instability in biological systems and thus in yields, and green revolution approaches to reducing this instability in the garden or field only delay its ultimate expression, and will lead to greater instability in economic and social systems.

THE CONTROL AND ORGANIZATION OF CROP DEVELOPMENT

The international plant breeding system is the source of green revolution varieties, and understanding its organization gives insights into the nature of the varieties themselves (Jahnke et al., 1987:27). The first level in the system is basic scientific knowledge and technological innovation in plant science provided by commercial and university research in the industrial world. Techniques and breeding material are then picked up by applied international research organizations, epitomized by the International Agricultural Research Centers (IARCs) of the Consultative Group on International Agricultural Research (CGIAR),[2] in which research is organized primarily by commodity and by region, and to some extent by discipline. The CGIAR is headquartered in Washington, D.C., and is controlled by the Western industrial nations. The IARCs send plant material to National Agricultural Research Centers (NARCs) in the Third World for either direct release or further breeding for local or regional conditions.

While biotechnology, through tissue culture and induced mutation, has been contributing to the creation of new crop varieties for some time, the latest techniques, most notably genetic engineering, promise to revolutionize research and development in this area. Whatever its ultimate contribution to African agricultural development, genetic engineering promises to be even more removed from the influence of African farmers and less appropriate for sustainable agriculture than conventional green revolution research, because it requires more technical and capital resources, and it is much more under the control of private business interests (Buttel et al., 1985; Gould, F., 1988). Whether genetic engineering or more conventional methods of creating new crop varieties are used, traditional landraces, their wild and weedy relatives, and associated microorganisms are now widely acknowledged to be the main source of the genetic diversity needed for future agricultural production. This is true for the development of new varieties by plant breeders, not only for Africa and the rest of the Third World, but especially for the industrial north (Edwards, 1987; Kloppenburg and Klienman, 1987; Plucknett et al., 1987:16–18). It is also true for the maintenance of traditionally based production (Oldfield and Alcorn, 1987).

The success of new green revolution varieties in Africa will be measured by the extent to which they replace landraces in farmers' fields (Plucknett et al., 1987:96). The greater the success, the more indigenous genetic diversity would depend on *ex situ* conservation in gene banks. The world gene bank system is administered by the International Board for Plant Genetic Resources (IBPGR) housed at the FAO in Rome, but controlled by the CGIAR in Washington, D.C. A world network of base seed collections at gene banks has been designated by IBPGR to serve as conservation centers for major crops. Of the 127 base collections in 1987, 81 are in industrialized countries, 29 at IARCs, and only 17 in Third World countries, including only one African gene bank housing several collections, in Ethiopia (Fowler et al.,

1988:269-270; IBPGR, 1987:27-32). Objections by Third World countries that this leads to lack of control over their own genetic resources is countered by the argument that as a matter of scientific ethics, there is free exchange of germplasm between plant breeders world wide (although not from gene banks to farmers). The place where genetic diversity is maintained, whether in gene banks or the gardens and fields of African farmers, is a major difference between the green revolution and indigenous agriculture.

INDIGENOUS AGRICULTURE AND THE GREEN REVOLUTION

Indigenous agriculture is often dismissed by green revolution proponents as inadequate to meet the needs of a growing population. Richards has pointed out how "cultural evolutionist" models continue to result in misunderstanding and undervaluing African agriculture, and in the promotion of inappropriate green revolution development (1985:138-140; see also 1986: Chapter 2).

Replacement of many locally adapted varieties or landraces by a much smaller number of widely adapted green revolution varieties has led to increased production at the price of decreased diversity in crop genetics and field ecosystems. This results in increased instability, i.e. increased variation in yield from year to year, when subject to environmental fluctuations, e.g., in water supply or pest and pathogen attacks (Cleveland and Soleri, 1989, n.d.). The green revolution varieties also require more inputs and the replacement of varieties which succumb to evolving pests and pathogens, thus increasing yield instability further due to failure in the supply infrastructure. This increased yield instability means increased risk for farmers, especially those with limited resources, and therefore often increases inequity. In addition, the destruction of existing diversity within indigenous agriculture, and the dependence on non-renewable resources, Western technology, and economic growth means that production based on these new varieties is not sustainable.

The new, more sustainable and equitable green revolution for Africa based on new crop varieties is likely to be unsustainable and inequitable because it fails to address realistically the trade-off between production on the one hand and stability and diversity on the other.

CROP GENETIC DIVERSITY AND PRODUCTION STABILITY

Traditional African crops (both indigenous and introduced) are characterized by a large degree of intraspecific variation (that is, many different varieties or landraces within each crop species). In addition, each variety is genetically heterogeneous, that is contains a large amount of genetic variation.[3] This diversity is expressed in a range of phenotypic characteristics and makes crops more able to cope with environmental variability in both space and time (Clawson, 1985).

In contrast, relatively few varieties of each green revolution crop are bred and released, with each variety developed for production over much wider areas than landraces. Homogeneity, or a small amount of genetic variability, is the outcome of these breeding programs which emphasize increased production under optimal and stable environments in which yield per unit of labor and land increase.

The lack of genetic diversity leads to the inability of crops to respond to changes in the environment (social, biotic, and abiotic). Thus the need to create relatively homogenous agricultural environments that are maintained with a package of energy intensive inputs which often includes commercial fertilizers, insecticides, fungicides, and herbicides, irrigation, and mechanization. In addition, the yield per unit of capital and energy inputs and yield per unit of degraded soil, water, or genetic resources seldom appear to be considered as criteria in such breeding programs.

Plant breeders commonly work under the assumption that adaptability to a wide range of environments is correlated with stability of yield through time, and therefore use the former as a proxy for the latter in selecting for stability (Buddenhagen, 1985; Flinn and Garrity, 1986). In more favored environments, where new varieties are commonly evaluated, this means that low variability in yield between different test locations is correlated with low variation in yield through time at a given location (Flinn and Garrity, 1986:7). However, in marginal (e.g. non-irrigated) environments (subject to water stress, drought, and flooding) there is high variability in yield at different locations and through time (Lynam et al., 1986) and landraces typically perform better here.

For example, photoperiod sensitivity, which varies in some landraces with latitude, has many advantages in highly variable rainfall regimes (Smith and Francis 1986:229), such as those which characterize savanna Africa (Kassam, 1976). Green revolution varieties are often photoperiod insensitive so that they can be grown at many different latitudes and in different seasons. This makes them less resistant to drought, because they are programmed to develop according to schedule regardless of environmental conditions. They do not have a long vegetative period in which to take advantage of variable rainfall. So without irrigation or adequate rainfall, productivity is much less than is the case for landraces under similar circumstances. Modern, short-duration, photoperiod insensitive varieties of rice have lower yield and higher variability of yield than do traditional varieties in long rainy season, highly erratic rainfall areas of Asia (Flinn and Garrity, 1986:8-9).

Resistance to pests and disease offers another example of the trade-off between production and stability. Breeding for green revolution varieties emphasizes high levels of resistance to a few strains of pests or pathogens to achieve high production. This results in fairly rapid evolution of the pest or pathogen to overcome the varieties' resistance (Gould, F., 1988).

Overall, green revolution varieties often last only a few years before they need to be replaced. High yields depend on a "varietal relay race," a steady stream of new varieties produced by the research establishment, because "even superstars in the varietal relay race eventually succumb to new diseases, pests, or other environmental challenges," and if the race falters, "crop yields would dip" (Plucknett et al., 1987:19, 21, 184). The rapid replacement of varieties as they fail is so important to maintaining yield stability that Lipton and Longhurst even state that "if there is a Green Revolution, it is fast and responsive breeder-farmer interaction, not this or that vulnerable variety" (1985:17). Although landraces, too, are replaced as environments (social, biotic, and abiotic) change, it is a much slower process which maintains a high level of genetic diversity and does not depend on massive investments of resources (see Oldfield and Alcorn, 1987).

In Africa the inappropriateness of green revolution varieties in the past is evidenced by the fact that the great majority of the many varieties sent there by IARCs and others have not been as productive as the local varieties, either as field crops or breeding stock (Jahnke et al., 1987; Eicher, 1984). In Sierra Leone, for example, "Three of the most successful improved varieties now offered by IADPs [Integrated Agricultural Development Projects] ...are selections from local strains rather than HYVs [high yielding varieties]" developed by IARCs (Richards 1986:26). Increasing awareness of these problems has led to emphasis on the fact that "adoption of widely adapted varieties at best buys time for national programs working to develop varieties with high yields and stable performance under specific ecological conditions and market preferences" (Flinn and Garrity, 1986:7).

DIVERSITY IN GARDEN AND FIELD

Much of our Western scientific knowledge of crop production is based on the study of industrial varieties grown as sole crops. In Africa, however, the great majority of food production is in mixed or multiple cropping systems. These systems combine many different crop species as well as different varieties of each species, i.e., they possess intraspecific as well interspecific diversity (Clawson, 1985). For example, in Northern Nigeria 25 crops are grown in 200 different crop combinations (Norman, 1972:74), in northern Ghana a single field may have as many as a dozen different crop mixtures, some in an area as small as 0.01 acre (Lynn, 1937:20). The number of species increases with the intensity of land use and increasing inputs of labor and resources epitomized by gardens (Cleveland and Soleri, 1987). One survey in southern Nigeria found a total of 146 species (range:18–54) in 84 compounds (household gardens) (IITA 1986:31). Another study in this region found a mean of 47 species in four compounds (Lagemann, 1977:35). In a sample of small-scale women farmers in Malawi only four varieties make up the majority of beans planted, yet they maintain an average of 16–19 varieties per household (mean = 13) (Ferguson and Sprecher, 1987).

There has been increasing study of mixed cropping systems by Western science as their potential for sustained high productivity has been recognized. Mixed cropping often produces more total, but less of any one crop compared with yields in sole stands. Yet in a major publication on multiple cropping published in 1986, there is general consensus that Western science remains largely ignorant of it (Francis, 1986). While evaluation methods for selection of two crop mixtures have been developed, interactions in systems with three or more species are little understood (Smith and Francis, 1986), and in fact most research on intercropping in Africa has been done on just two crops (*see* e.g. Keswani and Ndunguru, 1982). The study of *indigenous* multiple cropping "represents a fundamental change in the organization of agricultural research" because there are too many variables to break the system down into components for conventional plot research (Lynam et al., 1986:261).

Another problem in attempting to apply standard approaches to crop breeding for multiple cropping systems is that in the marginal conditions which characterize many African farms, the level of environmental variability swamps genetic differences, making selection under atypical conditions of more optimal environments, like those of research stations, necessary (Smith and Francis, 1986). This points to the necessity of selecting varieties for each specific multiple cropping system, yet to do this using current research methods and infrastructure would require a large investment of resources.

CONCLUSION

The production oriented goals of a new green revolution for Africa promoted by the development establishment rest, as we have seen, on the same assumptions of unilineal agricultural development and unlimited resources for perpetual economic growth upon which the original green revolution was founded. Existing diversity in crop genetic resources, field ecosystems, and social organization is increasingly to be replaced with simpler green revolution systems that increase production over the short run. The short-term instability inherent in such an approach is to be mitigated with ever increasing investments in sophisticated research, new crop varieties, inputs, and infrastructure, thus increasing, long-term instability and risk even further (Ehrenfeld, 1987). The technology and resources needed to maintain this response will be increasingly concentrated in the industrialized world, beyond the control of African governments and farmers.

Proponents of a green revolution for Africa admit that "resource requirements for moving the food sector are immense" (Mellor et al., 1987:357), yet it seems unlikely that the large investments needed to begin and sustain a green revolution in Africa will be forthcoming. Africa's foreign debt is now $40 billion, with annual debt service of $3 billion, and annual development assistance is only $8 billion (World Bank, 1987:239-243).

Goals of environmental sustainability and social equity are incompatible with such an approach to agricultural development. By failing to understand indigenous African agriculture holistically, ecologically, and non-ethnocentrically with a view to enhancing it, this approach destroys the diversity that begets long-term stability.

This does not mean that traditional indigenous agriculture can feed Africa's growing population. These systems did not evolve under conditions like those that exist today. Demographic, environmental, social, and economic conditions have changed drastically, and indigenous systems need to adapt more rapidly than they have before. To do this, Western science can be helpful, but it must be a science which does not tautologically reinforce its own assumptions and theories. This means that it must discard the present approach of the agricultural development establishment, which says, for example, that "on-farm social science research has an important role in *support* of the biological science effort" (Mellor et al., 1987:363, emphasis added). Rather, social science has an important role to play in grounding biological science in the ecological and sociocultural realities as they are experienced by African farmers, in helping Africa to take charge of her own development, and in elucidating some of the ethnocentric assumptions, both tacit and explicit, on which the current drive by the development establishment for a new green revolution in Africa rests. This approach appears to offer a realistic alternative with some hope of achieving sustainability and equity in African agriculture.

NOTES

1. I thank Ellen Messer, Gary Nabhan, Thomas Painter, Stephen Reyna, and especially Daniela Soleri for helpful comments on previous drafts of this chapter; John Nieder-

hauser, John Peacock, Steven Smith, and Robert Voight for discussions on plant breeding in agricultural development; and Doris Sample for re-typing several drafts. I am fully responsible for this chapter.
2. Four international regional institutes dominate food crop research in Africa, ICRISAT, IITA, WARDA and IRAT, and all are part of CGIAR except IRAT, which is French (Eicher, 1984:12). However, bilateral and multilateral assistance to national agricultural research in Africa is also very important (Jahnke et al., 1987:63) and deserves more attention than I can give it here.
3. This is true for even self-pollinated crops. For example, one study of 25 lines of 15 different landraces of common bean (*Phaseolus vulgaris*) in northern Malawi found considerable variability in all 25 quantitative characteristics examined (Martin and Adams, 1987a). The progeny of a single heterozygous seed segregated into 60 unique seed types (Martin and Adams, 1987b).

REFERENCES

Brady, N. C.
1985 Toward a Green Revolution for Africa. Science 227:1159.
Buddenhagen, Ivan
1985 "Maize Disease in Relation to Maize Improvement in the Tropics." In Breeding Strategies for Maize Improvement in the Tropics. International Expert Consultation, Florence and Bergamo, Italy. Relazioni e Monografie Agrarie Subtropicali e Tropicali, Nuovo Serie N. 100. FAO and Istituto Agronomico per l'Oltremare, Firenze.
Buttel, Frederick, Martin Kenney, and Jack Kloppenburg, Jr.
1985 "From Green Revolution to Biorevolution: Some Observations on the Changing Technological Bases of Bases of Economic Transformation in the Third World." Economic Development and Cultural Change 33:31-55.
CGIAR (Consultative Group on International Agricultural Research)
1987 "Farming systems research in the CGIAR. An interview with Donald L. Plucknett, Scientific Advisor, CGIAR Secretariat." News from CGIAR 6(3):5-6.
Christensen, Cheryl, et al.
1981 Food Problems and Prospects in Sub-Saharan Africa: The Decade of the 1980's. Foreign Agricultural Economic Report No. 166. Washington, D.C.: U.S. Department of Agriculture.
Clawson, David L.
1985 "Harvest Security and Intraspecific Diversity in Traditional Tropical Agriculture." Economic Botany 39(1):56- 67.
Cleveland, David A.
1991 "Development Alternatives and the African Food Crisis." In Confronting Change: Stress and Coping in African Food System, Vol. 2. R. Huss-Ashmore and S. Katz, eds. New York: Gordon and Breach.
Cleveland, David A., and Daniela Soleri
1987 "Household Gardens as a Development Strategy." Human Organization 46(3):259-270.
1989 Diversity and the New Green Revolution. Diversity 5(2&3):24-25.
n.d. Production, Diversity, and Stability in Agricultural Development. Manuscript.

Clough, Paul, and Gavin Williams
    1987   Decoding Berg: The World Bank in Rural Northern Nigeria. In State, Oil,
           and Agriculture in Nigeria. M. Watts, ed. Pp. 168-201. Berkeley: Institute
           of International Studies, University of California.
Edwards, Ian
    1987   "Biotech Industry Should Consider Impact of Plant Patents on Future of
           Crop Improvement." Genetic Engineering News 7(8):4,31.
Ehrenfeld, David
    1987   "Implementing the Transition to a Sustainable Agriculture: An Opportu-
           nity for Ecology." Ecological Society of America Bulletin 68(1):5-8.
Eicher, Carl K.
    1984   "International Technology Transfer and the African Farmer: Theory and
           Practice." Working Paper 3/84. Harare, Zimbabwe: Department of Land
           Management, University of Zimbabwe.
Ferguson, Anne E. and Susan Sprecher
    1987   "Women and Plant Genetic Diversity: The Case of Beans in the Central
           region of Malawi." Paper presented at the annual meeting of the American
           Anthropological Association, Chicago, Illinois.
Flinn, J. C. and G. L. Denning
    1982   "Interdisciplinary Challenges and Opportunities in International Agricul-
           tural Research." IRRI Research Paper Series, Number 82. Manila, Philip-
           pines: International Rice Research Institute.
Flinn, J. C. and D. P. Garrity
    1986   "Yield Stability and Modern Rice Technology." IRRI Research Paper Se-
           ries, Number 122. Manila, Philippines: International Rice Research Insti-
           tute.
Fowler, Cary, Eva Lachkovics, Pat Mooney, and Hope Shand
    1988   The Laws of Life: Another Development and the New Biotechnologies.
           Development Dialogue 1988(1-2):1-350.
Francis, Charles A., editor
    1986   Multiple Cropping Systems. New York: Macmillan.
Goldsmith, Edward
    1987   "Open Letter to Mr. Conable, President of the World Bank: You can Only
           be Judged on Your Record." The Ecologist 17(2/3):58-65.
Gould, Fred
    1988   "Evolutionary Biology and Genetically Engineered Crops." BioScience
           38(1):26-33.
Gould, Stephen Jay
    1981   The Mismeasure of Man. New York: W. W. Norton and Company.
Harrison, Paul
    1987   The Greening of Africa: Breaking Through in the Battle for Land and
           Food. NY: Penguin Books.
Holden, Constance
    1987   "World Bank Launches New Environmental Policy." Science 236:769.
IBPGR (International Board for Plant Genetic Resources)
    1987   Annual Report 1986. Rome: 1986.
IITA (International Institute of Tropical Agriculture)
    1986   Annual Report and Research Highlights 1985. Ibadan, Nigeria: IITA

Jahnke, Hans E., Dieter Kirschke, and Johannes Lagemann
  1987 "The Impact of Agricultural Research in Tropical Africa." CGIAR Study
       Paper Number 21. Washington, D.C.: Consultative Group on International
       Agricultural Research, The World Bank.
Kassam, A. H.
  1976 Crops of the West African Semi-Arid Tropics. Hyderabad, India: Interna-
       tional Crops Research Institute for the Semi-Arid Tropics.
Keswani, C. L. and B. J. Ndunguri, editors
  1982 Intercropping: Proceedings of the Second Symposium on Intercropping in
       Semi-Arid Areas, held at Morogoro, Tanzania, 4-7 August 1980. Ottowa,
       Canada: International Development Research Centre.
Kloppenburg, Jack, and Daniel L. Kleinman
  1987 Seeds and Sovereignty. Diversity, No. 10:29-33.
La-Ayane, S.
  1985 Economics of Agricultural Development in Tropical Africa. Chichester,
       U.K.: John Wiley & Sons.
Lagemann, Johannes
  1977 Traditional African Farming Systems in Eastern Nigeria: An Analysis of
       Reaction to Increasing Population Pressure. Munich: Weltform-Verlag.
Lal, Rattan
  1987 Managing the Soils of Sub-Saharan Africa. Science 236:1069-1076.
Lawrence, Peter
  1988 The Political Economy of the "Green Revolution" in Africa. Review of Af-
       rican Political Economy No. 42:59-75.
Lipton, Michael, and Richard Longhurst
  1985 Modern Varieties, International Agricultural Research, and the Poor.
       CGIAR Study Paper No. 2. Washington, D.C.: CGIAR, The World Bank.
Lynam, John K., John H. Sanders, and Stephen C. Mason
  1986 "Economics and Risk in Multiple Cropping." In Multiple Cropping Sys-
       tems. Charles Francis, editor. Pp. 250-266. New York: Macmillan
Lynn, C. W.
  1937 Agriculture in North Mamprusi. Bulletin No. 34. Accra, Ghana: Depart-
       ment of Agriculture.
Martin, Gregory B. and M. Wayne Adams
  1987a "Landraces of Phaseolus vulgaris (Fabaceae) in Northern Malawi. I. Re-
       gional Variation." Economic Botany 41(2):190-203.
  1987b "Landraces of Phaseolus vulgaris (Fabaceae) in Northern Malawi. II. Gen-
       eration and Maintainance of Variability." Economic Botany 41(2):204-
       215.
Mellor, John W., Christopher L. Delgado, and Malcom J. Blackie
  1987 "Priorities for Accelerating Food Production in Sub-Saharan Africa." In
       Accelerating Food Production in Subsaharan Africa, J. Mellor, C. Del-
       gado, and M. Blackie, eds. Pp. 353-375. Baltimore: John Hopkins Univer-
       sity Press for IFPRI.
Mellor, John W. and Sarah Gavian
  1987 "Famine: Causes, Prevention, and Relief." Science 235:539-545.

Norman, D. W.
 1972 An Economic Survey of Three Villages in Zaria Province, 2. Input-Output
      Study Vol. i. Text. Samaru Miscellaneous Paper 37. Zaria, Nigeria: Insti-
      tute for Agricultural Research, Samaru, Ahmadu Bello University.
Oldfield, Margery L. and Janis B. Alcorn
 1987 "Conservation of Traditional Agroecosystems." BioScience 37(3):199–
      208.
Orr, David W.
 1988 Food Alchemy and Sustainable Agriculture. Bioscience 38:801–802.
Plucknett, Donald L., Nigel J. H. Smith, and N. Murhti Anishetty
 1987 Gene Banks and the World's Food. Princeton, New Jersey: Princeton Uni-
      versity Press.
Richards, Paul
 1985 Indigenous Agricultural Revolution: Ecology and Food Production in
      West Africa. London: Hutchinson.
 1986 Coping with Hunger: Hazard and Experiment in an African Rice-Farming
      System. London: Allen & Unwin.
Smith, Margaret E. and Charles A. Francis
 1986 "Breeding for Multiple Cropping Systems". In Multiple Cropping Sys-
      tems. Charles A. Francis, ed. Pp. 219–249. New York: Macmillan.
Todaro, Michael P.
 1985 Economic Development in the Third World. 3rd ed. New York: Longman.
World Bank
 1981 Accelerated Development in Sub-Saharan Africa: An Agenda for Action.
      Washington, D.C.: World Bank.
 1984 Toward Sustained Development in Sub-Saharan Africa: A Joint Program
      of Action. Washington, D.C.: World Bank.
 1987 World Development Report 1987. New York: Oxford University Press for
      the World Bank.

CHAPTER 13

What is to be Done?
An Historical Structural
Approach to Warfare
and Famine

S. P. Reyna

Consider the recent past: one torpid, New York city August in the 1970s I taught a motley and sympathetic crew, attracted to the groves of academe not so much by the prospect of anthropological exotica as by that of keeping their cool in Ivy-league air-conditioning. I was delighted to discover a student from Nigeria. This was because my first job as a professor had been there, during the civil war between Nigeria and its breakaway southeastern province, Biafra. People who have been in the same place eventually compare stories, especially if these are war stories.

My student said he had been an officer in the Biafran army. He recalled that he had returned to his village when the war was almost over. There was famine. One day a plane attacked. His brother was too weak to flee. So he threw him on his back and ran from the village to the forest, zigzagging, trying to outwit the plane. He was soon exhausted from the weight of his brother. He felt a fear of the unseen plane, because to see it he would have had to slow down, and peer back over his shoulder. Eventually, as he ran, he sensed quiet. The plane had gone. He stopped running. His gasping for breath seemed wildly cacaphonic to him in the forest, now still. Panting, standing alone, he felt exultant. then he became aware of moisture. It tickled as it moved down his neck. He looked back. A small fragment of something the plane had dropped had made a hole in his brother's head. The plane had won.

There are those who believe that the past is a poor predictor of the future. Of course, one response to these timid souls is that the past, for good or bad, is the *only* predictor of the future there is. So that, like it or not, you have to return to the past—to memories of a man fleeing with his burden of kinship—no matter how difficult this may be, for clues to the future. This is exactly what this essay does. It is organized into three parts. The first asks what has happened recently in the modern world and argues, on the basis of the response to this question, that a dangerous passage from the modern into the post modern world is in the offing. The second asks what should be done given such a prospect and suggests that it might be appropriate to formulate a historical structural approach to explain this impending transition. The third section returns to the Africa of the Nigerian student—to its wars and famines—to create a preliminary theory of these phenomena and, perhaps, to gain thereby some understanding of future prospects.[1]

WHAT HAPPENED?

World Bank documents are exemplars of bureaucratic discretion, so it catches our attention when one announces that globally 730 million people appeared to be malnourished during the 1980s (1986:1). George Kent reported that eighteen to twenty million of these perished, directly or indirectly, each year as a result of this condition (1984:26).[2] Such numbers are enormous, but they themselves may not be particularly important, for there are reasons to believe that they are but symptoms of an underlying malignancy.

Ironically, the discussion of these reasons begins with what appears to be the best of news. There has been tremendous industrial expansion over the past few centuries. This is perhaps the sole actuality agreed upon by both political economists (Mandel, 1980) and more conventional economists (Rostow, 1978). Expansion has brought a huge increase in the delivery of goods and services, and a rise in the standards of living for many in industrial nations. As a consequence, it was believed in the mid-20th century, that a new type of social concern had been spawned—that of adjusting to this "great and quite unprecedented affluence" (Galbraith, 1958:1). Anticipation of the delights of making such adjustments gave birth to a whole new industry, modernization theory, that specialized in the production of manuals instructing readers as to the proper procedures for achieving industrial "take off" (Rostow, 1962). Sometimes, however, good news is bad news.

In 1972 the Club of Rome published *The Limits of Growth*, which warned that:

> If the present growth trends in world population, industrialization, pollution, food production, and resource depletion continue unchanged, the limits to growth on this planet will be reached sometime within the next 100 years. The

most probable result will be a rather sudden and uncontrollable decline in both population and industrial capacity [Meadows et. al., 1972:23].

The Club of Rome, a loose group of European industrialists, had commissioned social scientists associated with Dennis and Donella Meadows to advise them on the future. Meadows and associates informed their patrons that their world might be at risk in the late 21st century, circa A. D. 2072. Such bad news, as might be expected, created something of a *frisson* in those used to the good times. So the very next year, *Models of Doom: A Critique of the Limits to Growth*, appeared. It claimed that the Meadows group suffered from an "almost Messianic faith" in "modern systems dynamics" (Cole, 1973:9). Then, revealing similar proclivities, they formulated their own systems models which found the Meadows' views to be unduly pessimistic. Everybody was relieved. The good times would roll on into a rosy future. What has happened since then?

One of the things which has occurred has been the continuation of studies exploring issues raised by the Meadows. First, there is clear evidence that global demand for products and services will continue to experience extraordinary growth throughout the next century. This is in part indicated by the enormous population growth rates which have occurred, and will continue to occur, especially in the Third World. Each additional person born requires an additional supply of goods and services. In the U.S. this bundle is large, including 40,000 pounds annually of new minerals per person (Harf and Trout, 1986:130). In 1990 the world population was estimated at 5.3 billion. In 2090, the latest United Nations projections predict it will be 11.3 billion (UNFPA, 1990). This is an enormous number of new people who will demand a huge bundle of products.

Firms might be expected to supply greater quantities of goods and services over the course of the forthcoming century, even in the absence of such increased demand. This is because of the exigencies of profit maximization. Any business's viability is determined by its profitability. Thus it is driven to achieve the highest, i.e., maximized profits. Profits, however, are powerfully influenced by market share. This is "the sales of the product or products of a firm as a proportion of the sales of the product or products of the industry as a whole . . ." (Bannock et al., 1972:297). The major way a business captures market share is by reducing its prices to levels below that of its competition; either by skimping on labor costs or by achieving some technological innovation that allows it to produce more cheaply. When it does so, it sells more. This means that businesses normally contrive ways to increase sales to maximize profits. This, of course, contributes to industrial growth.

All of which means that industrial expansion will continue, and in so doing will consume raw materials at rates which are now unprecedented. Exhaustion of different resources will be one consequence of such consumption levels. Consider non-renewable resources. The *Global 2000 Report* (1980) analyses the life expectancies of seventeen minerals critical to industrial activity and conservatively predicts that the reserves of the vast bulk of these will be exhausted in less than one hundred and fifty years (Ibid.:29). Oil, because it is the major energy source, is a *sine qua non* of contemporary manufacturing and transportation. Further, it is vital to the maintenance of large populations, because it is an essential component of the fertilizers necessary for the enormous yields required to feed these people. The fate of oil is clear. Production ceases at the end of the 21st century, regardless of whether one operates with optimistic or pessimistic estimates (Hubbert, 1971:69). Let us now briefly consider renewable resources. The world annually experiences the deforestation of c. 22,0000,000 hectares, as well as the degradation of 11 million hectares of arable land (J. Spiller: personal communication).

Furthermore, not only will raw materials begin to be exhausted in the 21st century, but their use may come to transform the environment in threatening ways. Nowhere is this more significant than in the Greenhouse Effect, where pollutants from industrial activities alter the chemistry of the atmosphere globally, threatening to raise temperatures. This has led to projections that by the mid 21st century "the amount of warming and associated changes in climate would begin to sharply increase the economic and environmental costs of world production, not only in agriculture but in other sectors as well. The main impact would . . . be . . . to reduce the capacity of the global system to produce economic and environmental goods and services" (Crosson, 1989:119).

What will such events mean for the quality of life of the majority of those inhabiting the earth, the Third World poor? An attempt to address this question is, in fact, this essay's chief concern. Some idea of what direction a response will have to take is indicated by the findings of the Food and Agriculture Organization (FAO), which detected a widening gap in per capita food consumption between developed and developing countries. People in developed nations eat an average of 3,390 calories a day. While those in the least developed nations consume only 1,800 calories a day (WDF, 1987a:1). A caloric intake of only 1,800 calories is generally regarded as marginal for most adults. What the FAO reported, thus, was a process of nutritional marginalization.

Hunger, resource over-utilization, pollution; these are some of the things which have increasingly happened since the Meadows' first document, and they have helped to fix it as a boundary between radically different conceptions of the human prospect. Prior to the Club of Rome report sensible people might contemplate a comfortable future of increasing affluence based upon industrial growth. But the Meadows had warned that such expansion consumes enormous and increasing amounts of raw materials and that their over utilization threatened any rosy prospects. Subsequent studies of resource utilization trends and their consequences have turned earlier optimists into Cassandras, who warn that pressures on global resources "have surpassed many natural thresholds, including the capacity of forests to tolerate pollution, of the atmosphere to absorb waste gases, and of cropland to sustain intensive cultivation" (WFD, 1987b:3).

Hard charging Vandals in the 5th century do not seem to have stopped and contemplated what they provoked. Nor do aggressive businessfolk of the late 20th century appear to realize that they have helped to create one of those rare "moments of transition from one historical system to another . . ."(Wallerstein, 1986:16). However, unlike the Vandals and their ilk, we must now stop and comprehend the significance of what has just been said. Transition always involves dissolution, as one system gives way to another. So while the good news is that there will be continued industrial growth, the bad news is that this will lead to the dissolution of existing economic and political systems. Hunger, as noted earlier, is included in this prospect. This raises a question: what is to be done?

WHAT IS TO BE DONE?

In a tract entitled *What is to Be Done*, Lenin surveyed Russia at the turn of the 20th century, during a time that he called the "Third Period." The beginning of the 20th century was for Lenin, just as its end is for us, a time of "dissolution" (1988:298). Faced with such a situation, he urged that what should be done was to "Liquidate the Third Period!" (1988:300). This poses a question: Should social analysts, in their enthusiasm to fight the present dissolution, respond in a Leninist fashion? I unequivocally respond to this question with both "no" and "yes."

Two Leninisms

If, by responding in a Leninist fashion, it is meant that sensible persons should plan violence; then I think that the response should be a clear "no". Consider the following: in the Algerian War French paratroopers regularly shocked the genitalia of their opponents with powerful electrodes. Algerian guerrillas responded to this and other provocations, on at least one occasion, by slashing open the belly of a pregnant woman, killing her infant and then returning it to its open womb. South African soldiers are rumored to have roasted one of their prisoners alive and American troops in Viet Nam heartily barbecued "suspect" villages with napalm. Such unpleasantries, inevitable in warfare, are only its small change. Contemporary forces of military destruction have so evolved since Lenin's time that their application with vigor means either almost unimaginable suffering or armageddon. There are a number of studies suggesting that there is a considerable chance of major conflict during the next century. This literature begins by observing that Europe went from ancient empires to feudalism as a result of the onslaughts of the barbarians, and from feudalism to capitalism in the wars of nation-states; and then from such observations it infers that social transformations often have been violent.[3] If this conclusion is even remotely cogent, then gratifying the impulse to resolve problems of the impending dissolution by planning violence, increases the risk of total inferno. The Lenin of violence was always terrifying, and never more so than in the present circumstances.

But Lenin had also said in *What is to Be Done* that "Without a revolutionary theory there can be no revolutionary movement" [1988:40]. He was quite specific in his word selection, using the term theory instead of ideology; and by "theory", being a firm positivist, he meant scientific theory. There is a special urgency for intellectuals to become Leninist in this second sense, because the formulation of theories that explain the complex of circumstances producing dissolution may be the only way of achieving an understanding of how to avoid global war and famine. So the question "what is to be done" resolves itself into what type of analyses will usefully guide action through the dissolution of contemporary worlds.

Historical Structuralism

Elsewhere (Reyna, 1990) I have described historical structuralism as a positivist methodology interested in understanding social dynamics.[4] The following pages apply this approach to an understanding of the approaching transition. This is done by first developing the notions of structure and history; second, by sketching a rough model of the industrial and Third Worlds; and third, by deriving certain propositions, based upon the conclusions of the *What's Happening* section, that predict what some of the history of this model might be.

I believe it is useful to think that social structures occupy different "levels." These levels are composed of concepts about the parts and relationships between the parts of organizations. Structural concepts vary in the degree of their generality and abstractness, and it is out of such variation that different levels may be constructed. Generality refers to the variety of phenomena denoted by a concept. Red is less general than color. Abstractness refers to the distance of a concept from observed events. Walking is less abstract than instantaneous velocity.[5]

Social structures may be thought of as constructed from concepts occupying at least two levels above the ground, with the "ground" being events in the world. Closest to the ground is a level of concepts built up, in Radcliffe-Brown's terms, from observations of "actually existing social relations" (1965:90). Concepts at this level tend to be lower in generality and abstraction. Then, as Levi-Strauss insisted, there is a second, higher, level that has "nothing to do with empirical reality" and "everything to do with models that are built up after it" (1973:375). This level is distinguished from the first by concepts of greater generality and/or abstraction. The first level might be termed that of institutions; the second that of models. Finally, the two levels may be seen to be higher or lower parts in the same edifice when, through the processes of induction or deduction, models are inferred from institutions or institutions deduced from models.

A frequent criticism of structuralism is that it ignores history. However, in historical structuralism, just as there are two related levels of structure, so there are two related levels of structural history. The notion of process is a key to understanding such history. The more general view of process is of a "series of . . . regularly occurring actions . . ."(McGraw-Hill, 1969:1173). Social processes are regularly reoccurring actions within social structures; and because these actions are events strung out across time, they constitute the history of the structures in which they occur, i.e., they are structural history. Such histories may be observed at the level of institutions or at the level of models.

Historical structuralism has two general goals. The first is to arrive at a set of propositions which express the structure and history of models. This proposition set is a "theory." It can be formulated by using induction to raise the scope and abstraction of concepts which represent a number of institutions. The second goal is to explore the validity of the theory. Essential to this process is the establishment of the degree of "fit" between what the propositions of the theory assert to be the organization and history of a model and what is actually observed to be its organization and history. Clearly the closer the correspondence, i.e., the fit, between what is asserted and observed the more valid the theory.[6] The presentation of a model of how affluent industrial nations may be related to the impoverished, underdeveloped world will help illustrate how historical structuralism works.

The model to be proposed is not my own, but a synthesis of the work of certain French structural Marxists, such as Althusser and Balibar (1970), and world system theorists, such as Wallerstein (1974, 1978) and Chase-Dunn (1989). Their model is that of a world system. A system, as used here, is a set of structures. A world system, which may not include the entire globe (Wallerstein, 1974:301), is an international structure whose parts are articulated.

The concept of articulation has a checkered history in political economy (Wolpe, 1980). Here it merely means that the parts of a structure are linked, permitting among other things, the processes of its reproduction to occur. Reproduction refers to processes which recreate any structure or system of structures (Althusser and Balibar, 1970: 254–270). The reproduction of a structure or system may produce contradictions. The notion of contradiction is based upon an irony: the processes which maintain structures, change them. A contradiction is a process that helps to reproduce a structure or system, and by doing so moves it toward its dissolution.

I believe that what makes a system a *world* system is the existence of two main parts. These are the core, the wealthy, industrial world; and the periphery, the hungry Third World. Core and periphery each contain many structures. These can be usefully thought of as existing at local, regional, national, and multinational levels.[7] A farm family growing cotton on a few acres in Chad is a local institution. The person who comes to collect these farmers' taxes is part of a regional institution, the *Prefecture*. The state corporation, *Compagnie Cotonnière Tchadienne (COTONTCHAD)*, that buys the farm's cotton is part of a national institution which buys all cotton throughout the country. The French technical experts who advise *COTONTCHAD* on operations and policies are seconded from their development agency, called the *Fonds d'Assistance et Cooperation*, which is a French national institution. The French firm Lacoste, which buys *COTONTCHAD's* cotton, is a multinational textile manufacturer. Finally the American gentleman who buys an Izod shirt manufactured by Lacoste from a regional retail institution is in his turn part of a local institution, the much maligned American family. There are a huge number of local, regional, and national institutions in the core and periphery. A complete analysis of core and periphery would consider all of these.

There is a strong belief, however, that the economic actions of many core and periphery institutions are expressions of a certain type of model, called the capitalist mode of production, or capitalism for short. This model of production consists of "capitalists," those who control production by combining capital and land, which they own, with labor, which they buy from the other part in the structure, the "proletariat," who are free, propertyless workers (Marx, 1981). The core is articulated with the periphery, because in order for capitalists to reproduce capital they must acquire land from the periphery. The notion of "land, " for those unfamiliar with economic terminology, is broader than in its conventional usage. It denotes *any* raw material which is transformed during production into a finished commodity.

A crucial point to grasp is that the periphery is the *sole* source of many agricultural products and natural resources that are the raw materials used by capital in the core. This means that the core becomes increasingly dependent on the periphery for its land (Perlman and Murray, 1982:112) as production expands, which implies that should the supply of peripheral land be gravely diminished, then capital would experience difficulties with its reproduction. Thus the core is articulated with the periphery not so much because it wants to be but because it has to be.

What might be the history of this articulation? In order to respond to this question I integrate Marxian views concerning the main process of capitalism with the conclusion of the first section. Mandel expresses the Marxist position when he says "the basic laws of motion of the capitalist system are those of capital accumulation . . ." (1980:8). Clearly, industrial growth is an expression of capitalist accumulation.

Marx had also said that capitalist accumulation involved "a tendency towards absolute development of the productive forces . . ." (1981:273). The notion of productive forces is a complicated one in political economy, but it might usefully be thought of as the "factors of production . . . characterizing a . . . society . . ." at a particular time (Godelier, 1972: 335). Land is a major factor of production. Thus what Marx was saying was that in order for capitalist accumulation to occur, increased production had to occur; and that in order for increased production, the productive forces had to be developed, or increased. Of course, and this is utterly critical, land is finite and its increased use increases pollution; both of these combine to raise production costs.

This means that what capitalists do to accumulate capital (develop productive forces by consuming land in increasing amounts), threatens their reproduction (due to the increasing production costs consequent upon increasing land scarcity and pollution). There would thus appear to be something of a contradiction between capital and land, for the same process, capitalist accumulation, which helps to reproduce capital, does so by removing the conditions for its continuation. Furthermore, it is entirely reasonable to suspect that this contradiction will become more pronounced as raw materials grow scarcer and pollution more serious throughout the next century. The conclusion of the first section of this essay was that contemporary economic and political systems might experience dissolution because of the consequences of industrial growth. This is another way of saying that over the next century there will be an intensification of the contradiction between capital and land.

What are likely to be the consequences of this intensification? Certainly, competition between core nations will increase as production becomes more difficult. This can heighten instability among core Great Powers as they strive to maintain or improve their positions among their rivals. The core nations which enjoy assured markets, sources of investment, and especially the increasingly scarce raw materials in the periphery will be able to compete

348   S. P. REYNA

effectively in these rivalries. Core powers achieved such advantages in the past by implementing policies that permitted them greater control in the affairs of peripheral polities. Bergesen performed a study of the relationship between colonial expansion in the periphery and core events which found that "Colonialism expands when there is instability within the core. . . " (1980:119).

According to one count there were one hundred and twenty wars between 1945 and 1976 (Kende, 1978). All of these, with five exceptions, were in the Third World. This meant that there were "11.5 wars" being fought "every single day of the past 32 years" in the periphery (Ibid.: 228). The need to increase core political control in the periphery is likely to keep warfare frequent in these regions, and perhaps even make it more frequent. There are two reasons for this.

The first reason follows from the fact that if a polity seeks to control in significant ways another polity or polities, then it must be prepared to use force. There is ample evidence supporting this generalization. Certainly, one of the effects of Western expansion was "to generate warfare . . . :"(Ferguson and Whitehead, 1990:6). Imperial expansion produced four major types of wars. The first occurred when the forces of a core nation directly engaged those of a peripheral polity. This happened when a core nation established direct control in a peripheral polity. Cortez' campaign against Montezuma in Mexico in the 16th century is an example of such conflict. The second type of war that occurred was between peripheral elites, acting as surrogates of core nations, and other segments of peripheral society. These wars seem to have often resulted from the elites' attempt to expropriate natural resources from their owners. Such wars were continual between Native Americans and the European elites in North America. They occurred between *pieds noirs* and Algerians in Algeria, and between settlers and Mau Mau in Kenya. The third type of war that occurred was between indigenous peripheral peoples who sought to preserve or acquire some advantage, where one or both sides to the conflict were aided by core powers who, for some reason, believed that this assistance was in support of their interests. The wars between the Iriquois and Huron in the 17th century are an example of such hostilities, because they were fought to acquire beaver hunting territories to participate in the fur trade (Wolf, 1982). A fourth type of war occurred when an emerging power in the periphery challenged an existing Great power in the core. The United States War of Independence in the 18th century is an example of such conflict.[8] All four of these types of wars would be expected if the core establishes greater political control in the periphery.[9]

There is a second reason for frequent warfare in the periphery. This has to do with the fact "that the majority of the Third-world countries are barely capable of reaching a level of economic development at which even the basic needs of the population are met . . . ," which "causes renewed power and political struggles and intensifies the conflict between rival ideologies" (Steinbach, 1982: 22). Today there is a "transfer of capital" from the periphery to the core "via debt and interest payments," so "that many of the least developed states are actively regressing in terms of GNP per capita . . ."(Thomas, 1989:2). Intensification of the land/capital contradiction will mean that peripheral nations will experience even greater population growth than their core counterparts, under conditions of increasing resource scarcity and pollution in the future. This can only further exacerbate conflicts within peripheral nations.

Thus I am suggesting that the history of the core-periphery articulation might be expressed by the following three propositions:

(1)   The contradiction between capital and land will intensify over the next hundred years.

(2)   Intensification of this contradiction can increase the need for core nations to exercise greater political control in peripheral areas.

(3)   Increased core attempts to exercise control in the periphery, in conjunction with stagnant or decreased peripheral development, will maintain or increase the frequency and intensity of peripheral warfare.[10]

Historical structuralism has been applied in the past few pages to speculate upon the causes of peripheral warfare. In the next section it will be used to inquire into the consequences of such hostilities for famine.

FAMINE AND WARFARE

In this section I formulate a most preliminary theory of the famine and warfare tormenting Africa. This is accomplished by examining A.A. Sen's theory of famine and suggesting how it might be broadened; next by establishing the nature of the relationship between African warfare and famine; and finally, by offering five propositions that integrate certain aspects of Sen's theory with our findings concerning the causes and consequences of warfare.

Famine

Sen's is the most significant recent theoretical achievement in the analysis of famine (1976, 1977, 1981) because it challenges one of the oldest explanations of famine. This approach derives from Adam Smith (1776). Its common-sense logic runs: people die in famines from starvation, which is due to lack of food; so, obviously, famines result from food availability declines [or FADs, as Sen likes to abbreviate them]. J. Mellor and S. Gavin reveal the continuing acceptance of this explanation, when they matter-of-factly state, in the influential journal *Science*, that "The underlying cause of famine is crop failure . . . ," and crop failure is, of course, a FAD (1987:539). Sen begins his analysis by observing that "some of the worst famines have taken place with no significant decline in food availability per head . . . ," as, for example, in Africa; and that "the elimination of starvation" in certain countries, notably China, "seems to have taken place even without a dramatic rise in food availability per head . . ." (Ibid.:7). This leads him to conclude that famine occurs in situations of insufficient ingestion of food, but that such "Starvation is the characteristic of some people not *having* enough food to eat. It is not the characteristic of there *being* not enough food to eat " (Ibid.:1; emphasis in the original); and, he insists, the system of exchange entitlements largely determines how much food people have. Sen is thus offering an entitlement theory of famine.

Exchange entitlements are for Sen the amount of goods and services a person is entitled to in exchange for what he or she has. One is entitled to goods or services when one enjoys an authorized right to them. The exchange entitlements available to a person in a society are the result of the relationships between three concepts: entitlement sets, endowments, and exchange entitlement mapping. The entitlement set of a person "consists of a set of alternative commodity bundles, any one of which the person can decide to have" (Ibid.:46). The endowment of a person is the "ownership bundle" (Ibid.:45) of that person; i.e., his or her "land, labor, power, and . . . other resources . . ." (Ibid.:47). A person is entitled to that which he or she can get in exchange for his or her endowments given a certain entitlement mapping [E-mapping, for short]. This is a mathematical function which "specifies the set of alternative commodity bundles that the person can command respectively for each endowment bundle" (Ibid.:46). People starve, regardless of food availability, when their endowments, given the prevailing E-mapping, cannot be exchanged for sufficient calories to subsist.

Based on the preceding, Sen's theory of famine may be stated in four propositions:

(1)   The entitlement sets of people equal the amount of commodities they may receive in exchange for their endowments.

(2)   Entitlement sets are influenced by endowments and E-mapping.

(3)   Declines in endowments and E-mappings mean collapses in entitlement sets.

(4)   Famines occur subsequent to collapses in entitlement sets, resulting in large numbers of people who are not entitled to enough food to survive.

How has this theory been received?

Most commentators find Sen's argument "persuasive," though some also add: "As far as it goes" (Ravallion, 1987:2). There seem to have been two sorts of criticisms; one more general, and the other rather specific.[11] The broader concern, advanced by Ravallion, is that exchange entitlement theory "begs the important question" of the causes of shifts "in the conditions of exchange" which give "rise to entitlement failure" (Ibid.:2). Ravallion is suggesting that entitlement theory has too narrow a scope.[12]

Ravallion's concern seems valid. Sen formally explains famine in terms of entitlement sets which are determined by endowments and the prevailing E-mapping. What is absent is any theoretical consideration of the forces which control endowments and E-mappings. Such forces exist, and Sen is well aware that they do, for he says that "The exchange entitlement mapping . . . will depend on the legal, political, economic and social characteristics of a society" (1981:41). However, just how this political economy operates is left out of the theory, i. e., is simply unspecified. Clearly, these political and economic forces are important because they control the forces (endowments and E-mappings) that control the forces (entitlement sets) that produce famine. What has just been argued is not that Sen's existing theory is invalid, but that it would be enhanced if it considered how political and economic forces influenced entitlements.

The second line of criticism has been presented by Kula, who insists that "the real reason for most famines, which are mentioned in Sen's writings, is one of those 'secondary factors,' war and its complicated politics . . ." (1988:112). The importance of warfare for understanding famine had been noted by Basu (1986) in his explanation of the great Bengal Famine of 1943. Sen had used this famine, in which 1.5 million perished, to support his own views. He argued that it occurred because exchange entitlements declined "violently" (1981:75), and even though the famine occurred during World War II, nowhere does the war figure in his analysis. Basu, however, suggested that,

"Because of the war, the area [Bengal] was practically sealed off for imports. With total disregard to the interests of the civilian population the provincial government had practically destroyed the internal transport and did prohibit internal trade. They and their commercial collaborators started forced purchase of the existing stocks of supplies to feed the growing number of the army, and the industrial and civilian work force needed for the war effort. That had caused the spiraling of prices and speculative hoarding by the government agents and the grain-traders. Government purchases and exports continued at the same time to lead to the total destruction of the market, with the foodgrain disappearing from the market totally at one time while prices skyrocketed . . ." (1986:602).

Basu was saying that war led to policies (prohibition of internal trade, grain purchases, etc.) that had consequences (hoarding) that led to changes in the E-mapping (skyrocketing prices) that produced starvation.

Such reviews of Sen's theory encourage efforts to expand the scope of his original position, and suggest that one way to doing so would be to include war in broader formulations of the political economy of entitlements. In the section which follows I first explore African evidence linking war and famine and then offer a preliminary historical structuralist theory that builds upon Sen's work to account for certain African famines.

Warfare

E. Messer has emphasized in the *World Hunger Report* (1990) that there is, indeed, a connection between hunger and organized violence, especially in Africa. Watts does the same in this volume. The *Review of African Political Economy* devoted a special issue to the topic (1985). Griffith has said that the "relationship between famine and war in Africa" is "obvious" (1988:59); and, in this spirit, Shindo offers the mono-causal proposition, for Africa and beyond, that "famine is the product of war . . ." (1985:7).

Such statements jump the gun, because systematic empirical analyses of the nature and dimensions of the connections between African famine and war are rare. P. Shipton (1990) has just performed an excellent review of the literature concerning African famines and food security. His discussion is based upon approximately four hundred references. Only three of these focus upon war and famine. The following paragraphs first seek to consider if there has been an association between warfare and famine; and second how the former can produce the latter.

A Chi Square analysis was performed to ascertain whether a war/famine relationship could be established for the African subcontinent. Forty nations were included in this exercise. These included all countries, with the exception of South Africa and island nations such as Madagascar. The period under examination was the thirty years between 1960 and the present. Warfare was defined as armed conflict producing one thousand or more deaths per year (Sivard, 1989). Famine was operationalized as large scale loss of life, social disruption, and economic chaos produced by lack of food (Mellor and Gavin, 1987). Each country was examined to see whether it had one or more wars and/or famines between 1960 and 1990. Table 1 reports upon the results of this analysis. [Appendix 1 presents the sources of information used to con-

Table 1.   Warfare and Famine in Sub-Saharan Africa (Excluding South Africa): 1960 – Present

	War Absent	War Present	Total
Famine Absent	13	5	(18)
Famine Present	8	14	(22)
Total	(21)	(19)	(40)

$x^2 = 5.078$
$p < .025$

struct Table 1.] A first finding that follows from an examination of Table 1 is that war and famine have been frequent: 22, or 55%, of all nations had experienced at least one famine; 19, or 48%, of all of these countries had also endured at least one war.

A second, and central, finding that emerges from calculation of the Chi Square is that the association between war and famine is *not* due to chance. Rather, where there was war, there was likely to be famine, as was the case in fourteen (or 74%) of the countries; and where there was no war, there was not likely to be famine, as was the case in thirteen or (62%) of the countries. A third finding of the analysis is that there was a fair number of nations—eight (or 38%)—which experienced famine in the absence of war.

These findings suggest three conclusions. First, those who asserted a relationship between war and famine were absolutely correct. The two go together in Africa, a bit like love and marriage in romantic novels. Second, Africa has been horribly famine prone. So much that famines readily occurred, even in the absence of warfare. Third, mono-causal explanations of famine solely in terms of war, such as that of Shindo, are too simple. More supple accounts are needed: ones sensitive to the reality that at some times famines occur in the absence of war, while at other times war may occur and not produce famine.

Chi Square analysis can only establish association. In what follows below I shall show that there is reason to suspect that war and famine are associated because they are causally related. Relationships may be said to be causal if they exhibit two properties; spatio-temporal ordering and production (Bunge, 1959). A relationship exhibits the first property if there is an organization in space and time of the events which compose the relationship: i.e., A comes first in space and time, and is followed by B which comes second, etc. . . . A relationship possesses the second property if, in some way, the ante-

354 S. P. REYNA

cedent events create, in the sense of "make happen", the subsequent events in the relationship. To illustrate what is meant by causality consider that the knockout of a boxer is composed of two events, the punch (A) and the unconsciousness (B). These display an invariant spatio-temporal relationship. First somebody is hit, i.e., A occurs: then the person hit collapses, i.e., B occurs. Further, B occurs because A creates a shock in the brain of the person hit that removes consciousness, i.e., A produces B. This is causality. Evidence from six African nations which have experienced wars over the three decades since 1960 suggests that warfare can, indeed, deliver a "knockout punch."

I begin with Nigeria. Oil had been discovered in Nigeria and was about to be produced when, between 1967 and 1970, the federal government of Nigeria engaged in a major civil war with its breakaway southeastern region, Biafra. In part the conflict was a petroleum war, because easterners believed, even though the oil was in their area, that its revenues would be diverted to other regions. So to prevent this from occurring, among other reasons, they seceded and created Biafra. As many as a million people, mainly in the east, died in the ensuing hostilities (Cervenka, 1987:72). Britain, the United States, the Soviet Union, and France, in pursuit of their interests, intensified the conflict, contributing to this extremely high level of mortality.

Southeastern Nigeria is a forested area of especially high population density. In the early phases of the war there was no famine in the region. However, the federal government decided in 1967 upon a policy of "total war" (Stremlau, 1978:78), whose objectives included a blockade of the east and the destruction of food crops. Britain, the United States, and the Soviets decided that they would enjoy greater influence with this emerging oil producing power if they supported the federal government. They did this by supplying very considerable technical expertise and war material to the federal armed forces, transforming the latter from an inept military institution into a capable one, and vastly increasing its capacity to wage "total war." France, on the other hand, calculated differently and threw its lot in with the Biafrans, providing them with military supplies and thus increasing their ability to kill federal soldiers.

The success of the government's total war strategy has been documented a number of times, though perhaps most effectively by Jacobs (1987). By late 1969 there was little food left that had been produced in Biafra, and very, very little else entered through the increasingly effective blockage. As a consequence Biafra starved. Clearly, in the Nigerian Civil war, the war came first, followed by the famine which occurred because of the reduction of food supplies produced by the military operations of crop destruction and blockade. Equally clearly, the capacity to conduct military operations, and hence

the intensity of combat, was raised as a result of core powers seeking to enhance their control of an oil rich region.

It has been reported that there has been a total of 7000 war and war related
deaths since 1970 in Chad (Watts, this volume), a figure which probably terribly underreports the fatalities. Armed conflict began in 1966 and continues
in sporadic fashion today, meaning that the country has been at war with itself, or its neighbor Libya, for 80% of its post-independence history. In fact,
there have been two major conflicts. The first, from 1966 through 1978, was
between political factions in the northern part of the country and the national
government that was then dominated by southerners. Then in 1978 the north
beat the south, and there began a competition which continues today between
warlords of various northern political factions.

Chadian government revenues rarely covered expenditures during this period, and at least in the 1960s and 1970s, their military forces were rather
ragtag. How could Chad keep fighting under these conditions? One answer
to this question is that it did so with a lot of help from a friend in high places.
The wars have been heavily financed and to a considerable extent fought by
France. French money, weapons, and elite troops like the Foreign Legion
were poured into Chad, at least in part, as the result of a strategy of maintaining influence throughout Francophone Africa by militarily supporting existing regimes. Gallic logic is simple: they will listen to France, because they
need France.[13] Thus, Chadians fought, and in good measure continue to do
so, because they were given forces of destruction by a core power as part of
its policy of maintaining control in the African periphery.

Parts of Chad have experienced famine at least twice since Independence:
once in 1973-74 and a second time in the early 1980s. Let us consider the
first famine. Severe drought occurred prior to the 1973-74 famine. Precipitation was far below normal in the northern two thirds of the country from 1969
through 1974. These were sahelian, sub desert, and desert regions dominated
by livestock production. Prolonged absence of rains devastated pastures and
completely dried up most surface waters. The combined absence of fodder
and drinking water produced huge herd losses. The herders in these northerly
areas would be the segment of the Chadian society most seriously touched by
famine, suggesting that perhaps the famine is better explained by meteorological rather than military events. However, there seems to have been sufficient food in the country to have adequately fed the pastoralists. This was
because, though southern Chad received less than normal rain, what did fall
was enough to permit substantial cereal harvests. Unfortunately, the food
was in the south, the hungry folk were in the north, and the two areas were at
war.

The causes of famine here appear to be different from those that produced the famine in Biafra, for there does not seem to have been a conscious strategy of sealing off an area and starving it out. Rather, military operations in northern and central Chad made travel in these areas problematic. Roads, always difficult in Chad under the best of conditions, were either physically impassable or most dangerous. This meant that private merchants, parastatal commercial organizations, such as the *Société Nationale de la Commercialisation du Tchad* [SONACOT], had the gravest difficulties operating in the north. As a result far less grain was transported into these regions than was the case in normal times. The ensuing extreme scarcity of cereals meant that their prices rose steeply. This occurred at a time when herders flooded the market with their animals, hoping to sell them before they died. This, of course, led to a collapse of livestock prices.

Chadians who succumbed to famine seem to have perished in one of two ways. First, there were those in locations where no cereals had been transported and who had lost their animals. So, lacking food, they perished. In other areas where people had lost their animals some cereals had been brought in, but unfortunately, these folk could afford to purchase little food because of the exceptionally high cereal prices and low livestock prices. So, lacking money, they starved.

The preceding suggests an ordering of events: first there was combat, which was followed by famine. the first event also produced the second, because fighting meant that either people did not have enough food available to survive, or they did not have enough money to buy enough food to survive. Thus, there appears to have been both spatio-temporal ordering and production in the war/famine relationship, suggesting that they were causally related.

Angolans, as well as Chadians, have fought a great deal since 1960. In the period 1961 to 1974, led by the *Movimento Popular Libertação de Angola* [MPLA], the *Frente Nacional de Libertaçgo de Angola* [FNLA], and *União Nacional para a Independêndença Total de Angola* [UNITA], they struggled for Independence against Portugal. Then, in the 1980s they bore the burden of a destablilization strategy devised by South Africa. Angola has had to fight South Africa on two fronts. Most often it has had to engage UNITA, which has evolved into a counter-revolutionary movement. Training and financial assistance are provided to UNITA by the South Africans. Weapons, in considerable numbers, have come from the United States. All too frequently Angola also had to engage the South African Defense Force [SADF] in the 1980s. Military and civilian casualties as a result of fighting UNITA and SADF have been enormous. Rusk estimates that well over 300,000 people perished from war or war-induced famine between 1980 and 1986 (1987:37).

Rusk, citing the accounts of missionaries, further reports on certain tactics that can produce famine. One of the most important of these is that "UNITA guerrillas plant mines in the fields and paths down to the waterholes. They aim to disrupt peasant farming . . . . When a farmer goes to the fields or a mother and her children go for water, the mines explode, sending shrapnel in every direction, killing or wounding everyone in a hundred feet radius" (1987:39). UNITA's favorite mine is the American Claymore.

Rusk's evidence suggests that famine is produced due to disruptions to farming; that is to say planting, weeding, harvesting, etc. do not occur, or do not occur in a timely fashion, because of farmer fears of being turned into confetti by an American mine. This suggests a causal relationship between Angolan war and famine. First, there are mining operations, then there is the hunger, resulting from disruptions in food-production.

Mozambique was Portugal's colony in southeast Africa. Like Angola and Chad it has engaged in almost continual warfare since the 1960s. From 1964 to 1974, led by the *Frente de Libertação de Moçambique* [FRELIMO], it fought a war of liberation against Portugal. Then in the 1980s it had to bear the brunt of South Africa's destabliization strategy. South African surrogates in Mozambique are those of a counter revolutionary organization called the *Movimento Nacional de Resistência de Moçambique* [RENAMO, or MNR]. RENAMO was originally a creature of the Rhodesian intelligence service. Subsequent to the fall of Rhodesia in 1980, it was taken over by the South African military.

RENAMO is a grotesque institution. It lacks ties to, or legitimacy with, the people among whom it operates. Further, because South Africa's goals in Mozambique are those of destabilization, the *idée fixe* of RENAMO in the 1980s was to intensify insecurity by heightening terror. To implement such goals RENAMO "killed . . . people and stuffed their bodies down wells to poison what little water there was . . ." (Hanlon, 1984: 227), while reserving for officials and teachers the prospect of having their "ears and perhaps lips and breasts cut off . . .: (Ibid.:228). There are also reports that it forced children to kill their relatives, to cook them, and then to consume them (Nordstrom 1989). Not unexpectedly in this situation war and war related deaths in Mozambique have been enormous, with estimates in excess of 400,000 since 1981 (Watts, this volume).

The late 1970s and early 1980s reveal a significant relationship between drought, war, and famine in the Mozambiquan provinces of Gaze and Inhambane. These are the two southernmost provinces, closest to South Africa, and hence most vulnerable to RENAMO. Both provinces suffered drought in

1989-90, but neither experienced famine. This was because "FRELIMO had run a successful relief effort . . ."(Hanlon, 1984:252). RENAMO at this time was virtually shattered, in part due to the collapse of support from Rhodesia, internal political disputes, and defeat at the hands of FRELIMO (Ibid.:221). However, its operational capacities improved following South African support for it that began in late 1980, so much so that its actions tended to be dramatically successful" in the years 1981-83 (Ibid.:224).

Drought again hit Gaze and Inhambane provinces in 1983. This was in areas that were "badly affected" by RENAMO (Ibid.:252). Here people following the drought lost much of "their remaining foodstocks and cattle" (Ibid.:252), because RENAMO operations concentrated upon "economic targets and disrupting transport" (Ibid.:227). This meant that it regularly attacked "transportation links, farms, and relief convoys" (Rusk, 1987:40). "Crops [were] burned in the field and in peasant grain stores:" (Hanlon, 1984:227). This time famine did not occur as RENAMO was able to prevent the government from conducting effective relief operations.

What is revealing about this Mozambiquan famine of 1983 is that, like the earlier Chadian debacle, it shows how drought alone may not be sufficient to provoke famine. Rather, it appears to have been a combination of factors, brought upon by RENAMO operations, that produced it. This combination included reductions in food supplies, as in Angola, and the disruption of food distribution and relief, as in Chad and Biafra. First, drought reduced food supplies. Then combat further reduced them apparently to starvation levels. Concomitantly fighting disrupted the food distribution systems so that the deficit could not be made up. Finally, at the end of this dismal sequence, people starved. In this interpretation, drought caused food shortages; but war caused conditions that added to the original shortages, producing famine.

Before leaving southern Africa it should be noted that the United States has also played a role in the region's hostilities. Since World War II, American policy vis-à-vis the increasingly racist and repressive South African government has been one of covert, and occasionally overt, support (Love, 1985:13). This is in large measure because South Africa supplies the United States with a large number of minerals; because it is strategically situated along sealanes upon which other resources are shipped; and because it has been a source of profitable investment.[14] Thus, when South Africa began to destabilize its neighbors in the 1980s, the United States initiated a policy of "constructive engagement." This policy sought to maintain American influence in south African affairs by not criticizing Sough African military aggression and even, in some cases, directly supporting it. Thus the United States regularly armed UNITA throughout the 1980s; and, as late as 1988, it appears to have "been sponsoring not one but two covert operations in support of" Renamo (Africa Confidential, 1988:1). Thus the greatest of core powers has aided and abetted a regional hegemon's military lusts in order to maintain its influence in a resource rich corner of the periphery. It is time now to consider Ethiopia.

The drama of Ethiopian famine has been told many times and in many ways (see Clay and Watts, this volume). Nowhere in Africa since 1974 has there been more intense warfare, largely involving secessionist movements, as in Eritrea and Tigray, as well as against the neighboring countries of Somalia and Sudan. Estimates of mortality from war and war related famine regularly appear on the order of a million persons since 1974 (Watts, this volume).

No one denies that war has been a "main cause" of famine (Vestal, 1985:8). Ethiopian tactics have included "direct ground and air attacks on people, livestock, villages, and other economic targets such as grain silos and crop fields . . . ." (Pasha, 1988:36). The ordinance used in these attacks includes "napalm" and "500 kilo cluster bombs" (Ibid.:36). Mining of paths leading to fields as well as the mining of the fields themselves are reported (Ibid.:36). Ethiopia has raised to a fine art the blockading of food deficit areas (Clay, this volume). Such scorched earth policies appear to cause famine in Ethiopia in the same ways as they did in the countries previously discussed. First there is war, then there is famine; and famine is produced because combat operations reduce food production, and then as food runs out, blockades insure that it is not replaced.

The foreign policies of the United States and the Soviet Union have their place in these famines. The Horn of Africa, in which Ethiopia is situated, has long been considered to be of strategic significance because it commands access to the Red Sea and because its control was thought to be vital for assuring the movement of Middle Eastern oil. Hence, core powers have long vied for influence in the region. Since the second World War and the decline of Britain, the Americans Russians have been the major competitors for this control. Provisions of military assistance was a major method used by these powers to attain their ends. This began in 1953, when the United States agreed to train and equip the Ethiopian army through a Military Assistance Advisory Group (MAAG). A decade later, Ethiopia had already received 73 billion dollars in military aid from the MAAG (Ottawa, 1982:27). Subsequent to 1974, Ethiopia moved into the socialist camp, and in 1977 the Soviet Union began to provide military assistance. This is reported to have totaled 2 billion dollars between 1977 and 1980. the crucial point in all this is that Ethiopia is a desperately poor country and normally would not have the means to wage extensive and protracted war. However, great power competition for influence in the region gave the Ethiopian government ample means to conduct lengthy combat operations, and it was these which were a cause of famine.

Consider one final case, that of the Republic of Sudan. This case is instructive because it shows how famine can occur as a result of war in areas that should have food surpluses. The Sudan has enormous areas of arable land and therefore has very considerable agricultural potential. Unlike other countries in the Sahel and the Horn of Africa, it escaped the 1973-74 famine for reasons that are described by O'Brien and Gruenbaum (this volume). But then changes in development policies and war occurred. O'Brien and Gruenbaum have documented the role of these new policies in Sudanese famine (this volume). I briefly explore the role of warfare.

Sudan has experienced friction between an Islamic north and a non-Islamic south on and off since the 1960s. However, since 1984 and the fall of Nimeiry, the more fundamentalist national government in Khartoum has taken a harder line toward the south, especially with regard to its intentions of imposing *sharia* law there. This has produced active civil war. The Sudanese Peoples' Liberation Army [SPLA] was organized in 1983 in the south, under the leadership of John Gaurang. During 1987-88, according to one source, Sudan "enjoyed its best harvest of the past decade" (Van Voorhis, 1988:29). Yet for that year "the total number of deaths" due to famine in the south "was estimated to be at least 250,000 . . ." (Ibid.:29). The "chief cause" of this suffering "was the continuation of the civil war . . . (Ibid.:30). War produced famine in much the same way it had done elsewhere by "denying farmers access to their fields and by intercepting food assistance" (Van Arsdale, 1989:65).

Again in the Sudan, as in the preceding five cases, the actions of core powers have contributed to famine. Sudan is perceived to be the "back door" to Egypt, and Egypt is considered to be a key supporter of Western interests in the Middle East. Western officials believe that if the Sudan were to become hostile, Egypt would be vulnerable, and an insecure Egypt would make it much more difficult to defend Western oil interests throughout the Middle East. This had led the competing core powers eagerly to court Sudan for their camps, and the courting gifts, here as elsewhere, come in the form of military assistance. So in the midst of famine, "The U.S. AID officials refused to condemn Khartoum for the use of food as a weapon . . . In the meantime U.S. and Arab states continue to supply arms to . . . the Sudanese military, while the Soviets supply the Ethiopians who in turn supply the SPLA" (African Rights Monitor, 1988:87).

The foregoing analysis is exceedingly tentative, yet at the same time singularly suggestive. Warfare, as predicted in Proposition 3 (see p. 349), seems to have been intensified in each of the six cases as a result of core attempts to exercise control in the periphery, in at least partial support of their resource interests. Furthermore, each case of warfare was of the third type associated with core expansion, that of hostilities between indigenous peoples aided and abetted by core powers. The English and French armed their Iroquois and Huron allies in the 17th century so that they would fight each other for control of beaver territories, the better to supply their sponsors with pelts for a rising European fur industry. Americans, British, French, and the Soviets arm their allies in the late 20th century to secure their oil and/or mineral and other economic interests. Finally, this warfare does appear to cause famine in the six cases under examination, and it does so primarily by reducing food supply in one of two ways. The first way is for combat to reduce the amount of food produced by crippling agricultural production or by destruction of foodstuffs. The second way is for combat to reduce the amount of food distributed to the region, usually by crippling normal marketing systems and relief measures.

A WORLD SYSTEM FAMINE THEORY

These findings, tentative though they are, can be integrated with Sen's entitlement theory. This is because fluctuations in food supply appear to influence endowments and E-mappings. Specifically, decreases in food supply decrease endowments and E-mappings. Remember that endowments are peoples' "ownership bundles." One thing that people own is some portion of the food they raise. So any decrease in peoples' food production is a decrease in their endowments. When animals or crops are destroyed by fighting this means that their owners' endowments decrease. E-mappings should be understood to decrease in the sense that bundles of endowments bring fewer entitlements than they did in the past, a process that is expressed by the inflation and hoarding provoked by a reduced food supply. A final point to grasp is that decreased endowments and E-mappings mean decreased entitlement sets.

Now we are in a position to integrate warfare and entitlements into a common causal sequence that results in famine. The sequence runs as follows: warfare produces declines in food production and distribution in areas experiencing combat; these declines produce decreases in food supply; the decreased food supply produces decreases in endowments and E-mappings; decreased endowments and E-mappings produce decreased entitlement sets; and it is these final decreases that produce the starvation that kills people in famines. The preceding, suggested though by no means confirmed by the cases reviewed, may be expressed as two propositions:

(1) Warfare can produce declines in entitlement sets.

(2) Declines in entitlement sets can produce famines.

These propositions explain how war may cause famine. They do not explain how war might be caused.

So now it is time to return to the propositions at the end of the section on Historical Sructuralism and incorporate them with the two propositions just derived, to elaborate upon how African famine might be maintained, or increased, in frequency over the next hundred or so years. The resulting explanation articulates events in core structures with those in peripheral ones, and so is at a world systems level of analysis. For this reason it might be called a world systems theory.

CONCLUSION

The theory consists of five propositions. Three, from the Historical Structuralism section of the essay, pertain to the nature of the core-periphery articulation. Two, just formulated, consider the effects of this articulation upon famine.

(1) The contradiction between capital and land will intensify over the next hundred years.

(2) Intensification of this contradiction can increase the need for core nations to exercise political control in peripheral nations.

(3) Increased core attempts to exercise control in the periphery in conjunction with stagnant or decreased peripheral development, will maintain, or increase the frequency and intensity of warfare in the periphery.

(4) More frequent warfare can produce more frequent declines in the entitlement sets of people in different regions of peripheral nations.

(5) If there are more frequent regional declines in individual entitlement sets, then there will be more frequent famines.

There is a dismal logic to this syllogism. If propositions 1 through 3 are valid, then warfare increases in the periphery. If warfare occurs, and proposition four is valid, then famine occurs.

The theory just presented, like all theories, is incomplete, contains anomalies, and is subject to modification. Perhaps most importantly, although it is concerned with how warfare can produce famine, it does not consider the relationship of poverty to warfare and famine. A more complete analysis would explore the articulation between core capital accumulation and peripheral impoverishment, warfare, and famine.

Currently eighteen to twenty million people appear to die each year of hunger related causes. This is an almost unimaginable slaughter, one that appears to be merely a symptom of a world system rushing toward its dissolution. If the theory of warfare and famine just presented proves correct, then the horrors of the future will dwarf those of today. This returns us to the nagging question, "What is to be done?"

There is an ethos in all societies with which I am familiar that insists you nurture your kin. If this means throwing your brother, your sister, your mother, or your father on your back and running with them in time of danger—then you do it. They are yours. Unfortunately, especially in the core, there is increasingly a counter-ethos that encourages one to throw one's parents in a nursing home when they become ripe, and to "use" everybody else.

I believe that current events have made us all ultimately kin. This is because—except for a very few, fabulously wealthy—we are all perilously racing through dark forests, chased by predatory states in the service of an industrial capitalism grown malignant. If we do not bear the burden of a global kinship, then what is to be done is to bury the dead.

NOTES

1. An earlier version of this essay was presented at the 1988 Annual Meetings of the American Anthropological Association. I an grateful to R. E. Downs for his critiques of it. Its faults are my own.
2. The World Bank and Kent figures are rough assessements. There is no reason to believe that they are inflated. The Kent estimates suggest that approximately 3,500 times more people perish from hunger related deaths each yer than did Americans from combat in the entire Viet Nam War.
3. Reviews of the literature which discuss the prospects for war and in the 21st century can be found in Thompson (1988) and Goldstein (1988).
4. The term "structural history" is already associated with Braudel, and some readers may be bothered by the introduction of a new concept of "historical structuralism." The latter term seems appropriate because it directs attention to what is most important — structures, which as part of their operation have histories.
5. The notions of abstractness and generality used in the text are those of Wallace (1971).
6. Space considerations preclude lengthy discussion of validation procedures in historical structuralism. I am, however, generally sympathetic to Fischer's adductive approach (1970).
7. Note that the concept of "level" is employed in two ways throughout the essay. On the one hand it denotes different degrees of generality and abstraction; on the other it specifies the geographic focus of a structure. If a structure operates in a small area, it is said to function at the local level. If it operates throughout a country, it is said to be at the national level.
8. Rosh conducted a study of arms production in the Third World, and found that regional hegemons, countries like Iraq or Brazil, "are engaging in large-scale arms production to pursue political, military, and economic mobility" (1990:70). This suggests that the fourth type of war identified in the text may be especially significant; and, in fact, the dispute in the summer of 1990 between Iraq and the industrial nations is an example of just such a conflict.
9. Rosecrance argues, contrary to the position expressed in the text, that warfare is a thing of the past (1986). However, his analysis ignores Third World conflict, frequent and bloody

since 1945, as well as the security implications of rapidly rising population and pollution under conditions of increasing resource scarcity. I believe his position is not credible in the absence of consideration of these topics.

10. The proposition in the text suggesting that warfare will be frequent in the periphery does not imply that every war there will be directly over resources. Perlman and Murray discount the possibility of core/periphery resource wars (1982). Their arguement, however, is based upon a single case, that of Japan in the 1950s, and ignores the impact of increasing resource scarcity. It consequently seems to over-simplify a complex structural situation in which resource scarcity has a place.

11. Critical reviews of entitlement theory can be found in Basu (1986), Bowbrick (1986), Mitra (1982), Rangasami (1985), Srinivasan (1983), Woldemeskel (1990).

12. Watts, in this volume, is concerned that the narrow scope of Sen's theory inhibits understanding of "longer term processes of social reproduction."

13. Accounts of the French role in Chadian wars can be found in Buijtenhuijs (1981) and Chapelle (1980).

14. Assessment of the strategic importance of South Africa to the United States can be found in Bowmann(1985). South Africa has reserves of eleven of the twenty-seven minerals identified by the United States Geological Survey as critical to industrial societies.

REFERENCES

Africa Confidential
  1988   Mozambique: Plausible Deniability. Africa Confidential. 29(24):1-2.
Africa Watch
  1990   Somalia: A Government at War with Its Own People. New York: Human Rights Watch.
African Rights Monitor
  1988   The Denial of Food: Sudan and the Shari'a. Africa Today. 35(3-4):86-87.
Akong'a, J.
  1988   Drought and Famine Management in Kitui District, Kenya. In D. Brokensha and P. Little, eds., Anthropology of Development and Change in East Africa. Boulder, CO: Westview.
Allen, C.
  1987   An African Success Story. Africa Report. 32(1):22-24.
Althusser, L. and E. Balibar, eds.
  1970   Reading Capital. London: New Left Books.
Bannock, G., R. E. Baxter, and R. Ress
  1972   Dictionary of Economics. Harmondsworth: Penguin.
Basu, D. R.
  1986   Sen's Analysis of famine: A critique. Journal of Development Studies. 22(3):598-604.
Bergesen, A.
  1980   Cycles of Formal Colonial Rule. In T. K. Hopkins and I. Wallerstein, eds., Processes of the World System. Beverley Hills, CA: Sage Publications.
Bertram, C.
  1982   Introduction. In C. Bertram, ed., Third World Conflict and International Security. London: Archon Press.

Bobb, F. S.
  1988 Historical Dictionary of Zaire. Metuchen, NJ: Scarecrow Press.
Bonner, R.
  1989 A Reporter at Large: Famine. New Yorker. March 13: 85-101.
Boston Globe
  1990 Liberian Rebels Arrive for Peace Talks. 12 July 1990: 10.
Bowbrick, P.
  1986 The Causes of Famine: A Refutation of Professor Sen's Theory. Food Pol-
        icy. 11(2):105-25.
Bowman, L.
  1985 The Strategic Importance of South Africa to the United States: An Ap-
        praisal and Policy Analysis. In Aluko, O. and T. M. Shaw, eds., Southern
        Africa in the 1980s. London: George Allen and Unwin.
Buijtenhuijs, R.
  1981 Guerre de guérilla et révolution en Afrique noire: les leçons du Tchad.
        Politique Africaine. 1:23-33.
Bunge, M.
  1959 Causality, The Place of the Causal Principle in Modern Science.
        Cambridge, MA: Harvard University Press.
Burdette, M.
  1978 Zambia: Between Two Worlds. Boulder, CO: Westview.
Carrithers, M.
  1990 Is Anthropology Art or Science? Current Anthropology. 31(3):263-82.
Cathie, J. and H. Dick.
  1987 Food security and Macroeconomic Stabilization: A Case Study of
        Botswana. Tubingen: J. C. Mohr.
Cervenka, Z.
  1987 The Effects of Militarisation on African Human Rights. Africa Today.
        34(1&2):69-85.
Chapelle, J.
  1980 Le peuple Tchadien: Ses racines, sa vie quotidienne, et ses combats. Paris:
        Harmattan.
Chase-Dunn, C.
  1989 Global Formation, Structures of the World Economy. Cambridge, MA:
        Basil Blackwell.
Clapham, C.
  1986 The Horn of Africa. In Duignan, P. and R. H. Jackson, eds., Politics and
        Government in African States, 1960-1985. London: Croom Helm.
Clay, J. W. and B. K. Holcombe
  1985 Politics and the Ethiopian Famine, 1984-85. Cambridge, MA, Cultural
        Survival: Transaction Books.
Cole, H. S. D., C. Freeman, M. Jahoda, & K. L. R. Pavitt
  1973 Models of Doom: A Critique of the Limits to Growth. New York: Universe
        Books.
Crosson, P.
  1989 Greenhouse Warming and Climate Change: Why should we care? Food
        Policy. 14(2):107-119.

Davidson, B.
   1981 No Fist is Big Enough to Hide the Sky: The Liberation of Guinea Bissau
         and Cape Verde. London: Zed Press.
Decalo, S.
   1987 Historical Dictionary of Togo. Metuchen, NJ: Scarecrow Press.
   1989 Psychoses of Power: African Personal Dictatorships. Boulder, CO:
         Westview.
Delancy, M. W.
   1988 Cameroon. Boulder, CO: Westview.
De Saint-Paul, M. A.
   1988 Gabon: The Development of a Nation. London: Routledge Chapman Hall.
Downing, T. E., K. Gilu, and C. Kamau, eds.
   1989 Coping With Drought in Kenya: National and Local Strategies. Boulder,
         Co: Lynne Rienner.
Dunn, D. E. and B. Tarr
   1988 Liberia: A National Polity in Transition. Metuchen, NJ: Scarecrow Press.
Engberg, L. E., J. H. Sabry, and S. A. Berkerson.
   1987 Production Activities, Food Supply, and Nutritional Status in Malawi.
Fatton, R.
   1987 The Making of a Liberal Democracy: Senegal's Passive Revolution,
         1975–85. Boulder, CO: Lynne Rienner.
Ferguson R. B. and N. L. Whitehead
   1989 Warfare in the Tribal Zone. Unpublished Manuscript. New York: Harry
         Frank Guggenheim Foundation.
Finnegan, W.
   1989 A Reporter at Large: Mozaqmbique. New Yorker. May 22:43–76; May
         29:69–96.
Fischer, D. H.
   1970 Historians' Fallacies: Toward a Logic of Historical Thought. New York:
         Harper and Row.
Gailey, H.
   1987 Historical Dictionary of the Gambia. Metuchen, NJ: Scarecrow Press.
Galbraith, J. K.
   1958 The Affluent Society. Boston, MA: Houghton Mifflin.
Giorgis, D.
   1989 Red Tears. Trenton, NJ: Red Sea Press.
Global 2000
   1980 The Global 2000 Report to the President. United States Council on Envi-
         ronmental Quality and the Department of State. Washington, DC: Govern-
         ment Printing Office.
Godelier, M.
   1972 Structure and Contradiction in Capital. In R. Blackburn, ed., Ideology in
         Social Science. London: Fontana.
Goldstein, J. S.
   1988 Long Cycles: Prosperity and War in the Modern Age. New Haven, CT:
         Yale University Press.
Griffiths, I. L.
   1988. "Famine and War in Africa." Geography. 73(1):59–61.

Hanlon, J.
  1984 Mozambique: The Revolution Under Fire. London: Zed Press.
Harf, J. and B. Trout
  1986 The Politics of Global Resources: Energy, Environment, Population, and
        Food. Durham, NC: Duke University Press.
Holm, J. and R. Morgan
  1983 Coping with Drought in Botswana: An African Success. Journal of Mod-
        ern African Studies. 23:463-82.
Hubbert, M. K.
  1971 Energy Resources of the Earth. Scientific American. September: 61-79.
ICIHI
  1985 Famine: A Man-Made Disaster. New York: Vintage.
Imperato, P. J.
  1989 Mali: A Search for Direction. Boulder, CO: Westview.
Jacobs, D.
  1987 The Brutality of Nations. New York: Alfred Knopf.
Katjavini, A.
  1988 A History of Resistance in Namibia. Paris: UNESCO.
Kelly, M. P.
  1986 A State in Disarray: Conditions of Chad's Survival. Boulder, CO:
        Westview.
Kende, I.
  1978 Wars of Ten Years (1967-1976). Journal of Peace Research.
        3(XV):227-41.
Kent, G.
  1984 The Political Economy of Hunger: The Silent Holocaust. New York:
        Praeger.
Kitching, G.
  1980 Class and Economic Change in Kenya. New Haven: Yale University Press.
Kula, E.
  1988 The Inadequacy of the Entitlement Approach to Explain and Remedy Fam-
        ine. Journal of Development Studies. 25(1):112-16.
Lan, D.
  1985 Guns and Rain: Guerrillas and Spirit Mediums in Zimbabwe. Berkeley,
        CA: University of California Press.
Lemarchand, R.
  1970 Rwanda and Burundi. New York: Praeger.
Lenin, N.
  1988 (1902) What is to Be Done? Harmondsworth: Penguin.
Lévi-Strauss, C.
  1973 Social Structure. In Bohannon, P. and M. Glazer, eds., High Points in An-
        thropology. New York: Alfred Knopf.
Lewis, B. C.
  1989 The Ivory Coast. Boulder, CO: Westview.
Liniger-Goumaz, M.
  1988 Historical Dictionary of Equatorial Guinea. Metuchen, NJ: Scarecrow
        Press.

Love, J.
   1985 The U.S. Anti-Apartheid Movement: Local Activism in Global Politics.
          New York: Praeger.
Mamdani, M.
   1982 Karamoja: Colonial roots of Famine in Northeast Uganda. Review of Afri-
          can Political Economy. 25:66-73.
Mandel, E.
   1980 Long Waves of Capitalist Development. Cambridge: Cambridge Univer-
          sity Press.
Marx, K.
   1981 Capital. Vol. III. New York: Vintage.
McGraw-Hill
   1969 McGraw-Hill Dictionary of Scientific and Technical Terms. New York:
          McGraw-Hill.
Meadows, D. H., D. L. Meadows, R. Randers, and W. Behrens.
   1972 The Limits to Growth. New York: Universe Books.
Mellor, J. W. and S. Gavin
   1987 Famine: Causes, Prevention, and Relief. Science. 235:539-45.
Messer, E.
   1990 Food Wars: Hunger as a Weapon of War. In Brown University World Hun-
          ger Program, The Hunger Report.
Mitra, A.
   1982 The Meaning of Meaning.. Economic and Political Weekly. 27:488-9.
Mtewa, M.
   1986 Democratic Theory and Public Policy. Schenkman.
Nordstrom, C.
   1989 Clean Theories/Dirty Wars. Unpublished Paper. Washington, DC: Annual
          Meetings American Anthropological Association.
Nzongola-Ntalaja
   1987 Revolution and Counter Revolution in Africa: Essays in Contemporary
          Politics. London: Zed Press.
Obbo, C.
   1988 What Went Wrong in Uganda? In Hansen, H. B. and M. Twaddle, eds.
          Uganda Now: Between Decay and Development. London: James Curry.
O'Connor, A.
   1988 Uganda: The Spatial Dimension. In Hansen, H. B. and M. Twaddle. eds.,
          Uganda Now: Between Decay and Development. London: James Curry.
OED
   1989 The Oxford English Dictionary. Oxford: Clarendon Press.
Orobator, S. E.
   1983-4 Western Sahara: The Collapse of Irredentism. Journal of African Stud-
            ies. 10(4):137-45.
O'Toole, T. E.
   1987 Historical Dictionary of the Republic of Guinea. Metuchen, NJ: Scarecrow
          Press.
Ottaway, M.
   1982 Soviet and American Influence in the Horn of Africa. New York: Praeger.

Perlman, R. and A. Murray
 1982 Resources and Conflict: Requirements and Vulnerabilities of the Industrialized World. In C. Bertram, ed., Third World Conflict and International Security. London: Archon Press.
Radcliffe-Brown, A. R.
 1965 Structure and Function in Primitive Society. New York: Macmillan.
Rangasami, A.
 1985 Failure of Exchange Entitlements Theory of Famine. Economic and Political Weekly. XX(41): 1747-52; (42):1797-1800.
Ravallion, M.
 1987 Markets and Famines. Oxford:Clarendon Press.
Reyna, S. P.
 1990 Wars Without End: The Political Economy of a Precolonial African State. Hanover, NH: University Press of New England.
ROAPE
 1985 Review of African Political Economy. 33.
Rosecrance, R.
 1986 The Rise of the Trading State. New York: Basic Books.
Rosh, R. M.
 1990 Third World Arms Production and the Evolving Interstate System. Journal of Conflict Resolution. 34(1):57-73.
Rostow, W. W.
 1962 The Process of Economic Growth. New York: Norton.
 1978 The World Economy: History and Prospect. Austin, TX: University of Texas Press.
Roth, P. A.
 1989 Ethnography Without Tears. Current Anthropology. 30(5):555-70.
Rusk, J. D.
 1987 African Rights Monitor: Warfare and Human Rights in Angola and Mozambique. Africa Today. 34(4):33-43.
Sen, A. K.
 1976 Famines as Failures of Exchange Entitlements. Economic and Political Weekly.
 1977 Starvation and Exchange Entitlements: A General Approach and its Application to the Great Bengal Famine. Cambridge Journal of Economics. 1.
 1981 Poverty and Famines: An Essay of Entitlement and Deprivation. Oxford. Clarendon Press.
Shepard, G. W.
 1987 Global Majority Rights: The African Context. Africa Today. 34(1&2):13-27.
Shindo, E.
 1985 Hunger and Weapons: The Entropy of Militarisation. Review of African Political Economy. 33:6-22.
Shipton, P.
 1990 African Famines and Food Security: Anthropological Perspectives. Annual Review of Anthropology. 19.
Sivard, R. L.
 1989 World Military and Social Expenditures, 1989. 13th Ed. Washington, DC: World Priorities.

Smith, A.
  1937 (1776) An Inquiry into the Nature and Causes of the Wealth of Nations. New York: Modern Library.
Srinivasan, T. N.
  1983 Review of Sen, A. K. American Journal of Agricultural Economics. 65:200-1.
Steinbach, U.
  1982 Sources of Third World Conflict. In C. Bertram, ed., Third World Conflict and International Security. London: Archon Press.
Stremlau, J. J.
  1978 The International Politics of the Nigerian Civil War, 1967-1970. Princeton: Princeton University Press.
Tholomier, R.
  1988 Djibouti: Pawn of the Horn of Africa. Metuchen, NJ: Scarecrow Press.
Thomas C.
  1989 Introduction. In Thomas, C. & P. Saravanamuttu, eds., Conflict and Concensus in South/North Security. Cambridge: Cambridge University Press.
Thompson, W. R.
  1988 On Global War: Historical-Structural Approaches to World Politics. Columbia, SC: University of South Carolina Press.
Tucker, V.
  1985. Military Attacks, Drought, and Hunger in Mozambique. Review of African Political Economy. 33:89-91.
UNFPA
  1990 The State of the World Population. New York: United Nations Population Fund. United Nations.
Van Arsdale, P. W.
  1989 The Ecology of Survival in Sudan's Periphery: Short Term Tactics and Long Term Strategies. Africa Today. 36(3&4):65-79.
Van Voorhis, B.
  1989 Food as a Weapon for Peace: Operation Lifeline Sudan. Africa Today. 36(3&4): 29-43.
Vestal, T. M.
  1985 Famine in Ethiopia: Crisis of Many Directions. Africa Today. 32(4):6-17.
Wallace, W.
  1971 The Logic of Science in Sociology. Chicago: Aldine.
Wallerstein, I.
  1974 The Modern World System. Vol. 1., Capitalist Agriculture and the Origins of the European World Economy in the 16th Century. New York; Academic Press.
  1978 World System Analysis: Theoretical and Interpretive Issues. In Kaplan, B. H., ed., Social Change in the Capitalist World Economy. Beverly Hills, CA:Sage.
  1986 Japan and the Future Trajectory of the World System: Lessons from History. Unpublished paper. Binghamton, New York: Braudel Center, SUNY-Binghamton.
WDF
  1987a World Development Forum. 9:3.
  1987b World Development Forum. 17:1.

Weinstein, W.
  1976 Historical Dictionary of Burundi. Metuchen, NJ: Scarecrow Press.
Woldemeskel, G.
  1990 Famine and the Two Faces of Entitlement: A Comment on Sen. World De-
        velopment. 18(3):491–5.
Wolpe. H.
  1980 ed., The Articulation of Modes of Production. London:Routledge & Kegan
        Paul.
World Bank
  1986 Poverty and Hunger: Issues and Options for Food Security in Developing
        Countries. Washington, DC: World Bank.

Index

INDEX NOTE

Note: Page numbers followed by f indicate figures.

Price control, 242, 244, 245, 246
Price fixing, 227, 230
Price incentives, 233
Price intervention, 245
Price manipulation, 236, 253
Prices
  dependence on, 252
  food, 232
  after harvest, 238
  increased, 234, 235
  in Kumasi, 246
  from market traders, 230
  reduced, 243
Pricing, and food production, 247
Processed corn products, 245
Production methods, during
    drought, 103
Production of food. *See* Food pro-
    duction
Production stability, crop genetic
    diversity and, 330-332
Productive resources, women's
    control over, 274
Profit, of food traders, 235, 236
Proletarianization, 47
Property rights, 30
Propositions, in ontological ac-
    quiescence versus science,
    73, 74
Public works, 55
Purchased lands, 240
Purchase of food, 247
Purchasing power, of nomads, in
    drought, 125

R

Radio, 238
Rainfall
  in Ethiopia, 159
  in Guinea-Bissau, 205

[Rainfall]
  before 1968-1974 WoDaaBe
    drought, 130
  in Sahel, 80, 123
  in Sudan, 93, 94
  WoDaaBe herders and, 126
Rainfed agricultural development
    project, 3, 91-115
Rain-making rites, 51
Rainy season
  coping strategies for, 216-217,
    221-223
  subsistence during, 127
Reagan administration, 49
Red Cross, 50
Regional market system, 253
RENAMO, 35, 357-358
Reproduction, crises of, 44
Research, on Ethiopian famine,
    156, 157-159, 162, 164-165
Resettlement, as cause of Ethio-
    pian famine, 148, 162,
    164-168
Resources
  access to, 32
  control over, 32
Response to famine, 38, 39
Retailers, 232, 236, 243
Rice, 215, 252
Rights to resources, in Chadian
    societies, 294, 295, 297, 305,
    307, 309, 311, 312, 317,
    318, 319
Risk(s)
  corn as, 245
  of green revolution, 334
  and Kumasi violence, 243
  price, 238
  of storage, 236
  of traders, 234

For Product Safety Concerns and Information please contact our EU
representative GPSR@taylorandfrancis.com
Taylor & Francis Verlag GmbH, Kaufingerstraße 24, 80331 München, Germany